PROSPECTS FOR
MIDDLE EASTERN AND
NORTH AFRICAN ECONOMIES

Also by Nemat Shafik

ECONOMIC CHALLENGES FACING MIDDLE EASTERN AND NORTH AFRICAN COUNTRIES: Alternative Futures

REVIVING PRIVATE INVESTMENT IN DEVELOPING COUNTRIES: Empirical Studies and Policy Lessons (*editor with A. Chhibber and M. Dailami*)

Prospects for Middle Eastern and North African Economies

From Boom to Bust and Back?

Edited by

Nemat Shafik

Foreword by Heba Handoussa

in association with
ECONOMIC RESEARCH FORUM FOR THE
ARAB COUNTRIES, IRAN AND TURKEY

First published in Great Britain 1998 by
MACMILLAN PRESS LTD
Houndmills, Basingstoke, Hampshire RG21 6XS and London
Companies and representatives throughout the world

A catalogue record for this book is available from the British Library.

ISBN 0-333-71400-8 hardcover
ISBN 0-333-71401-6 paperback

First published in the United States of America 1998 by
ST. MARTIN'S PRESS, INC.,
Scholarly and Reference Division,
175 Fifth Avenue, New York, N.Y. 10010

ISBN 0-312-17633-3

Library of Congress Cataloging-in-Publication Data
Prospects for Middle Eastern and North African economies : from boom
to bust and back? / edited by Nemat Shafik ; foreword by Heba
Handoussa.
   p.   cm.
Includes bibliographical references and index.
ISBN 0-312-17633-3 (cloth)
1. Middle East—Economic conditions—1979–   2. Africa, North–
–Economic conditions.   3. Economic policy—Middle East.   4. Economic
policy—Africa, North.   I. Shafik, Nemat.
HC415.15.P76 1997
330.956—DC21   97–13672
                                                                          CIP

© Economic Research Forum 1998

All rights reserved. No reproduction, copy or transmission of this publication may be made without written permission.

No paragraph of this publication may be reproduced, copied or transmitted save with written permission or in accordance with the provisions of the Copyright, Designs and Patents Act 1988, or under the terms of any licence permitting limited copying issued by the Copyright Licensing Agency, 90 Tottenham Court Road, London W1P 9HE.

Any person who does any unauthorised act in relation to this publication may be liable to criminal prosecution and civil claims for damages.

The authors have asserted their rights to be identified as the authors of this work in accordance with the Copyright, Designs and Patents Act 1988.

This book is printed on paper suitable for recycling and made from fully managed and sustained forest sources.

10   9   8   7   6   5   4   3   2   1
07 06 05 04 03 02 01 00 99 98

Printed and bound in Great Britain by Antony Rowe Ltd, Chippenham, Wiltshire

> The findings, interpretations, and conclusions expressed in this volume are entirely those of the authors and should not be attributed in any manner to the World Bank, to its affiliated organizations, or to members of its Board of Executive Directors or the countries they represent.

To Maissa Hamza

Contents

List of Figures, Tables, and Boxes   ix
Foreword   xv
Notes on the Contributors   xvii

1   Prospects for Middle Eastern and North African Economies: An Overview
  Nemat Shafik   1

PART I   THE CHANGING INTERNATIONAL CONTEXT   13

2   The World Economy and its Implications for the Middle East and North Africa, 1995–2010
  E. Mick Riordan, Uri Dadush, Jalal Jalali, Shane Streifel, Milan Brahmbhatt, and Kazue Takagaki   15

3   The Arab Economies, the Uruguay Round Predicament, and the European Union Wildcard
  Ishac Diwan, Chang-Po Yang, and Zhi Wang   47

4   The World Trade Organization, the European Union, and the Arab World: Trade Policy Priorities and Pitfalls
  Bernard Hoekman   96

PART II   ECONOMIC GROWTH, THE STATE, AND THE PRIVATE SECTOR

5   From Boom to Bust – and Back? The Crisis of Growth in the Middle East and North Africa
  John Page   133

6   The State and Economic Transition in the Middle East and North Africa
  John Waterbury   159

7   Supporting Private Sector Development in the Middle East and North Africa
  Robert E. Anderson and Albert Martinez   178

PART III SECTORAL ISSUES: HUMAN RESOURCES, POVERTY, AND THE ENVIRONMENT

8   A Human Capital Strategy for Competing in
    World Markets
    *Fredrick L. Golladay, Sue E. Berryman, Jon Avins,
    and Laurence Wolff*   197

9   Poverty in the Middle East and North Africa
    Willem van Eeghen   226

10 Environmentally Sustainable Development in
    the Middle East and North Africa
    Hamid Mohtadi   262

11 Environmental and Natural Resource Management
    in the Middle East and North Africa
    Bjorn Larsen   288

Index   313

List of Figures, Tables, and Boxes

Figures

2.1	Per capita GDP growth, various regions, 1981–90	17
2.2	Volatility of the purchasing power of exports, various regions, 1970–93	20
2.3	Volatility of the purchasing power of exports, Middle East and North Africa, 1970–93	21
2.4	Nonoil exports as a share of total, Middle East and North Africa, 1970–92	26
2.5	Composition of nonoil exports, Middle East and North Africa, 1970–93	27
2.6	Option for nonoil export growth	33
2.7	Nonoil export growth, 1981–2010	40
2.8	Real effective exchange rates, Middle East and North Africa and competitor countries, 1980–94	42
3.1	Aggregate welfare impacts and levels of trade under the three simulations	64
4.1	Per capita nonoil exports from various regions, 1989 and 1995	107
4.2	Per capita nonoil exports from various countries, 1988 and 1995	108
4.3	Intraindustry trade with the European Union, 1989–94	111
5.1	GDP growth, 1960–85, and GDP per capita, 1960	134
5.2	GDP growth, 1965–89, and income inequality	135
5.3	Investment as a share of GDP, 1960–85, and GDP per capita, 1960	137
5.4	GDP per capita and primary enrollment, 1960	138
5.5	Average education stock, 1960–85, and GDP per capita, 1960	139
5.6	Accounting for differences in growth due to differences in accumulation, 1960–91	141
5.7	Investment and GDP growth, Middle East and North Africa, 1970–89	142
5.8	Total factor productivity FP growth, 1960–90, and GDP per capita, 1960	144

5.9	Public and private investment, various regions, 1970–88	146
5.10	Quota coverage, various regions, 1985–88	148
5.11	Total aid, worker remittances, and foreign direct investment in the Maghreb, 1970–90	149
5.12	Total aid, worker remittances, and foreign direct investment in the Mashreq, 1970–90	150
5.13	Total factor productivity growth, 1960–89, and share of manufactured exports in total exports, 1960–85	152
5.14	Changes in real trade, various regions, 1960–94	153
6.1	Pathways to institutional change	165
7.1	Per capita income growth, various regions, 1965–93	179
7.2	Share of public enterprises in economic activity, various countries, 1986–91	180
7.3	Privatization transactions, various countries, 1983–93	183
7.4	Foreign direct investment inflows, various regions, 1982–93	185
8.1	Earnings gaps between U.S. college graduates and high school graduates, 1965, 1975, and 1985	203
9.1	Change in poverty and real GDP per capita, various countries	236
10.1	Environmental indicators at different country income levels	263
10.2	Economic development and the environment in the Middle East and North Africa	264
11.1	Net national savings rates in the Middle East and North Africa and East Asia, 1972–92	290
11.2	Share of heavy fuel oil in primary energy consumption, Middle East and North Africa, 1991	297
11.3	Toxic pollution from industry, Middle East and North Africa, 1990	299

Tables

2.1	Sources of foreign exchange, Middle East and North Africa, 1970–93	18
2.2	Population growth, Middle East and North Africa, 1970–2010	19
2.3	Distribution of exports, Middle East and North Africa, 1970–92	25
2.4	Nonoil exports by Standard Industrial Trade Classification, Middle East and North Africa, 1970–92	27

List of Figures, Tables, and Boxes

2.5	Share of merchandise exports in nonoil exports, Middle East and North Africa, 1970–92	28
2.6	Required growth in GDP and exports, Middle East and North Africa, 1995–2010	32
2.7	Trade performance, Middle East and North Africa, 1985–90	37
3.1	Trade and factor intensity by region, 1992	51
3.2	Net trade flows from the Middle East and North Africa, 1992	54
3.3	Production, trade, and factor income in the Middle East and North Africa, 1992	55
3.4	Macroeconomic impacts of the three simulations	57
3.5	Simulation design: L9(34) orthogonal table, combination of elasticity estimates	62
3.6	Sensitivity analysis, first simulation	62
3.7	Sensitivity analysis, second simulation	63
3.8	Sensitivity analysis, third simulation	63
A3.1	Change in prices by sector, first simulation	72
A3.2	Change in sectoral exports by destination, first simulation	74
A3.3	Structural change, first simulation	76
A3.4	Factor reallocation, first simulation	78
A3.5	Change in prices by sector, second simulation	80
A3.6	Change in sectoral exports by destination, second simulation	82
A3.7	Structural change, second simulation	84
A3.8	Factor reallocation, second simulation	86
A3.9	Change in prices by sector, third simulation	88
A3.10	Change in sectoral exports by destination, third simulation	90
A3.11	Structural change, third simulation	92
A3.12	Factor reallocation, third simulation	94
4.1	Average unweighted tariffs of countries undertaking liberalization efforts, mid-1980s and early 1990s	99
4.2	Trade taxes, various countries, 1993	100
4.3	Nonoil exports to the world, Middle East and North Africa and Central and Eastern Europe, 1989 and 1995	109
4.4	Share of traditional and nontraditional products in exports to the European Union, Middle East and North Africa and Central and Eastern Europe, 1989 and 1994	110

4.5	Exports after outward processing, Central and Eastern Europe and Middle East and North Africa, 1989 and 1994	112
4.6	Bound and applied tariffs, Egypt and Tunisia	117
4.7	Sectoral coverage of specific services commitments, various countries	117
5.1	Output, growth, and investment, 1960–85	140
7.1	Investor ratings, various countries, 1980–94	184
7.2	Government borrowing, Middle East and North Africa, 1980–93	188
8.1	Traditional instruction and its effects on learning	207
8.2	Traditional and new approaches to working and learning	209
8.3	Gross enrollments, Middle East and North Africa, 1992	210
8.4	Public spending on education, Middle East and North Africa, 1990	214
9.1	Poverty in the Middle East and North Africa, 1985, 1990, and 1994	227
9.2	Poverty in various regions, 1985 and 1990	228
9.3	Incidence, depth, and severity of poverty, various countries	229
9.4	Income inequality, various countries	231
9.5	Social indicators, various countries, 1993	232
9.6	Growth to poverty elasticities, selected countries	237
9.7	Growth and income redistribution as components of changes in poverty, Jordan, Morocco and Tunisia	238
9.8	Poverty and income inequality, Jordan, Morocco, and Tunisia	239
10.1	Estimated pollution loads by sector, Middle East and North Africa	266
10.2	Road transportation and air pollution, selected cities	268
10.3	Oil, economic openness, and energy consumption	273
10.4	Policies for changing environmental behavior	282
11.1	Trends in human exposure, Middle East and North Africa, 1980–2004	294
11.2	Potential reductions in emissions from fossil fuel use	298

Boxes

6.1	Regional conflicts in the Middle East and North Africa	169
8.1	Using context to learn concepts	208
8.2	Iran's Islamic Azad University	219

9.1	With perfect transfers, poverty could be eliminated	230
9.2	Tunisia uses quality differentiation to distribute food subsidies	243
11.1	Tunisia: sustaining employment with effective natural resource management	293
11.2	Morocco and Tunisia: energy efficiency and pricing policies	296

Foreword

The Economic Research Forum for the Arab Countries, Iran and Turkey (ERF) is an independent, nonprofit networking institution based in Cairo that promotes and funds policy-oriented research. The ERF develops and coordinates research activities for a core constituency of research fellows primarily from the region but also operating out of institutions elsewhere in the world. An important part of the ERF's mandate is to contribute to capacity building in economic research and to the policy debate in the Middle East and North Africa.

This volume of thematic studies by international scholars is the second to be published by the ERF as part of its efforts to disseminate the findings of ongoing research on the Arab countries, Iran, and Turkey. The papers here provide a unique combination of empirical analysis and policy insights on a range of issues that will determine the region's economic future. The book is complemented by a companion volume of country studies by development thinkers in the region titled *Economic Challenges Facing Middle Eastern and North African Countries: Alternative Futures*. We hope that both books will contribute to the debate in the region about its economic future and inform policy decisions in these countries in the coming years.

This book and its companion volume could not have been produced without the efforts of a number of people. Gillian Potter, the publications director of the ERF, helped identify publication outlets for the books. Nemat Shafik helped plan the workshop in Tunisia and commissioned many of the papers. Paul Holtz, of American Writing Corporation, edited the manuscript. Azeb Yideru kept track of numerous authors around the world with great efficiency. Without the efforts of these people, this important book and its companion volume would not have seen the light of day.

HEBA HANDOUSSA
Managing Director
Economic Research Forum
for the Arab Countries, Iran and Turkey

Notes on the Contributors

Robert E. Anderson is Senior Private Sector Development Specialist on the Private Sector and Finance Team, Europe and Central Asia–Middle East and North Africa Technical Department, at the World Bank.

Albert Martinez is Principal Private Sector Development Specialist on the Private Sector and Finance Team, Europe and Central Asia –Middle East and North Africa Technical Department, at the World Bank.

Jon Avins is Operations Officer on the Human Resources and Social Development Team, Europe and Central Asia–Middle East and North Africa Technical Department, at the World Bank.

Sue E. Berryman is Senior Education Specialist on the Human Resources and Social Development Team, Europe and Central Asia – Middle East and North Africa Technical Department, at the World Bank.

Milan Brahmbhatt is Economist in the Analysis and Prospects Division, International Economics Department, at the World Bank.

Uri Dadush is Division Chief in the Analysis and Prospects Division, International Economics Department, at the World Bank.

Ishac Diwan is Regional Coordinator for the Middle East and North Africa in the Economic Development Institute at the World Bank.

Willem van Eeghen is Senior Economist in the Middle East and North Africa Region at the World Bank.

Fredrick L. Golladay is Principal Human Resources Economist on the Human Resources and Social Development Team, Europe and Central Asia – Middle East and North Africa Technical Department, at the World Bank.

Bernard Hoekman is Senior Economist on the Private Sector and Finance Team, Europe and Central Asia–Middle East and North

Africa Technical Department, at the World Bank and Research Fellow at the Centre for Economic Policy Research.

Jalal Jalali is Economist in the Analysis and Prospects Division, International Economics Department, at the World Bank.

Bjorn Larsen is Environmental Economist in the Environment Division, Europe and Central Asia–Middle East and North Africa Technical Department, at the World Bank.

Hamid Mohtadi is Associate Professor of Economics at the University of Wisconsin and Research Fellow at the Economic Research Forum for the Arab Countries, Iran and Turkey.

John Page is Chief Economist in the Middle East and North Africa Regional Office at the World Bank.

E. Mick Riordan is Economist in the Analysis and Prospects Division, International Economics Department, at the World Bank.

Nemat Shafik is Research Fellow at the Economic Research Forum for the Arab Countries, Iran and Turkey and manager of the Private Sector Team in the Middle East and North Africa Region at the World Bank. While editing this book she was a Visiting Associate Professor at the Wharton School of the University of Pennsylvania.

Shane Streifel is Economist in the Commodity Policy and Analysis Unit, International Economics Department, at the World Bank.

Kazue Takagaki was a consultant on leave from Marubemi Trading Company when this volume was written.

Zhi Wang is Agricultural Economist in the Department of Applied Economics at the University of Minnesota.

John Waterbury is Director of the Center of International Studies at Princeton University.

Laurence Wolff is Principal Operations Officer in the Human Resources Division, Middle East and North Africa Country Department I, at the World Bank.

Chang-Po Yang is Senior Resident Economist at the World Bank field office in Cairo.

1 Prospects for Middle Eastern and North African Economies: An Overview

Nemat Shafik

The economies of the Middle East and North Africa are at a crossroads. After a decade of poor growth performance, a conjuncture of forces promises to change the region's economic outlook. Globalization of the world economy, revolutions in transport and communications, and increasingly liberalized trade are creating new competitive pressures and new opportunities. Meanwhile, the end of the Cold War, the aftermath of the Gulf conflict, the evolving Middle East peace process, and the rise of fundamentalism are challenging traditional regimes and policies. Young populations with poor employment prospects are calling for change, and opposition groups have become increasingly vocal. Navigating these turbulent waters will require that the region's leaders, business people, and citizens have a purposeful vision of the way ahead.

This volume presents the results of work sponsored by the Economic Research Forum for the Arab Countries, Iran and Turkey (ERF) and by the World Bank to contribute to such a vision. Most of the papers in this volume were presented at a workshop held in Tunis in June 1995 that brought together economists, human resource specialists, and environmentalists from almost every country in the region to discuss the major long-term issues facing the Middle East and North Africa. The comparative papers in this volume on the changing international context, human resource development, the role of the private sector, and the environment were prepared mainly by World Bank staff as background papers to a regional study called *Claiming the Future: Choosing Prosperity in the Middle East and North Africa* (World Bank, 1995).

By their nature, these thematic papers look across countries and may imply homogeneity in what is actually a very heterogeneous region. Readers more interested in country-specific analysis should refer to the country studies by scholars from the region, which are presented in a companion volume called *Economic Challenges Facing*

Middle Eastern and North African Countries (Shafik, 1997). Those studies analyze the implications of international developments at the local level, the key policy challenges facing national governments, and the political and institutional obstacles to reform for Egypt, the Gulf Cooperation Council (GCC) countries, Iran, Jordan, Lebanon, Morocco, Palestine, Sudan, Syria, Tunisia, and Turkey.

A number of cross-cutting themes recurred throughout the workshop and across the papers: the increasingly tough international environment that the region's countries face; uncertainty about how the region will integrate with the world economy and where future growth will come from, and the role that regionalism will play; the enormous shift in thinking about the role of human capital and natural resources in development; the decline of old institutions and the emergence of more efficient but often inequitable alternatives; and debate about the appropriate pace of change. Each of these issues is discussed in turn.

AN INCREASINGLY TOUGH EXTERNAL ENVIRONMENT

The chapters on the changing world economy, including the implications of the Uruguay Round, conveyed a sense that the region is rapidly falling behind in an increasingly competitive world. In Chapter 3 Ishac Diwan, Chang-Po Yang, and Zhi Wang estimate the impact of the Uruguay Round and find negative effects for Middle Eastern and North African countries, most of which have benefited from preferences and distortions in world trade such as the Multifiber Agreement. How can a region where wages tend to exceed productivity and skills find a competitive niche?

A favorable international environment was central to the region's past economic success, as noted in Chapter 2 by E. Mick Riordan, Uri Dadush, Jalal Jalali, Shane Streifel, Milan Brahmbhatt, and Kazue Takagaki. During 1960–85 Middle Eastern and North African countries outperformed all other developing regions except East Asia in output growth. In some ways the rapid growth of this era was similar to other regions, with the early and "easy" stages of import-substituting industrialization bringing economic improvements in the postcolonial period. But more important, the windfall brought about by the oil price shocks of the 1970s resulted in a massive transfer of wealth to both oil exporters and their neighbors (who benefited from migrant remittances and aid flows). At its peak in 1977–82 the windfall's effect on oil producers was equivalent to an almost 50 percent increase in their national incomes (Askari, Bazzari, and Tyler, 1997). Spillovers were equivalent to a 35–40 percent increase in GDP for the region as a whole. This windfall enabled a massive increase in public investment – in state-owned enterprises, infrastructure, and human capital – that fueled growth until oil prices collapsed in 1986.

Although the external environment for most developing countries has not been more favorable since the 1960s, the conditions for Middle Eastern and North African countries are increasingly tough. Riordan *et al.* describe the increasingly integrated global market – characterized by rapid growth in world trade, the increasing importance of outsourcing by multinational corporations, and a boom in capital flows to developing countries. The chapter also analyzes the degree to which Middle Eastern and North African countries have not participated in these trends – trade integration has actually declined, nonoil exports are flat, outsourcing has been insignificant, and the region has attracted only 3 percent of foreign direct investment (FDI) and less than 1 percent of total portfolio flows to developing countries.

The differences in integration with the world economy across the region's countries are significant – with countries such as Algeria, Egypt, Iran, Iraq, and Syria the most disengaged while Morocco, Tunisia, and Jordan are the most closely linked to international markets. These differences are apparent in the country studies, which reflect the very different issues faced by economies at various stages of the reform process. The more closed economies in the region still need to undergo significant trade liberalization to subject domestic producers to competitive pressures from the world economy (see Handoussa and Kheir-El-Din, 1997; Karshenas, 1997; Sukkar, 1997). Meanwhile, the more advanced reformers are struggling with issues such as how to find competitive niches in increasingly integrated world markets (see Kanaan, 1997; Hamdouch, 1997; Lahouel, 1997). And all countries in the region will have to ensure that integration with the world economy is accompanied by the creation of sound social institutions to ensure that those who lose from the process are few and well protected.

Trade liberalization is the first step toward remedying the region's isolation from broader trends in the global economy. In Chapter 4 Bernard Hoekman assesses the progress made under the Uruguay Round and the trading options open to Middle Eastern and North African countries. The Uruguay Round, he concludes, will subject firms in the region to increasing competitive pressures that, combined with the loss of preferences, will force considerable restructuring. The region's governments have not yet used the World Trade Organization (WTO) as a means of signaling commitments to trade liberalization. Hoekman argues that such binding commitments, along with free trade agreements with the European Union, would lock in the policy reforms that private investors demand. Private investment, in turn, will facilitate the region's integration with world markets.

EVOLVING REGIONAL OPTIONS

The menu of regional options has broadened for the Middle East and North Africa. In the past regionalism was a by-product of Arab nationalism and was driven by political, not economic, motives. The numerous attempts at Arab regionalism produced very little true integration (for example, intraregional trade never exceeded 9 percent of total regional trade) with the exception of labor migration to the major oil exporters and the remittances these workers sent home (Shafik, 1994). Arab regionalism failed for a number of reasons – the dominance of primary production in most regional economies created few trading opportunities, the region trades very little in general, and protectionist interests in most countries have resisted liberalization efforts, both regional and multilateral (Shafik, 1995). And although there are calls for greater intra-Arab economic cooperation, most authors in the volume focus on broader regional and global alternatives.

Today there are at least two new regional options on the table – one brought about by the peace process (the so-called Triangle proposal) and the other by fears of political instability along the southern rim of the Mediterranean (the European Union's Mediterranean Initiative). The Triangle proposal – to forge a Benelux-style integration arrangement between Israel, Jordan, and Palestine – was advocated by Israel's foreign minister, Shimon Peres, and a group at Harvard University proposed a free trade area among the three countries by 2010 that would be open to accession by other countries in the region (Lawrence *et al.*, 1995). But estimates of the quantitative impact of such an arrangement are small (in the hundreds of millions of dollars) and the political costs are potentially very large (since many Arabs fear Israeli hegemony under such an arrangement because the Israeli economy is many times larger than those of its neighbors). Thus the prospects for the Triangle are limited, although partial and ad hoc arrangements are likely to emerge in the medium term.

The European Union's Mediterranean Initiative is probably the most economically interesting and politically palatable option for the region. Empirical estimates of the impact of free trade arrangements with Europe show significant gains (Rutherford, Ruström, and Tarr, 1993, 1995). Interestingly, most of the benefits come not from the reduction of tariffs (since most Middle Eastern and North African countries already have free access to the market for manufactures in Europe) but from the harmonization of standards and reduction of trading costs from improved infrastructure, financed by aid from the European Union. The greatest gains result when trade liberalization vis-a-vis Europe is combined with broader liberalization vis-a-vis the rest of the world. The adjustment costs from integration with the Union are significant (especially for the region's more closed economies) but vary by sector, with tradables tending to gain at the expense of nontradables.

Some of the chapters in this volume evince ambivalence about the terms at which integration (be it with the rest of the world or with the European Union) is being offered. Few concessions are expected from Europe on agriculture and textiles – the two most important sectors for Middle Eastern and North African exporters. In the countries most advanced in their integration with the European Union – Turkey and Tunisia – there is a disturbing lack of public discourse and empirical analysis guiding policy choices. But there is also a sense that regionalism is at best a complement to the inevitable pressures to exploit the opportunities that integration with the world economy might bring. The only real choice is how fast to begin adjusting.

WHERE IS FUTURE GROWTH GOING TO COME FROM?

The authors agree that a key issue is how to move from stabilization to growth in the region. Although macroeconomic stabilization in countries like Egypt, Jordan, Morocco, and Tunisia cannot be taken for granted, the low-level equilibrium that has emerged in these countries has meant stagnant wages and little improvement in living standards. The causes of such low productivity growth in the region remains a puzzle – Is it policies? The role of the public sector? Or the weakness of institutions? In Chapter 5 John Page explores the depth of the productivity collapse (especially compared with East Asia's experience) and focuses on weak investment in tradable sectors, where international competition raises efficiency.

The importance of growth for reducing poverty is emphasized in Willem van Eeghen's chapter, which surveys the achievements on poverty reduction in Middle Eastern and North African countries. He finds strong evidence that growth has been the most important factor in determining the relatively small number of poor in the region and holds the key to further poverty reduction in the future. The differences in poverty performance across countries is dramatic – with fast-growing economies like Morocco and Tunisia achieving dramatic reductions in poverty while slow-growing countries have seen a sharp increase in the number of poor.

Nevertheless, macroeconomic stability is still an issue in several Middle Eastern and North Africa countries. Lebanon has achieved a tentative macroeconomic stability, but the situation is fragile because of the enormous investment requirements of the government's ambitious reconstruction program (Corm, 1997). Syria, which has managed to replace past aid flows from the Gulf and the Soviet Union with oil revenues, still faces an external constraint because of its arrears to foreign creditors (Sukkar, 1997). As in Sudan, Syria's outstanding debt must be addressed if private investors are to have sufficient confidence in the macroeconomic situation to provide needed capital (Elbadawi, 1997).

What can we learn from countries, like Turkey, that have stabilized, are among the most advanced reformers, and have been the most successful at generating growth and exports? Turkey's productivity gains and export success relied on several instruments – a competitive exchange rate, preferential access to credit for exporters, fiscal incentives, and reduced protection. The productivity gains that resulted from greater competition, investment, and innovation explain about 42 percent of Turkey's growth from 1978–92 (Togan, 1997). But despite its success in creating an outward-oriented export sector, Turkey has not yet been able to reform poorly performing public enterprises, whose losses are putting enormous pressure on the government deficit and threatening macroeconomic stability.

The chapters in this volume reveal considerable debate about the appropriate role of the private and public sectors and some skepticism on whether the private sector can "carry the ball" on growth. There is frequent emphasis on the need to build institutions that can serve the public interest in the context of a private sector-led economy. The private sector in many of the region's countries is characterized by extensive rent-seeking. Privatization of public enterprises in competitive markets is important, but sound governance and regulation by the public sector where private markets are imperfect is equally important. In Chapter 7 Robert E. Anderson and Albert Martinez show how the region's countries have lagged in privatization and created distorted environments for private sector development. But they argue that the region's private sector is the product of government policies, so there is no reason to believe that the energies devoted to rent-seeking in the past will not be channeled to productivity gains in the future if incentives change.

INTEGRATING EDUCATION AND THE ENVIRONMENT

The chapters in the volume make some headway in explicitly integrating human capital and natural resource concerns with the region's development strategies. Most countries in the region have come to recognize that, in addition to physical capital, human and natural capital are essential to the region's economic future. There is also growing appreciation of the need to build social capital, particularly in war-torn societies (such as Lebanon and Sudan) where civic institutions have been destroyed.

Because most Middle Eastern and North African countries are unlikely to compete with low-wage countries like India and China, developing skills and moving into higher value-added activities must be a central part of any country's development strategy. This means that quality will become far more important in education systems that in the past have focused on increasing access. In Chapter 8 Frederick L. Golladay, Sue E. Berryman, Jon Avins, and Laurence Wolff highlight the changing international context in which education systems in the region must respond to very different skill requirements. These pressures are already being felt in many countries where labor markets are increasingly bifurcated and those in the middle (civil servants, public enterprise employees, secondary school graduates) are being squeezed out. In countries like Egypt, Lebanon, Sudan, Syria, Tunisia, and Turkey there are emerging pressures on education systems and a need to "catch up" by providing better access to schooling and improving quality. In Chapter 9 Willem van Eeghen also emphasizes that while most of the region's governments have been successful in reducing poverty of incomes, they have failed to reduce poverty of opportunities by improving access to education (especially for girls and in rural areas).

Similarly, more prudent management of natural resources, especially water, is increasingly urgent. The mining of nonrenewable resources such as oil and of renewables such as clean air, water, and soils has reached unsustainable levels in many Middle Eastern and North African countries, as noted in Chapter 10 by Hamid Mohtadi and Chapter 11 by Bjorn Larsen. Mohtadi analyzes how oil income enabled countries to finance inward-oriented industrialization that was both energy- and pollution-intensive. The economic implications of moving away from such methods of production are enormous – as oil, mining, and water-intensive agriculture decline in importance, new sources of income will have to be found. Larsen analyzes natural resource depletion and savings behavior in the region and finds that much of the windfall from past resource extraction has been consumed. Savings rates will have to increase dramatically if living standards are to be maintained or improved.

Moreover, the costs of environmental neglect are rising in many countries. Larsen estimates that almost 25 percent of the region's population is exposed to air pollution levels that exceed World Health Organization (WHO) guidelines. Some 45 million people lack access to safe water, and 85 million survive without adequate sanitation. Millions of life-years are lost as a result of air and water pollution. Mohtadi delineates the role of property rights, public information, education, and democratization in addressing these critical environmental issues.

THE DECAY OF INSTITUTIONS

There is considerable discussion on the collapse or corruption of institutions, with the region's low-wage civil servants increasingly susceptible to bribes and much of the private sector resorting to informal channels to evade burdensome regulations. There is an urgent need for institutional upgrading and reduced transactions costs for the private sector as key issues for the future. In particular, as governments withdraw from the commercial sphere there is a need to build the capacity to regulate the private sector in new areas such as natural monopolies, environmental protection, and the provision of infrastructure and social services.

The emergence of informal structures that are more efficient (but often less equitable) is a common phenomenon in several countries. For example, in Lebanon the decline of the middle class, the growing inequality of incomes, and the weakness of the state have resulted in a growing bifurcation of society and a reliance on informal institutions (Corm, 1997). Standards in Egyptian schools have deteriorated rapidly as underpaid public sector teachers devote their energies to private tutoring. The nascent Palestinian administration has yet to take shape and needs to develop the structures of a modern state (Abed, 1997). And countries like Sudan have experienced a complete breakdown of public institutions after decades of war (Elbadawi, 1997). Democratization – which through elections provides a mechanism for the ruled to change the ruler – is discussed in some chapters, but there is little optimism about the immediate prospects for political and social restructuring of this magnitude in many countries.

There is, however, a strong sense that more energy should be devoted to understanding the role of institutions in the region and their role in economic reform. In Chapter 6 John Waterbury provides an interesting framework for thinking about the relationship between the quality of governance and progress on economic reform. He concludes that there are multiple pathways, each with different degrees of government quality and economic policy. Institutional change is inevitable, but the pathway taken determines whether it will be a coherent and orderly process or one driven by crises and upheaval. Waterbury also makes a special plea for protecting civil society from states more concerned with suppressing religious opposition than with building the institutions required for political and economic development.

CAN GRADUALISM WORK?

Countries in the region tend to prefer gradualist approaches that allow phasing of the inevitable adjustment costs. But does today's fast-paced world economy enable gradualist strategies to succeed? Waterbury draws a distinction between the rate of change and the quality of change. If the rate of reform is inadequate, the challenge is to create the political will and sense of urgency required to speed it up. But if the quality of change is the issue, the solution may be more structural, involving institutions, governance, and culture. He argues that while Middle Eastern and North African countries are characterized by a kind of political exceptionalism that will make the transition to greater accountability and democratization difficult, they are not exceptional when it comes to economic reform. This combination is likely to spawn a continued preference for gradualism, even if punctuated by periodic crises.

How can Middle Eastern and North African countries achieve economic success with gradualist reform strategies? There is a clear link to the credibility of institutions. Attracting investors usually requires up-front commitments, but promises about the future direction of economic policy may be adequate if they are made by credible public institutions. Few governments in the region have this kind of credibility with their own private sector, much less with foreign investors. Thus international mechanisms for securing credibility – such as association or customs union agreements with the European Union, as discussed by several authors, or through international credit agencies or guarantee instruments, as mentioned by Riordan *et al.* – may be the only way to proceed gradually while still attracting the private capital that is essential for future growth.

References

Abed, George,T., 1997. "The Palestinian Economy: Alternative Futures," in Nemat Shafik (ed.), *Economic Challenges Facing Middle Eastern and North African Countries*, London: Macmillan.

Askari, Hossein, Maha Bazzari, and William Tyler, 1997. "Policies and Economic Potential in the Countries of the Gulf Cooperation Council," in Nemat Shafik (ed.), *Economic Challenges Facing Middle Eastern and North African Countries*, London: Macmillan.

Corm, Georges, 1997. "Reconstructing Lebanon's Economy," in Nemat Shafik (ed.), *Economic Challenges Facing Middle Eastern and North African Countries*, London: Macmillan.

Elbadawi, Ibrahim A., 1997. "Sudan: Toward a Strategic Vision for Peace and Development," in Nemat Shafik (ed.), *Economic Challenges Facing Middle Eastern and North African Countries*. London: Macmillan.

Hamdouch, Bachir, 1997. "Adjustment, Strategic Planning, and the Moroccan Economy," In Nemat Shafik, (ed.), *Economic Challenges Facing Middle Eastern and North African Countries*, London: Macmillan.

Handoussa, Heba, and Hanaa Kheir-El-Din, 1997. "A Vision for Egypt in 2012," in Nemat Shafik, ed., *Economic Challenges Facing Middle Eastern and North African Countries*. London: Macmillan.

Kanaan, Taher H., 1997. "The State and the Private Sector in Jordan," in Nemat Shafik (ed.), *Economic Challenges Facing Middle Eastern and North African Countries*, London: Macmillan.

Karshenas, Massoud, 1997. "Structural Adjustment and the Iranian Economy," in Nemat Shafik (ed.), *Economic Challenges Facing Middle Eastern and North African Countries*, London: Macmillan.

Lahouel, Mohamed Hedi, 1997. "Competition Policies and Deregulation in Tunisia," in Nemat Shafik (ed.), *Economic Challenges Facing Middle Eastern and North African Countries*, London: Macmillan.

Lawrence, Robert *et al.*, 1995. "Toward Free Trade in the Middle East: The Triad and Beyond," Cambridge, Mass. : Harvard University.

Rutherford, Thomas, E.E. Ruström, and David Tarr. 1993. "Morocco's Free Trade Agreement with the European Union: A Quantitative Assessment," Policy Research Working Paper 1173, Washington, D.C. : World Bank.

——1995. "The Free Trade Agreement Between Tunisia and the European Union," Policy Research Department, Washington, D.C. : World Bank.

Shafik, Nemat, 1994. "Integration by Migration?", *Digest of Middle East Studies*, 3(2).

—— 1995. "Learning from Doers: Lessons on Regional Integration for the Middle East," in Hanaa Kheir-El-Din (ed.), *Economic Cooperation in the Middle East: Prospects and Challenges*, Cairo: Dar Al-Mostaqbal Al Arabi.

—— (ed.), 1997. *Economic Challenges Facing Middle Eastern and North African Countries*, London: Macmillan.

Sukkar, Nabil, 1997. "Syria: Strategic Economic Issues," in Nemat Shafik,(ed.), *Economic Challenges Facing Middle Eastern and North African Countries*, London: Macmillan.

Togan, Sübidey, 1997. "Determinants of Economic Growth in Turkey," in Nemat Shafik (ed.), *Economic Challenges Facing Middle Eastern and North African Countries*, London: Macmillan.

World Bank, 1995. *Claiming the Future: Choosing Prosperity in the Middle East and North Africa*, Washington, D.C.: World Bank.

Part I

The Changing International Context

2 The World Economy and its Implications for the Middle East and North Africa, 1995–2010

E. Mick Riordan, Uri Dadush, Jalal Jalali, Shane Streifel, Milan Brahmbhatt, and Kazue Takagaki

The next fifteen years will be critical to fulfilling the long-term potential of the Middle East and North Africa. For too long the countries in the region have relied on oil revenues – which are now declining – and resisted market-oriented reforms. Yet a far-reaching economic reorientation is essential if the region is to reap the benefits of a changing global economy. Exports must be diversified to secure additional foreign currency. Public sectors should shrink to foster private sector activity and increase competitiveness. Peace must be achieved to attract investment. Population growth rates must be brought under control. And regional and global integration should be used as a springboard for growth. The benefits of reform come quickly, as some countries in the region have learned. Countries that squander these opportunities risk being left behind in the twenty-first century.

A decline in the world oil market, regional strife, and slow progress in instituting market-based reforms have caused real export earnings per capita to drop in the Middle East and North Africa. As populations in the region grow, per capita incomes will fall further unless nonoil sources of revenue are developed.

Nonoil merchandise exports hold the greatest potential for growth in foreign currency earnings. But if the region's public sectors continue to stifle efficiency and initiative, the contribution of nonoil merchandise exports will likely remain small. Reforms that improve international competitiveness would enable countries in the region to build on several favorable aspects in the external environment, including the increasing importance of reverse linkages between industrial and developing countries, the liberalization of trade with and increased financial assistance from the European Union (EU), the possible consolidation of the peace process, the rapid growth in world demand for nonoil goods and services, and the ability to repatriate flight capital.

A WORRYING OUTLOOK

Because the region's nonoil exporting countries depend heavily on the oil exporters, foreign exchange earnings in all the Middle Eastern and North African countries are adversely affected by a decline in oil export earnings. But with little growth in real oil prices expected through 2010, oil export earnings are expected to grow by just 2–2.5 percent a year.

Declining per capita export and foreign exchange earnings

During the 1980s growth in the Middle East and North Africa averaged 0.4 percent a year and real per capita gross domestic product (GDP) fell by 2.7 percent a year – the largest such decline in any developing region outside the transition economies (Figure 2.1). Among the major oil exporters per capita GDP fell by more than 2 percent a year, while GDP for the more diversified exporters rose by about 3.5 percent a year between 1980 and 1994. Real per capita export earnings for the region dropped by more than 4 percent a year between 1980 and 1993, however, and the import purchasing power of per capita revenues fell by more than 7 percent a year.

The sharp decline and recent stagnation in the region's oil revenues have affected foreign exchange earnings both directly and through a multiplier effect on other sources of foreign exchange earnings (Table 2.1). Indeed, of the region's important sources of revenue, only tourism and worker remittances advanced in real terms over the past decade, and gains in both areas were modest. Nonoil merchandise exports have suffered from the effects of Dutch disease and from the lack of dynamism caused by limited product diversification. Earnings on overseas assets also have fallen, as fiscal difficulties have induced the major oil exporters in the Gulf area to liquidate substantial amounts of foreign holdings. This trend was accentuated by the Gulf

Figure 2.1 Per capita GDP growth, various regions, 1981–90

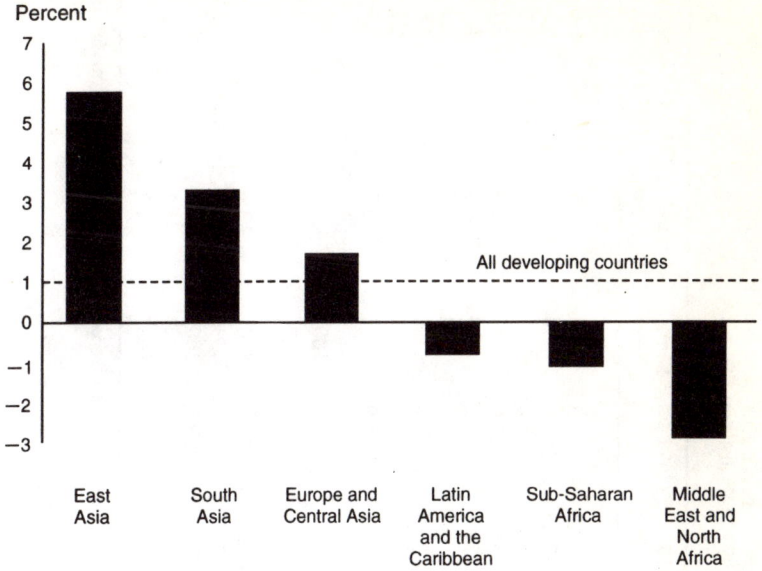

Source: World Bank data.

war and by lower returns stemming from the recent recessions in industrial countries. Worker remittances to the region's labor-surplus countries are tied to economic conditions in the oil-exporting countries, and have subsided from earlier peaks. Finally, official grants, particularly from Arab OPEC sources, have fallen, in part because of changing political circumstances but also because of the drop in oil revenues.

Rapidly growing populations

Since 1970 the population of the Middle East and North Africa has doubled, increasing by 3 percent a year. This growth rate far exceeds the 1.8 percent annual average experienced by all developing countries – even those in Sub-Saharan Africa. Population growth has been most rapid in the oil-exporting countries, with population growth of more than 5 percent a year in the countries of the Gulf Cooperation Council (GCC).[1] Among the nonoil exporters, populations nearly doubled between 1970 and 1995 (Table 2.2). Rapid growth and demographic

Table 2.1 Sources of foreign exchange, Middle East and North Africa, 1970–93 (real 1987 U.S. dollars)

Source	1970	1974	1984	1990	1993	Share (percent)	Growth, 1970–93 (percent)	Growth, 1980–93 (percent)
Current account revenues (billion dollars)	172.8	173.3	155.0	192.8	210.3	100.0	0.9	−1.0
Merchandise exports	162.0	142.8	91.2	138.0	156.0	74.2	−0.2	−0.5
Fuels (oil and other)	142.0	140.0	62.5	100.0	125.0	59.4	−0.6	0.0
Nonoil merchandise	20.0	2.8	28.7	38.0	31.0	14.8	1.9	−2.1
Services exports	5.1	13.6	19.7	19.8	22.2	10.6	6.7	−1.3
Tourism	1.8	4.0	5.5	6.7	7.8	3.7	6.6	0.3
Factor income receipts	2.0	8.5	27.1	20.8	18.0	8.6	10.0	−2.8
Worker remittances	1.3	3.4	10.6	7.5	9.1	4.3	8.8	1.2
Official transfers	2.4	5.0	6.3	6.7	5.0	2.2	3.2	−3.4
Real per capita revenues[a] (dollars)	128	115	76	80	76	100[b]	−2.2	−4.2
Maghreb	132	65	45	53	45	6[b]	−4.6	−3.4
Mashreq	14	21	30	33	37	50[b]	4.3	0.2
Gulf Cooperation Council	1,020	1,100	435	410	435	570[b]	−3.6	−6.2
Other Gulf countries[c]	82	50	37	33	25	33[b]	−5.0	−7.2
Israel	140	245	330	387	380	500[b]	4.4	0.6
Oil exporters	160	140	80	80	75	99[b]	−3.2	−5.2
Nonoil exporters	30	50	60	75	78	103[b]	4.2	0.3

Note: Real merchandise exports reflect appropriate trade deflators. Nonmerchandise components have been converted to real terms using U.S. private consumption deflator.
a. Regional average. *b.* Percentage of regional aggregate. *c.* Iran, Iraq, and Yemen.
Source: U.N. Comtrade database; IMF and World Bank data.

Table 2.2 Population growth, Middle East and North Africa, 1970–2010 (million)

Region	1970	1990	Growth, 1970–90 (percent)	1995	2010[a]	Growth, 1990–2010[a] (percent)
Total	134.2	246.0	3.0	282.0	400.0	2.5
Maghreb	36.2	62.7	2.8	70.3	95.0	2.0
Mashreq	43.3	71.5	2.5	80.4	107.6	2.0
Gulf Cooperation Council	7.7	22.1	5.4	25.0	39.4	3.0
Other Gulf countries[b]	44.1	85.1	3.3	100.0	152.0	3.0
Israel	3.0	4.6	2.2	5.6	6.8	2.0
Memorandum items						
Oil exporters	100.6	189.2	3.2	216.4	311.4	2.5
Nonoil exporters	33.6	56.8	2.7	65.6	88.6	2.2
All low- and middle-income countries	2,850	4,050	1.8	4,450	5,625	1.2

a. Projected
b. Iran, Iraq, and Yemen.
Source: World Bank data and projections.

change have led to a rise in food and other import requirements, increased demands for sanitation and other infrastructure, caused living standards to decline, generated high unemployment, and resulted in increasing social unrest.

World Bank projections suggest that although population growth will slow moderately, the region will need to accommodate 120 million new inhabitants – a 40 percent increase – by 2010 (World Bank, 1994b). To achieve growth rates in per capita income equal to those expected in industrial countries (about 2.5 percent a year), let alone compensate for earlier declines in living standards or absorb new entrants to the labor force, GDP in the region will need to grow by 5 percent a year in the coming decade. Given the uncertain outlook in the oil market, this massive increase in population suggests that prospects for gains in per capita income are not bright.

Volatile export earnings

The dominance of fuels in the region's export mix has led not only to sluggish growth, but also to extreme instability in foreign earnings.

Figure 2.2 Volatility of the purchasing power of exports, various regions, 1970–93

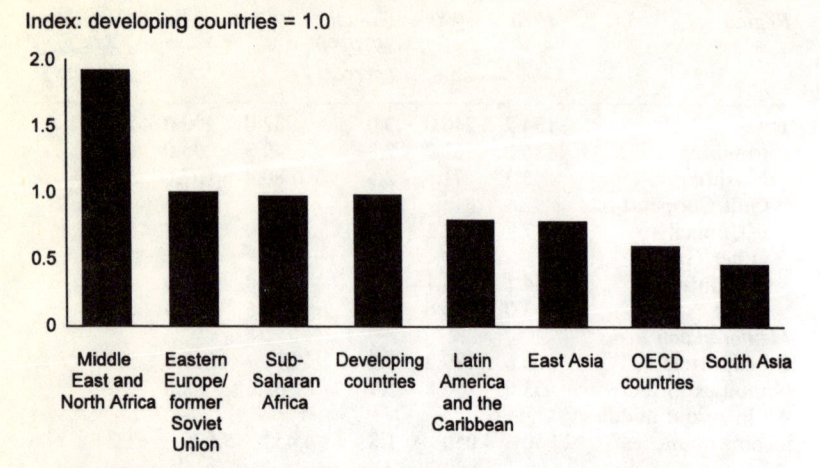

Index: developing countries = 1.0

Middle East and North Africa	~1.9
Eastern Europe/former Soviet Union	~1.0
Sub-Saharan Africa	~0.95
Developing countries	~0.95
Latin America and the Caribbean	~0.8
East Asia	~0.75
OECD countries	~0.6
South Asia	~0.45

Note: The measure of volatility used is the standard error (%) of a time trend regression of the purchasing power of exports.
Source: World Bank data.

During 1970–93 the purchasing power of exports (defined as exports of goods and all factor and nonfactor services, adjusted for inflation by the U.S. private consumption deflator) in the region was twice as volatile as that for other developing regions, and nearly four times as high as that of industrial countries (Figure 2.2). Instability for the oil exporters exceeds that of the nonoil exporting group by a factor of three, with the more diversified economies of Israel, Morocco, and Tunisia displaying distinctly smoother patterns of export growth (Figure 2.3). The oil market will continue to be subject to enormous uncertainty, both on the demand side (because of the potential for energy conservation and possible development of alternative sources of power) and on the supply side (the return of Iraq to the market, possible advances in exploration or product technologies), suggesting that export earnings in the region will remain volatile.

Prospects for revenue by source

Oil

Fuel exports are the most important link to the global economy and the most significant determinant of regional economic performance.

Figure 2.3 Volatility of the purchasing power of exports, Middle East and North Africa, 1970–93

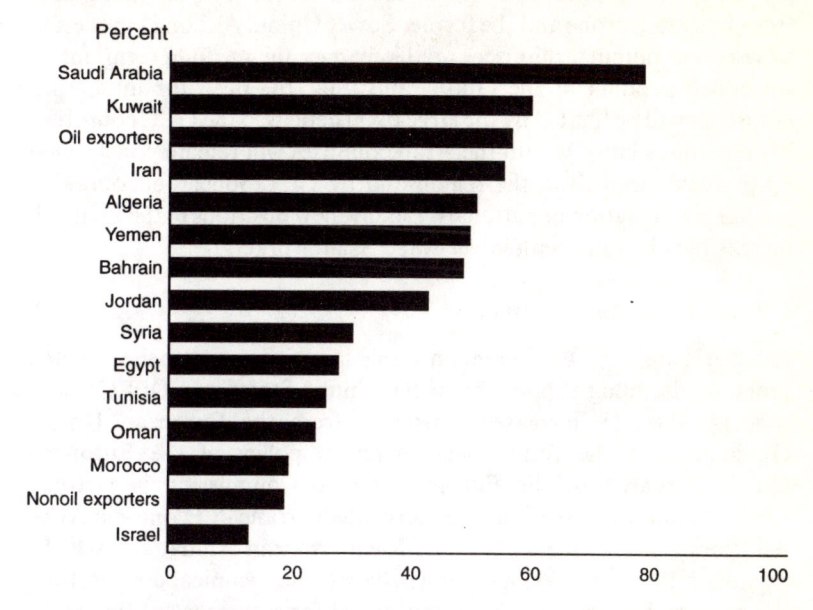

Country	Percent
Saudi Arabia	~80
Kuwait	~60
Oil exporters	~58
Iran	~55
Algeria	~50
Yemen	~48
Bahrain	~47
Jordan	~42
Syria	~30
Egypt	~28
Tunisia	~25
Oman	~23
Morocco	~20
Nonoil exporters	~18
Israel	~12

Note: The measure of volatility used is the standard error (percentage) of a time trend regression of the purchasing power of exports.
Source: World Bank data.

Fuel exports accounted for as much as 96 percent of the region's merchandise export earnings in 1981, and for about 80 percent in recent years. For major oil exporters fuel exports have consistently represented more than 90 percent of merchandise exports.

The World Bank projects little growth in real oil prices and a rate of growth of oil export earnings of 2–2.5 percent through 2010. The sluggish outlook for long-run oil earnings will adversely affect the entire region. Oil exporters and importers in the Middle East and North Africa are linked through three important channels: worker remittances, intraregional trade, and development assistance from the Gulf members of OPEC to several countries of the Mashreq.[2]

Worker remittances

Several economic and political trends suggest that no further growth in the level of real remittances to the Middle East and North Africa is likely over the medium term. Despite recovery in industrial countries, demand for immigrant labor will decline in Europe because of structural unemployment in the European Union and the recent flow of immigrants from Eastern Europe and the former Soviet Union. Although moderate increases in nominal oil prices are likely over the medium term, infrastructure spending in the Gulf – and thus, the need for immigrant laborers – will be limited by the large fiscal deficits in the GCC countries. Movement of labor within the Arab countries will remain constrained by political tensions in the region and by GCC policies encouraging greater participation of nationals. Finally, new positions in the Gulf will increasingly be filled with lower-wage Asian workers.

Official development assistance

Aid levels are expected to remain stable in real terms over the next ten years, as declining support from the United States and OPEC countries is offset by increased assistance from the European Union. Guidelines for the future Mediterranean policy of the European Union, prepared by the European Union Commission in October 1994, envision the creation of a Euro-Mediterranean Economic Area. An important element of this Mediterranean Initiative will be expanded flows of development assistance and technical cooperation. With the end of the Cold War and hoped-for settlement of the Arab-Israeli conflict, external aid will be increasingly based on recipient countries' commitment to economic reforms rather than their geopolitical importance. There are also renewed moves – championed by Japan – to link development assistance to military spending in the recipient country. Each of these factors will likely carry important implications for the distribution of development funds.

Earnings on overseas assets

Over the past decade the deficit on goods and nonfactor service trade in the Middle East and North Africa became the largest of the developing regions, averaging an annual $19.5 billion during 1990–93. Drawdowns of external assets – including reserves, short-term borrowings, and increased arrears – have been the principal modes of financing this deficit. Kuwait, whose budget deficit represents 15 percent of GDP, spent about $60 billion on the Gulf war, drawing down its $100 billion reserve fund. Given the long-term outlook for oil prices and for only slow reform among the major oil exporters, additional drawing down of revenues is likely throughout the region.

Tourism

Tourism is one of the few sources of foreign earnings that advanced in real terms during the 1980s (albeit at a sluggish rate of 0.3 percent a year), and it represents an important source of foreign exchange for Egypt, Israel, Jordan, Morocco, and Tunisia. Although potentially a growth area for wider segments of the region, tourism's small relative importance in total revenues suggests that even robust growth in revenues will be unable to offset the expected stagnation in oil trade. And for tourism to grow, perceptions of the region as a war zone must be reduced.

Other commercial services

One of the more vigorous areas of growth in world trade over the past decade has been commercial services, and international trade in services – particularly long-distance provision of business and other support functions – is expected to lead the next stage of globalization. Commercial services exports in the Middle East and North Africa reached almost $30 billion in 1993, an amount equivalent to the value of nonoil merchandise exports. Transportation and tourism each account for about 30 percent and other services for 40 percent of the total. For several countries in the region (including Israel, Morocco, and the countries of the Mashreq) significant potential exists to build on this strong foundation. Most countries in the region are not currently well placed to participate in the burgeoning growth of global long-distance services, however, but are likely to find niches in services trade within the region.

WILL THE REGION PARTICIPATE IN THE GLOBALIZATION OF MARKETS AND PRODUCTION?

The existence of other sources of foreign exchange both facilitates and inhibits the region's ability to develop its nonoil merchandise export sector. The literature on Dutch disease tends to stress the disadvantages of other sources of foreign exchange. The first and most important effect – that exporters can avail themselves of the scale economies afforded by a larger domestic market for their products – cuts both ways. On the one hand, if earnings from oil, foreign aid, worker remittances, and other sources did not exist, domestic markets in the region would be much smaller and average costs higher. On the other hand, the domestic market tends to absorb supply that would otherwise be destined for export. The second effect seems to have been especially important in the Middle East and North Africa, where domestic markets are heavily protected (and profitable) in sectors with export potential and public sector companies enjoy quasi-monopoly positions.

The existence of large alternative sources of foreign exchange appears to have had two main adverse effects on the region's exports. First, despite significant unemployment, the cost of doing business in the region is high compared with other countries at similar stages of development.[3] Anecdotal evidence suggests that the cost of labor is at least 50 percent higher in Egypt than in China or India, and there is no indication that productivity is higher. Second, the direct accrual to the government of large rents has facilitated the development of large public sectors in the region. Large and inefficient government enterprises inhibit exports by competing with the private sector for markets and resources, by providing preferential treatment in customs and other regulations, and by creating a variety of opportunities for rent seeking. Red tape, high fees, and restrictive labor policies are often cited by exporters as important impediments to their activities. Domestic reforms will be critical if the economies of the Middle East and North Africa are to increase their nonoil exports.

Nonoil export performance and potential

Since 1970 crude oil, refined products, and natural gas have accounted for between 77 percent (in 1988) and 93 percent (in 1980) of total merchandise exports from the Middle East and North Africa. But for most countries in the region the share of nonoil exports in total exports has increased since the mid-1980s (Figure 2.4). Boosting the growth of these exports will be critical if gains in per capita incomes are to be achieved over the coming decade.

Since 1970 the value of nonoil merchandise exports has risen by more than ten times, from $3.4 billion in 1970 to $36.8 billion in 1992 (in nominal dollars; Table 2.3). Excluding Israel, which accounted for about a third of these exports, nonoil merchandise exports in the region stood at about $24 billion in 1992 – below the level in several East Asian countries and slightly less than Finland's total exports. Of the region's total nonoil merchandise exports in 1992, about 72 percent went to OECD countries, including 40 percent to the European Union, 14 percent to the United States, and 5 percent to Japan. If

Table 2.3 Distribution of exports, Middle East and North Africa, 1970–92
(billions of U.S. dollars)

	Total merchandise exports			Nonoil merchandise exports		
Region/country	1970	1980	1992	1970	1980	1992
Total	15.43	257.95	152.59	3.39	18.33	36.77
Total excluding						
Israel	14.69	252.66	139.47	2.65	13.04	23.73
Maghreb	1.68	20.26	68.08	0.92	3.59	7.74
Algeria	1.01	15.62	11.14	0.30	0.24	0.46
Morocco	0.49	2.40	3.98	0.49	2.29	3.85
Tunisia	0.18	2.24	4.04	0.13	1.06	3.43
Mashreq	1.20	6.60	120.95	0.94	2.60	4.20
Egypt	0.76	3.05	3.07	0.54	0.72	1.22
Jordan	0.03	0.57	1.22	0.03	0.57	1.22
Lebanon	0.20	0.87	0.84	0.20	0.86	0.83
Syria	0.20	2.11	3.09	0.17	0.45	0.94
Gulf Cooperation Council	5.59	162.7	9.39	0.35	4.88	9.94
Bahrain	0.27	3.60	3.46	0.06	0.23	0.69
Kuwait	1.90	19.85	6.69	0.11	2.21	0.33
Oman	0.21	3.75	5.43	0.02	0.14	0.49
Qatar	0.24	5.71	3.60	0.00	0.23	0.52
Saudi Arabia	2.42	109.11	42.77	0.02	0.89	4.62
United Arab Emirates	0.55	20.67	20.50	0.13	1.18	3.29
Other						
Iran	2.62	14.11	16.70	0.30	1.02	1.25
Iraq	1.10	26.28	4.20	0.06	0.24	0.13
Israel	0.73	5.29	13.12	0.73	5.29	13.04
Libya	2.37	21.92	8.10	0.00	0.00	0.32
Yemen	0.14	0.80	0.65	0.09	0.71	0.13

Source: U.N. Comtrade database.

Israel is excluded from this analysis, the U.S. share falls to 4.5 percent of total nonoil merchandise exports from the region.[4]

The main source of growth has been manufactured products, which rose from 30 percent of nonoil merchandise exports in 1970–72 to 50 percent in 1980–82 and 70 percent in 1990–92. Between 1970 and 1992 the EU's share in nonoil merchandise exports from the Middle East and North Africa fell from 52 percent to 43 percent, while exports to Japan and especially the United States rose. Compared with other groups in the Middle East and North Africa, exports by the Maghreb countries have been more oriented toward the OECD; exports to the

Figure 2.4 Nonoil exports as a share of total, Middle East and North Africa, 1970–92

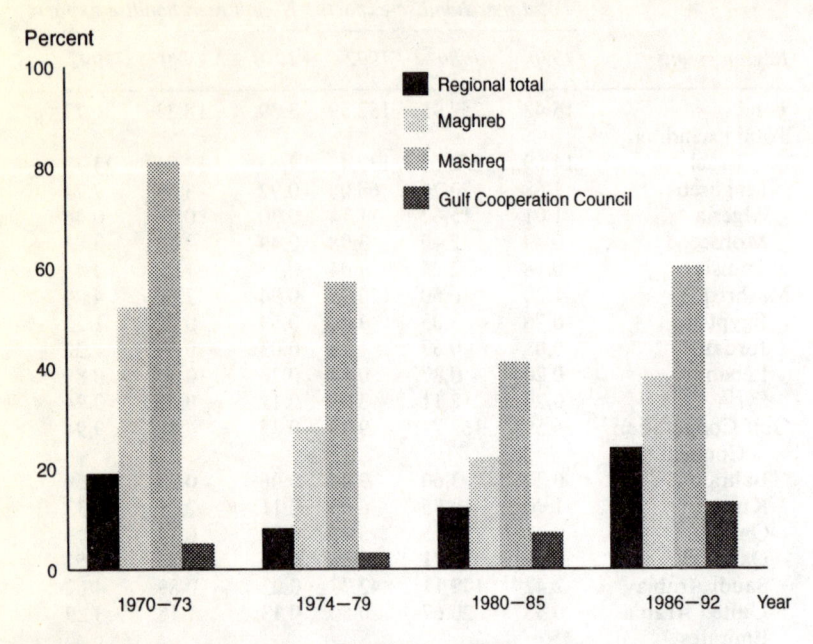

Source: U.N. Comtrade and U.N. Conference on Trade and Development data.

EU countries represented two-thirds of the group's nonoil merchandise exports in 1992.[5] GCC countries export only 45 percent of their nonoil merchandise exports to industrial countries.

The region's most important nonoil exports are shown in Table 2.4. Among nonoil merchandise exports, manufactures have been growing the fastest; the shares of food and other agricultural products have been falling (Table 2.5). In 1992 food accounted for 13 percent of onoil manufacturing exports from the region; other agricultural products accounted for only 2.7 percent. This evolution is even more pronounced when Israel is excluded from the region (Figure 2.5). Maghreb countries have experienced the greatest transformation of their economies, with the share of manufactures in their nonoil manufacturing exports increasing from 13 percent in 1970 to 37 percent in 1980 and 74 percent in 1992. The main components of manufactures exports from the region are clothing and textiles (30 percent), chemicals (27 percent), and machinery (14 percent).

Table 2.4 Nonoil exports by Standard Industrial Trade Classification, Middle East and North Africa, 1970–92 (billions of U.S. dollars)

Export	1970–72	1980–82	1990–92
Miscellaneous manufactured goods	0.10	1.34	5.09
Chemicals	0.09	0.99	4.91
Basic manufactures	0.43	2.13	3.97
Food and live animals	0.66	1.83	3.41
Machines and transport equipment	0.08	1.42	2.42
Crude materials excluding fuels	0.75	2.24	2.34
Goods not classed by kind	0.03	0.30	1.78
Animal, vegetable oils, and fats	0.06	0.16	0.23
Beverages and tobacco	0.08	0.11	0.17
Total	2.30	10.50	24.30

Note: Excludes Israel.
Source: U.N. Comtrade database.

Figure 2.5 Composition of nonoil exports, Middle East and North Africa, 1970–92

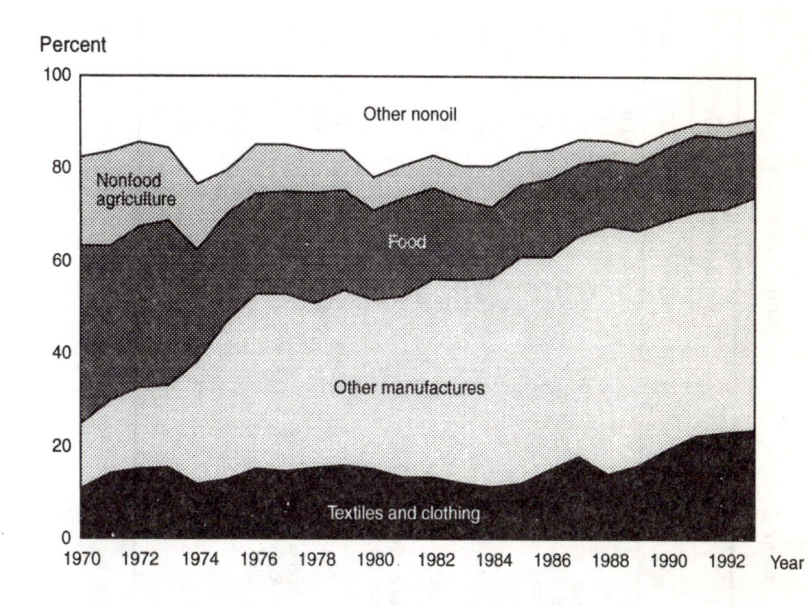

Note: Excludes Israel.
Sources: U.N. Comtrade and U.N. Conference on Trade and Development data.

Table 2.5 Share of merchandise exports in nonoil exports, Middle East and North Africa, 1970–92 (percent)

Region/country	Manufactures 1970	Manufactures 1980	Manufactures 1992	Clothing and textiles 1970	Clothing and textiles 1980	Clothing and textiles 1992	Food 1970	Food 1980	Food 1992	Nonfood agriculture 1970	Nonfood agriculture 1980	Nonfood agriculture 1992
Total	32.9	57.5	76.5	11.0	13.4	18.5	37.1	18.7	13.0	15.5	6.8	2.7
Total excluding Israel	24.7	51.6	71.7	10.9	15.0	23.3	38.6	19.5	15.4	19.1	7.0	2.7
Maghreb	13.2	36.7	73.5	3.5	18.6	34.9	55.1	28.6	17.9	4.3	2.1	1.4
Algeria	18.2	44.2	92.5	3.6	0.4	0.1	72.5	20.8	2.4	1.6	0.4	0.1
Morocco	7.9	20.5	58.9	3.0	11.1	34.6	50.1	32.1	27.5	4.8	2.3	2.2
Tunisia	26.3	67.7	86.8	5.3	37.2	52.5	43.6	23.0	10.8	6.8	2.0	0.7
Mashreq	26.0	42.1	61.3	10.3	11.9	23.0	30.7	25.4	15.0	39.6	18.4	9.3
Egypt	22.4	34.8	69.5	12.7	18.3	32.7	26.6	19.9	14.2	50.1	31.1	5.1
Jordan	14.3	32.0	55.7	0.0	1.4	3.7	42.9	34.1	5.5	4.8	0.5	1.1
Lebanon	48.5	58.8	70.4	9.2	8.3	13.0	28.8	29.0	19.1	15.3	2.7	3.9
Syria	8.5	33.0	29.6	5.9	12.9	19.3	44.1	23.0	25.9	45.8	42.4	39.4
Gulf Cooperation Council	39.7	69.8	76.7	0.0	2.1	8.3	14.4	7.0	9.3	3.4	0.8	0.8
Bahrain	38.5	50.9	55.6	0.0	0.9	5.2	30.8	0.9	0.8	0.0	0.0	0.3
Kuwait	66.7	79.0	81.1	0.0	3.1	2.4	16.7	5.2	4.7	3.3	1.4	2.8
Oman	3.0	91.3	81.9	0.0	1.1	22.3	6.1	6.5	8.1	0.0	0.0	0.0
Qatar	50.0	98.3	97.0	0.0	0.9	18.3	25.0	0.9	0.0	0.0	0.0	0.3
Saudi Arabia	70.3	87.5	81.8	0.0	1.6	0.6	16.2	8.8	8.8	8.1	0.9	0.8
United Arab Emirates	13.8	41.9	71.2	0.0	3.1	16.9	10.3	8.9	13.4	3.4	1.1	1.0
Other												
Iran	47.8	70.8	49.0	41.1	58.1	36.6	17.8	10.6	35.3	26.1	14.1	7.4
Iraq	29.8	50.8	43.8	2.1	1.1	6.3	42.6	18.4	50.0	23.4	7.9	0.0
Israel	59.5	72.3	87.0	11.4	9.2	8.0	32.4	16.9	7.9	3.5	6.2	2.7
Libya	54.5	82.0	96.4	0.0	0.7	0.2	0.0	13.3	1.1	18.2	2.7	2.0
Yemen	0.0	30.4	16.5a	0.0	0.0	0.0a	50.0	26.1	57.0a	25.0	21.7	19.0a

Note: Data for 1970 and 1980 are likely to be overstated since they are based on partner data and some non-OECD countries have not reported their imports.
a. 1989 data.
Source: U.N. Comtrade database.

Clothing and textiles

Exports of clothing grew from just $30 million a year in the early 1970s to $3.9 billion a year by the early 1990s, of which $3.4 billion went to the European Union and $400 million went to the United States. The bulk of these exports were from Morocco and Tunisia, which shipped about $1.6 billion and $1.5 billion worth of clothing, respectively. The rest was exported from Egypt and several GCC countries.

Although the expansion of clothing exports has been impressive, the value of shipments overstates the sector's contribution to net foreign exchange earnings. During the 1980s, for example, Tunisia increased its annual net exports of clothing from $300 million to $1.1 billion. But because annual net imports of textiles increased from $200 million to $800 million over the same period, net exports of clothing and textiles only increased from $60 million in the early 1980s to $300 million in the early 1990s – a much less impressive jump. The more modest contribution to foreign earnings of net exports largely reflects the outsourcing practices of EU multinational corporations operating under export processing arrangements.

The expansion of clothing and textiles exports that has taken place, mainly in Morocco, Tunisia, and Syria, has occurred under the protective umbrella of the Multifiber Arrangement (MFA), which restricts exports by more efficient producers (especially those in Asia) to the OECD countries. Under the Uruguay Round agreements the MFA will be phased out by 2005. Under free trade, garment-exporting countries in the Middle East and North Africa will face stiff competition from the more efficient manufacturers in low-wage countries such as Bangladesh and China. However, the European Union's Mediterranean Initiative will allow some countries in the Middle East and North Africa to continue to enjoy preferential access to EU markets. The interim period before the MFA phaseout should be regarded as a window of opportunity for these countries to make their garment industries increasingly more efficient so that in time they will be able to compete with lower-cost exporters.

Chemicals

Chemical exports from the region are dominated by petrochemicals from the GCC countries, but also include inorganic chemicals (mainly phosphatic fertilizers) from Jordan, Morocco, and Tunisia. Chemical exports grew from less than $100 million a year in the early 1970s to about $1 billion a year in the early 1980s and $4.9 billion a year by the early 1990s. Products contributing to this expansion include plastic materials and other organic chemicals, whose export values grew twentyfold and elevenfold, respectively.

Countries in the Middle East and North Africa maintain a strong comparative advantage in petrochemical production, and favorable circumstances in the external environment could enable this sector to serve as a driving force for expansion of nonoil manufacturing exports from several countries in the region. All the GCC countries, as well as Iran, are determined to expand their petrochemical industries quickly. Iran has the world's second largest supply of gas reserves, and is located favorably. Algeria would also like to develop some of its natural gas reserves into higher value-added petrochemicals. Both countries have found it difficult to finance these large, capital-intensive projects, however.

An increase in fuel prices would raise the region's comparative advantage in these industries. But increases in supply from Russia and several Central Asian states – which collectively hold enormous reserves of natural gas – would hurt development of the sector in the Middle East and North Africa.

Petrochemicals do not currently face particularly high tariffs in the OECD countries, and the tariffs that do exist are being reduced under the General Agreement on Tariffs and Trade (GATT). For exporters of phosphatic fertilizers, however, the reduced protection of agricultural products in the European Union under the Uruguay Round will likely soften demand in that market. Moreover, the planned free trade agreements with the European Union are not likely to lead to major boosts in these exports from the Middle East and North Africa. Better growth potential exists in Southeast Asia, which has been the main importer of petrochemicals from the Middle and North Africa and which may experience rapid growth in demand. A reduction in the high import tariffs in Korea and Thailand (put in place to protect domestic industries, which depend on imported feedstock) would benefit the Middle East and North Africa. In the longer run, demand for manufactured fertilizers is likely to grow in China, India, and the countries of Sub-Saharan Africa, which cannot currently afford such products.

Other sectors

Some potential may exist for growth in selected nonoil primary commodity exports, especially in foods. During the early 1990s food and live animal exports amounted to about $3.4 billion a year, of which more than half were fruit and vegetable exports (mainly from Morocco and Iran) and about a quarter were fish exports (mainly from Morocco and Tunisia). Such exports have doubled in nominal value over the past decade, and more than quadrupled over the past twenty years. Although for the region as a whole population is likely to grow as fast as food production, several countries (including Iran, Morocco, and Tunisia) are likely to find niche markets of rapid growth among both industrial and developing countries. But prudent management of scarce resources – including water, arable land, and the dwindling fish stock – will be required to support sustainable growth in such exports.

The required growth of nonoil exports

With an outlook for slow growth in fuel exports and moderate advances in services and transfers over the next decade, nonoil merchandise exports will have to become the driving force behind regional growth. How rapidly must these exports expand if per capita incomes in the region are to grow? One approach to addressing this question suggests that for the more diversified economies, nonoil exports will need to grow twice as quickly as they did in the past and that oil exporters will need to increase nonoil exports by a factor of ten if per capita incomes are to advance by 2.5 percent a year, the rate of growth anticipated in industrial countries (Table 2.6). By growing at 2.5 percent a year, the countries of the Middle East and North Africa would return to their peak per capita income of 1979-80 by 2005.

Given country-specific population projections prepared by the World Bank (2.5 percent a year for the region over 1995–2010) and desired growth of 2.5 percent in per capita incomes, GDP must grow by 5 percent a year. Applying an income elasticity of import demand of 1.5 – about the level for noncredit constrained developing countries and several industrial countries – and assuming that no change occurs in the real external balance as a share of output, the derived import and matching export growth for the region is 7.5 percent.[6] The results of the analysis suggest a segmentation of the Middle East and North Africa into three groups (Figure 2.6a–c). For the first group of countries the required growth in exports for 1995–2010 is either below the performance achieved over the past decade (Tunisia, Israel) or readily attainable given a favorable external environment (Morocco, Jordan). Although the targeted growth in per capita GDP lies above the

Table 2.6 Required growth in GDP and exports, Middle East and North Africa, 1995–2010 (percent)

Region/country	GDP Population growth, 1995–2010[a]	GDP Actual growth, 1980–93	GDP Required growth 1995–2010[b]	Derived import/ export growth 1995–2010[c]	Contribution of oil exports, 1995–2010[d]	Nonoil exports Amount, 1992 (millions of U.S. dollars)	Nonoil exports Share in total exports, 1992	Nonoil exports Actual growth, 1980–93	Nonoil exports Required growth, 1995–2010
Total	2.5	1.0	5.0	7.5	1.9	36,768	24.1	4.2	23.3
Maghreb	2.0	2.5	4.5	6.8	2.1	7,744	15.0	6.0	31.1
Algeria	2.1	2.1	4.6	6.9	2.4	462	4.1	4.5	108.2
Morocco	1.8	3.0	4.3	6.4	0.1	3,852	96.9	3.8	6.5
Tunisia	1.8	3.8	4.3	6.5	0.4	3,430	84.9	10.5	7.2
Mashreq	2.0	3.8	4.5	6.7	1.3	4,202	50.0	1.1	10.9
Egypt	1.6	4.0	4.1	6.1	1.5	1,250	39.6	0.5	11.5
Jordan	2.8	2.8	5.3	8.0	0.0	1,215	100.0	4.3	8.0
Syria	3.3	3.6	5.8	8.7	1.3	940	50.0	6.7	15.0
Gulf Cooperation Council	3.1	0.0	5.6	8.4	2.2	9,941	10.6	2.5	57.9
Bahrain	2.0	2.0	4.5	6.8	2.0	695	20.0	10.5	23.8
Kuwait	2.4	−4.5	4.9	7.4	2.4	330	4.9	−18.0	101.8
Oman	3.8	8.6	6.3	9.4	2.3	490	9.0	11.0	79.3
Saudi Arabia	3.3	0.2	5.7	8.6	2.2	4,619	10.8	10.8	58.9
United Arab Emirates	1.8	0.7	4.3	6.5	2.1	3,292	16.1	6.5	27.2
Other Gulf countries	2.8	−0.2	5.3	8.0	2.4	1,387	5.5	−0.5	112.4
Iran	2.7	3.4	5.2	7.7	2.3	1,253	7.5	−1.0	72.2
Iraq	3.0	−12.0	5.5	8.2	2.4	134	3.2	1.4	179.8
Israel	1.3	4.2	3.8	5.7	0.0	13,040	99.4	5.8	5.7
Memorandum items									
Oil exporters[e]	2.8	0.0	5.3	8.0	2.2	13,075	10.8	4.9	55.9
Diversified economies[f]	1.9	3.8	4.4	6.6	0.4	23,693	83.1	3.0	7.4

a. Projected. b. Growth required to achieve 2.5 percent annual growth in *per capita* incomes.
c. Assumes income elasticity of import demand at 1.5 and no change in real external balance (that is, growth in exports matches growth in imports).
d. Assumes growth in fuel exports of 2.5 percent a year; share of fuels in exports applied to this figure to calculate contribution toward required growth.
e. Excludes Egypt, which is grouped with diversified economies.
f. Egypt, Israel, Jordan, Morocco, Syria, and Tunisia.
Source: World Bank data.

Figure 2.6 Options for nonoil export growth
(a) Readily achievable (b) Policy-supported (c) Paradigm change

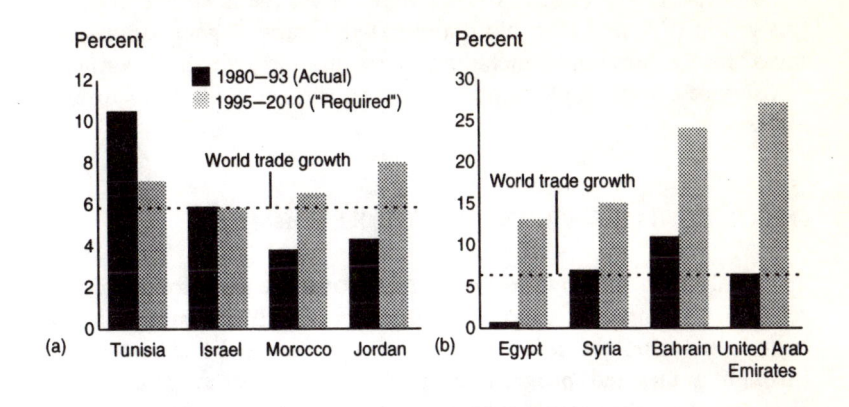

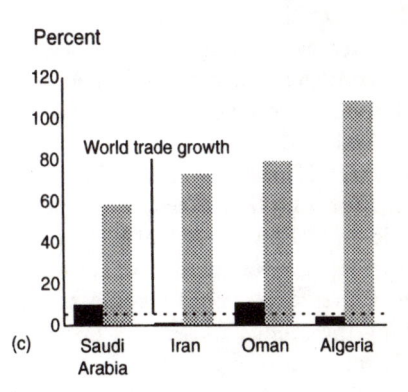

Source: World Bank data.

historic average for these countries, actual output will likely exceed annual population gains of 2.5 percent. For the second group of countries, including Bahrain, Egypt, Syria, and the United Arab Emirates, targeted exports are within reach of recent performance but will require significant promotion efforts, including the adoption of policies geared at improving competitiveness and diversifying the product and market mix. For the third group of countries, comprising economies in which fuel accounts for more than 90 percent of exports, nonoil exports will need to grow by more than 50 percent a year if income growth is to outpace population growth. The problem is clearly more acute for countries with large population and import requirements, including Algeria, Iran, and Iraq. Because targets for nonoil exports are unlikely to be achieved over the next several years, this group will need to explore alternative means of generating additional foreign exchange, including increasing the growth of commercial service exports and earning higher returns on holdings of foreign assets.

OPPORTUNITIES ABOUND – FOR REFORMERS

The analysis in previous sections underscores the need for structural reforms to improve export performance. Such measures should include reducing the role of public enterprises in the export sector through a targeted program of privatization, encouraging private investment in the export sector by maintaining a competitive real exchange rate, and reducing barriers to imports. These measures would increase incentives for domestic producers to identify niches in which they can compete internationally and relieve demand pressures on scarce domestic production factors (such as skilled workers and entrepreneurial talent).

While these structural measures are being implemented, policy-makers should consider adopting other measures to promote exports. Governments could publicize the potential investment opportunities of an export sector that has liberalized its trade regime and privatized public enterprises. Other steps could include adjusting the fee structures and improving the quality of services provided by public enterprises that provide services to exporters.

Countries in the Middle East and North Africa that vigorously pursue reforms may be able to take advantage of the EU's Mediterranean Initiative, which offers the possibilities of expanded free trade and foreign investment, substantially increased official financial flows, and enhanced regional integration. The possible consolidation of the peace process could help reduce the widespread perceptions of risk held by both overseas and domestic investors, thereby encouraging higher levels of capital flow in support of private sector activity. Countries that introduce reforms may be able to develop selected niches within the region, particularly in commercial services. Financial support for the development of these niches could come from the gradual repatriation of the substantial stock of flight capital (overseas assets not officially recorded in external balance statistics). Trade liberalization, increased financial assistance from the European Union, movement toward EU standards, and enhanced foreign direct investment flows could greatly strengthen the potential for the Mediterranean countries to break from the stagnation that has characterized their economies for the past fifteen years. Whether the internal political consensus will make the most of these opportunities remains to be seen.

The Mediterranean Initiative

The increasing global economic role played by developing countries implies growing economic feedback from developing to industrial countries, making the links between them increasingly important. Indeed, the gains to industrial countries from increased trade integration with developing countries are potentially larger than the gains from additional integration among industrial countries, since the cost – price differences between developing and industrial countries can be more than twice as large as the differences between industrial countries. Beyond a more efficient use of resources, medium- to long-term gains from increased investment and innovation and higher productivity growth (as a result of increased market size, competition, and technology spillovers) are likely to be substantial. The scope for gains from trade integration will expand with the increasing tradability of services.

Partly in response to these trends, but also because of increased concern about instability and migration from the south (particularly from North Africa), the European Union has put forward the Mediterranean Initiative, which could emerge as one of the more positive long-term elements in the external environment for the Middle East and North Africa. Guidelines for the future Mediterranean policy of the European Union envision the creation of a Euro–Mediterranean Economic Area of 600–800 million people and thirty to forty countries over the next ten to fifteen years. Within the area, free trade and foreign investment would be expanded, official financial flows from the European Union would be increased, and regional integration would be enhanced. The basic objectives of the Mediterranean Initiative are to achieve reciprocal free trade in manufactured goods between the countries of the European Union and the countries of the Middle East and North Africa by 2010, develop preferential and reciprocal access for agricultural products of interest to both parties, and expand technical, economic, social, cultural, and financial cooperation. A key benefit of such an agreement is that it provides a policy blueprint to which governments in the Middle East and North Africa can credibly commit themselves. Credibility results both from the formal nature of the treaty and the availability of financial and technical assistance from the European Union to help implement the agreement.

The European Union currently has association agreements with Cyprus, Malta, and Turkey and cooperation agreements with Algeria, Egypt, Israel, Jordan, Lebanon, Morocco, Syria, and Tunisia. These agreements allow free access to EU markets for most manufactured exports. (The agreement with Israel is the only one that currently provides for reciprocal free trade in manufactures.) Voluntary restraint agreements and quotas on sensitive products (including some categories of textiles and clothing) have gradually been relaxed. Agricultural products from Mediterranean countries receive preferential access to EU markets; the products vary from country to country.

The trade performance of the Mediterranean countries in 1985–90, particularly in relation to the European Union, is summarized in Table 2.7.[7] Merchandise export growth averaged 7.3 percent in 1985-90; exports to the European Union grew by just over 6 percent. As a result the Mediterranean countries' share of exports to the European Union fell by just over 3 percentage points, to 60 percent in 1990. These regional figures obscure widely different performance by different groups of Mediterranean countries, however.

Countries that implemented fewer reforms (Algeria, Egypt, Lebanon, and Syria) experienced weak growth in exports (1.7 percent a year), and the share of the European Union in their exports fell by nearly 5 percentage points during 1985–90, to 64.5 percent in 1990. The decline in the EU share of exports was, however, entirely due to the decline in exports of oil and other commodities: exports of manufactures to the European Union grew rapidly (38 percent a year), so that by 1990 two-thirds of manufactured exports were to the European Union. Because manufactures accounted for such a small share of total exports, however, this rapid growth did little to increase overall export growth.

Economies that have initiated wider-ranging structural reforms and that had a larger share of manufactures in their exports (Israel, Morocco, and Tunisia) achieved average annual export growth of more than 15 percent, and the share of the European Union in their exports increased by about 3 percentage points, to 55.5 percent in 1990. For these countries rapid growth in manufactures exports to the European Union played a major role in their

Table 2.7 Trade performance, Middle East and North Africa, 1985–90 (percent)

	Merchandise exports			Manufactures exports			Share of manufactures in exports		
	Average growth, 1985–90		Share of European Union in exports	Average growth, 1985–90		Share of European Union in exports	Exports to world		Exports to European Union
Region/country	To world	To European Union	1990	Change, 1985–90	To world	To European Union	1990	Change, 1985–90	1990	Change, 1985–90	1990	Change, 1985–90
Total	7.3	6.1	60.0	−3.4	20.2	25.8	53.7	10.9	43.3	18.7	38.8	22.2
Maghreb	5.6	5.5	70.1	−0.2	28.7	32.8	82.2	11.8	30.6	19.2	35.9	24.5
Algeria	0.6	−0.5	65.8	−3.7	50.0	62.3	95.8	31.3	10.3	8.9	15.0	13.7
Morocco	17.5	19.0	72.8	4.4	26.5	31.0	76.1	12.3	56.0	17.2	58.6	22.4
Tunisia	17.7	18.4	82.3	2.3	24.2	25.2	81.9	3.0	69.6	16.5	69.3	16.9
Mashreq	3.9	1.1	56.9	−8.1	12.9	9.8	32.7	−5.0	22.6	7.7	13.0	4.4
Egypt	0.0	−2.2	62.2	−7.5	20.4	15.4	41.9	−9.9	21.8	13.2	14.7	8.3
Jordan	4.9	−12.1	12.4	−17.6	4.1	−9.7	18.4	−19.1	49.1	−1.9	72.9	9.3
Lebanon	7.4	3.7	24.0	−4.6	7.5	17.0	22.9	7.9	56.3	0.4	53.8	24.4
Syria	14.8	12.4	71.2	−7.9	15.5	26.2	29.7	10.6	6.0	0.2	2.5	1.1
Israel	15.2	16.2	42.3	1.8	17.2	21.1	37.3	5.7	83.8	7.0	73.9	13.9
Memorandum items												
Reformers[a]	15.6	16.9	55.5	3.1	19.2	23.6	51.5	8.7	72.9	10.4	67.7	16.5
Other countries[b]	1.7	0.2	64.5	−4.8	27.2	38.1	65.8	22.3	13.6	9.1	13.8	11.0

a. Israel, Jordan, Morocco, and Tunisia.
b. Algeria, Egypt, Lebanon, and Syria.
Source: U.N. Comtrade database.

overall export expansion. For both groups of countries manufactures exports to the European Union grew more rapidly than exports to the rest of the world, while exports of nonmanufactures grew more slowly.

An important benefit to be derived from the proposed initiatives in trade may be the stimulative effects in competitiveness and efficiency that might accompany increased EU access to the Middle East and North Africa in trade and investment. The agreement will require participating countries not to discriminate between foreign (EU) and domestic firms. Nondiscrimination may not be sufficient to ensure that domestic firms have adequate opportunities to compete with European Union-based exporters for the local market, however. Elimination of existing policies that unnecessarily reduce the competitiveness of domestic firms will also be necessary. It is crucial that trade and other barriers to competition that affect non-EU firms are also reduced, with a view to limiting the trade diversion costs of an agreement with the European Union. Indeed, if tariffs and other barriers to trade against the rest of the world are reduced at the same time and at the same pace as barriers to EU suppliers, the additional adjustment costs will be small and the potential gains from liberalization will be greatly enhanced.

Another area being developed under the initiative is that of "cooperation," which is likely to entail:

- Movement toward harmonization between indirect tax and customs procedures; competition policy; corporate, banking, accounting, and tax laws; intellectual property rights; and technical, consumer protection, workers rights, safety, and environmental standards.
- Movement toward liberalization of capital movements.
- Strengthened cooperation and dialogue over a range of other areas, including the environment, energy, social policy and poverty, and industrial policy (training, subcontracting, technology transfer, and so on).

The peace process

A more peaceful climate in the region is a prerequisite for increased domestic and foreign investment, trade, and tourism, and lower military expenditures. Recent peace agreements between Israel, the Palestine Liberation Organization, and Jordan and ongoing talks between

Israel and Syria are encouraging in this respect. According to some estimates, Israel, Jordan, and Syria may eventually be able to redirect 5 percent of GDP from military expenditures to more productive sectors, generating as much as 1 percent additional output growth. Even more important in the medium term, foreign perceptions of risk are likely to improve as a result of peace in the Middle East.

Global and regional niches in goods and services trade

World trade will be a major engine of growth over the next ten to fifteen years. Economic reform, participation in the Mediterranean Initiative, and lower foreign perceptions of risk should allow some Middle Eastern and North African countries to participate in the growth of global trade in both nonoil merchandise and commercial services. Moreover, under appropriate circumstances the region's strategic location on the important Europe – Asia trade route could offer opportunities for development of trade and services.

Growth in market demand for nonoil exports, measured as the weighted average of trade partner import volumes, is likely to increase by almost 50 percent over the coming decade, registering annual gains of more than 6 percent. Across geographic export markets demand for manufactured products will be the driving force behind world trade growth. Private sector trade analysts, among them the WEFA Group (1995), expect manufactures import volumes to rise almost threefold by 2010 (annual growth of 7 percent). Trade in nonoil commodities is expected to double (5 percent annual growth), and trade in fuels is expected to increase by 50 percent (2.5 percent annual growth). From a simple demand-side perspective, potential exists for further growth in the Middle East and North Africa's nonoil merchandise exports.

The main contributions to stronger growth in market demand are expected to come from industrial countries, which account for more than two-thirds of the market. Expansion in Europe (where the recently expanded European Union accounts for more than 55 percent of nonoil exports by Middle Eastern and North African countries), recovery and deregulation of markets and distribution systems in Japan, and continued strong imports by the United States suggest strong demand for exports. Also of significance are the robust conditions in developing countries, especially in Asia, and the expected rebound in the transition economies, where pent – up demand is anticipated to support strong advances in imports of almost 7 percent a year (Figure 2.7).

Figure 2.7 Nonoil export growth, 1981–2010

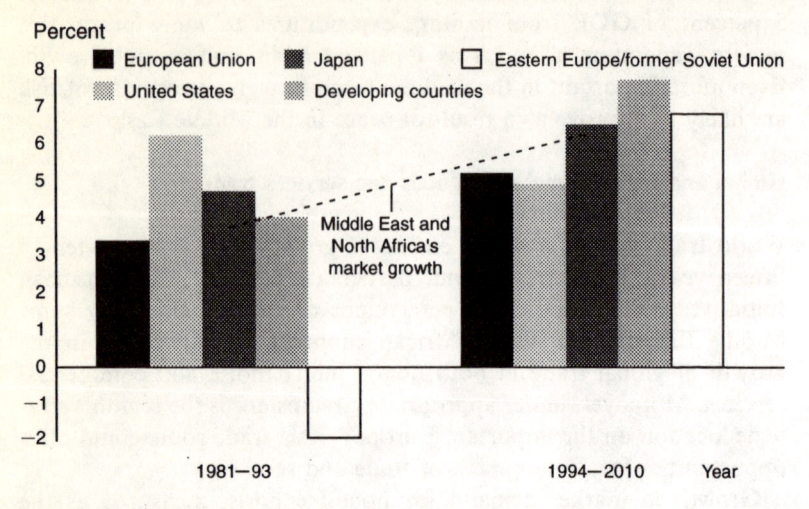

Source: World Bank data.

As import demand by the European Union continues to rise rapidly (at rates of 6–7 percent over the next several years), the diversified economies of the region (Morocco and Tunisia, and to a lesser degree Egypt and Jordan) may be well placed to benefit from market expansion. Except for Egypt, all these countries have supported stable real exchange rates and attracted increasing amounts of export-oriented foreign direct investment. These factors, together with their geographic location, their experience in contracted production for EU multinationals, the establishment and operation of free trade zones, and improvement of product standards to meet EU criteria suggest that significant potential exists for rapid expansion of clothing and textiles exports, as well as diversification into other light (assembly-type) production and trade. An optimistic assessment might also consider the possibility of tighter integration of outsourced production with "just in time" networks of contractors and suppliers linked through high-tech channels of telecommunications and logistics.

Rapid growth in export markets and in world trade provides other opportunities for several Middle Eastern and North African countries. Strong demand for manufactured fertilizers and other low-end hydrocarbon-based products in Asia and over time in certain Sub-Saharan African countries presents opportunities for GCC producers of petrochemicals. GATT-negotiated reductions in tariffs and other forms of restrictions in industrial countries may open up markets for high-end products as well. Growth in specialty markets in both industrial and developing countries represents an opportunity for diversified exporters, particularly producers of fruits, vegetables, spices, and fish. The European Union, Eastern Europe, and the republics of the former Soviet Union may be attractive markets for citrus and other fruits and vegetables.

There may also be a great deal of potential for leveraging the region's strategic location on key trade routes. The route between Europe and East Asia and the Gulf, which the Suez Canal straddles, is thought to be on a trend growth path that is 75 percent above that of world trade, making it one of the most dynamic in the world. Since 1980 canal dues have increased by 8.7 percent a year, reaching a record $2 billion during 1993. With the onset of economic recovery in Europe, continued robust activity in East Asia, the opening of markets in South Asia (particularly India), the likely recovery of the economies of Eastern Europe and the former Soviet Union, and the hoped-for normalization of conditions in the Gulf, the movement of cargo between these areas is likely to grow by more than 9 percent a year.

These trends provide opportunities for the countries of the region to engage in (or subcontract out) processing and assembly of goods shipped between Europe and Asia, providing local content in the context of free trade areas and attracting Asian "trans-plants" for weight-gaining manufactures. Growth in traffic through the Suez Canal may also stimulate the development of trade- and logistics-related services, entrepot activities, and freight forwarding, processing, and distribution. Increased stability in the region could help reduce the high insurance costs associated with the Middle East, currently an important constraint to such activities. Development of intermodal transport facilities could follow from peace agreements in the region, and a variety of land routes, including new railway lines, could be developed. Use of cross-border pipeline networks could also increase as a result of the peace process.

Repatriation of flight capital

Although estimates of the stock of flight capital may be misleading, there is no doubt that the stock of flight capital is large in the Middle East and North Africa. In contrast with other developing regions, however, capital has started to flow back to the region (except for the

GCC countries), attracted by the early liberalization of current and capital accounts by countries undergoing adjustment. Governments have been the main beneficiaries of these flows. To the extent that they delay fiscal and financial market reforms, such flows may prove to be a mixed blessing in the short term. In the longer term, however, repatriation of flight capital offers some promise, particularly if such funds can be attracted through foreign direct investment and equity flows in support of private sector activity.

CLAIMING THE PROMISE

Developments on the supply side will likely play the critical role in determining whether the export potential of the Middle East and North Africa is realized. Competition from such countries as China, Indonesia, and, increasingly, India and Pakistan represents a serious challenge to the region. Real effective exchange rates of these countries have fallen relative to exchange rates in the Middle East and North Africa (Figure 2.8), and changes associated with the phasing out of the MFA will favor basic clothing and textiles exports from more efficient suppliers at the expense of higher-cost suppliers in the Middle East and North Africa. Competition with the transition economies of Eastern Europe in basic and light manufacturing will

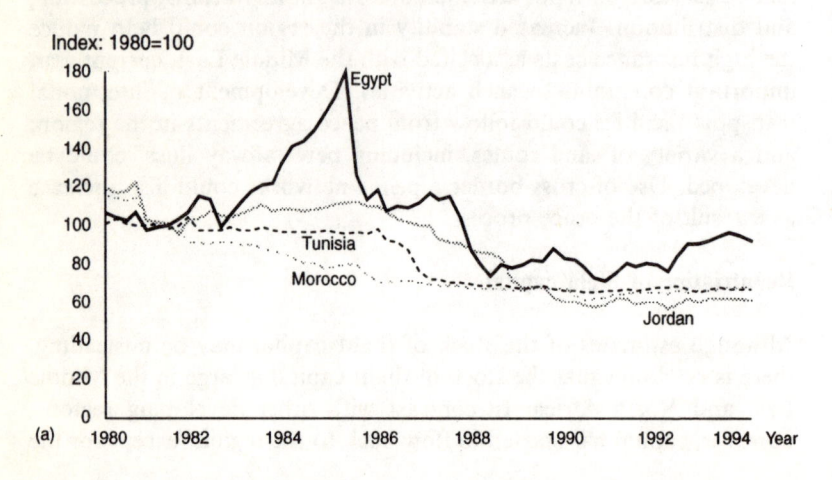

Figure 2.8 Real effective exchange rates, 1980–94
(a) Middle East and North Africa (b) Competitor countries

Index: 1980=100

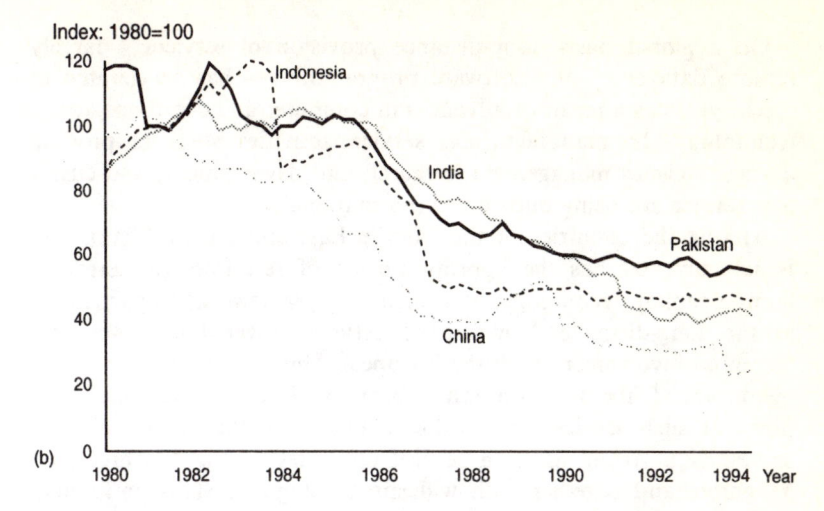

(b)

Source: IMF data.

also be a concern as private sector activity there rises as a share of GDP (and exports). The quality of Eastern European output has improved as new technologies have been adopted, and large investments have been made in the region by Western multinationals. Recent policy decisions in that region regarding exchange rate management, as well as trends in foreign direct investment, have enhanced the potential for continued gains in Western markets. Moreover, recent statistics suggest that trade among the countries of Eastern Europe is reviving, which may reflect increasing linkages between newly invigorated private sector entities and the establishment of cross-border production ties.

With its high endowment of skilled labor and surplus stock of unskilled labor, Middle Eastern and North African countries (particularly those in the Maghreb and Mashreq) could reap benefits from fast growth in commercial services trade in the coming decade, particularly in long-distance services. Services exports also hold the potential to provide domestic employment opportunities (albeit on a small scale). But policy must be supportive for services trade to flourish. Regulatory barriers to entry in service industries need to be minimized, and attention must be paid to harmonizing domestic regulatory regimes with those of the major trading partners. A transparent, liberal foreign direct investment regime must be adopted and intellectual property rights must be protected if countries hope to benefit fully from the internationalization of services.

On a global basis, long-distance provision of services – largely remote data entry and software programming – has accelerated in recent years as a result of advances in computer and communications technology. In manufacturing, service activities such as product design, logistics management, research and development, and customer service are being outsourced internationally.

Among the countries of the Middle East and North Africa only Israel currently has the appropriate set of resources (in terms of human capital, technology, and regulatory framework) to participate in the long-distance provision of services. Over the longer-term increased involvement with the European Union and stronger implementation of liberalization and reform could help support increased flows of such services from other countries in the region. Human capital is a strong asset in several countries of the Mashreq and Maghreb, and together with widespread language skills in French, English, and Arabic could provide a platform for growth in long-distance service transactions with Europe and North America, as well as within the region, particularly with the GCC countries.

The potential for increasing trade in services within the region is encouraging, and increasing specialization of countries should help boost these flows in the coming years. Finance and Islamic banking, Arab language-based publishing, computer software and hardware development, and transportation and distribution networks all represent areas of potential growth. In the Maghreb Tunisia could become a regional center for medical services, engineering, and other consulting activities. In the Mashreq Lebanon could emerge as a financial center, and Jordan has the capacity to build on its strengths in health care, transport, and other professional activities. In the GCC Bahrain has long been established as an offshore banking and commercial hub; Kuwait and the United Arab Emirates are exploring diversification into Islamic banking and related support services.

Notes

1. The GCC countries are Bahrain, Kuwait, Oman, Qatar, Saudi Arabia, and the United Arab Emirates.
2. The Mashreq countries are Egypt, Jordan, Lebanon, and Syria.
3. As in the classic manifestation of Dutch disease, foreign exchange windfalls have raised the price of domestic production factors, including labor and land, relative to the price of traded products, whose price is set in the international market.

4. The remainder of this analysis of the region's nonoil merchandise exports excludes Israel from aggregate statistics.
5. The Maghreb countries are Algeria, Morocco, and Tunisia.
6. Historical import elasticities for the region varied widely during 1970–93, from 0.2 in Yemen to 2.9 in Saudi Arabia. For developing countries as a group import elasticities have averaged 1.1, with more credit-constrained regions such as Sub-Saharan Africa averaging 0.2; Latin America, 0.9; and East Asia, about 1.2. Among industrial countries income elasticities range between 0.9 (Japan) and 2.0 (United States), and average 1.3. Hence the assumption in the forward-looking export analysis for the Middle East and North Africa is somewhat optimistic regarding creditworthiness for the region, and closer to the higher end for the likely range of import demand (and required export growth).
7. For the rest of this section the Mediterranean countries are defined as Algeria, Morocco, Tunisia (Maghreb), Egypt, Jordan, Lebanon, Syria (Mashreq), and Israel. The 1985-90 period was chosen because it is probably more representative of underlying trends than one containing data from the early 1990s. Trade patterns in the early 1990s were temporarily disrupted by the recessions that affected OECD regions. Comparisons ending in 1993, the trough of the recession in Europe, show, for example, major declines in exports to Europe from the Middle East and North Africa that are likely to be temporary. A second reason for excluding more recent data is the greater potential for incompleteness. Finally, European trade statistics in 1993 are heavily distorted by a change in data collection procedures.

References

Boltho, Andrea, 1994. "China's Emergence: Prospects, Opportunities and Challenges," International Economics Department, Washington, D.C. : World Bank.

Chopra, Ram, 1994. "Three Challenges for Economic Management in the MENA Region," paper prepared for the Center for Strategic and International Studies–World Bank conference on economic challenges in the Middle East and North Africa, held at the World Bank (September 23-24), Washington, D.C.

Dadush, Uri, Mick Riordan, Jalal Jalali and Kazue Takagaki, 1994. "Egypt in the Global Economy," International Economics Department, Washington, D.C. : World Bank.

EIU (Economist Intelligence Unit), 1992. "International Tourism Forecasts to 2005," *Special Report*, 2454, London, EIU.

——— 1994–5. "Country Profile" and "Country Report," Middle Eastern and North African countries, various issues, London.

Euromoney, various issues.

Goldin, Ian, Mylene Kherallah, 1994. "The Uruguay Round and International Trade in Agricultural Products: Implications for Arab Countries," paper prepared for the annual seminar of the Arab Fund for Economic and Social Development, Kuwait (January 17-18 1995).

IMF (International Monetary Fund). various issues. *International Financial Statistics*, Washington, D.C.: IMF.

────── Various issues. *Balance of Payments Statistics*, Washington, D.C.: IMF.

IMF (International Monetary Fund), Various issues. *Direction of Trade Statistics*, Washington, D.C.: IMF.

Mitchell, Donald O., and Merlinda D. Ingco. 1993. *The World Food Outlook*, International Economics Department, Washington, D.C.: World Bank.

Odell, Peter R. and Kenneth E. Rosing, 1983. *The Future of Oil: World Resources and Use*, London: Kogan Page.

Oil and Gas Journal, various issues.

Page, John M. 1994. "Restoring Sustained Growth in the MENA Region," Paper prepared for the Center for Strategic and International Studies–World Bank conference on economic challenges in the Middle East and North Africa, held at the World Bank, (September 23-24), Washington, D.C.

Russell, Sharon Stanton and Michael S. Teitelbaum, 1992. *International Migration and International Trade*, World Bank Discussion Paper, 160. Washington, D.C. : World Bank.

Standard and Poor's, 1994. *International Financing Review* (January 8).

────── 1995. *Creditweek International*, (January 2).

United Nations, Commodity Trade Statistics (Comtrade) database.

UNFAO (United Nations Food and Agriculture Organization), AgroStat database.

UNIDO (United Nations Industrial Development Organization), Industry statistics database.

U.S. Department of Energy, various issues. *Annual Energy Outlook*, Washington, D.C. : World Bank.

WEFA Group. 1995. *World Outlook*, Executive Summary, Philadelphia.

World Bank, 1992. "Attracting Private Investment." Middle East and North Africa Technical Department, Industry and Energy Division, Washington, D.C. : World Bank.

────── 1994a "Private Sector Development in Egypt: The Status and the Challenges," paper prepared for a conference on private sector development in Egypt: Investing in the future, (October 9- 10), Cairo.

────── 1994b. *World Population Projections 1994– 95*, Baltimore, Md.: Johns Hopkins University Press.

────── 1995a. "Commodity Markets and the Developing Countries (February and May), " A World Bank Quarterly, Washington, D.C. : World Bank.

────── 1995b. "Financial Flows and the Developing Countries (February and May)," A World Bank Quarterly, Washington, D.C. : World Bank.

────── 1995c. *Global Economic Prospects and the Developing Countries*, Washington, D.C. : World Bank.

3 The Arab Economies, the Uruguay Round Predicament, and the European Union Wildcard[1]

Ishac Diwan, Chang-Po Yang, and Zhi Wang

The recently completed Uruguay Round and the parallel rise of regional trading blocs promise to hasten the ongoing globalization of the world economy. Although these developments create market opportunities, they also increase competition. What lies ahead for the Middle East and North Africa? This chapter uses a multiregion, multisector computable general equilibrium model to examine the impact of the Uruguay Round on the Middle East and North Africa's welfare, trade, production, factor returns, and employment. It also examines the effects of the emergence of an enlarged European market incorporating Eastern Europe and Turkey, and the possibility of the Middle East and North Africa joining this emerging trading bloc.

These are revolutionary times in the global economy. The lives of workers in different parts of the world are increasingly intertwined. The embrace of market-based development strategies by many developing and post-centrally planned economies, the opening of international markets, and great advances in the ease with which goods, capital, and ideas flow around the world are bringing new opportunities to billions of people. Are these favorable developments from the point of view of the economies of the Middle East and North Africa? The stakes are clearly high. During the 1970s and early 1980s labor migration and official aid were sources of growth. Now, other sources of foreign exchange will have to be found to finance import needs. The globalization of trade promises to open new markets, but it also increases competition. East Asia's export-led boom started in the 1970s when international competition was nearly nonexistent; by the 1980s these countries were able to upgrade their exports and take advantage of an increasingly educated workforce by moving away from labor-intensive industries and up the technology ladder. In a fast-changing international environment, will such a strategy be available to Middle Eastern and North African countries as the twenty-first century approaches?

Three groups of countries have emerged over the past two decades. In the first group, rich countries, a continually upgraded labor force is increasingly specializing in high value- added products, while production of labor-intensive goods has been shifting to lower-income countries. The rapid structural transformation has created social dislocations, with the less-skilled workers being left behind. This trend is reflected in rising wage inequality in the United States and high unemployment in Europe. These developments have strengthened protectionist forces, but there are powerful lobbies for greater openness. Exports from OECD countries to developing countries – computers, planes, and other research-intensive products – have become an important engine for growth, accounting in 1994 for 80 percent of the growth in exports.

A second group of countries specializes in the production of medium-skill goods. The newly industrialized economies of East Asia were the first to use cheap exports as an engine for growth. They have managed to upgrade their workers' skills with massive investments and good education policies and are now producing sophisticated industrial products that can ensure good earnings for their workforce. These newly industrialized countries have been joined by a few reformers – Chile, Mexico, and Turkey. The transition economies of Eastern Europe are now trying to join this group. Their success will be determined by their ability to attract capital and convert their extensive human and physical capital endowments into assets that can produce the goods demanded by the global marketplace.

A third group is made up of low-income countries. These countries have large pools of surplus unskilled labor and are geared toward producing labor-intensive exports based on cheap wages. The improvement in these countries' economies has been dramatic. In 1992 foreign direct investment in China accounted for nearly a quarter of all foreign investment in developing countries. The combined share of Indonesia, Malaysia, Singapore, and Thailand was 27 percent; that of the Middle East was only 1.5 percent. Increasingly, poor workers will crowd the market at its low end, putting downward pressures on unskilled workers' wages the world over.

What do these developments imply for the Middle East and North Africa? Ideally, the Arab world should stay ahead of the third (low-income) group. Competing with China and India would mean lower wages and rising social tensions, and fewer opportunities to take advantage of a well-educated labor force (Diwan and Walton, 1995). Instead, Middle Eastern and North African countries should expand exports of semi-skilled goods and aim to catch up with the second group. The region has about ten years to manage such a conversion, since the Uruguay Round agreements will apply fully by 2005. Most Arab countries have the necessary labor and infrastructure, and capital could be attracted. But in order to compete with the newly industrialized countries (NICs), the countries in the region need to reform their economies. In some labor-rich parts of the region (Egypt, Syria) trade reforms, privatization, and public sector retrenchment have barely started. The formal private sector, particularly the industrial sector, is small and protected. The situation is aggravated by the advantages that Eastern European and Turkish firms will receive as their countries enter into customs union agreements with the European Union (EU).

Against this background, this chapter examines how the Uruguay Round trade liberalization agreements will affect the Middle East and North Africa's external trade environment, how the emergence of an enlarged EU market incorporating Eastern Europe and the former Soviet Union would affect the Middle East and North Africa, and how free trade relations with the European Union would help the region regain some of its privileged access to EU markets in preparation for greater competition from Asia. In all cases the impacts of these relations on the Middle East and North Africa's trade, production, factor returns, and employment are examined using a multi-region, multisector computable general equilibrium model for world trade and production (see Appendix 3.1, p. 67, for a description of the model).

This family of models has limitations for the study of a heterogeneous group of countries. Nevertheless, the results are striking enough to raise some important concerns. The Uruguay Round is likely to lead to important losses for the Middle East and North Africa that will be magnified by the formation of a EU bloc incorporating Eastern Europe and the former Soviet Union but not the Middle East and North Africa. However, if Middle Eastern and North African countries manage to adjust their policies and join the emerging EU market, the static losses will be reduced, with significant effects on the structure of trade, production, and employment. We also speculate on the long-term dynamic effects, which are likely to go well beyond the relatively small static gains.

INITIAL CONDITIONS AND TRADE PATTERNS IN THE MAJOR REGIONS

Our computable general equilibrium model is constructed around a nine-region, ten-sector social accounting matrix estimated for 1992 (see Wang, 1994) based on the Global Trade Analysis Project database developed by Hertel (1996).[2]

Factor endowments

Data on factor endowments, intensity, cost, and relative size for the economic regions included in the model reveal several salient features of the global economy (Table 3.1). The three industrial regions (North America, the European Union, and Japan) contain only about 15 percent of the global labor force but possess 74 percent of the capital stock. More than 60 percent of the global labor force resides in the two low-income developing regions with just 5 percent of the world's capital. This uneven distribution of factor endowments induces enormous differences in factor cost and intensity among these regions.

Developing Asian countries and other developing countries, as defined in the model, are poorly endowed with capital relative to labor. They have the lowest capital–labor ratios (capital stock per worker), the largest shares of agricultural labor (more than 60 percent of their labor force works in agriculture), and the highest rental–wage ratios. The reverse is true for Japan, the European Union, and North America. The newly industrialized countries, Eastern Europe and the former Soviet Union, and the Middle East and North Africa fall somewhere between these two extremes. Their share of agricultural labor is much larger than that of industrial countries but only one-third that of low-income countries. Their labor costs are about one-seventh the levels in industrial countries but more than five times those in low-income countries. Compared with the developing world, these regions have higher skills and capital. But compared with industrial countries, they have much lower capital intensity and a higher relative capital–labor price.

Table 3.1 Trade and factor intensity by region, 1992

	North America	European Union	Japan	Middle East and North Africa	Eastern Europe and former Soviet Union	Newly industrialized countries	Asian developing countries	Other developing countries	Other OECD countries
GDP and trade flows (billion U.S. dollars)									
GDP	6,480.14	6,552.15	3,651.54	576.41	810.03	1,574.96	786.74	744.93	1,527.52
Exports	516.68	612.66	384.94	162.90	75.70	408.27	222.29	144.59	341.61
Imports	553.21	770.41	326.32	177.62	83.27	459.13	175.21	169.73	343.59
Relative size in the world economy (percent)									
GDP	28.54	28.86	16.08	2.54	3.57	6.94	3.47	3.28	6.73
Exports	18.01	21.35	13.41	5.68	2.64	14.23	7.75	5.04	11.90
Imports	18.09	25.19	10.67	5.81	2.72	15.01	5.73	5.55	11.23
Trade dependency (percent)									
Exports/output ratio	4.62	5.44	5.53	15.70	5.24	12.38	14.36	9.58	11.79
Imports/absorption	4.94	6.81	4.74	16.87	5.74	13.71	11.68	11.04	11.88
Share in world factor endowment (percent)									
Land	16.15	5.69	0.31	3.86	18.25	8.23	10.26	26.14	11.11
Agricultural labor	0.28	0.77	0.33	1.79	2.30	2.79	47.27	38.69	5.79
Unskilled labor	8.77	10.73	4.58	3.36	11.15	8.63	24.99	20.01	7.79
Skilled labor	16.85	13.03	4.15	4.28	19.31	6.05	13.39	13.38	9.57
Total labor	5.69	6.41	2.59	2.73	7.91	5.70	34.02	27.89	7.05
Capital	25.80	30.10	17.78	2.44	3.61	6.68	2.72	3.11	7.77
Factor share in regional value-added (percent)									
Land	0.35	0.41	0.86	2.78	1.34	2.86	7.58	3.49	1.52
Agricultural labor	0.60	2.36	1.41	1.56	1.31	2.44	12.33	18.22	1.14

Table 3.1 Cont'd.

	North America	European Union	Japan	Middle East and North Africa	Eastern Europe and former Soviet Union	Newly industrialized countries	Asian developing countries	Other developing countries	Other OECD countries
Factor share in required value-added (percent) [Contd.]									
Unskilled labor	35.42	40.02	42.23	20.70	32.40	28.76	22.68	23.75	36.42
Skilled labor	27.94	23.19	15.14	18.25	26.25	14.27	8.51	10.19	19.69
Total labor	63.96	65.57	58.77	40.51	59.96	45.47	43.51	52.16	57.25
Capital	35.69	34.02	40.37	56.70	38.71	51.67	48.90	44.35	41.23
Skill distribution of regional labor force (percent)									
Agricultural labor	2.23	5.51	5.79	29.91	13.27	22.39	63.50	63.40	37.51
Unskilled labor	68.38	74.30	78.31	54.56	62.52	67.09	32.59	31.83	49.02
Skilled labor	29.39	20.19	15.90	15.53	24.22	10.52	3.91	4.76	13.46
Labor cost (thousands of U.S. dollars)									
Agricultural labor	11.52	17.46	12.97	0.41	0.39	1.12	0.15	0.26	0.25
Unskilled labor	22.16	22.00	28.73	3.01	2.06	4.41	0.54	0.67	6.02
Skilled labor	40.68	46.92	50.74	9.31	4.31	13.94	1.68	1.93	11.84
Average wage	27.37	26.78	31.32	3.21	2.38	4.67	0.34	0.47	4.64
Capital intensity (thousands of U.S. dollars per worker) and relative factor price									
Capital/labor ratio	126.57	131.16	191.41	24.93	12.73	32.69	2.23	3.11	30.74
Rental/wage ratio	0.44	0.40	0.36	5.61	5.07	3.48	50.36	27.36	2.34

Source: Authors' calculations.

Structure of production and trade

An examination of the sectoral composition of production, income, demand, and trade in the Middle East and North Africa shows the region to be a net exporter of mineral and energy products as well as wearing apparel (Tables 3.2 and 3.3). The small surplus in the apparel sector is due to exports to North America and the European Union. The region is a net importer of all other products – particularly food and agricultural commodities. Exports are concentrated in the energy and mineral sector (70 percent); labor-intensive and medium-skill manufacturing constitute about 15 percent of exports. Machinery and transport equipment account for more than 35 percent of imports.

Because of its heavy dependence on oil production and exports, the Middle East and North Africa is the most trade-dependent of all regions (as measured by export share in gross output and import share in total demand at the sectoral level see Table 3.1). At the sector level 60 percent of its mineral and energy output is absorbed by the world market, while more than 60 percent of its demand for machinery and equipment is met by foreign suppliers. East Asia is also dependent on exports, especially in labor-intensive manufactures: nearly 80 percent of its apparel and other light manufactures are sold on the world market. But only half its machinery and equipment is imported. By contrast, trade dependence is low in North America, the European Union, Japan, and Eastern Europe and the former Soviet Union. More than 30 percent of the demand for apparel and nearly half the demand for other light manufactured goods in the North American market comes from outside (33 percent for both for the European Union). Nearly a quarter of industrial countries' technology-intensive products are exported.

The Middle East and North Africa is an important trade partner of the European Union. It accounts for 13 percent of the union's exports and 9 percent of its imports. The trade structure revealed by these figures is consistent with conventional international trade theory. At one end, the two low-income regions are major competitors in labor-intensive manufactured exports with middle-income countries (the newly industrialized countries, Eastern Europe and the former Soviet Union, and the Middle East and North Africa) and important importers of capital- and technology-intensive products. At the other end, the OECD is a major supplier of capital-intensive goods and a major importer of labor-intensive and primary products. The newly industrialized countries are in an intermediate position: they are important

Table 3.2 Net trade flows from the Middle East and North Africa, 1992 (billions of U.S. dollars)

Sector	North America	European Union	Japan	Eastern Europe and the former Soviet Union	Newly industrialized countries	Asian developing countries	Other developing countries	Other OECD countries	Total
Agricultural products	−1.91	0.23	0.07	0.00	−0.21	−0.18	−0.78	−0.79	−3.58
Mineral and energy products	14.45	34.75	26.02	1.61	16.26	3.78	4.25	4.81	105.93
Wood and paper products	−0.79	−1.81	−0.09	−0.20	−0.42	−0.37	−0.15	−1.01	−4.82
Food processing	−1.34	−4.08	0.22	−0.07	−1.47	−0.66	−0.68	−1.10	−9.18
Textiles	−0.25	−1.99	−0.69	0.10	−1.23	−0.72	−0.52	−0.28	−5.60
Wearing apparel	0.61	2.99	−0.02	0.03	−0.16	−1.25	−0.15	−0.05	2.00
Other light manufactures	0.15	−1.15	−0.46	0.02	−0.48	−0.29	−0.14	−0.30	−2.65
Manufactured intermediates	−0.30	−9.38	−1.19	−0.37	−0.29	0.33	0.74	−1.31	−11.76
Machinery and equipment	−11.53	−25.36	−10.52	−0.23	−2.38	−0.37	0.01	−3.07	−53.45
Services	−6.68	−10.97	3.61	−0.08	−2.98	−0.82	−0.25	−3.68	−21.85
Total	−7.59	−16.78	16.97	0.82	6.65	−0.55	2.33	−6.8	−4.96

Source: Authors' calculations.

Table 3.3 Production, trade, and factor income in the Middle East and North Africa, 1992 (percent)

Sector	Outputs	Exports	Imports	Skilled labor/ unskilled labor	Skilled labor/ capital	Unskilled labor/ capital
				Factor ratio in value added		
Agricultural products	4.97	1.44	3.75	0.03	0.02	0.53
Mineral and energy products	18.06	69.47	4.67	0.97	0.06	0.07
Wood and paper products	2.89	0.21	3.24	0.21	0.12	0.56
Food processing	8.36	1.22	6.73	0.28	0.12	0.42
Textiles	1.64	1.03	4.30	0.21	0.12	0.59
Wearing apparel	1.66	2.95	1.67	0.12	0.16	1.26
Other light manufactures	0.78	0.74	2.29	0.26	0.13	0.48
Manufactured intermediates	6.26	6.02	13.58	0.35	0.20	0.58
Machinery and equipment	4.38	3.37	35.02	0.54	0.43	0.79
Services	51.01	13.56	24.74	1.05	0.60	0.57
Total	100.00	100.00	100.00	0.88	0.32	0.37

Source: Authors' calculations.

suppliers of manufactured goods and both purchasers and suppliers of capital-intensive products. Eastern Europe and the former Soviet Union and the Middle East and North Africa are special cases. All are closely tied to the European Union and face an uncertain future. Their shares of the services sector and their endowment of skilled labor are similar to that of OECD countries, while their agricultural labor force is much smaller than that of low-income countries. Their comparative advantage lies in low- to medium-skilled sectors, but they are different from the low-income countries in important ways. Their exports depend heavily on mineral and energy products, and their labor and semi-skilled intensive goods compete with both the newly industrialized countries and developing countries. They could move up the ladder and catch up with the newly industrialized countries, or they could fall behind and be forced to compete with Asian and other developing countries in labor-intensive products.

These structural characteristics are the starting point for assessing what further structural changes in trade, production, wages, employment, and real absorption may take place among the regions, particularly the Middle East and North Africa, after the Uruguay Round trade liberalization.

THE IMPACT OF THE URUGUAY ROUND AND THE EU OPTION ON THE MIDDLE EAST AND NORTH AFRICA

Simulations were run to examine the impact of the Uruguay Round on the Middle East and North Africa; the impact of a magnified Uruguay Round with free trade between Eastern Europe and the former Soviet Union and the European Union (but with the Middle East and North Africa remaining outside this free trade area); and the impact of the Middle East and North Africa joining the enlarged European Free Trade Area. For each scenario the computable general equilibrium model generates results on the impact on social welfare, terms of trade, volume of trade, output, real wages paid to each labor category, and other factor returns. Trade creation impacts were assessed by calculating the change in intraregional trade within the free trade area; trade diversion impacts were assessed by calculating the change in interregional trade between the rest of the world and the free trade area. The results of the simulations should be regarded as controlled experiments rather than as forecasts. Actual trade and output patterns will be influenced by much more than just trade liberalization; domestic macroeconomic and income policies will be particularly important.

The first simulation

The implementation of the Uruguay Round will generate very different macroeconomic effects across regions (Table 3.4). In the first simulation social welfare (measured by the Hicksian equivalent variation) increases in North America, the European Union, and Asia but declines in the Middle East and North Africa and in Eastern Europe and the former Soviet Union. The Round leads to a loss in social welfare of $2.6 billion a year for the Middle East and North Africa and $1.7 billion for Eastern Europe and the former Soviet Union. Asia experiences a welfare gain of $8.7 billion.

North America and the European Union enjoy both an improvement in terms of trade and an expansion in real trade volume. The reverse takes place in the Middle East and North Africa. Its terms of trade will deteriorate by as much as 3.6 percent, and its volume of

Table 3.4 Macroeconomic impacts of the three simulations
(percentage change from base)

	North America	European Union	Middle East and North Africa	Eastern Europe and the former Soviet Union	Asian developing countries
First simulation					
Social welfare					
(billions of U.S. dollars)	11.33	11.39	−2.55	−1.73	8.67
As a percentage of 1992 GDP	0.18	0.18	−0.45	−0.22	1.10
International terms of trade	2.23	2.52	−3.56	−3.108	−0.63
Exports/output	0.27	0.12	−0.07	0.05	0.70
Imports/absorption	0.16	0.12	−0.11	−0.01	0.45
Real exports	4.19	2.18	−0.12	0.57	10.41
Real imports	5.56	3.43	−1.18	−0.99	8.98
Second simulation					
Social welfare					
(billions of U.S. dollars)	11.09	11.72	−2.90	0.51	8.03
As a percentage of 1992 GDP	0.17	0.18	−0.51	0.46	1.02
International terms of trade	2.18	2.39	−3.91	2.03	−0.77
Exports/output	0.27	0.18	−0.08	0.65	0.70
Imports/absorption	0.16	0.14	−0.12	0.31	0.44
Real exports	4.17	3.02	−0.18	9.41	10.19
Real imports	5.51	4.13	−1.40	9.72	8.67
Third simulation					
Social welfare					
(billions of U.S. dollars)	10.12	15.52	−2.62	0.25	7.51
As a percentage of 1992 GDP	0.16	0.24	−0.46	0.03	0.96
International terms of trade	2.00	2.75	−0.18	1.58	−0.88
Exports/output	0.27	0.25	0.82	0.64	0.70
Imports/absorption	0.15	0.18	0.11	0.30	0.43
Real exports	4.02	3.95	4.19	9.29	10.08
Real imports	5.23	5.33	2.94	9.21	8.42

Note: See text for descriptions of the simulations.
Source: Authors' calculations.

trade also declines. Eastern Europe and the former Soviet Union and Asia also suffer terms of trade losses but gain in export growth. For

Eastern Europe and the former Soviet Union the negative price effect dominates the positive volume effect (leading to a net loss), while in Asia the volume effect dominates the terms of trade effect (leading to a net gain).

The details of price changes at the sectoral level show that the Middle East and North Africa's main export, minerals and energy, has nearly flat export prices, while the export prices of textiles and apparel shows a marked fall (Table A3.1, pp. 71–2). The reduction in prices is a consequence of greater competition resulting from the phasing out of the Multifiber Arrangement (MFA). The picture is also gloomy on the import side. There is a 28 percent increase in the region's import prices of food and agricultural commodities that is related to the reduction of agricultural subsidies in industrial countries. Finally, the prices of capital- and skill-intensive manufactured goods is projected to rise, a consequence of the expected increase in global demand for these products. While the overall terms of trade facing the nonindustrial world deteriorate, the Middle East and North Africa is harder hit that those regions, which have more diversified trade structures.

Differences in production and consumption structures between the Middle East and North Africa and Asia help explain the different impact on the two regions. In the Middle East and North Africa, a net food importer, food imports account for 12 percent of food consumption. In Asia food imports account for only 3–4 percent of domestic consumption. The 28 percent increase in agricultural import prices induced by the Uruguay Round will have strong adverse welfare effects in the Middle East and North Africa. Apparel accounts for only 3 percent of the region's exports, while it accounts for 15 percent of East Asia's. In the past most Arab countries were exporting below their MFA quotas, while most of their Asian competitors were bound by theirs. As the quota under the MFA is eliminated, the quota-rents that were available in the past will evaporate.

An examination of changes in real export flows by sector and destination shows that trade is diverted away from Middle Eastern and North African producers (Table A3.2, pp. 73–4). The region's exports (except to Japan, East Asia, and the newly industrialized countries) decline in almost every sector. More than $0.5 billion of the region's apparel exports to North America and the European Union will be replaced by exports from East Asia and the newly industrialized countries. More than $2.8 billion in total trade between the European Union and the Middle East and North Africa is diverted to other regions (EU exports to the Middle East and North Africa decrease by $1.8 billion, the Middle East and North Africa's exports to the EU drop by $1 billion). Export expansion in industrial countries occurs mainly in capital- and skill-intensive sectors, with North America also gaining in agricultural exports.

The most striking change in the region induced by the Uruguay Round is the expansion of agriculture (Tables A3.3 and A3.4, pp. 75–8). Semi-skilled, capital-intensive manufacturing will also increase, but at the expense of unskilled, labor-intensive manufacturing. In both sectors output expands and imports fall. But the labor-intensive manufacturing sectors are unable to hold on to their production factors in the face of a global expansion of low-cost unskilled labor, and both output and exports fall. The small expansion of the semiskilled and capital-intensive manufacturing sectors appears to be driven more by push factors in the low-skill sectors than by a pull from the more skilled industries.

From a global prospective the largest structural change induced by the Uruguay Round occurs in the textile and apparel sectors. Apparel output falls, and imports in OECD countries increase sharply. Developing countries expand their production and exports, with Asia increasing its output by 39 percent and exports by 57 percent. Powerful structural changes also occur in agriculture. The output of agricultural products falls by about 5 percent in Japan and the newly industrialized countries, while imports rise by about 25 percent in Japan and 53 percent in the newly industrialized countries as trade protection in these regions is reduced. The European Union sees a 34 percent reduction in its agricultural exports as a result of cuts in domestic subsidies.

What does all this mean for income distribution in the Middle East and North Africa and elsewhere? The changes in factor prices are consistent with intuition and the aggregate welfare changes discussed above. Returns to arable land would decline in Japan, the European Union, and the newly industrialized countries and increase in North America, the Middle East and North Africa, Eastern Europe and the former Soviet Union, and the rest of Asia. Returns to labor and capital decline in the Middle East and North Africa and Eastern Europe and the former Soviet Union but rise elsewhere. Once the effects of rural–urban migration are played out, skilled labor ends up as the main loser in the Middle East and North Africa because unskilled wages are pushed up by the rise in agricultural terms of trade. In other regions the wages of rural and urban unskilled labor increase as well, except for a slight decline in Eastern Europe and the former Soviet Union.

The second simulation

The establishment of a free trade area for Eastern Europe and the former Soviet Union and the European Union would worsen the external environment for the Middle East and North Africa and cost the region an additional $0.35 billion in social welfare loss over the first simulation (see Table 3.4). Eastern Europe and the former Soviet Union would gain $0.5 billion rather than lose $1.7 billion, as in the first simulation. This turnaround reflects these countries' gain of preferential access to the EU market, which would improve terms of trade. Trade creation between that region and the European Union is nearly $10 billion, and only $2.7 billion of trade is diverted from other regions. An additional $0.4 billion of trade between the European Union, Eastern Europe and the former Soviet Union, and the Middle East and North Africa will be diverted to other regions (above the loss due to the Uruguay Round, see Tables A3.5–A3.8, pp.79–86).

These results illustrate the risk that the Middle East and North Africa faces of falling behind and, ultimately, being shut out of the emerging global economy. The static effects of trade liberalization are usually small and can easily be overtaken by dynamic effects. Still, it is worrisome that our estimates of the static effects are negative and quite large for the Middle East and North Africa. One option that the region can follow to soften the effect of the international environment and facilitate policy reform is to imitate Eastern Europe and regain preferential access to the EU market. But it must use this opportunity to get ready for the increased globalization introduced by the Uruguay Round. The question then is whether a policy that pursues active engagement in the emerging European bloc can facilitate the implementation of domestic policy changes.

The third simulation

The Middle East and North Africa would suffer a welfare loss of $2.6 billion if it joined the enlarged EU free trade area (see Table 3.4). This is a marginal gain of $0.3 billion relative to the second simulation. Thus the European option does not appear to be a highly valuable opportunity.

This small welfare effect should not, however, mask the significant shift in trade and production structures involved (Tables A3.9–A3.12, pp. 87–94). Real exports would rise by nearly 6 percent and become more open, since export–output and import–absorption ratios would rise. The region also enjoys slightly improved terms of trade. Returns to factors improve relative to the first and second simulations. Compared with the current situation, land and unskilled labor gain, while capital and skilled labor suffer a slight decline. The small aggregate effects that would accompany large structural changes suggest that trade diversion creates large inefficiencies, with cheap international imports being replaced by more expensive imports from Europe. At the same time, customs revenues would fall and need to be replaced by new taxes. For gains from a closer association with Europe to be large, integration must transcend the pure static trade motive.

Trade creation exceeds trade diversion for the enlarged EU free trade area. Total trade creation is estimated at $43 billion; total trade diversion is about $15 billion. The difference between trade creation and diversion varies considerably among the three regions, however. For the European Union there is no trade diversion at all (other region's exports to the EU market would increase by more than $22 billion). For Eastern Europe and the former Soviet Union the ratio of trade diversion to trade creation is 0.23, while for the Middle East and North Africa it is 0.77. The reason for the much larger trade diversion in the Middle East and North Africa seems to be its high levels of protection compared with the European Union and Eastern Europe and the former Soviet Union after the Uruguay Round (Hoekman, 1995).

SENSITIVITY ANALYSIS

Further simulations were carried out to evaluate how sensitive the analysis of the three simulation results are to changes in the important elasticities underlying the model. These simulations were designed to embody different combinations for the various underlying elasticities, with each of the main parameters having three point values (Table 3.5).

The results for the first simulation are show in Table 3.6. Clearly, the simulation's main conclusions appear to be quite robust. While the predicted impacts of policy changes will be quantitatively affected by

Table 3.5 Simulation design: L9(34) orthogonal table, combination of elasticity estimates

Simulation	Substitution elasticities between domestic and foreign products	Substitution elasticities among different import sources	Transformation elasticities (domestic sale through exports)
1	Low	Low	Low
2	Low	Central	Central
3	Low	High	High
4	Central	Low	Central
5	Central	High	High
6	Central	High	Low
7	High	Low	High
8	High	Central	Low
9	High	High	Central

Table 3.6 Sensitivity analysis, first simulation (percentage change from base)

Simulation	Social welfare[a]	Share of 1992 GNP	Terms of trade	Real exports	Real imports
Central case	−2.55	−0.45	−3.56	−0.12	−1.18
1	−4.01	−0.70	−3.94	0.69	−1.36
2	−3.11	−0.54	−3.81	0.58	−0.97
3	−3.09	−0.54	−4.26	0.47	−0.99
4	−2.61	−0.46	−3.22	−0.16	−1.25
5	−2.25	−0.39	−3.22	−0.10	−1.03
6	−3.62	−0.63	−4.22	−0.06	−1.68
7	−2.10	−0.37	−2.90	−0.21	−1.01
8	−3.40	−0.59	−3.61	−0.34	−1.78
9	−2.70	−0.47	−3.79	−0.41	−1.46
Mean (1–9)	−2.99	−0.52	−3.66	0.05	−1.28
Standard deviation	0.632	0.11	0.469	0.415	0.309
Coefficient of variation	0.211	0.21	0.128	–	0.242

a. Percentage change based on billions of U.S. dollars.
Source: Simulation results.

variations in the size of elasticities, they all carry the same signs and show a narrow range of variations (with coefficient of variation below 0.3). The results for the second simulation are shown in Table 3.7. The results are also quite robust, with the predicted impacts carrying the same signs and variations within a narrow range. Finally, the sensi-

Table 3.7 Sensitivity analysis, second simulation (percentage change from base)

Simulation	Social welfare[a]	Share of 1992 GNP	Terms of trade	Real exports	Real imports
Central case	−2.90	−0.51	−3.91	−0.18	−1.40
1	−4.54	−0.79	−4.45	0.77	−1.56
2	−3.47	−0.61	−4.22	0.61	−1.12
3	−3.37	−0.59	−4.66	0.47	−1.12
4	−2.96	−0.52	−3.54	−0.22	−1.47
5	−2.57	−0.45	−3.52	−0.18	−1.25
6	−4.08	−0.71	−4.72	−0.08	−1.91
7	−2.36	−0.41	−3.12	−0.32	−1.22
8	−3.80	−0.67	−4.04	−0.39	−2.01
9	−3.04	−0.53	−4.15	−0.54	−1.72
Mean (1–9)	−3.35	−0.59	−4.05	0.01	−1.49
Standard deviation	0.707	0.123	0.551	0.477	0.337
Coefficient of variation	0.211	0.209	0.136	−	0.226

a. Percentage change based on billions of U.S. dollars.
Source: Simulation results.

Table 3.8 Sensitivity analysis, third simulation (percentage change from base)

Simulation	Social welfare[a]	Share of 1992 GNP	Terms of trade	Real exports	Real imports
Central case	−2.62	−0.46	−0.18	4.19	2.94
1	−4.04	−0.71	0.31	2.24	0.31
2	−3.09	−0.54	−0.59	3.01	1.63
3	−2.89	−0.51	−0.61	3.29	2.25
4	−2.82	−0.49	−0.39	3.95	2.47
5	−2.69	−0.47	−0.58	4.75	3.40
6	−3.83	−0.67	1.14	2.60	1.19
7	−2.44	−0.43	−0.71	5.79	4.23
8	−3.40	−0.59	1.20	2.45	1.09
9	−2.92	−0.51	0.20	5.43	4.10
Mean (1–9)	−3.12	−0.55	0.00	3.72	2.30
Standard deviation	0.531	0.09	0.757	1.326	1.383
Coefficient of variation	0.170	0.169	−	0.356	0.601

a. Percentage change based on billions of U.S. dollars.
Source: Simulation results.

tivity tests for the third simulation are show in Table 3.8. As with the first two simulations, the predicted impacts on aggregate welfare, GNP, and terms of trade vary within a narrow range despite large variations in the size of the main parameters of the model. However, unlike the other two simulations, there are significant variations in the behavior of trade (with imports and exports showing coefficient of variations greater than 0.3). This suggests that although strong qualitative conclusions can be drawn regarding changes in real imports and exports, the magnitude obtained must be interpreted with caution.

Figure 3.1 Aggregate welfare impact and levels of trade
(a) First simulation (b) Second simulation (c) Third simulation

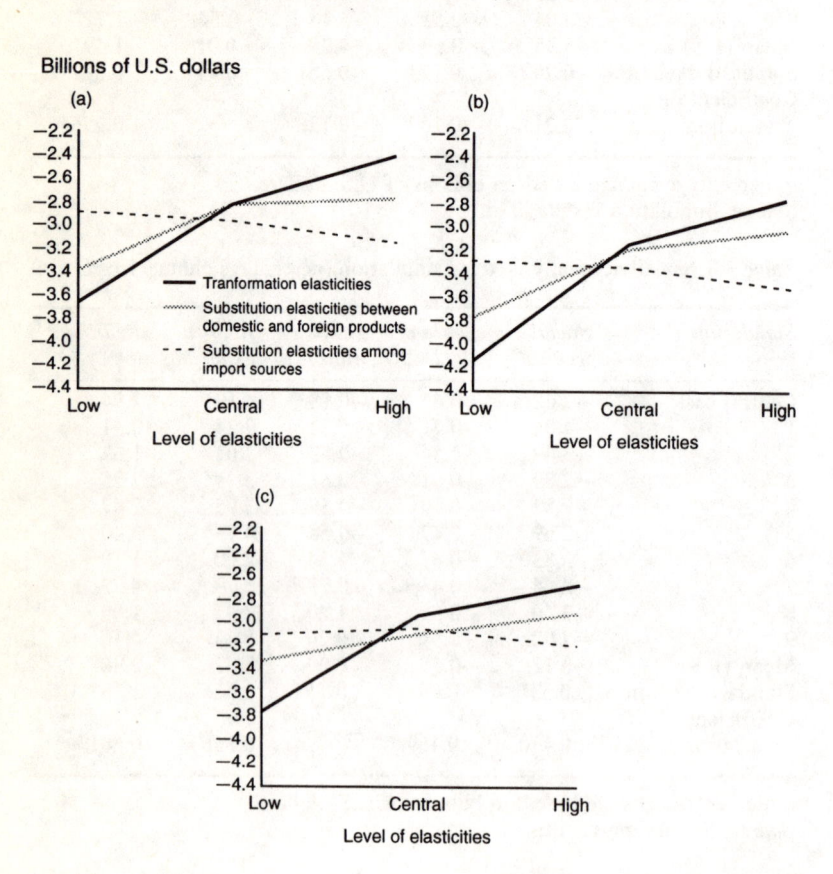

Source: Authors' calculations.

The effects of changes in different elasticities on aggregate welfare are shown in Figure 3.1. As transformation elasticities increase (or decrease), the predicted impact on aggregate welfare gains increases (or decreases). This pattern appears to prevail for all three simulation scenarios. This result is consistent with economic intuition: the more easily a region can shift its resources between production for domestic sales and exports, the more it will gain (or the less it will lose) from a change in trade policy. Similarly, but to a lesser extent, as the substitution elasticities between domestic and foreign products increase (or decrease), aggregate welfare also improves (or worsens). But an increase in the substitution elasticities among import sources appears to be associated with decreases in aggregate welfare. Overall, transformation elasticities seem to be affect aggregate welfare more than the other two sets of elasticities.

CONCLUSION

The simulation results suggest that because of its factor endowments and initial conditions in production and trade, the Middle East and North Africa will experience a social welfare loss following the implementation of the Uruguay Round equivalent to 0.5 percent of its 1992 GDP. These static losses will be higher if a free trade area is established between the European Union and Eastern Europe and the former Soviet Union, and the Middle East and North Africa remains outside the association. The combined welfare losses would be somewhat smaller if the Middle East and North Africa joins the enlarged free trade area.

The simulation results further suggest that by fostering competition, especially from low-income countries, the Uruguay Round will exert downward pressure on real wages for Arab workers (real wages will drop 0.7 percent), divert trade to other regions (0.1 percent of 1992 exports), worsen the region's terms of trade (by 4 percent), and increase the need for radical policy adjustments. The specific outcomes would be magnified by the formation of a free trade area comprising European Union and Eastern Europe and the former Soviet Union. This predicament will mainly be caused by the elimination of agricultural subsidies (leading to higher import prices) and the phaseout of the MFA (exacerbating competition in labor-intensive industries). The loss of preferred access to the EU market in favor of the middle- income and medium-skilled economies of Eastern Europe and the former Soviet Union would leave the Middle East and North Africa further behind these countries, make it more difficult to move up the technology ladder, and complicate the task of attracting investment. These short-term losses could turn into long-term decline if they unleash a vicious circle of social instability and capital flight.

The globalization of world trade leaves the Middle East and North Africa with little choice but to accelerate economic reforms. Countries in the region should dismantle their protective walls to benefit from global trade. The net effect of access to markets abroad – but also more competition – depends on whether the economy is flexible and adept enough to gain sufficient markets abroad to compensate for those lost at home. Such a structural change will take time and requires a supporting social environment in which workers and other production factors can be reallocated from traditional sectors and into new industries.

The EU option provides a window of opportunity, but other beneficial aspects of deeper links with the EU must be developed if its gains are to be valuable. At least four areas require the attention of the region's policymakers:

- *Increased aid.* The European Union could help the region move toward a more open trade regime (for example, by converting import substituting sectors, retraining displaced workers, and transferring new technologies) and would make available adjustment finance (the Union has already pledged to increase development assistance by nearly $10 billion in the context of its Mediterranean initiative).
- *Openness.* It is hoped that the European Union will refrain from using new protectionist devises such as exaggerated antidumping claims, picky quality standards, or restrictive rules of origin.
- *Better policies.* A closer association with Europe could help establish the credibility of reform programs in the region. As the region increases its exports it will become increasingly important to reform domestic policies. But a clear timetable for convergence in policies is needed to anchor expectations. And to minimize the losses due to trade diversion, the opening to Europe should be accompanied by wide-scale economic liberalization.
- *Regional stability.* If the peace process progresses, the European option offers a mechanism for integrating Israel with the region, easing regional tensions and increasing stability.

Appendix 3.1 A Multiregion, Multisector General Equilibrium Model of World Production and Trade

The model uses nine regions to represent the world economy. Each region is assumed to have basically the same structure. Ten production sectors are posited in each region. Five primary factors of production are assumed for each region: agricultural land, rural labor, capital, unskilled labor, and skilled labor. The division between skilled and unskilled labor is basically a white-collar and blue-collar distinction. Primary factors are assumed to be mobile across sectors but immobile among regions. Rural labor and urban unskilled labor cannot be substituted but are linked by rural-urban migration flows, which are driven by the urban-rural wage differential.[3]

ECONOMIC AGENTS AND FACTOR ENDOWMENTS

Three demand side agents are assumed for each region: a private household, a public household, and an investor. Factor endowments are assumed to be owned by households and are set exogenously. Private households are assumed to sell the three categories of labors, to rent capital to firms, and to divide fixed proportions of their factor returns into savings and expenditures on final consumption goods from firms. Investors collect savings from households, government, and firms, accounting for foreign capital inflows and outflows. Investors are also assumed to spend total regional saving on capital goods, which are assumed to consist of fixed proportions of the ten composite goods for gross investment.

PRODUCTION

There is one competitive firm in each sector for every region that produces just one product. Production is characterized by two-level nesting. At the first level there is a Leontief-type production function.

Firms are assumed to use a composite of primary factors of production according to a constant elasticity of substitution (CES) cost function and fixed proportion intermediate inputs for the ten composite goods. Strong separability of the production function is assumed at this level. There is no substitution between the composite primary factor and the ten composite intermediates. Technology in all sectors is assumed to exhibit constant return to scale, implying constant average and marginal costs. At the second level the four primary factors of production are assumed to substitute smoothly through a CES value-added function. The degree of substitution among them depends on their base year share in production and on the elasticity of substitution, which is assumed to be constant. The firm's output is assumed to be sold on the domestic market or exported to other regions through a constant elasticity of transformation (CET) function.

DEMAND

Agents in each region are assumed to value products from different regions as imperfect substitutes (the Armington assumption). Private households in each region are assumed to maximize a Stone–Grey utility function over the ten composite goods, subject to their budget constraints. Government spending and investment decisions in each region are based on Cobb–Douglas utility functions, which generate constant expenditure shares for each composite commodity. In each region intermediate inputs for the firms, household consumption, government spending, and investment demand constitute total demand for the same Armington composite of domestic products and imported goods from different sources. A two-level nested CES aggregation function is specified for each composite commodity in each region. The total demand is first divided between domestically produced and imported goods. Then the expenditure on imports is further divided according to geographical origin under the assumption of cost minimization. Sectoral import demand functions for each region are derived by the duality method. Complete trade flow matrices for all trade partners are part of the model solution.

INTERNATIONAL SHIPPING

There is an international shipping industry in the model that transports products from one region to another. Each region is assumed to allocate a fraction of the output of its transportation and service sector to satisfy the demand for shipping generated by interregional trade. The global shipping industry is assumed to have a unity elasticity of substitution among supplier sources. The margins associated with this activity are commodity- and route-specific. In equilibrium the total value of international transportation services at the world price equals the sum of the export proportions of the service sector's output from each region.

TRADE-DISTORTING POLICY

The government in each region is assumed to impose sector-specific, ad valorem import tariffs, export subsidies, and indirect taxes.

PRICE SYSTEM

There are average output prices, composite good prices, domestic good prices, export prices, import prices, f.o.b. prices, and c.i.f. prices in each region for goods in the same sector. The average output price is a tax-inclusive CET aggregation of domestic and export prices. The composite good price is a tax-inclusive CES aggregation of domestic and import prices, which in turn is an aggregation of tariff-inclusive import prices from different sources. The f.o.b. price of each Armington good is the firm's export price plus the export subsidy. This is the price that sellers receive. The c.i.f. price is the seller's price plus international transportation margins. An exchange rate, as a conversion factor, translates world market prices into domestic prices.

EQUILIBRIUM

Equilibrium is defined as a set of prices and quantities for goods and factors in all regions such that demand equals supply for all goods and factors, each industry earns zero profit, and gross investment equals aggregate saving in each region.

CHOICE OF NUMERAIRE

Like other computable general equilibrium models, only relative prices matter. The absolute price level is set exogenously. A price index equal to the share of domestic supplies at the base year multiplied by their price in each region is used as the numeraire. The advantage of this choice of normalization is that it closely relates the equilibrium exchange rate defined in the model to the concept of real exchange rate in trade theory (de Melo and Robinson 1989).

CHOICE OF MACROECONOMIC CLOSURE

There are three major macroeconomic balances in each region: the government deficit (surplus), aggregate savings and investment, and the balance of trade. Although each agent has a balanced budget in equilibrium, there is no presumption that bilateral trade flows between any two regions is balanced. These flows are determined endogenously. Government deficit or surplus is the difference between revenue and expenditures, with real spending fixed exogenously but revenue dependent on taxes on trade and domestic production. Thus deficits or surpluses can also be determined endogenously. Because we are interested in the impact of trade liberalization, the balance of trade (and thus the domestic saving and investment gap) are held constant in all the simulations.

Notes

1. The authors are grateful to Hanaa Khaireddine for her detailed review; Arvind Panagariya, Sherman Robinson, Michael Walton, and Adrian Wood for helpful conversations; and the participants at the June 1995 Economic Research Forum workshop in Tunisia for comments.
2. The nine regions are North America (the United States and Canada), the European Union (twelve member countries), Japan, the Middle East and North Africa, Eastern Europe and the former Soviet Union, the newly industrialized countries (Argentina, Brazil, Hong Kong, Republic of Korea, Malaysia, Singapore, Taiwan), Asian developing countries (China, Indonesia, the Philippines, and Thailand), other developing countries (the rest of Latin America, South Asia, and Sub-Saharan Africa), and other industrial countries (Australia, New Zealand, and countries in the European Free Trade Area). The ten sectors are agricultural products, minerals and energy, wood and paper products, food processing, textiles, wearing apparel, other light manufactures, manufacture intermediates, machinery and transportation equipment, and transportation, service, and construction, a portion of which is allocated to international shipping. All trade figures reported in this section refer to interregional trade. Intraregional trade flows are treated as another source of domestic demand.
3. The model is based on Wang, 1994; a detailed algebraic description can be found in Wang and Slagle, 1996.

References

Armington, Paul S. 1969, "A Theory of Demand for Products Distinguished by Place of Production." *IMF Staff Papers* 16: 159–76.

Balassa, Bela. 1965. "Trade Liberalization and Revealed Comparative Advantage," *The Manchester School* 33: 99–124.

Brook, A., D. Kendrick, and A. Meeraus. 1988. *GAMS: A User's Guide*. San Francisco, Calif.: Scientific Press.

de Melo, Jaime and Sherman Robinson, 1989. "Product Differentiation and the Treatment of Foreign Trade in Computable General Equilibrium Models of Small Economies," *Journal of International Economics*, 27: 47–67.

Diwan, Ishac, and Mike Walton, 1995. "Opening Up and Distribution in the Middle East and North Africa: The Poor, the Unemployed, and the Public Sector," Washington, D.C.: *World Bank*

Harrison, Glenn W., Thomas F. Rutherford, and David G. Tarr. 1995. "Quantifying the Uruguay Round." In Will Martin and Alan Winters (eds.), *The Uruguay Round and the Developing Economies*, Washington, D.C.: World Bank.

Hertel, Thomas W.(ed.), 1996. *Global Trade Analysis: Modeling and Applications,*. Cambridge: Cambridge University Press.

Hoekman, Bernard. 1995. "The WTO, the EU, and the Arab World: Trade Policy Priorities and Pitfalls," Washington, D.C.: World Bank

Kreinin, E. Morderchai, 1991. *International Economics: A Policy Approach*, 6th eds, New York: Harcourt Brace Jovanovich.

Leamer, E., 1984. *Sources of International Comparative Advantage,*. Cambridge, Mass.: MIT Press.

Lewis, Jeffrey D., Sherman Robinson and Zhi Wang, 1995. "Beyond the Uruguay Round: The Implication of an Asian Free Trade Area," *China Economic Review – An International Journal*, 6(1): 35–90.

Shoven J. B. and J. Whalley. 1992. *Applying General Equilibrium*, Cambridge Surveys of Economic Literature, Cambridge: Cambridge University Press.

Wang, Zhi, 1994. "The Impact of Economic Integration Among Taiwan, Hong Kong, and China: A Computable General Equilibrium Analysis," Ph.D dissertation. Department of Applied Economics, University of Minnesota, St. Paul.

Wang, Zhi and James Slagle, 1996. "An Object-Oriented Approach to Formulate Applied General Equilibrium Models," *Journal of Economic Dynamics and Control* 20: 209–36.

Whalley, J., 1985. *Trade Liberalization Among Major World Trading Areas*. Cambridge, Mass.: MIT Press.

Table A3.1 Change in prices by sector, first simulation (percentage change from base)

	North America	European Union	Japan	Middle East and North Africa	Eastern Europe and former Soviet Union	Newly industrialized countries	Asian developing countries	Other developing countries	Other OECD countries
World import prices (c.i.f)									
Agricultural products	2.175	4.348	7.134	27.564	19.682	8.784	13.097	22.783	2.934
Mineral and energy products	1.020	0.760	1.053	0.926	1.060	1.116	1.383	1.021	0.850
Wood and paper products	2.169	1.500	1.249	1.674	1.795	1.580	1.886	1.462	1.738
Food processing	1.106	1.962	1.881	7.407	10.034	2.240	3.467	5.027	1.512
Textiles	−2.108	−2.398	1.919	1.750	1.371	2.052	2.266	1.882	1.637
Wearing apparel	−8.971	−4.879	3.136	2.845	1.689	3.762	1.518	2.616	2.624
Other light manufactures	1.471	1.429	1.125	1.258	1.197	1.732	1.344	1.142	1.211
Manufactured intermediates	1.762	1.360	1.425	1.646	1.592	1.885	1.770	1.543	1.580
Machinery and equipment	1.595	1.218	0.843	1.172	1.048	1.380	1.286	1.236	1.160
Services	0.625	0.608	0.626	0.546	0.551	0.631	0.608	0.600	0.557
World export prices (f.o.b.)									
Agricultural products	9.791	23.971	−4.583	4.275	4.926	−0.015	9.427	2.880	5.610
Mineral and energy products	0.906	0.695	2.836	0.646	0.524	1.115	2.125	0.808	0.646
Wood and paper products	0.623	1.883	3.247	1.368	0.850	2.239	2.689	1.064	1.742
Food processing	2.062	5.071	0.166	2.100	2.322	0.845	2.219	2.970	2.700
Textiles	1.705	1.139	2.322	−1.364	−0.067	0.891	−0.295	−1.481	0.350
Wearing apparel	2.336	3.007	1.129	−7.023	−6.137	−8.300	0.369	−9.770	−5.620
Other light manufactures	0.909	1.017	2.833	0.898	0.594	0.912	1.655	1.409	0.968
Manufactured intermediates	1.227	1.587	3.102	1.691	0.847	1.366	2.041	1.384	1.280
Machinery and equipment	0.701	1.055	2.541	1.387	0.477	0.959	0.830	1.305	0.583
Services	0.593	0.479	0.694	0.782	0.474	0.706	1.005	0.631	0.536

Domestic consumer prices								
Agricultural products	3.51	2.17	-13.92	4.38	7.87	-9.17	2.69	1.87	4.15
Mineral and energy products	0.22	0.11	0.13	-0.38	-0.36	0.84	0.17	-0.17	-0.04
Wood and paper products	0.07	-0.39	0.39	-0.17	-0.33	0.59	-0.45	-0.04	-1.37
Food processing	1.10	0.95	-4.88	2.23	2.75	-3.98	1.07	0.77	1.22
Textiles	-0.71	-1.77	-1.73	0.49	-0.17	-1.19	-4.65	-0.15	-0.65
Wearing apparel	-7.01	-6.41	-0.68	1.25	1.02	-0.14	-13.06	-1.97	0.28
Other light manufactures	-0.43	-0.68	-1.00	0.16	-0.64	-0.24	-5.52	-0.33	-1.94
Manufactured intermediates	-0.36	-0.59	0.17	0.04	-0.43	0.05	-0.36	-0.51	-1.23
Machinery and equipment	-1.00	-0.80	0.04	-0.04	-0.31	-0.56	-3.19	-0.91	-1.53
Services	0.19	0.171	0.55	-0.40	-0.19	0.96	0.65	-0.06	0.16

Source: Authors' calculations.

Table A3.2 Change in sectoral exports by destination, first simulation (change from base in billions of U.S. dollars)

	North America	European Union	Japan	Middle East and North Africa	Eastern Europe and former Soviet Union	Newly industrialized countries	Asian developing countries	Other developing countries	Other OECD countries	Total
North America										
Agricultural products	—	−0.878	2.952	−0.275	−0.127	3.677	0.518	−0.033	−0.183	5.651
Mineral and energy products	—	0.242	0.042	−0.004	0.015	0.245	0.074	0.154	0.121	0.889
Wood and paper products	—	0.002	0.446	0.024	0.001	0.346	−0.045	0.039	0.047	0.862
Food processing	—	−0.026	0.300	0.091	0.092	−0.203	0.150	0.306	−0.023	0.687
Textiles	—	−0.223	0.008	−0.006	0.60	0.067	0.039	0.037	0.058	−0.020
Wearing apparel	—	−0.405	−0.009	0.002	0.002	−0.005	−0.013	−0.155	0.029	−0.553
Other light manufactures	—	−0.251	0.053	0.003	0.005	0.543	0.091	0.021	0.096	0.559
Manufactured intermediates	—	1.675	0.590	0.016	0.003	0.285	0.243	0.166	0.298	3.276
Machinery and equipment	—	1.826	1.256	0.401	0.018	3.335	−1.254	0.380	3.074	9.038
Services	—	−0.304	0.753	−0.016	−0.024	0.345	0.316	0.040	−0.109	1.001
Total	—	1.658	6.393	0.237	−0.014	8.636	0.119	0.956	3.407	21.391
European Union										
Agricultural products	0.093	—	−0.114	−0.813	−0.584	−0.103	−0.221	−0.480	0.227	−1.995
Mineral and energy products	0.165	—	0.197	−0.019	0.018	0.051	0.222	0.102	−0.124	0.611
Wood and paper products	0.209	—	0.055	−0.053	0.00	0.061	−4.78	−0.005	0.00	1.043
Food processing	0.406	—	0.437	−1.105	−0.882	0.042	0.059	−0.539	0.080	−1.663
Textiles	−0.216	—	0.056	0.029	0.126	0.228	0.316	0.076	0.099	0.714
Wearing apparel	−1.047	—	0.162	−0.032	−0.015	−0.027	−0.003	−0.053	0.169	−0.845
Other light manufactures	−0.198	—	0.228	0.015	0.044	0.362	0.067	0.041	0.322	0.882
Manufactured intermediates	1.211	—	0.634	−0.082	0.047	1.198	0.245	0.231	1.663	5.148
Machinery and equipment	4.766	—	0.895	0.175	−0.055	2.307	0.313	0.780	−0.022	9.160
Services	−0.231	—	0.452	0.050	−0.081	0.106	0.052	0.099	−0.226	0.220
Total	5.159	—	3.002	−1.836	−1.382	4.180	1.049	0.198	2.903	13.275
Middle East and North Africa										
Agricultural products	−0.007	−0.070	−0.038	—	0.015	0.075	0.018	0.005	−0.001	−0.002
Mineral and energy products	−0.433	−0.422	0.835	—	−0.060	0.185	0.063	−0.067	−0.138	0.039
Wood and paper products	0.00	0.003	0.00	—	−0.003	0.005	0.00	0.00	0.002	0.007

Food processing	−0.012	0.00	−0.042	—	0.005	0.004	−0.003	0.005	−0.003	−0.045
Textiles	−0.011	0.025	0.00	—	−0.012	0.003	0.00	0.00	−0.004	0.00
Wearing apparel	−0.126	−0.444	0.00	—	0.011	0.004	0.00	0.004	0.046	−0.503
Other light manufactures	−0.028	0.010	0.00	—	−0.003	0.006	0.00	0.00	0.00	0.002
Manufactured intermediates	−0.014	0.088	0.051	—	−0.011	0.156	−0.011	0.052	0.013	0.324
Machinery and equipment	0.168	−0.041	0.002	—	−0.007	−0.012	−0.029	0.004	0.045	0.130
Services	−0.056	−0.110	0.140	—	−0.007	0.00	0.005	−0.002	−0.018	−0.049
Total	−0.518	−0.961	0.950	—	−0.072	0.426	0.044	−0.002	−0.059	−0.193
Eastern Europe and the former Soviet Union										
Agricultural products	−0.004	−0.117	−0.012	0.010	—	−0.061	0.004	0.007	−0.007	−0.181
Mineral and energy products	0.006	0.396	0.011	0.003	—	0.009	0.014	0.016	−0.035	0.418
Wood and paper products	0.014	0.090	0.003	0.005	—	0.00	−0.002	0.012	0.015	0.139
Food processing	0.015	0.068	−0.078	0.007	—	−0.020	0.00	−0.003	−0.020	−0.031
Textiles	−0.10	−0.074	0.002	0.001	—	0.008	0.023	0.002	0.004	−0.044
Wearing apparel	−0.059	−1.058	0.011	0.003	—	0.003	0.003	0.00	0.311	−0.786
Other light manufactures	−0.004	0.015	0.00	0.00	—	0.002	−0.002	0.00	−0.009	0.003
Manufactured intermediates	−0.005	0.409	0.140	0.014	—	0.009	0.018	0.008	0.125	0.682
Machinery and equipment	−0.019	−0.055	0.003	0.015	—	0.046	0.017	0.055	0.128	0.190
Services	−0.007	−0.009	0.038	0.001	—	0.003	0.015	0.002	−0.011	0.033
Total	−0.073	−0.334	0.082	0.059	—	0.00	0.090	0.099	0.501	0.424
Asian developing countries										
Agricultural products	−0.292	−0.560	−0.493	−0.018	−0.002	3.276	—	−0.047	−0.066	1.799
Mineral and energy products	−0.170	−0.048	−0.233	−0.008	−0.007	−0.382	—	−0.001	−0.003	−0.852
Wood and paper products	−0.100	−0.053	0.197	−0.022	0.00	−0.198	—	−0.009	0.058	−0.127
Food processing	−0.321	0.048	−0.489	0.067	0.078	−0.336	—	−0.027	−0.029	−0.010
Textiles	0.405	1.003	−0.021	−0.016	−0.009	−0.095	—	0.60	0.008	1.276
Wearing apparel	16.030	12.800	−0.010	−0.163	−0.116	−1.613	—	−0.136	−0.114	26.680
Other light manufactures	−0.489	−0.355	0.006	−0.010	−0.004	−1.021	—	−0.011	0.055	−1.828
Manufactured intermediates	−0.110	0.041	0.052	−0.013	0.00	−0.426	—	0.002	0.003	−0.451
Machinery and equipment	−1.401	−0.174	0.301	0.011	0.005	−1.437	—	0.003	0.281	−2.411
Services	−0.066	−0.051	0.060	−0.017	−0.013	−0.037	—	−0.014	−0.044	−0.182
Total	13.486	12.651	−0630	−0.189	−0.067	−2.269	—	−0.239	0.150	22.893

Source: Authors' calculations.

Table A3.3 Structural change, first simulation (percentage change from base)

	North America	European Union	Japan	Middle East and North Africa	Eastern Europe and the former Soviet Union	Newly industrialized countries	Asian developing countries	Other developing countries	Other OECD countries
Outputs									
Agricultural products	2.55	−1.26	−5.10	1.70	0.55	−4.87	0.46	0.29	0.30
Mineral and energy products	0.37	0.26	−0.71	−0.02	0.58	−0.25	−2.43	−0.93	0.77
Wood and paper products	0.21	−0.18	−0.25	0.27	0.18	0.72	−2.19	−0.41	0.79
Food processing	0.04	−0.55	1.07	0.23	0.32	2.09	−1.72	−0.25	0.53
Textiles	−6.73	−1.92	1.56	−1.03	−2.67	9.03	4.01	4.33	−4.45
Wearing apparel	−22.75	−17.05	−0.49	−2.68	−4.95	10.34	38.67	10.16	−6.30
Other light manufactures	0.27	0.64	1.98	−0.68	−1.49	3.73	−5.90	−0.11	−3.03
Manufactured intermediates	0.13	0.14	0.04	1.26	0.71	0.23	−2.22	−0.64	0.10
Machinery and equipment	0.48	0.77	0.33	0.76	0.34	0.61	−4.99	−0.70	0.81
Services	0.05	0.14	0.09	−0.29	−0.10	−0.17	0.20	−0.24	−0.08
Exports									
Agricultural products	19.99	−34.00	20.36	−0.12	−8.16	18.35	16.81	0.54	4.59
Mineral and energy products	4.38	2.19	2.21	−0.03	2.52	−0.23	−3.83	−1.23	2.44
Wood and paper products	3.48	5.22	3.64	2.06	2.96	4.41	−1.50	−0.29	6.98
Food processing	2.76	−6.09	12.54	−2.31	−0.82	15.72	−5.89	2.53	4.46
Textiles	−0.34	4.20	8.94	−0.03	−2.79	19.11	7.46	14.51	−3.35
Wearing apparel	−14.79	−7.01	0.00	−10.47	−17.37	16.46	57.08	26.37	−18.14
Other light manufactures	4.44	3.57	6.57	−1.42	0.14	5.74	−4.73	0.94	0.26
Manufactured intermediates	5.36	4.66	3.94	3.36	3.58	2.56	−2.70	0.98	4.60
Machinery and equipment	4.61	3.91	2.26	2.39	2.25	2.28	−5.93	1.47	3.80
Services	0.75	0.19	−0.77	−0.22	0.28	−0.46	−0.99	−0.47	0.15

Imports

Agricultural products	0.89	−5.41	24.78	−11.67	−5.92	52.65	17.57	−7.58	2.56
Mineral and energy products	−2.11	0.08	2.85	−0.59	−0.66	0.98	6.21	1.29	−0.53
Wood and paper products	0.83	5.01	5.19	−1.79	1.01	1.52	12.72	0.78	8.13
Food processing	3.88	0.85	4.94	−4.90	−9.05	−0.24	36.27	0.95	−0.57
Textiles	3.56	10.45	0.07	−1.85	2.41	2.25	38.80	3.19	1.76
Wearing apparel	54.13	37.07	8.53	−4.15	2.98	−12.82	59.53	−12.38	5.72
Other light manufactures	0.63	1.75	4.70	−0.77	3.57	0.50	13.38	2.90	4.93
Manufactured intermediates	5.48	4.89	6.56	−0.91	0.03	3.40	2.21	2.66	4.44
Machinery and equipment	4.57	3.20	7.68	−0.33	−0.05	1.58	4.90	1.25	2.77
Services	−2.02	−0.63	2.58	−0.08	−1.32	0.96	6.40	0.48	−0.92

Source: Authors' calculations.

Table A3.4 Factor reallocation, first simulation (percentage change from base)

	North America	European Union	Japan	Middle East and North Africa	Eastern Europe and the former Soviet Union	Newly industrialized countries	Asian developing countries	Other developing countries	Other OECD countries
Unskilled labor									
Mineral and energy products	0.57	0.26	−0.86	0.25	0.65	−0.89	−2.72	−0.93	0.83
Wood and paper products	0.36	−0.17	−0.35	0.44	0.22	0.20	−2.41	−0.42	0.83
Food processing	0.19	−0.54	0.95	0.40	0.37	1.58	−1.95	−0.25	0.58
Textiles	−6.62	−1.91	1.48	−0.85	−2.63	8.46	3.73	4.32	−4.41
Wearing apparel	−22.68	−17.05	−0.56	−2.55	−4.92	9.83	38.37	10.16	−6.26
Other light manufactures	0.46	0.66	1.86	−0.48	−1.45	3.22	−6.14	−0.12	−2.97
Manufactured intermediates	0.29	0.16	−0.12	1.44	0.75	−0.31	−2.52	−0.65	0.15
Machinery and equipment	0.65	0.81	0.19	0.90	0.37	0.14	−5.24	−0.72	0.86
Services	0.24	0.17	−0.05	−0.13	−0.04	−0.74	−0.09	−0.29	−0.02
Skilled labor									
Agricultural products	5.91	−4.71	−21.96	4.44	1.51	−11.70	2.45	2.11	0.88
Mineral and energy products	0.36	0.13	−0.82	0.28	0.64	−0.47	−2.44	−0.74	0.77
Wood and paper products	0.15	−0.30	−0.31	0.47	0.21	0.63	−2.13	−0.22	0.76
Food processing	0.00	−0.66	0.98	0.43	0.36	1.96	−1.69	−0.08	0.51
Textiles	−6.84	−2.05	1.52	−0.81	−2.64	8.95	4.06	4.54	−4.48
Wearing apparel	−22.85	−17.16	−0.52	−2.52	−4.93	10.33	38.80	10.39	−6.33
Other light manufactures	0.23	0.52	1.91	−0.45	−1.46	3.69	−5.85	0.09	−3.04
Manufactured intermediates	0.06	0.03	−0.07	1.47	0.74	0.14	−2.21	−0.44	0.08
Machinery and equipment	0.42	0.68	0.24	0.93	0.36	0.59	−4.95	−0.51	0.78
Services	0.00	0.02	0.00	−0.10	−0.06	−0.24	0.25	−0.06	−0.10

Capital								
Agricultural products	5.86	−4.62	−21.84	4.21	1.45	−11.47	2.51	1.97	0.87
Mineral and energy products	0.28	0.28	−0.57	−0.05	0.54	−0.06	−2.35	−0.94	0.75
Wood and paper products	0.07	−0.15	−0.60	0.14	0.12	1.03	−2.04	−0.42	0.75
Food processing	−0.06	−0.52	1.20	0.13	0.28	2.33	−1.61	−0.26	0.50
Textiles	−6.91	−1.89	1.79	−1.17	−2.74	9.42	4.16	4.32	−4.50
Wearing apparel	−22.91	−17.03	−0.26	−2.87	−5.03	10.81	38.94	10.15	−6.35
Other light manufactures	0.15	0.68	2.17	−0.80	−1.56	4.14	−5.76	−0.13	−3.06
Manufactured intermediates	−0.02	0.19	0.19	1.11	0.64	0.57	−2.12	−0.66	0.06
Machinery and equipment	0.34	0.84	0.50	0.58	0.26	1.03	−4.85	−0.72	0.77
Services	−0.09	0.20	0.28	−0.49	−0.17	0.23	0.35	−0.29	−0.12

Source: Authors' calculations.

Table A3.5 Change in prices by sector, second simulation (percentage change from base)

	North America	European Union	Japan	Middle East and North Africa	Eastern Europe and the former Soviet Union	Newly industrialized countries	Asian developing countries	Other developing countries	Other OECD countries
World import prices (c.i.f.)									
Agricultural products	2.034	7.960	7.118	27.817	16.961	8.743	13.047	22.870	3.404
Mineral and energy products	1.035	0.937	1.066	1.089	3.077	1.137	1.413	1.078	1.125
Wood and paper products	2.304	1.596	1.311	1.872	2.003	1.648	1.950	1.621	2.069
Food processing	1.235	3.548	1.956	7.837	7.251	2.389	3.609	5.351	2.095
Textiles	−9.906	−2.705	2.049	2.048	1.790	2.100	2.309	2.039	2.158
Wearing apparel	−9.101	−5.775	3.081	2.945	2.022	3.652	1.419	2.661	3.579
Other light manufactures	1.520	1.517	1.209	1.438	1.359	1.746	1.368	1.293	1.482
Manufactured intermediates	1.914	1.603	1.595	1.899	1.743	1.988	1.922	1.721	1.928
Machinery and equipment	1.711	1.282	0.943	1.362	1.264	1.474	1.402	1.384	1.388
Services	0.701	0.962	0.704	0.646	0.634	0.704	0.684	0.678	0.643
World export prices (f.o.b.)									
Agricultural products	9.760	23.677	−4.713	3.806	31.114	−0.347	9.191	2.401	5.436
Mineral and energy products	0.948	1.116	2.885	0.661	1.847	1.132	2.102	0.798	0.636
Wood and paper products	0.674	2.257	3.307	1.287	1.762	2.271	2.677	1.066	1.722
Food processing	1.950	5.224	0.178	1.684	14.703	0.699	2.061	2.696	2.451
Textiles	1.677	1.817	2.323	−1.571	1.102	0.879	−0.370	−1.679	0.105
Wearing apparel	2.331	3.718	1.089	−7.492	−2.528	−8.492	0.033	−10.035	−6.194
Other light manufactures	0.930	1.450	2.856	0.880	3.222	0.914	1.582	1.266	0.870
Manufactured intermediates	1.257	1.925	3.152	1.685	3.036	1.395	2.008	1.328	1.203
Machinery and equipment	0.756	1.385	2.605	1.398	2.610	0.996	0.842	1.151	0.508
Services	0.663	0.570	0.754	0.861	0.750	0.769	1.057	0.700	0.626

Domestic consumer prices								
Agricultural products	3.47	1.16	-13.96	4.33	11.06	-9.25	2.57	1.65	4.32
Mineral and energy products	0.22	0.12	0.11	-0.39	-0.33	0.84	0.19	-0.15	0.00
Wood and paper products	0.07	-0.41	0.39	-0.15	-0.46	0.59	-0.44	-0.03	-1.33
Food processing	1.10	0.49	-4.89	2.24	2.74	-3.99	1.04	0.70	1.37
Textiles	-0.68	-2.08	-1.72	0.63	-2.25	-1.18	-4.63	-0.15	-0.42
Wearing apparel	-7.09	-7.13	-0.69	1.46	-4.12	-0.08	-12.85	-1.85	0.73
Other light manufactures	-0.43	-0.86	-0.97	0.22	-2.98	-0.23	-5.48	-0.26	-1.78
Manufactured intermediates	-0.34	-0.68	0.18	0.13	-1.36	0.07	-0.27	-0.45	-1.12
Machinery and equipment	-0.97	-0.86	0.01	0.07	-2.12	-0.50	-3.05	-0.78	-1.39
Services	0.19	0.21	0.55	-0.42	0.10	0.95	0.66	-0.06	0.12

Source: Authors' calculations.

Table A3.6 Change in sectoral exports by destination, second simulation (change from base in billions of U.S. dollars)

	North America	European Union	Japan	Middle East and North Africa	Eastern Europe and the former Soviet Union	Newly industrialized countries	Other developing countries	Asian developing countries	Other OECD countries	Total
North America										
Agricultural products	—	−1.122	2.963	−0.271	0.101	3.647	−0.049	0.496	−0.166	5.600
Mineral and energy products	—	0.240	0.041	0.00	0.006	0.240	0.154	0.072	0.133	0.886
Wood and paper products	—	0.001	0.453	0.027	−0.006	0.343	0.040	−0.048	0.056	0.866
Food processing	—	−0.254	0.383	0.111	0.007	−0.158	0.320	0.154	0.018	0.581
Textiles	—	−0.251	0.010	−0.003	−0.004	0.068	0.039	0.037	0.067	−0.038
Wearing apparel	—	−0.429	−0.008	0.003	−0.007	−0.007	−0.149	−0.013	0.037	−0.571
Other light manufactures	—	−0.276	0.061	0.005	−0.014	0.541	0.023	0.090	0.114	0.544
Manufactured intermediates	—	1.540	0.630	0.027	−0.045	0.324	0.182	0.257	0.338	3.254
Machinery and equipment	—	1.612	1.319	0.505	−0.294	3.485	0.441	−1.223	3.266	9.111
Services	—	−0.228	0.757	−0.026	0.015	0.314	0.019	0.304	−0.132	1.023
Total	—	0.834	6.611	0.377	−0.241	8.797	1.020	0.126	3.731	21.255
European Union										
Agricultural products	0.066	—	−0.122	−0.824	−0.299	−0.119	−0.486	−0.225	0.207	−1.802
Mineral and energy products	0.066	—	0.177	−0.052	0.478	0.019	0.066	0.210	−0.175	0.788
Wood and paper products	0.169	—	0.045	−0.074	0.382	−0.005	−0.024	−0.007	0.735	1.222
Food processing	0.257	—	0.341	−1.202	0.350	−0.064	−0.701	0.028	−0.093	−1.083
Textiles	−0.265	—	0.031	−0.042	0.848	0.178	0.045	0.288	0.034	1.116
Wearing apparel	−1.084	—	0.080	−0.074	0.348	−0.075	−0.073	−0.005	0.135	−0.748
Other light manufactures	−0.351	—	0.167	−0.019	0.972	0.280	0.014	0.058	0.192	1.313
Manufactured intermediates	0.994	—	0.564	−0.165	1.793	1.032	0.128	0.190	1.473	6.010
Machinery and equipment	3.910	—	0.713	−0.133	5.097	1.809	0.492	0.092	−0.683	11.296
Services	−0.249	—	0.442	0.011	0.099	0.085	0.063	0.047	−0.337	0.159
Total	3.511	—	2.437	−2.574	10.067	3.140	−0.477	0.676	1.488	18.270
Middle East and North Africa										
Agricultural products	−0.005	−0.138	0.037	—	0.024	0.079	0.006	0.020	0.011	0.040
Mineral and energy products	−0.407	−0.377	0.868	—	−0.126	0.195	−0.061	0.060	0.089	−0.064
Wood and paper products	0.00	0.004	0.00	—	−0.005	0.005	0.00	0.00	0.003	0.006

82

Food processing	−0.008	−0.036	−0.036	—	0.001	0.007	0.006	−0.002	0.00	−6.609
Textiles	−0.009	0.009	0.00	—	−0.024	0.003	0.00	0.00	0.00	−0.019
Wearing apparel	−0.105	−0.571	0.00	—	0.00	0.005	0.005	0.00	0.058	−0.609
Other light manufactures	−0.026	0.008	0.00	—	−0.009	0.006	0.00	0.00	0.002	−0.019
Manufactured intermediates	−0.008	0.066	0.057	—	−0.026	0.160	0.056	−0.008	0.020	0.317
Machinery and equipment	0.179	−0.041	0.003	—	−0.034	−0.010	0.005	−0.029	0.048	0.121
Services	−0.058	−0.101	0.139	—	0.00	−0.003	−0.004	0.004	−0.021	−0.044
Total	−0.447	−1.176	0.995	—	−0.199	0.446	0.012	0.046	0.031	−0.291

Eastern Europe and the former Soviet Union

Agricultural products	−0.031	2.205	−0.070	−0.039	—	−0.112	−0.010	−0.016	−0.174	1.753
Mineral and energy products	−0.011	0.611	−0.015	−0.009	—	−0.014	−0.003	0.003	−0.227	0.335
Wood and paper products	0.009	0.077	−0.011	−0.004	—	0.00	0.010	−0.004	−0.011	0.064
Food processing	−0.141	2.149	−0.251	−0.041	—	−0.125	−0.017	−0.051	−0.237	1.285
Textiles	−0.034	0.446	−0.004	−0.007	—	−0.010	−0.0067	0.006	−0.055	0.335
Wearing apparel	−0.142	2.168	−0.004	−0.002	—	−0.002	0.00	0.00	−0.134	1.884
Other light manufactures	−0.051	0.134	−0.006	0.00	—	0.00	0.00	−0.002	−0.053	0.019
Manufactured intermediates	−0.084	1.512	−0.042	−0.028	—	−0.065	−0.033	−0.124	−0.072	1.064
Machinery and equipment	−0.061	0.576	−0.002	−0.027	—	0.00	0.002	−0.116	−0.016	0.356
Services	−0.011	−0.057	0.028	−0.002	—	0.00	0.00	0.013	−0.029	−0.057
Total	−0.557	9.820	−0.377	−0.160	—	−0.329	−0.059	−0.292	−1.007	7.038

Asian developing countries

Agricultural products	−0.288	−0.668	−0.475	−0.014	0.028	3.320	—	−0.046	−0.058	1.800
Mineral and energy products	−0.161	−0.044	−0.197	−0.007	−0.012	−0.369	—	0.00	0.008	−0.782
Wood and paper products	−0.093	−0.049	0.206	−0.020	−0.002	−0.193	—	−0.009	0.062	−0.099
Food processing	−0.279	−0.062	−0.436	0.078	0.011	−0.296	—	−0.021	−0.008	−1.014
Textiles	0.417	0.942	−0.013	−0.10	−0.026	−0.086	—	0.001	0.021	1.247
Wearing apparel	16.160	11.561	0.070	−0.132	−0.271	−1.524	—	−0.128	0.008	25.745
Other light manufactures	−0.377	−0.350	0.033	−0.006	−0.051	−0.956	—	−0.009	0.084	−1.631
Manufactured intermediates	−0.093	0.029	0.072	−0.008	−0.016	−0.399	—	0.005	0.013	−0.398
Machinery and equipment	−1.348	−0.176	0.321	0.017	−0.066	−1.340	—	0.010	0.300	−2.282
Services	−0.066	−0.046	0.065	−0.018	−0.003	−0.041	—	−0.016	−0.046	−0.171
Total	13.871	11.137	−0.354	−0.121	−0.408	−1.882	—	−0.213	0.348	22.415

Source: Authors' calculations.

Table A3.7 Structural change, second simulation (percentage change from base)

	North America	European Union	Japan	Middle East and North Africa	Eastern Europe and the former Soviet Union	Newly industrialized countries	Asian developing countries	Other developing countries	Other OECD countries
Outputs									
Agricultural products	2.50	−1.60	−5.11	1.65	4.17	−4.94	0.44	0.25	0.34
Mineral and energy products	0.37	0.26	−0.74	0.07	−0.20	−0.02	−2.29	−0.77	0.94
Wood and paper products	0.22	−0.13	−0.25	0.31	−0.73	0.76	−2.08	−0.35	0.89
Food processing	0.04	−0.58	1.08	0.24	0.85	2.07	−1.75	−0.25	0.54
Textiles	−6.80	−1.82	1.50	−1.37	0.88	8.80	3.73	4.19	−4.37
Wearing apparel	−23.07	−18.14	−0.57	−3.43	11.06	9.69	37.27	9.65	−6.10
Other light manufactures	0.23	1.24	1.90	−0.65	−5.83	3.71	−5.43	−0.12	−2.92
Manufactured intermediates	0.15	0.21	0.04	1.36	−0.63	0.32	−2.00	−0.54	0.19
Machinery and equipment	0.50	1.02	0.33	0.80	−1.67	0.73	−4.78	−0.65	0.72
Services	0.05	0.13	0.09	−0.31	−0.14	−0.17	0.18	−0.26	−0.10
Exports									
Agricultural products	19.84	−30.81	19.54	−1.77	79.21	17.17	16.82	−0.18	3.73
Mineral and energy products	4.36	2.62	2.11	0.06	2.02	−0.12	−3.50	−0.96	2.64
Wood and paper products	3.49	6.11	3.61	1.78	1.37	4.56	−1.16	−0.05	7.06
Food processing	2.34	−3.68	12.41	−3.49	29.98	15.30	−5.92	2.19	3.70
Textiles	−0.64	6.57	8.66	−1.23	22.80	18.86	7.32	14.16	−4.14
Wearing apparel	−15.27	−6.20	−0.42	−12.71	43.84	15.27	55.17	25.01	−19.74
Other light manufactures	4.32	5.31	6.33	−1.59	0.91	5.71	−4.22	0.69	0.04
Manufactured intermediates	5.32	5.44	3.90	3.30	5.44	2.72	−2.38	1.05	4.42
Machinery and equipment	4.65	4.82	2.25	2.23	4.16	2.44	−5.61	1.08	3.42
Services	0.77	0.14	−0.77	−0.20	−0.48	−0.42	−0.92	−0.40	0.21

Imports								
Agricultural products	1.39	−2.08	24.86	−11.91	6.91	52.50	17.09	−8.21	0.99
Mineral and energy products	−2.11	0.44	2.94	−0.99	6.57	0.91	5.95	0.97	−1.13
Wood and paper products	0.65	5.19	5.19	−2.09	13.54	1.38	12.40	0.34	7.44
Food processing	3.39	3.89	4.79	−5.41	6.85	−0.70	35.35	0.18	−2.01
Textiles	3.23	12.06	−0.09	−2.46	19.59	1.90	37.91	2.55	1.16
Wearing apparel	54.90	40.60	8.96	−3.71	2.98	−12.34	60.79	−12.43	3.70
Other light manufactures	0.63	1.88	4.68	−1.08	20.36	0.43	13.19	2.39	4.48
Manufactured intermediates	5.26	5.73	6.33	−1.19	11.54	3.23	1.90	2.26	3.90
Machinery and equipment	4.46	3.39	7.60	−0.47	12.04	1.50	4.71	1.03	2.47
Services	−2.08	−0.54	2.56	−0.24	1.02	0.79	6.01	0.18	−1.20

Source: Authors' calculations.

Table A3.8 Factor reallocation, second simulation (percentage change from base)

	North America	European Union	Japan	Middle East and North Africa	Eastern Europe and the former Soviet Union	Newly industrialized countries	Asian developing countries	Other developing countries	Other OECD countries
Unskilled labor									
Mineral and energy products	0.57	0.23	−0.89	0.37	0.03	−0.85	−2.57	−0.78	1.01
Wood and paper products	0.36	−0.12	−0.35	0.51	−0.60	0.24	−2.29	−0.36	0.93
Food processing	0.19	−0.59	0.96	0.43	1.01	1.55	−1.97	−0.26	0.59
Textiles	−6.70	−1.82	1.41	−1.17	1.01	8.23	3.46	4.19	−4.33
Wearing apparel	−23.00	−18.14	−0.64	−3.29	11.18	9.19	36.99	9.64	−6.07
Other light manufactures	0.42	1.24	1.78	−0.43	−5.67	3.20	−5.66	−0.13	−2.86
Manufactured intermediates	0.31	0.21	−0.11	1.56	−0.48	−0.23	−2.28	−0.55	0.24
Machinery and equipment	0.68	1.06	0.19	0.96	−1.56	0.25	−5.02	−0.67	0.77
Services	0.24	0.14	−0.05	−0.14	−0.02	−0.75	−0.11	−0.30	−0.04
Skilled labor									
Agricultural products	5.79	−5.95	−22.01	4.34	11.77	−11.88	2.31	1.85	−1.00
Mineral and energy products	0.35	0.11	−0.85	0.39	0.05	−0.42	−2.29	−0.57	0.95
Wood and paper products	0.15	−0.25	−0.31	0.53	−0.58	0.66	−2.01	−0.16	0.88
Food processing	0.00	−0.70	1.00	0.45	1.03	1.94	−1.71	−0.07	0.54
Textiles	−6.91	−1.95	1.46	−1.14	1.03	8.72	3.79	4.41	−4.38
Wearing apparel	−23.17	−18.25	−0.60	−3.27	11.20	9.68	37.42	9.88	−6.12
Other light manufactures	0.19	1.10	1.82	−0.41	−5.65	3.67	−5.37	0.09	−2.92
Manufactured intermediates	0.08	0.08	−0.07	1.59	−0.46	0.22	−1.98	−0.33	0.18
Machinery and equipment	0.44	0.92	0.24	0.98	−1.54	0.70	−4.73	−0.45	0.71
Services	−0.01	0.00	0.00	−0.11	0.04	−0.25	0.23	−0.06	−0.11

Capital

Agricultural products	5.74	−5.84	−21.88	4.10	11.48	−11.64	2.36	1.71	0.98
Mineral and energy products	0.28	0.29	−0.60	0.03	−0.35	−0.01	−2.21	−0.78	0.91
Wood and paper products	0.08	−0.07	−0.07	0.17	−0.98	1.08	−1.93	−0.36	0.84
Food processing	−0.07	−0.54	1.22	0.13	0.67	2.32	−1.64	−0.26	0.50
Textiles	−6.98	−1.76	1.72	−1.52	0.60	9.20	3.87	4.18	−4.42
Wearing apparel	−23.23	−18.09	−0.34	−3.64	10.72	10.17	37.53	9.64	−6.16
Other light manufactures	0.11	1.30	2.09	−0.79	−6.05	4.12	−5.29	−0.13	−2.96
Manufactured intermediates	0.00	0.28	0.19	1.20	−0.88	0.67	−1.90	−0.55	0.14
Machinery and equipment	0.37	1.12	0.50	0.59	−1.96	1.15	−4.65	−0.67	0.67
Services	−0.09	0.21	0.29	−0.53	−0.43	0.24	0.32	−0.31	−0.15

Source: Authors' calculations.

Table A3.9 Change in prices by sector, third simulation (percentage change from base)

	North America	European Union	Japan	Middle East and North Africa	Eastern Europe and the former Soviet Union	Newly industrialized countries	Asian developing countries	Other developing countries	Other OECD countries
World import prices (c.i.f.)									
Agricultural products	1.821	10.766	6.926	24.890	17.118	8.629	13.027	22.845	3.603
Mineral and energy products	1.047	0.923	1.064	3.025	2.672	1.131	1.402	1.077	1.179
Wood and paper products	2.490	1.583	1.310	2.129	2.489	1.682	1.972	1.840	2.627
Food processing	1.453	3.659	2.047	5.706	8.161	2.573	3.717	5.867	2.778
Textiles	−1.584	−2.881	2.247	2.542	2.946	2.104	2.245	2.212	2.905
Wearing apparel	−9.059	−6.434	3.007	3.347	2.441	3.529	1.293	2.689	4.090
Other light manufactures	1.543	1.472	1.279	1.667	1.738	1.733	1.351	1.453	1.773
Manufactured intermediates	2.096	1.645	1.690	2.280	2.169	2.068	1.966	1.958	2.369
Machinery and equipment	1.841	1.202	1.004	1.766	1.794	1.501	1.470	1.548	1.739
Services	0.741	0.765	0.756	0.685	0.677	0.747	0.731	0.716	0.672
World export prices (f.o.b.)									
Agricultural products	9.565	23.209	−4.924	26.176	29.961	−0.747	8.897	1.881	5.150
Mineral and energy products	0.894	1.703	2.844	0.681	1.964	1.088	2.045	0.792	0.599
Wood and paper products	0.629	3.002	3.286	2.921	2.094	2.233	2.580	1.001	1.720
Food processing	1.830	5.698	0.131	7.556	14.622	0.545	1.938	2.522	2.304
Textiles	1.507	3.132	2.145	0.413	1.093	0.771	−0.481	−1.853	−0.114
Wearing apparel	2.214	4.567	0.936	−3.343	−2.852	−8.632	−0.158	−10.205	−6.557
Other light manufactures	0.889	2.019	2.803	2.056	3.270	0.877	1.483	1.186	0.725
Manufactured intermediates	1.200	2.530	3.066	3.029	3.118	1.331	1.910	1.280	1.138
Machinery and equipment	0.607	2.081	2.547	2.049	2.778	0.980	0.810	1.103	0.431
Services	0.720	0.587	0.769	0.926	0.886	0.800	1.057	0.775	0.741

Domestic consumer prices								
Agricultural products	3.43	−0.04	−14.03	7.40	10.82	−9.33	2.47	1.44	4.41
Mineral and energy products	0.23	0.09	0.13	−0.67	−0.38	0.85	0.22	−0.13	0.04
Wood and paper products	0.08	−0.47	0.40	−0.74	−0.48	0.60	−0.42	0.00	−1.26
Food processing	1.11	0.02	−4.90	2.89	2.71	−4.00	1.00	0.64	1.46
Textiles	−0.63	−2.45	−1.68	−1.79	−2.06	−1.15	−4.62	−0.14	−0.13
Wearing apparel	−7.10	−7.85	−0.68	−3.26	−3.88	−0.03	−12.69	−1.77	1.05
Other light manufactures	−0.39	−1.12	−0.94	−2.16	−2.89	−0.21	−5.45	−0.20	−1.59
Manufactured intermediates	−0.31	−0.80	0.19	−2.31	−1.34	0.11	−0.20	−0.37	−0.98
Machinery and equipment	−0.90	−1.05	0.03	−3.19	−2.03	−0.45	−2.92	−0.66	−1.19
Services	0.19	0.27	0.55	0.00	0.10	0.94	0.67	−0.05	0.08

Source: Authors' calculations.

Table A3.10 Change in sectoral exports by destination, third simulation (change from base in billions of U.S. dollars)

	North America	European Union	Japan	Middle East and North Africa	Eastern Europe and the former Soviet Union	Newly industrialized countries	Asian developing countries	Other developing countries	Other OECD countries	Total
North America										
Agricultural products	—	−1.342	2.970	−0.228	0.112	3.661	0.502	−0.042	−0.147	5.486
Mineral and energy products	—	0.294	0.050	−0.104	0.005	0.256	0.073	0.167	0.153	0.894
Wood and paper products	—	0.073	0.462	−0.088	−0.005	0.356	−0.047	0.050	0.078	0.879
Food processing	—	−0.279	0.438	−0.077	0.022	−0.117	0.156	0.347	0.054	0.544
Textiles	—	−0.263	0.014	−0.050	−0.003	0.077	0.037	0.048	0.082	−0.058
Wearing apparel	—	−0.442	−0.004	−0.026	−0.006	−0.003	−0.013	−0.131	0.044	−0.581
Other light manufactures	—	−0.256	0.070	−0.045	−0.012	0.547	0.091	0.029	0.141	0.566
Manufactured intermediates	—	1.596	0.673	−0.287	−0.040	0.417	0.272	0.232	0.411	3.273
Machinery and equipment	—	2.274	1.617	−3.104	−0.264	4.260	−1.067	0.719	3.929	8.364
Services	—	0.179	0.700	−0.154	0.014	0.262	0.291	0.00	−0.161	1.130
Total	—	1.834	6.989	−4.163	−0.179	9.717	0.296	1.417	4.586	20.496
European Union										
Agricultural products	0.049	—	−0.128	−0.668	−0.315	−0.128	−0.227	−0.489	0.210	−1.697
Mineral and energy products	−0.208	—	0.121	1.006	0.396	−0.062	0.178	−0.024	−0.427	0.980
Wood and paper products	0.074	—	0.020	0.607	0.340	−0.049	−0.019	−0.060	0.541	1.453
Food processing	−0.009	—	0.170	0.720	0.223	−0.241	−0.020	−0.855	−0.316	−0.328
Textiles	−0.362	—	−0.020	1.228	0.732	0.085	0.238	−0.012	−0.141	1.748
Wearing apparel	−1.124	—	−0.017	0.480	0.291	−0.129	−0.007	−0.096	−0.102	−0.704
Other light manufactures	−0.572	—	0.075	0.900	0.910	0.169	0.047	−0.021	0.00	1.509
Manufactured intermediates	0.510	—	0.381	2.605	1.635	0.689	0.062	−0.061	0.949	6.770
Machinery and equipment	1.682	—	0.220	10.635	4.631	0.459	−0.051	−0.257	−2.523	14.345
Services	−0.266	—	0.435	−0.242	0.108	0.076	0.044	0.052	−0.385	−0.178
Total	−0.226	—	1.257	17.270	8.950	0.868	−0.205	−1.823	−2.193	23.899
Middle East and North Africa										
Agricultural products	−0.039	2.520	−0.056	—	−0.018	−0.035	−0.071	−0.053	−0.160	2.060
Mineral and energy products	−0.098	0.376	0.823	—	−0.010	0.179	0.050	−0.048	−0.040	0.952
Wood and paper products	−0.002	0.006	0.00	—	0.018	0.003	0.00	−0.002	0.001	0.023

Food processing	−0.039	0.369	−0.092	—	0.003	−0.016	−0.005	−0.009	−0.018	0.192
Textiles	−0.035	0.479	−0.005	—	−0.002	−0.003	0.00	−0.005	−0.023	0.404
Wearing apparel	−0.401	1.943	0.00	—	0.033	−0.003	0.00	−0.004	−0.001	1.567
Other light manufactures	−0.049	0.085	−0.001	—	−0.004	0.003	0.00	−0.002	−0.010	0.021
Manufactured intermediates	−0.064	0.915	0.014	—	0.031	0.102	−0.046	0.011	−0.003	0.961
Machinery and equipment	0.118	0.409	0.00	—	0.063	−0.029	−0.033	−0.002	0.042	0.568
Services	−0.064	−0.039	0.122	—	0.00	−0.008	0.004	−0.007	−0.024	−0.017
Total	−1.002	7.062	0.804	—	0.134	0.193	−0.101	−0.121	−0.238	6.732
Eastern Europe and the former Soviet Union									
Agricultural products	−0.030	2.072	−0.069	−0.020	—	−0.111	−0.016	−0.010	−0.168	1.647
Mineral and energy products	−0.012	0.599	−0.017	0.033	—	−0.016	0.002	−0.003	−0.216	0.370
Wood and paper products	0.007	0.055	−0.017	0.072	—	0.00	−0.005	0.009	−0.012	0.107
Food processing	−0.140	2.110	−0.250	−0.015	—	−0.125	−0.052	−0.017	−0.231	1.281
Textiles	−0.033	0.424	−0.004	0.003	—	−0.010	0.005	−0.006	−0.051	0.328
Wearing apparel	−0.141	2.009	−0.004	0.00	—	−0.002	0.00	0.00	−0.120	1.741
Other light manufactures	−0.052	0.132	−0.007	0.002	—	0.00	−0.003	0.00	−0.050	0.022
Manufactured intermediates	−0.085	1.470	−0.046	0.042	—	−0.067	−0.129	−0.032	−0.050	1.104
Machinery and equipment	−0.063	0.507	−0.002	0.085	—	−0.004	−0.123	0.001	−0.007	0.394
Services	−0.014	−0.023	0.022	−0.009	—	0.00	−0.012	−0.001	−0.039	−0.052
Total	−0.562	9.356	−0.394	0.192	—	−0.336	−0.307	−0.061	−0.946	6.942
Asian developing countries									
Agricultural products	−0.282	−0.773	−0.465	−0.005	0.031	3.364	—	−0.043	−0.051	1.776
Mineral and energy products	−0.151	−0.035	−0.170	−0.025	−0.013	−0.352	—	0.001	0.022	−0.722
Wood and paper products	−0.082	−0.031	0.214	−0.067	−0.002	−0.183	—	−0.008	0.069	−0.089
Food processing	−0.248	−0.076	−0.409	−0.011	0.023	−0.268	—	−0.013	0.008	−0.995
Textiles	0.435	0.907	−0.001	−0.091	−0.022	−0.065	—	0.005	0.041	1.209
Wearing apparel	16.387	10.846	0.136	−0.518	−0.257	−1.440	—	−0.120	0.101	25.135
Other light manufactures	−0.286	−0.291	0.057	−0.077	−0.047	−0.892	—	−0.007	0.118	−1.425
Manufactured intermediates	−0.071	0.041	0.091	−0.106	−0.014	−0.358	—	0.012	0.027	−0.378
Machinery and equipment	−1.275	−0.165	0.342	−0.126	−0.061	−1.256	—	0.021	0.337	−2.184
Services	−0.067	−0.023	0.066	−0.030	−0.002	−1.042	—	−0.017	−0.047	−0.162
Total	14.360	10.399	−0.141	−1.055	−0.364	−1.491	—	−0.169	0.626	22.165

Source: Authors' calculations.

Table A3.11 Structural change, third simulation (percentage change from base)

	North America	European Union	Japan	Middle East and North Africa	Eastern Europe and the former Soviet Union	Newly industrialized countries	Asian developing countries	Other developing countries	Other OECD countries
Outputs									
Agricultural products	2.45	−2.02	−5.13	4.39	3.95	−5.02	0.41	0.21	0.34
Mineral and energy products	0.41	0.15	−0.72	−1.69	−0.19	−0.15	−2.16	−0.64	1.08
Wood and paper products	0.24	−0.09	−0.25	−1.44	−0.61	0.79	−2.02	−0.31	1.07
Food processing	0.06	−0.44	1.11	4.69	0.92	2.08	−1.75	−0.21	0.57
Textiles	−6.79	−1.55	1.45	10.06	0.92	8.56	3.43	4.07	−4.30
Wearing apparel	−23.15	−19.27	−0.60	−4.23	10.02	9.25	36.12	9.25	−6.21
Other light manufactures	0.35	1.28	1.95	−0.36	−5.62	3.75	−4.93	−0.06	−2.91
Manufactured intermediates	0.20	0.20	0.04	0.37	−0.50	0.38	−1.86	−0.42	0.32
Machinery and equipment	0.44	1.32	0.29	−0.59	−1.50	0.80	−4.61	−0.58	0.65
Services	0.05	0.12	0.10		−0.16	−0.17	0.16	−0.28	−0.13
Exports									
Agricultural products	19.47	−28.73	18.97	89.47	74.42	15.94	16.60	−1.14	2.71
Mineral and energy products	4.40	3.35	2.14	0.85	2.23	−0.06	−3.23	−0.76	2.71
Wood and paper products	3.54	7.27	3.67	6.98	2.30	4.63	−1.05	−0.09	7.24
Food processing	2.17	−0.64	12.50	9.84	29.92	15.07	−5.80	2.08	3.29
Textiles	−0.98	10.29	8.19	23.73	22.40	18.36	7.07	13.65	−4.96
Wearing apparel	−15.54	−5.83	−0.81	33.31	40.54	14.47	53.59	23.98	−21.08
Other light manufactures	4.49	6.11	6.35	1.74	1.04	5.76	−3.69	0.64	−0.44
Manufactured intermediates	5.35	6.13	3.75	9.63	5.66	2.67	−2.27	1.07	4.24
Machinery and equipment	4.27	6.13	2.12	10.42	4.63	2.53	−5.37	0.96	2.98
Services	0.85	−0.16	−0.74	−0.08	−0.44	−0.37	−0.87	−0.35	0.28

Imports							
Agricultural products	1.65	2.59	25.04	−5.89	6.59	52.41	16.41	−8.94	−0.27
Mineral and energy products	−2.41	1.53	2.86	8.07	7.42	0.77	5.68	0.63	−1.69
Wood and paper products	0.14	5.95	5.11	4.33	13.10	1.21	12.12	−0.16	6.38
Food processing	2.68	4.59	4.50	5.69	5.67	−1.22	34.68	−0.84	−3.20
Textiles	2.60	14.14	−0.60	8.28	17.70	1.62	37.27	1.95	0.15
Wearing apparel	55.03	44.31	9.02	−6.97	3.93	−12.03	61.84	−12.47	2.73
Other light manufactures	0.47	2.72	4.32	7.69	19.59	0.34	13.05	1.87	4.03
Manufactured intermediates	4.74	7.05	5.98	4.63	11.09	3.02	1.70	1.81	3.23
Machinery and equipment	4.18	4.15	7.34	3.08	11.33	1.43	4.52	0.80	2.02
Services	−2.27	0.16	2.37	−1.63	1.03	0.59	5.64	0.00	−1.37

Source: Authors' calculations.

Table A3.12 Factor reallocation, third simulation (percentage change from base)

	North America	European Union	Japan	Middle East and North Africa	Eastern Europe and the former Soviet Union	Newly industrialized countries	Asian developing countries	Other developing countries	Other OECD countries
Unskilled labor									
Mineral and energy products	0.61	0.10	−0.86	0.55	0.03	−0.80	−2.44	−0.65	1.15
Wood and paper products	0.38	−0.11	−0.34	−1.33	−0.48	0.27	−2.22	−0.32	1.12
Food processing	0.21	−0.47	0.99	−1.09	1.08	1.55	−1.96	−0.22	0.62
Textiles	−6.69	−1.57	1.37	5.09	1.04	7.98	3.17	4.05	−4.25
Wearing apparel	−23.09	−19.29	−0.67	10.36	10.13	8.74	35.84	9.23	−6.17
Other light manufactures	0.54	1.26	1.83	−3.83	−5.48	3.24	−5.16	−0.07	−2.85
Manufactured intermediates	0.36	0.19	−0.11	0.01	−0.36	−0.18	−2.14	−0.44	0.38
Machinery and equipment	0.61	1.34	0.15	0.65	−1.41	0.32	−4.85	−0.61	0.70
Services	0.24	0.12	−0.15	−0.28	−0.01	−0.75	−0.13	−0.33	−0.07
Skilled labor									
Agricultural products	5.67	−7.44	−22.09	11.73	11.13	−12.05	2.18	1.59	1.01
Mineral and energy products	0.40	−0.02	−0.82	0.69	0.05	−0.38	−2.15	−0.43	1.10
Wood and paper products	0.17	−0.22	−0.30	−1.20	−0.46	0.69	−1.94	−0.10	1.08
Food processing	0.02	−0.58	1.03	−0.97	1.10	1.94	−1.71	−0.03	0.59
Textiles	−6.90	−1.69	1.42	5.24	1.07	8.47	3.50	4.30	−4.30
Wearing apparel	−23.26	−19.39	−0.63	10.51	10.16	9.23	36.27	9.49	−6.22
Other light manufactures	0.32	1.14	1.87	−3.70	−5.45	3.70	−4.87	0.16	−2.89
Manufactured intermediates	0.13	0.07	−0.06	0.15	−0.33	0.27	−1.83	−0.20	0.33
Machinery and equipment	0.39	1.21	0.20	0.79	−1.38	0.78	−4.55	−0.38	0.65
Services	−0.01	−0.02	0.00	−0.13	0.02	−0.26	0.22	−0.08	−0.12

Capital							
Agricultural products	5.62	−7.31	−21.97	11.18	10.85	−11.81	2.23	1.45
Mineral and energy products	0.32	0.21	−0.58	−0.09	−0.33	0.05	−2.09	−0.65
Wood and paper products	0.10	0.80	−0.06	−1.95	−0.84	1.11	−1.88	−0.32
Food processing	−0.04	−0.38	1.25	−1.65	0.75	2.32	−1.65	−0.22
Textiles	−6.97	−1.46	1.68	4.38	0.66	8.96	3.57	4.06
Wearing apparel	−23.32	−19.20	−0.37	9.61	9.71	9.72	36.36	9.24
Other light manufactures	0.24	1.38	2.14	−4.48	−5.84	4.17	−4.80	−0.07
Manufactured intermediates	0.05	0.30	0.20	−0.67	−0.74	0.73	−1.76	−0.43
Machinery and equipment	0.31	1.45	0.46	−0.03	−1.78	1.23	−4.48	−0.60
Services	−0.09	0.24	0.29	−1.03	−0.43	0.24	0.29	−0.33

0.97
1.04
1.02
0.53
−4.36
−6.27
−2.95
0.27
0.59
−0.18

Source: Authors' calculations.

4 The World Trade Organization, the European Union, and the Arab World: Trade Policy Priorities and Pitfalls[1]

Bernard Hoekman

The credibility of economic reform in the Middle East and North Africa has been hampered by the slow place of implementation, which has impeded a strong private sector supply response. Membership in the World Trade Organization (WTO) and the European Union's offer to establish a Euro–Mediterranean economic area provide possible institutional frameworks that can greatly enhance the credibility of gradual reform strategies. But neither option is a panacea, and much depends on the willingness of the region's governments to exploit the opportunities embodied in these institutional options. Both avenues should be pursued simultaneously to limit the potential negative trade diversion effects of a preferential agreement with the European Union.

The long-term economic potential of the Middle East and North Africa has improved significantly in recent years as the peace process expands opportunities for investment and intraregional trade and cooperation.[2] The challenge facing many governments in the region is to adopt policies that will allow this potential to be realized by fostering private sector development and encouraging export-led growth. Many countries in the region are trying to reduce the state's role in the economy and shift away from import substitution and industrial protection strategies. Although some progress has been made, the pace of trade policy reform has varied substantially across countries, and many economies retain an anti-export bias. The gradual and tentative nature of reform has also created credibility problems in some countries, limiting the private sector's supply response.

Within the region North African countries like Morocco and Tunisia have made more progress in reform than their Middle Eastern and Arab counterparts. This variation is reflected in the growth of nontraditional exports. The share of phosphates in Morocco's exports and the share of olive oil in Tunisia's exports dropped from about 45 percent in 1980 to less than 20 percent in 1992 (World Bank, 1994). But the region as a whole has been lagging behind global policy developments in trade and investment. This shortfall is most clearly illustrated by comparing the recent export performance of Middle Eastern and North African countries with Central and Eastern European countries.

The main policy challenge facing the Middle East and North Africa is to implement much more far-reaching liberalization, privatization, and deregulation. The creation of the WTO and its three constituent elements – a revised and significantly expanded General Agreement on Tariffs and Trade (GATT), a new General Agreement on Trade in Services (GATS), and a new agreement on Trade-Related Intellectual Property Rights (TRIPs) – increases the urgency of this challenge. Implementation of the Uruguay Round agreements will increase competition in third markets. At the same time the WTO (which entered into force in January 1995) offers an opportunity to adopt better trade policies and improve trade institutions. Many countries in the region – including Algeria, Iraq, Jordan, Lebanon, Libya, Saudi Arabia, Syria, and Yemen – were not GATT contracting parties and thus are not members of the WTO.[3] Nonmembership in the WTO is likely to make it difficult for these countries to attract the foreign direct investment and technological know-how they need to diversify production and compete in world markets. Bahrain, Egypt, Israel, Kuwait, Morocco, Qatar, Tunisia, and the United Arab Emirates were GATT members by the end of the Uruguay Round. Regardless of whether they are a GATT contracting party, every country in the region will be affected by the trade liberalization agreed to under the Round. GATT members will also be confronted with a substantial number of policy and institutional changes that are required under the WTO (on customs valuation, product standards, intellectual property protection, and so on).

TRADE POLICY DISTORTIONS IN THE MIDDLE EAST AND NORTH AFRICA

Elements of the trade regime that inhibit the competitiveness of Middle Eastern and North African firms include high average rates of effective protection, substantial dispersion of such protection across industries, and nontransparent implementation of trade policies. High tariffs and the red tape associated with them constitute a tax on export production, both directly by raising input costs and indirectly by putting pressure on the real exchange rate. High levels of effective protection also reduce firms' incentives to enter world markets, since profit rates are often higher in sheltered domestic markets. These distortions have resulted in a somewhat dualistic economic structure, with export-oriented firms having few links to the rest of the economy and most firms concentrating on the domestic market. Export production in such a highly protected environment would require well-functioning duty drawback and temporary admission mechanisms, which are generally not available.

Agricultural trade tends to be significantly distorted in many countries in the region. One well-known example is Saudi Arabia, where large subsidies and import protection have been used to support domestic production of cereals and oilseeds. These efforts caused wheat production to rise from 3,000 tons in the mid-1970s to more than 4 million tons in 1992, more than half of which is exported. But direct subsidies for wheat alone total some $2.5 billion a year (Goldin and Kherallah, 1996). Agricultural subsidies are much smaller in other countries in the region, but many governments impose import quotas, license or ban specific products, use state monopolies for imports and distribution in conjunction with price controls, set high average tariffs for "sensitive" commodities, and provide input subsidies (including water and energy charges that often do not reflect scarcity values).

Import tariffs and protection

Many countries in the region maintain numerous tariff bands in their tariff schedules. Jordan, for example, has thirty-three rates ranging from 0–320 percent. In Egypt rates generally range from 0–70 percent, although some tariffs on motor vehicles are 160 percent. Tariffs in Morocco and Tunisia are lower, ranging from 0–35 percent in Morocco and 10–43 percent in Tunisia. Table 4.1 compares average unweighted tariffs for a number of countries in the region with those of countries in other parts of the world that have introduced liberal-

Table 4.1 Average unweighted tariffs of countries undertaking liberalization efforts, mid-1980s and early 1990s (percent)

Region/country (years)	Applied, mid-1980s	Applied, early 1990s	Post–Uruguay Round binding[a]
Middle East and North Africa			
Egypt (1989, 1993)	47.0	34.0	36.1
Jordan (1987, 1994)	33.4	30.5	[c]
Morocco (1983, 1990)	36.1	23.4	na
Tunisia (1987, 1990)	32.5	28.5	29.7
East Asia			
China (1986, 1992)	38.1	43.0	[c]
Indonesia (1985, 1990)	27.0	22.0	21.3
Korea, Rep. of (1984, 1992)	24.0	10.1	12.7
Malaysia (1985, 1993)	na	14.0	15.7
Latin America			
Argentina (1988, 1992)	29.4	12.2	20.3
Brazil (1987, 1992)	51.0	21.0	26.8
Chile (1984, 1991)[b]	15.0	11.0	20.0
Colombia (1984, 1992)	61.0	12.0	11.8
Costa Rica (1985, 1992)	53.0	15.0	na
Mexico (1986, 1991)	22.6	13.1	13.7
Peru (1984, 1992)	27.0	17.0	26.8
Venezuela (1989, 1991)	37.0	19.0	15.5
South Asia			
Bangladesh (1989, 1993)	94.0	50.0	na
India (1990, 1993)	128.0	71.0	52.6
Pakistan (1987, 1992)	68.9	64.8	na
Sri Lanka (1985, 1992)	31.0	25.0	28.3
Sub-Saharan Africa			
Côte d'Ivoire (1984, 1989)	26.0	33.0	na
Nigeria (1984, 1990)	35.0	32.7	na

na is not available.
a. Refers to date of full implementation of Uruguay Round tariff commitments; generally January 1999.
b. Uniform rates.
c. Not a GATT member as of April 1995.
Source: Dean, Desai, and Riedel, 1994; World Bank data.

ization programs since the mid-1980s. Average rates for the four Middle Eastern and North African countries are in the 23–34 percent range, and have fallen by less than in many comparator countries in other regions. Although the rates are lower than the average in the South Asian countries shown, they are substantially higher than in many Latin American countries. Moreover, they have been declining more slowly. This slow decline is perhaps the most important point, since levels of nominal tariffs are difficult to compare across countries.

Data on collected tariff revenue as a share of imports are shown in Table 4.2. This comparison is more revealing than the average statutory rate because it better reflects the actual tax burden on trade by allowing for exemptions and possible biases in customs classification

Table 4.2 Trade taxes, various countries, 1993 (percentage)

Country	Share of import duties[a] in total government revenue	Share of "other" taxes in total import tax revenue	Average collected tariff (revenue/ imports)
Bahrain	9.2	–	4.0
Egypt	10.0	8	14.9
Jordan	35.9	40	17.8
Morocco	17.7	52	17.5
Oman	3.2	-	3.0
Syria	10.0	25	16.4
Tunisia	28.3	46	18.7
United Arab Emirates	–	–	–
Yemen	20.2	3	19.1[b]
Israel	1.0	–	1.2
Turkey	4.4	78	2.5
Chile	9.9	–	9.7
Indonesia	5.2	–	4.9
Rep. of Korea	4.8	–	4.4
Malaysia	13.6	31	4.9
Mexico[c]	5.1	–	4.8

– Zero or negligible.
a. Does not include stamp duties.
b. Valued at the average parallel market exchange rate; the average collection rate was about 8 percent. The nominal 19.1 percent rate is indicative of the government's intentions, however.
c. 1990.
Source: IMF, 1994a, 1994b.

and valuation. The unweighted average burden in the Middle East and North Africa is about 17 percent (excluding Gulf countries – like Bahrain, Oman, and the United Arab Emirates – that pursue a zero or low tariff policy). This burden is considerably higher than the average for the comparator countries listed.

The high tariff burden means that import duties account for a much larger share of government revenue in Middle Eastern and North African countries than they do in countries with more outward-oriented economic strategies. The average share of revenue generated by trade taxes (excluding stamp duties) in the regional sample is 20 percent; for the comparators it is just 6 percent. Less distorting sources of revenue must be developed as part of efforts to further liberalize trade flows. The expected weakness of oil-related revenues in the medium term – given sluggish demand and the anticipated increase in supply following the recovery or reentry of producers like Iraq and Russia (World Bank, 1995a) – may perversely induce a greater reliance on trade taxes. This approach should be resisted, with priority instead being given to increasing indirect taxes, broadening the tax base, and reducing subsidies (especially those that encourage environmental degradation and inefficient use of scarce resources).

Effective rates of protection for manufacturing generally exceed nominal rates by a substantial margin. In addition to the nominal tariffs, imports are often also subject to a number of other taxes (see Table 4.2). In Jordan these include a 5 percent import licensing fee, a 4 percent tax earmarked for universities, a 2 percent tax for municipalities, a 6 percent consolidated fee, a 0.2 percent customs service fee, and a surcharge of either 3 percent on non-zero rated goods or 5 percent if no tariffs are applied. Yemen imposes mores than ten additional taxes and surcharges on imports. Morocco imposes a 15 percent import levy on most goods (capital goods face a 10 percent levy). Tunisia levies surcharges ranging from 10–30 percent on products that compete with domestic production. Egypt imposes a 1 percent statistical tax, a 2 percent service fee for goods subject to import duties of less than 30 percent, a 5 percent fee for other products, and a number of stamp duties. These kinds of additional fees on imports reduce the transparency of the tariff structure, especially since they often are not applied to all products.

The use of quantitative restrictions has been declining. In Morocco the production coverage of quantitative restrictions has fallen to zero, from 50 percent in the mid-1980s. In Tunisia only 20 percent of local production benefited from such barriers in 1994, down from 94 percent in the mid-1980s (Lahouel, 1997). Egypt also has eliminated most import quotas. Nontariff barriers to imports remain prevalent, however. Many industrial products, including processed foodstuffs, are subject to licensing requirements related to health and safety standards. These licenses tend to be granted by the relevant ministry (health for pharmaceuticals, agriculture for food, telecommunications for telecommunications equipment, interior for chemicals). More generally, imported products may require an import license (as in Jordan and Yemen). These licenses are often only granted after products have been approved by the relevant ministry or agency. This approval often requires inspection of the goods at customs, imposing costs on importers, delaying customs clearance, and subjecting importers to needless uncertainty.

Nonrecognition of internationally known certification bodies or international standards – as in Jordan and Egypt, for example – raises costs for importers and consumers and reduces the incentives for firms to use certification entities and adhere to the quality standards used in international trade. Current practices and procedures have led to claims that standards are being used as technical barriers to trade. Quality control inspections by Egypt's General Organization for Export and Import Control are an example. The organization inspects a sample of every consignment of goods entering Egypt subject to quality control – some 1,500 tariff lines, or 25 percent of the tariff schedule. Internationally recommended methods of testing and certification are ignored, and internationally recognized quality and certification marks (such as those of the European Union) may not be accepted. Even where international standards do guide domestic product standards, the relevant criteria for ascertaining whether they have been met may not be clearly defined in the appropriate regulations or statutes.

The administrative procedures and requirements associated with importing are generally burdensome, increasing the cost of imports substantially and thereby lowering the competitiveness of Middle Eastern and North African firms in world markets. Many government bodies can be involved in the import process, either collecting taxes or import duties or authorizing the release of imports. In Egypt, for example, these bodies include Customs, the Ministry of Health (pharmaceutical and medical devices), the Ministry of Supply (wheat), the General Organization for Veterinary Services (Ministry of Agriculture), the General Organization for Plant Protection and Quarantine (Ministry of Agriculture), the Atomic Energy Organization, the Industrial Control Authority (Ministry of Industry), and the General Organization for Export and Import Control.

Customs clearance is frequently cumbersome, with administrative controls that can delay customs clearance by anywhere from a few days to several weeks. In Lebanon eighteen signatures are required before goods can be released. In other countries in the region procedures can be even more complicated, to the extent that import licensing is required and product standards are enforced. Valuation procedures in particular give rise to uncertainty on the part of importers, since customs agencies usually expect underinvoicing. Customs officials in Jordan, for example, rely on the price lists and declared values of "bona fide" importers of particular goods to determine the value of goods. In Morocco reference prices are used to protect local production. If importers are found to have engaged in underinvoicing, fines can be imposed that are a multiple of the tariff that applies, and may be a multiple of the value of the goods concerned. Customs officials in a number of countries are allowed to keep 20–40 percent of these additional revenues, creating an incentive to find underinvoicing.

Export obstacles

Port service fees for the handling and storage of goods and the quality of the services provided are important factors raising the costs of exporters in the region. The companies that provide port services – loading and unloading of containers on ships, handling of containers, storage and warehousing – tend to be public monopolies. The cost per ton of handling a container in the port of Alexandria is two to three times that in other ports around the Mediterranean. Egyptian exporters have indicated that these companies' fees raise costs by more than 10 percent. Moreover, there is limited competition on the insurance premiums charged for trade coverage, making them higher than those confronting Egypt's competitors in world markets. Such costs raise prices and lower profits, reducing the competitiveness of Egyptian firms. Unlike the tariffs on intermediate inputs, the extra costs associated with customs clearance, quality control, customs valuation, and the monopoly service providers in the ports cannot be recovered through duty drawbacks and similar schemes. Thus they create a major disadvantage for firms seeking to export, and are a major disincentive for foreign firms investing in export-oriented production. Similar impediments prevail in many other countries in the region.

Many of the constraints to export development embedded in trade policies reflect the legacy of the ancien regime, which promoted large-scale public sector participation in and control of the economy. Some of the government agencies that impose significant transactions costs on traders had a mandate to control trade in the past. Although structural reforms incrementally whittled away the responsibilities of many of these agencies, they have made creative efforts to maintain their traditional role. In fact, one of the reasons some countries in the region (like Egypt) have stepped up efforts to enforce product standards and phytosanitary requirements in trade is that doing so perpetuates the control agencies.

Many countries in the region have concluded preferential trade agreements with one another. The trade flows covered by these agreements – mostly agricultural and raw materials – benefit from partial or complete exemptions from tariffs. For industrial products there is often a minimum local value-added criterion of 40 percent. Although many of these agreements were negotiated in the 1960s and 1970s, some are recent. A 1992 agreement between Lebanon and Jordan, for example, exempts animals, agricultural produce, and fruits and vegetables from customs duties and other taxes (such as surcharges). A positive list of industrial products is subject to a preferential tariff rate (two-thirds of the regular rate) but remains subject to all surcharges. Up to $5 million of goods used for exhibitions may enter free of duties and surcharges. The agreement also specifies that sales taxes will be levied on a national treatment basis. Such agreements are unlikely to benefit the countries involved, however. Many countries in the region have similar factor endowments, limiting the scope for intraindustry trade unless industries learn to specialize and compete in world markets. The partial coverage of the agreements prevents rather than stimulates trade flows between Arab states.

Progress and possibilities

The region has made some progress on trade liberalization since the late 1980s. For example, many countries have implemented reforms that reduce their anti-export bias. But much remains to be done, especially since competitor countries are moving faster. The efforts undertaken in many of the region's countries in recent years provide a strong base on which to build toward further integration with the world economy. The tradeoff in this regard is between the apparent political unfeasibility of rapid reforms and the opportunity costs of gradualism. The slower and less comprehensive is reform, the larger will be the gap between the region and the rest of the world. Greater gaps can also be expected between early reformers, such as Morocco and Tunisia, and later ones, like Egypt and Jordan. Unilateral reform efforts in Egypt and Jordan have so far been inadequate to induce a significant private sector supply response or to attract foreign direct investment (as opposed to short-term liquid capital). This is a major problem because a supply response is crucial to generating support for reform and inducing governments to continue reform efforts.

The next few years offer the region a window of opportunity to further implement structural reforms. Two developments are of particular importance. First, the external environment is expected to be relatively favorable over the next few years, with most major markets expected to show substantial growth. Increased economic activity will increase global demand for the region's output, especially oil. Peace in the region should also help attract potential investors. What is needed is an institutional framework that enhances the credibility of a gradual reform strategy by establishing a longer-term, credible vision of future economic policies and relationships in the region. The second development, the creation of the WTO and the European Union's offer to establish a Euro-Mediterranean economic area, is very relevant in this regard.

The problems constraining export-led growth in the region relate as much to institutional weaknesses as to policy measures. Thus changes in policy – although desirable and necessary – must be complemented by a reduction in and strengthening of implementing institutions. Reductions in the regulatory and administrative burdens confronting the private sector can be achieved relatively rapidly at low cost. The faster these changes are made, the sooner firms will be able to handle the reductions in protection. Significant up-front improvements in the administration of regulations will also help enhance governments' credibility. Given the constraints weak and costly support services impose on exporters' ability to compete in world markets, priority should also be given to enhancing services. This will require liberalization of access to service markets by foreign providers as well as privatization and demonopolization. The faster this is done and the more far-reaching the market opening, the sooner domestic firms will be able to handle import competition and diversify into world markets.

TRADE PERFORMANCE AND REFORM: COMPARING CENTRAL AND EASTERN EUROPE AND THE MIDDLE EAST AND NORTH AFRICA

The gradual and nontransparent approach to economic reform in many Middle Eastern and North African countries has created uncertainty for firms and undermined the credibility of the process. Traders in economies such as Egypt and Jordan often perceive that little has changed with respect to trade policy and administration. To assuage fears of reform, policymakers must ensure that adjustment costs are relatively short term and manageable, and convince interest groups that these costs will be offset by long-term benefits. Compensation schemes may be required during the transition for certain groups.

The reform experiences of countries in Central and Eastern Europe are relevant in this regard. They suggest that far-reaching reforms can have a dramatic effect on economic performance by inducing a reorientation and restructuring of production and trade to create and exploit competitive advantages, in the process generating private sector employment opportunities and fostering growth.

This section explores recent developments in the Middle East and North Africa's trade with the European Union to assess the potential impact of a significant reduction in protection. Most countries in Central and Eastern Europe have successfully reoriented and greatly expanded their exports to the European Union. Although comparing Central and Eastern Europe and the Middle East and North Africa is somewhat unfair given Eastern Europe's higher levels of industrialization and human capital, the two regions are similar enough to allow for an informative comparison. Many countries in both regions introduced reforms in the late 1980s, state intervention in the Middle East and North Africa was nearly as high as in Central and Eastern Europe, and both regions were directly affected by the collapse of Council for Mutual Economic Assistance-based trade. One notable difference between the regions is that Central and Eastern European countries that were GATT members were constrained in their ability to raise tariffs, having bound these at low levels upon accession. Low tariffs facilitated the negotiation of association agreements with the European Union (see below), illustrating one of the main potential benefits of GATT membership.

Middle Eastern and North African countries differ greatly in export performance

Middle Eastern and North African countries have been expanding non-oil, nontraditional exports. Per capita exports for the region were $287 in 1995, up from $188 in 1989 (Figure 4.1). The share of exports going to the European Union did not increase as significantly during this time, however. The region's exports to the European Union mainly

Figure 4.1 Per capita nonoil exports from various regions, 1989 and 1995

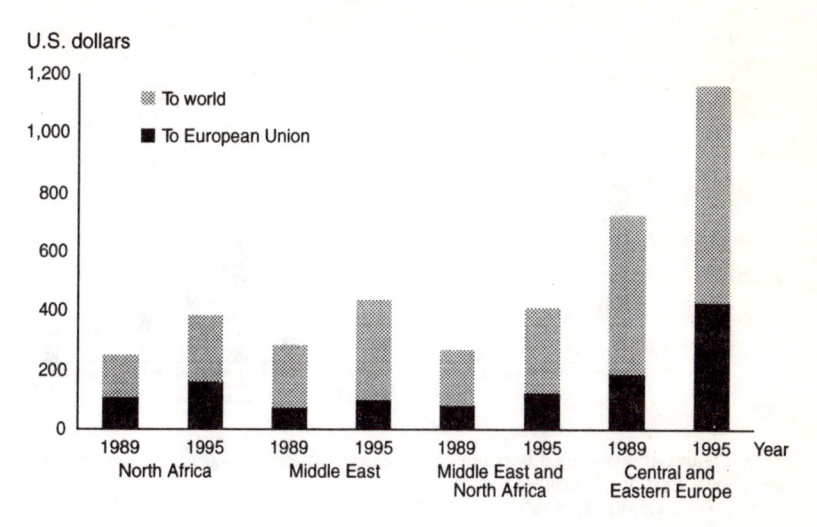

[Bar chart showing U.S. dollars on y-axis (0 to 1,200) with grouped bars for 1989 and 1995 across four regions: North Africa, Middle East, Middle East and North Africa, and Central and Eastern Europe. Each bar is divided into "To world" and "To European Union" components.]

Note: North Africa is Algeria, Morocco, and Tunisia; Middle East is Egypt, Israel, Jordan, Kuwait, Lebanon, Syria, and the United Arab Emirates; Central and Eastern Europe is Bulgaria, the Czech Republic, Hungary, Poland, Romania, and the Slovak Republic.
Source: U.N. Comtrade database.

come from North Africa, which exports most of its manufactured goods to Europe. For Middle Eastern countries the European Union is much less important (Figure 4.2). In Central and Eastern Europe aggregate exports to the world declined between 1989 and 1993 – reflecting a large drop in output and exports as firms adjusted to price liberalization and the demise of the Council for Mutual Economic Assistance. By 1995 per capita nonfuel exports, at $738, were some 40 percent above 1989 levels. In the process these countries managed to substantially reorient their trade. The share of the region's exports going to the European Union rose from 34 percent in 1989 to 58 percent in 1995. The region's average annual growth in exports to the European Union, at 14.8 percent, compares with the 6.9 percent growth of Middle Eastern and North African countries.

The data on per capita exports of nonfuel products highlights Israel's impressive performance, which reached $3,250 in 1995. This compares with an average of $740 for Central and Eastern Europe, $1,700 for the Czech Republic, $200–250 for Lebanon and Morocco, and $570 for Tunisia. During 1989–95 per capita exports of nonfuel

Figure 4.2 Per capita nonoil exports from various countries, 1988 and 1995

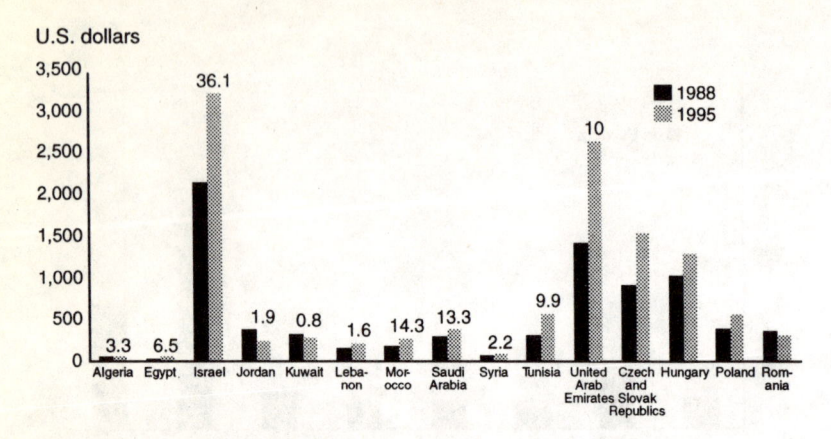

Note: Figures above shaded bars are each country's share in total nonoil exports from the Middle East and North Africa.
Source: U.N. Comtrade database.

products to the world fell for Jordan and Kuwait, while exports to the European Union declined for Algeria and Kuwait.

During 1989–95 total nonfuel exports by Central and Eastern European countries rose 5.4 percent a year, from $51.3 billion in 1989 to $70.6 billion in 1995 (Table 4.3). This compares with 9.7 percent growth for the Middle East and North Africa. With the exception of Algeria, Jordan, and Kuwait, all countries in the region experienced significant export growth. However, the share of exports going to the European Union has not been expanding, nor has the region's share in total EU imports (about 3 percent). About 65 percent of the Middle East and North Africa's market share in the European Union comes from oil and natural resources, mostly reflecting exports by Algeria, Kuwait, Saudi Arabia, and Syria (oil and related natural resources account for 90–95 percent of total exports to the European Union for these countries). Agricultural produce accounts for another 6 percent of the region's exports to the European Union. Thus other (manufactured) products account for less than one-third of total exports to the European Union. Much of the growth in exports of manufactures comes from textiles and clothing, an important sector for countries like Lebanon, Morocco, Tunisia, and the United Arab Emirates. For the region as a whole, garments account for 12.1 percent of total exports, compared with 16.6 percent for Central and Eastern Europe.

Table 4.3 Nonoil exports to the world, Middle East and North Africa and Central and Eastern Europe, 1989 and 1995 (millions of U.S. dollars)

Country	1989	1995	Annual growth rate (percent)
Middle East and North Africa	25,303 (45.2)	44,019 (44.3)	9.7
Algeria	1,476 (87.2)	1,676 (85.4)	2.1
Egypt	1,692 (46.0)	3,288 (42.6)	11.7
Israel	9,940 (38.2)	18,300 (32.7)	10.7
Jordan	1,167 (8.7)	985 (16.2)	−2.9
Kuwait	666 (21.5)	431 (17.2)	−7.5
Lebanon	519 (22.9)	811 (18.5)	7.7
Morocco	4,236 (68.0)	7,274 (69.1)	9.4
Saudi Arabia	4,631 (22.3)	6,735 (19.2)	6.4
Syria	879 (11.6)	1,140 (28.8)	4.4
Tunisia	2,431 (72.6)	5,039 (80.8)	12.9
United Arab Emirates	2,296 (19.5)	5,076 (17.0)	14.1
Central and Eastern Europe	51,326 (34.7)	70,558 (58.3)	5.4

Note: Numbers in parentheses are percentages of nonoil exports going to the European Union.
Source: IMF data.

A measure of the change in the structure of exports to the European Union is summarized in Table 4.4. There is a wide variation among Middle Eastern and North African countries. Algeria, Kuwait, Saudi Arabia, and Syria showed little change: the products that accounted for the lion's share of exports in 1989 were the same in 1994. Greater change occurred in Israel, Jordan, Lebanon, Morocco, Tunisia, and the United Arab Emirates. Of these, Jordan should be disregarded because the data are heavily influenced by one-time exports of gold and aircraft. Except for Kuwait and Lebanon, all countries registered

Table 4.4 Share of traditional and nontraditional products in exports to the European Union, Middle East and North Africa and Central and Eastern Europe, 1989 and 1994 (million ECU)

Region/country	Traditional products 1989	1994	Change (percent)	Nontraditional products 1989	1994	Change (percent)
Middle East and North Africa	25,349 (96)	28,260 (91)	2.2	1,146 (4)	2,731 (9)	19.0
Algeria	4,829 (99)	4,830 (97)	0	66 (1)	157 (3)	18.9
Egypt	2,271 (94)	2,323 (84)	0.5	157 (6)	435 (16)	22.6
Israel	2,366 (78)	2,575 (63)	1.2	648 (22)	1,494 (37)	18.2
Jordan	52 (60)	72 (53)	6.7	35 (40)	65 (47)	13.2
Kuwait	2,664 (98)	1,441 (96)	−13.1	47 (2)	64 (4)	6.4
Lebanon	45 (46)	28 (33)	−10.0	53 (54)	58 (67)	1.8
Morocco	2,320 (87)	2,953 (80)	4.9	345 (13)	735 (20)	16.3
Saudi Arabia	6,235 (98)	7,894 (94)	4.8	117 (2)	494 (6)	33.4
Syria	735 (95)	1,470 (94)	14.9	37 (5)	98 (6)	21.5
Tunisia	1,679 (85)	2,259 (75)	6.1	289 (15)	767 (25)	21.6
United Arab Emirates	1,397 (93)	477 (57)	−24.0	110 (7)	359 (43)	26.7
Central and Eastern Europe	10,247 (87)	18,352 (72)	12.4	1,548 (13)	7,179 (28)	35.9

Note: Numbers in parentheses are percentages of a country's total exports accounted for by traditional or nontraditional products (at the six-digit level) in a given year. Traditional products are defined as products accounting for ECU 3 million or more of exports to the European Union in 1989.
Source: EUROSTAT external trade database.

double-digit export growth in nontraditional exports. For many of these countries the share of nontraditional exports to the European Union as a share of total exports is significant. Thus a number of countries in the region have exhibited dynamism in diversifying their export base. The challenge is to increase the volume of exports to the European Union.

Central and Eastern Europe have exploited intraindustry trade opportunities

Intraindustry trade has been expanding rapidly between Central and Eastern Europe and the European Union (Figure 4.3).[4] Given the importance of natural resource exports for the Middle East and North Africa, intraindustry trade is quite low and has been relatively constant over time. It is significant only for Israel, followed by Tunisia. Thus there is considerable scope for fostering such trade by liberalizing access to markets. Intraindustry trade is important because it allows transfers of technology to occur. The association agreements with Central and Eastern Europe, for example, created incentives for EU suppliers and retailers to engage in outward processing trade. This type of trade involves shipping components or assemblies to a Central or Eastern European country where further processing occurs. The processed good is then exported back to the EU supplier or retailer. Such trade benefits from liberal access to the European Union and has been used intensively for sectors such as garments, electrical machinery, and

Figure: 4.3 Intraindustry trade with the European Union, 1989–94

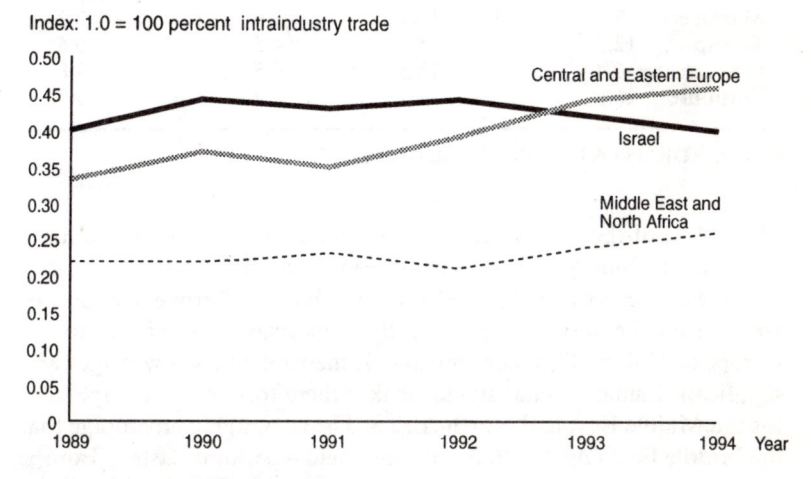

Index: 1.0 = 100 percent intraindustry trade

Source: U.N. Comtrade database.

furniture. As part of the subcontracting that is involved, EU counterparts often provide designs, monitor quality, take care of marketing, and so on. Thus outward processing trade is a good way for firms in Central and Eastern Europe to reduce the costs and risks associated with developing export markets while obtaining know-how from suppliers. Outward processing trade is frequently restricted, at least during the initial stages, to labor-intensive, low value-added activities. These activities can, however, create significant employment.

Following the implementation of the agreements with Central and Eastern European countries, exports after outward processing accounted for 17 percent of the region's exports to the European Union in 1994, up from 10 percent in 1989 (Table 4.5). By contrast, processed goods exports to the European Union represented only 1.7 percent of the Middle East and North Africa's exports in 1994, the same as in

Table 4.5 Exports after outward processing, Central and Eastern Europe and Middle East and North Africa, 1989 and 1994 (share in total exports to the European Union)

Export	Central and Eastern Europe 1989	1994	Middle East and North Africa 1989	1994
Total	10.4	17.1	1.6	1.7
Leather	38.9	30.8	8.0	7.0
Garments	60.8	76.6	15.6	10.8
Machinery	8.1	12.3	5.4	3.2
Transport	12.3	5.4	4.5	0.5
Instruments	6.4	15.3	6.5	3.8
Furniture	26.5	14.0	1.2	1.8

Source: EUROSTAT, COMEXT database.

1989. Most of the processing occurs in leather and footwear, clothing, electrical machinery, precision instruments, and furniture.

The data clearly reveal that Central and Eastern European countries are well on the way to exploiting their geographic proximity to the European Union. This, combined with their relatively low wages and significant human capital stocks, makes them formidable competitors for the Middle East and North Africa. The geographic advantage that the Middle East and North Africa once held – because Eastern Europe was effectively closed to open exchange with the West – has disappeared. The region must now compete head-to-head with Central and Eastern Europe. The two region's relatively similar labor costs will make this a particular challenge. Per capita incomes in Central and Eastern Europe – one proxy for such costs – are close to levels in the Middle East and North Africa. And Eastern Europe's ability to subcontract manufacturing products for export to the European Union gives it a significant competitive advantage. Just-in-time management practices make the availability of adequate service links (transport, harbor services, customs operations, telecommunications) fundamental to the decision on where to outsource. Many Middle Eastern and North African countries (particularly those around the Mediterranean) could become competitive locations for outsourcing by European companies once access to efficient producer services is made available. This will require significant changes in regulatory regimes and investment policies to enhance the contestability of markets.

THE URUGUAY ROUND: WORLD TRADE ORGANIZATION RULES AND DISCIPLINES

The changes required in the region's trade policies and institutions are clear; the challenge is creating a constituency that favors reforms and makes them politically feasible and self-sustaining. Although the main constraint to these efforts is the absence of internal support, external institutional mechanisms can be helpful. Two potential options are stronger links with the European Union and "deep" integration under the umbrella of the WTO.

The implications of the WTO and the Uruguay Round can be divided into two parts: the impact on the global economy through changes in demand and supply of goods and services, and the impact on trade policies and institutions in member countries. It is beyond the scope of this chapter to quantitatively assess the impact of the Uruguay Round and full implementation of the WTO agreements on the Middle East and North Africa, a difficult exercise in any event because many of the changes cannot be quantified (for example, changes in transparency and procedural rules and better enforcement of obligations). The most important agreements are on agricultural liberalization, reduced tariffs for industrial products, and the elimination of quantitative restrictions on imports of textiles and clothing.

The most comprehensive evaluation of the effects of the Uruguay Round using a computable general equilibrium model that distinguishes the Middle East and North Africa was done by Harrison, Rutherford, and Tarr (1996).[5] They find that the Round's effect on the region may be negative, reflecting the erosion of rents created by the Multifiber Arrangement (MFA) and the likely rise in global food prices resulting from lower export subsidies in OECD countries. Once capital stocks have adjusted, however, the region is expected to benefit from global liberalization, increasing aggregate welfare by up to $1.3 billion a year (not including possible adjustment costs). A key finding from the study, as well as from many other computable general equilibrium efforts, is that the impact of the Round is relatively small, and that much depends on government policies. Given the high average rates of protection that will continue to exist in many countries in the region after the Round is fully implemented, most of the potential gains will come from further liberalization of domestic, not foreign, markets. The commitments made by the region's countries in the Round illustrate that much remains to be done in this regard.

Turning to the Round's effects on trade policies and institutions, the WTO itself does not embody substantive rules regarding government policies – it is simply a formal institutional structure whose members negotiate and implement trade agreements. The rules are contained in the treaties it oversees (GATT, GATS, and TRIPs).

GATT-1994 disciplines

Many countries in the region are likely to require policy and institutional changes to fulfill WTO obligations. Major implications include:

- The most favored nation (MFN) and national treatment principles require that trade policies and their implementation must be *nondiscriminatory*. MFN requires nondiscrimination between foreign products; national treatment requires that foreign products be treated the same as domestic products in terms of internal indirect taxation and equivalent measures.
- The use of *quantitative restrictions* is heavily circumscribed, and the web of bilateral quantitative restrictions imposed under the Multifiber Arrangement will gradually be eliminated. Although this issue mainly affects OECD countries, some countries in the Middle East and North Africa – such as Egypt – maintain quantitative import restrictions for textiles and clothing and so will be affected by this change. Quantitative restrictions on agricultural imports are prohibited; in principle WTO members can only use tariffs to restrict imports of agricultural products, and all such tariffs are bound.[6]

- Governments must reduce export subsidies and support to agricultural production. Developing countries have been granted some flexibility in this connection; for example, input subsidies are permitted, as are export subsidies related to marketing services.
- Developing countries that have a per capita GNP above $1,000 are subject to GATT's *prohibition on export subsidies for industrial products*.
- By 2000, developing country WTO members must *eliminate all trade-related investment measures* (such as local content requirements, export performance rules, and so on) that violate GATT's national treatment principle or its prohibition on quantitative restrictions.
- If trade measures are imposed for balance of payments purposes, WTO rules require that price-based measures such as tariffs be used.
- The importer's invoice is the basis for *customs valuation*. However, developing countries that were not party to the 1979 Tokyo Round agreement on customs valuation can delay implementation of the agreement until 2000. Specific conditions are required for customs to be able to reject invoices when determining duties. Developing countries that value goods on the basis of officially established minimum values may request a reservation enabling them to retain such values on a limited and transitional basis, subject to the terms and conditions required by the other WTO members.
- The WTO's rules relating to *product standards and sanitary and phytosanitary measures* require that new regulations and conformity assessment procedures be based on international standards. An inquiry point must be created to answer questions regarding the product standards and sanitary or phytosanitary measures; applicable control and inspection procedures; quarantine, pesticide tolerance, and food additive approval procedures; and risk assessment methods used. Similar questions regarding technical regulations and conformity assessment procedures can be posed.
- There are many requirements concerning the procedures to be followed with respect to the *imposition of contingent protection* (safeguards, countervailing of subsidized imports, and antidumping). Space constraints prohibit a summary of these requirements, but the implications for the institutions that implement such mechanisms are significant (Hoekman, 1995).

GATS disciplines

- MFN status, national treatment, and market access are the key policy elements of the GATS. MFN is a general obligation. The sectoral coverage of national treatment and market access obligations is determined by country schedules. Six types of *market access restrictions* are prohibited under the GATS: limitations on the number of service suppliers allowed, the value of transactions or assets, the quantity of service output, the number of natural persons that can be employed, the type of legal entity through which a service supplier is permitted to supply a service (for example, branches or subsidiaries for banking), and the participation of foreign capital. Each GATS member negotiates which sectors are subject to market access and national treatment disciplines and what measures are kept in place for those sectors that violate market access or national treatment disciplines (see Hoekman, 1996).
- At least once a year, GATS members must inform the Council for Trade in Services of new laws or changes to laws, regulations, or administrative guidelines that significantly affect trade in services covered by their specific commitments (national treatment and market access).
- An inquiry point must be established to provide information to other members on all general application measures that affect the operation of the GATS.
- Judicial, arbitral, or administrative tribunals or procedures must provide for prompt, objective, and impartial review of administrative decisions affecting trade in services.
- Measures relating to qualification requirements and procedures, technical standards, and licensing requirements cannot unnecessarily restrict trade in services, should be based on objective and transparent criteria, and cannot be unnecessarily burdensome to ensure service quality.

Commitments for Middle Eastern and North African countries

Countries that were GATT-1947 signatories are committed to the various obligations noted above. The main effect on tariffs concerns the requirement under the Agreement on Agriculture to replace non-tariff barriers with tariffs. For industrial activities the main change is the requirement that a schedule of bound tariffs be presented that includes both tariffs and "other fees and charges." Egypt and Tunisia's post-Round bound tariff commitments are not significantly different from currently applied rates (Table 4.6) However, as noted earlier, tariffs in the region remain high, both absolutely – in terms of anti-export bias – and relative to other parts of the developing world.

Table 4.6 Bound and applied tariffs, Egypt and Tunisia (percent)

GATT member	Post-Uruguay Round bound average tariff rate (unweighted)		Current applied average tariff rates (unweighted)	
	Industry	Agriculture	Industry	Agriculture
Egypt	31	61	23	52
Tunisia	27	41	33	40

Source: Subramanian, 1995; WTO Integrated Database.

Middle Eastern and North African countries did little to open their service markets in the Uruguay Round. Commitments are only substantial for hotel and restaurant services (that is, tourism-related services), although as a group the region scheduled more service activities in their construction and financial offers than the average for developing countries (Hoekman and Primo Braga, 1996). Still, the average level and degree of liberalization in the commitments of the Arab countries is less than that of developing countries in general. The immediate implications of the GATS agreement for domestic service providers in Arab countries are quite limited. In Egypt, for example – the Arab country that maintains the fewest restrictions on market access and national treatment (Table 4.7) – most offers bind

Table 4.7 Sectoral coverage of specific services commitments, various countries (percent)

Type of coverage	High-income members	All other countries	Large developing countries	Arab countries					
				Algeria	Bahrain	Egypt	Kuwait	Morocco	Tunisia
Average share of sectors listed	53.3	15.1	29.6	0.65	2.58	16.77	28.39	23.23	8.39
No restrictions as a share of total possible	28.0	6.4	10.0	0.48	1.9	7.9	7.1	6.5	1.5

Source: Hoekman and Primo Braga, 1995.

the regulatory status quo for the scheduled sectors. The qualifications are extensive and include limitations on the share of foreign personnel in foreign-controlled enterprises (and even in the overall wage bill in maritime transport), foreign capital in several industries (49 percent in construction and related engineering services, tourism projects in the Sinai region, insurance), economic needs tests in tourism, opening of branches by foreign banks and insurance, the operations of representative offices, and so on.

Trade-related intellectual property rights

Protection of intellectual property rights is important for a number of reasons, including attracting foreign direct investment. The TRIPs agreement requires protection of trademarks (to last at least seven years, with equal treatment given to service and trademarks and a prohibition on compulsory licensing), geographical indications (prohibition on indications that mislead or constitute unfair competition), industrial designs, and layout designs of integrated circuits (to last at least ten years). For copyrights, members are required to comply with the substantive provisions of the 1971 Berne convention, with the exception of its obligations regarding the protection of moral rights, provision of rental rights, and protection against unauthorized recording of live performances. Computer software is to be protected as a literary work under the Berne Convention. Copyright protection is to last for at least fifty years. For patent protection, all signatories must comply with the substantive provisions of the 1967 Paris convention. Patent protection must be provided for almost all inventions, and must last at least twenty years after the filing date.

Intellectual property laws must also be enforced, which requires that customs authorities apply – and the judicial system enforces – the laws. Enforcement and dispute settlement procedures are spelled out in detail. Enforcement procedures under national laws must permit effective action against any act of infringement on intellectual property rights. Signatories must allow criminal procedures and penalties to be applied in cases of willful trademark counterfeiting or copyright piracy on a commercial scale, with penalties sufficiently large to act as an effective deterrent. Developing countries have five years to implement the provisions of the TRIPs agreement, with the exception of its national treatment and MFN requirements. If a developing country must extend patent protection to areas that are not currently protectable (such as pharmaceuticals or agricultural chemicals), the application of TRIPs disciplines to these areas may be delayed for another five years, for a total of ten.

Maximizing the potential benefits of WTO membership

Implementing the rules and principles of the WTO will help reduce the extent to which countries' trade policies distort incentives. But WTO membership is not a panacea. Full consistency with WTO requirements is neither necessary nor sufficient to ensure good trade policy; careful attention must be paid to institutional design. Although adherence to WTO rules and principles would clearly help increase the credibility of trade policy reform for Middle Eastern and North African governments, many of the WTO's disciplines are optional, either in the sense that members have discretion regarding the extent to which they apply or can choose whether to invoke them. A distinction can be made between the possibilities that exist for opting out of disciplines that are good – in that abiding by them is likely to enhance efficiency and welfare – and opting to use measures that are permitted but are likely to be detrimental to efficiency and welfare (Hoekman, 1996). Examples of good disciplines include setting limits on the magnitude and restrictiveness of tariff bindings, participating in the government procurement agreement, and agreeing to specific commitments under the GATS. Examples of bad disciplines include the possibility of demanding special and differential treatment, not binding tariffs at applied rates, implementing antidumping and countervailing duty legislation, using trade barriers on balance of payments grounds, negotiating free trade agreements that do not entail free trade, and severely limiting the extent to which service markets are opened to foreign competition.

The extent to which WTO options are invoked can have a large impact on the incentives facing firms and consumers. Each member government bears primary responsibility for limiting the extent to which the bad options are exercised and maximizing the extent to which the good options are exploited. Indeed, there is some degree of asymmetry here, since the adoption of good options is subject to pressure from trading partners but there is no such pressure with respect to bad ones. Autonomous decisions on trade policies are extremely important in determining the credibility of reform efforts. Such credibility can be substantially enhanced through WTO membership if governments so desire. But governments must make a conscious and autonomous decision to do so.

Actions that enhance the credibility of governments' trade policies include:

- Binding all tariffs at applied rates. If tariffs are lowered, they should automatically be bound at the new applied rate.
- Refraining from invoking GATT's special and differential treatment provisions. Full application of the agreements on customs valuation, standards, trade-related investment measures (as well as participation in the government procurement agreement), and adherence to the general rules relating to regional integration will increase the relevance of the WTO.
- Designing safeguard legislation that minimizes the scope for easy reimposition of protection and ensures that the economywide impact is considered before protection is imposed.
- Enhancing the transparency of policymaking by making an independent body responsible for evaluating the likely economic impact of proposed trade policies and monitoring their effects. Such a body could advise the government on the effects of trade policy on competition and national welfare and be required to prepare a regular, comprehensive report on the effects of trade and investment policies. The WTO's requirements concerning the Trade Policy Review Mechanism already imply that comprehensive description and analysis of trade policies should be made periodically. It makes good sense to build on this requirement and institutionalize such a domestic monitoring capacity.
- Initiating efforts to minimize the red tape associated with regulatory and customs procedures. Administrative burdens raise costs for traders and create uncertainty and opportunities for rent-seeking. Mutual recognition of standards and testing and conformity assessment procedures can greatly facilitate trade. Reducing the number of tariff bands and documents (in principle a single administrative document should be used) can help speed up customs clearance and reduce uncertainty.
- Expanding the scope of specific commitments on services under GATS auspices. As under the GATT, an important potential benefit of the GATS is the "anchor" effect. By binding its policies in the GATS, a government is in a better position to resist demands from interest groups to alter these policies in the future. The GATS imposes costs on backsliding – that is, on adopting more restrictive policies for services that are bound – by requiring countries to negotiate the withdrawal of specific commitments. In this context

even an offer to bind the status quo has a value to the extent that it improves the transparency of the regulatory regime and makes backsliding less likely. The lack of competition in services is an important factor underlying the difficulties many Middle Eastern and North African firms have competing in world markets. This raises the costs of services such as finance, insurance, transport, and handling and storage of goods, which are often much higher than in neighboring countries or in nations the region competes with. Similarly, the quality of the services provided is generally lower.

THE POTENTIAL ROLE OF AN EU AGREEMENT

As mentioned earlier, the absence of political support for liberalization and a perception on the part of governments that rapid liberalization could give rise to social unrest are important factors constraining policy reform in a number of Middle Eastern and North African countries. The problem with a cautious, gradual approach to reform is that it may be too slow, inducing the private sector to take a "wait and see" attitude. Ongoing developments in the external environment (globalization, the implementation of the Uruguay Round, the coming onstream of countries in Central and Eastern Europe and the former Soviet Union, the rapid growth of Asian economies) suggest that reform efforts must be accelerated. Closer relations with the European Union may help overcome some of the political constraints that have hindered reform in a number of Middle Eastern and North African countries.

A new approach

The Commission of the European Communities has proposed a Euro-Mediterranean economic area with Middle Eastern and North African countries. Such an arrangement would greatly expand the extent of cooperation between the region and the European Union, which currently is determined by agreements made during the 1970s. The commission has been authorized to negotiate agreements with the Mediterranean countries covering institutionalization of political dialogue, free trade in industrial products, reciprocal liberalization of trade in agriculture and services, and expansion of the scope for technical, economic, social, cultural, and financial cooperation. Negotiations with Egypt, Jordan, and Lebanon are expected to be completed in 1996. Agreements were reached with Tunisia and Morocco in 1995, and agreement on a customs union with Turkey was reached in early 1995. The European Union is also engaged in talks with the countries of the Gulf Cooperation Council on a free trade agreement, but this appears to be conditional upon the countries achieving a customs union (Zarrouk, 1996).

The basic objectives of the Euro-Mediterranean proposal, to be achieved gradually, are to achieve reciprocal free trade in manufactured goods by 2010, preferential and reciprocal access for agricultural products of interest to both parties, and free trade among the Mediterranean countries. The commission's proposal states that

> In order to be able to enter progressively into free trade with the Union and to take on board a wide range of trade-related Community regulations (customs, standards, competition, intellectual property protection, liberalization of services, free capital movements, etc.),- Mediterranean countries [require] four fundamental aspects... the need for long transitional mechanisms and secure safeguards; the need to obtain improved access for their agricultural exports; the need for increased financial flows; [and] the possibility to count on the Community's help to accelerate the modernization of their social and economic systems.

Basic elements of a Euro-Mediterranean agreement

The first Euro-Mediterranean agreement, negotiated with Tunisia, was signed in July 1995. An agreement with Morocco followed in October 1995. Negotiations are ongoing with Egypt, Jordan, and Lebanon. Although the terms of the EU agreements are similar, partner countries have considerable discretion in committing to changes in investment and services. The agreements have six major elements: free movement of goods; right of establishment and supply of services; payments, capital, competition, and other economic provisions (such as safeguards); economic, social, and cultural cooperation; financial cooperation; and political dialogue.

Trade

Free trade in goods is to be achieved over a twelve-year transition period, with partner countries granted great leeway in implementing tariff cuts. Little will change as far as agricultural trade is concerned. Negotiations to improve on existing agricultural concessions are to be initiated after January 1,2000. The EU commission's inability to significantly expand export opportunities was an important stumbling block for Morocco in finalizing its agreement. The relative importance of agriculture varies significantly across Mediterranean countries. It is least important to Jordan, where it accounts for 8 percent of GDP, and most important to Egypt, where it contributes some 20 percent of GDP.

Establishment and services

The right of establishment (that is, freedom to engage in foreign direct investment (FDI) and be treated as a national) is an objective of the Euro-Mediterranean agreements. No specific language is devoted to this subject in the Tunisian agreement, however, and no time path or target date is mentioned for its realization. This contrasts with the association agreements concluded with Central and Eastern European countries, where the European Union granted free entry and national treatment to firms from partner countries from 1992 on (except in air and inland water transport and maritime cabotage). Central and Eastern European countries also granted free entry and national treatment to EU firms, with transition periods for some sectors and activities. Liberalization of services is also an objective of the Association Council.

Competition policy, state aid, and government procurement

The Euro-Mediterranean agreements require partner countries to adopt the basic competition rules of the European Union, particularly on collusive behavior, abuse of dominant position, and competition-distorting state aid (Articles 85, 86, and 92 of the Treaty of Rome) as they affect trade between the European Union and each partner country. Until implementing rules are agreed, GATT rules on countervailing of subsidies will apply. The Association Council will adopt rules to enforce competition policy and subsidy disciplines after an initial five-year period. Despite the agreement to apply EU competition disciplines, antidumping measures can still be applied to trade flows between partners. Liberalization of government procurement is an objective of the Euro-Mediterranean agreement to be realized in the future.

Economic and financial cooperation

One-third of the articles of the Tunisian agreement deal with cooperation in economic, social, and cultural matters. The various articles are largely oriented toward upgrading Tunisian infrastructure (both physical and regulatory) and providing support for economic restructuring. This support will be in the form of technical assistance and advice as well as financial assistance. Under the agreement the European Union envisages earmarking a total amount of assistance – grants and loans – for all the Mediterranean partner countries. Individual allocations from this total will in part be endogenous, depending on country performance (including implementation of the agreement). The EC Commission initially requested ECU 5.5 billion for the region for a four-year period; ECU 4.7 billion was approved by the Association Council. An equivalent amount will be provided by the European Investment Bank.

IMPLICATIONS FOR THE MIDDLE EAST AND NORTH AFRICA

A key benefit of negotiating association agreements along these lines is that they provide a policy blueprint to which Middle Eastern and North African governments can credibly commit themselves. Credibility results from both the formal nature of a treaty and the availability of financial and technical assistance from the European Union to help implement the agreement.

Not much immediate improvement should be expected from the European Union in terms of market access for sensitive products. For clothing, Middle Eastern and North African countries currently have almost quota-free access. Access to EU agricultural markets will be difficult to improve significantly in the short run. Central and Eastern Europe's experience in this domain illustrates that obtaining better access will run into strong opposition by vested interests in the European Union. In any case improved access to EU markets is not the main benefit of the agreements – rather, it is the reduction in barriers to imports and increased foreign direct investment in goods and service sectors in partner countries. Central and Eastern European countries allowed EU-based firms to undertake operations in virtually every sector of economic activity. Although transitional arrangements and temporary exceptions were made, few sectors are excluded indefinitely (mainly agricultural land, natural resources, and historical monuments). Arguments favoring such an all-inclusive approach, with a short negative list of exceptions, are very strong. In many sectors – both goods and services – establishment is the most direct method of enhancing competition and efficiency.

Adoption of EU policies and regulations will have major implications for Middle Eastern and North African countries. These practices will help attract investment, facilitate exports, and enhance competition in domestic markets. The trend toward increasingly stringent product standards and regulations applied on a European Union-wide basis enhances the export payoff of associated countries harmonizing domestic product standards as much as possible with those of the European Union. The same applies to the use of EU customs procedures and documentation. Care must be taken that the adoption of regulations and directives does not conflict with a country's comparative advantage, however, especially on environmental and social policies.

An important caveat concerns the potential trade diversion costs that a free trade agreement with the European Union could entail. If external tariffs on products originating in the rest of world are not lowered concurrently, a free trade agreement may have large opportunity costs (Rutherford, Ruström, and Tarr, 1993). As noted earlier, the best strategy in this regard is if a link with the European Union is used as part of a broader effort to liberalize trade and investment regimes. Insofar as credibility problems exist, a free trade agreement with the European Union may do more than unilateral efforts to convince the private sector that planned reform efforts will be implemented. A supporting policy in this connection should be to critically review the rationale for regional agreements between Arab countries. The preferential trade agreements that many Middle Eastern and North African countries have concluded with one another should either be abolished or converted into full-fledged free trade agreements.

CONCLUSION

Despite the progress on policy reforms that has been made in recent years, the Middle East and North Africa remains more inward-oriented than many other parts of the world. Anti-export biases are strong, reflecting not only tariff policies but also the regulatory burdens and administrative red tape that confronts businesses. State intervention in the economy often remains pervasive. Only by allowing greater competition in domestic markets – by reducing barriers to imports and exports and by allowing foreign direct investment to occur – will the countries in the region be able to achieve sustainable real growth. Many countries have had trouble implementing far-reaching reform of trade and investment policies. External developments suggest that in the foreseeable future many – if not most – of the region's comparator and competitor countries will be more open, more encouraging of the private sector, and more dynamic. Central and Eastern Europe illustrates the challenge – not just in terms of being competitors, but also in terms of what must be done. Similar efforts are under way in Latin America and Asia.

Middle Eastern and North African countries face two key trade policy issues: adopting trade policies that foster integration with the world economy and establishing institutions that make these policies credible. Unless policies are credible, trade liberalization may achieve little in terms of private sector supply response. An important benefit of both the WTO and the EU option in this connection are their potential roles as a commitment device. The GATT and WTO provide a cheap and effective mechanism to lock in trade policy reforms and improve the transparency of policy implementation. By adopting and abiding by the rules of the game for the administration of trade laws and policies, the current problems associated with bureaucratic red tape would diminish significantly. By binding tariffs at applied levels, the scope for domestic firms to lobby for an increase in a specific tariff is greatly reduced, if not eliminated. This will force firms to use GATT-sanctioned mechanisms for temporary safeguard protection. If well designed, these mechanisms will not encourage rent-seeking expenditures or constitute a disincentive for firms to undertake the investment and adjustment efforts needed to enhance productivity.

One problem associated with the WTO is that its loopholes may substantially reduce the potential credibility effect. Developing countries are allowed to bind only a portion of their tariffs under the GATT, often at maximum or ceiling rates that exceed applied rates. Developing countries also benefit from special and differential treatment, which usually implies an exemption from specific rules or principles. Investment policies in general (as opposed to trade-related investment measures) are not covered by the WTO. The GATT allows for antidumping, a policy with almost no economic justification, which reduces the relevance of GATT rules with respect to safeguard actions. The GATT is weak on preferential rules of origin and allows trade restrictions to be imposed for balance of payments reasons rather than encouraging the use of alternative macroeconomic instruments. Disciplines on public procurement practices only apply to countries that want to be subject to them.

An agreement with the European Union to establish a free trade and investment area may help to offset many of the WTO's weaknesses and help overcome existing resistance to reform. An EU link can help assure potential investors in the Middle East and North Africa that although progress will be somewhat more gradual than in Eastern Europe, the region's governments are committed to far-reaching integration with the European Union. The European Union can offer a more binding and more credible road map than the WTO. Financial and technical assistance from the European Union is available to ease the process of transition and the adoption of EU norms. An EU agreement is not a panacea, however. In many ways an agreement will require only nondiscrimination or national treatment; that is, the obligation not to discriminate between foreign (EU) and domestic firms. This will often not be enough to ensure that a Middle Eastern or North African partner is a worthy recipient of foreign direct investment. Policies that unnecessarily reduce the competitiveness of domestic firms must be reduced or eliminated, including trade and other barriers to competition that affect non-EU firms. The latter is important to limit the trade diversion costs of an EU agreement. Indeed, governments should be encouraged to reduce tariffs and other barriers to trade against the rest of the world at the same time and at the same pace as barriers are reduced for EU suppliers. The additional adjustment costs of doing so are limited, while the potential gains from liberalization are great.

Notes

1. The author is grateful to Ishac Diwan, Hamid Mohtadi, Nemat Shafik, David Tarr, and Sübidey Togan for comments and suggestions, and to Faten Hatab and Ying Lin for research assistance.
2. This chapter defines the Middle East and North Africa region as Algeria, Bahrain, Egypt, Jordan, Iraq, Israel, Kuwait, Lebanon, Libya, Morocco, Oman, Qatar, Saudi Arabia, Syria, Tunisia, the United Arab Emirates, and Yemen. Iraq and Libya are not included in the analysis, however, due to lack of data.
3. When this chapter was written Algeria, Jordan, and Saudi Arabia were involved in accession talks.

4. Intraindustry trade is measured as:

$$\frac{\sum |x_i - m_i|}{\sum (x_i + m_i)}$$

where x and m are exports and imports of good i to and from a trading partner at the three-digit level.
5. See Goldin and Kherallah (1996) and Kirmani (1996) for qualitative discussions of agriculture and textiles and clothing.
6. Quantitative import restrictions, variable import levies, minimum import prices, discretionary import licensing, nontariff measures maintained through state trading enterprises, voluntary export restraints, and similar border measures are explicitly prohibited (Agreement on Agriculture, Article 4).

References

Dean, Judith, Seema Desai, and James Riedel, 1994. *Trade Policy Reform in Developing Countries since 1985: A Review of the Evidence*, World Bank Discussion Paper, 267, Washington D.C. : World Bank.

European Commission, 1994. "Strengthening the Mediterranean Policy of the European Union: Establishing a Euro-Mediterranean Partnership," Communication to the Council and the Parliament, Brussels.

Goldin, Ian and Mylene Kherallah, 1996. "The Uruguay Round and International Trade in Agricultural Products: Implications for Arab Countries," in Said El-Naggar (ed.), *The Uruguay Round and the Arab Countries*, Washington, D.C.: International Monetary Fund.

Harrison, Glenn, Thomas Rutherford, and David Tarr, 1996. "Quantifying the Uruguay Round," in Will Martin and Alan Winters (eds.), *The Uruguay Round and the Developing Economies*, Cambridge: Cambridge University Press.

Hoekman, Bernard, 1995. *Trade Laws and Institutions: Good Practices and the World Trade Organization*, World Bank Discussion Paper, 282, Washington D.C. : World Bank.

———1996. "Tentative First Steps: An Assessment of the Uruguay Round Agreement on Services," in Will Martin and Alan Winters (eds.), *The Uruguay Round and the Developing Economies*, Cambridge: Cambridge University Press.

Hoekman, Bernard and Carlos Primo Braga, 1996. "Trade in Services, the GATS, and the Arab Countries," in Said El-Naggar (ed.), *The Uruguay Round and the Arab Countries*. Washington, D.C.: International Monetary Fund.

IMF (International Monetary Fund), 1994a. *Government Finance Statistics Yearbook*. Washington, D.C.

———1994b. *International Financial Statistics*, Washington, D.C. : International Monetary Fund.

Kirmani, Naheed, 1996. "The Uruguay Round and International Trade in Textiles and Clothing," in Said El-Naggar (ed.), *The Uruguay Round and the Arab Countries*, Washington, D.C.: International Monetary Fund.

Lahouel, Mohammed, 1997. "Competition Policies and Regulation: The Case of Tunisia," in Nemat Shafik (ed.), *Perspectives on Middle Eastern and North African Economies*, London: Macmillan.

Rutherford, Thomas, E.E. Ruström and David Tarr, 1993. "Morocco's Free Trade Agreement with the European Community: A Quantitative Assessment," Policy Research Working Paper, 1173, Washington, D.C. : World Bank.

Subramanian, Arvind, 1995. "Effects of the Uruguay Round on Egypt," Washington, D.C. International Monetary Fund.

World Bank, 1994. "Kingdom of Morocco – Republic of Tunisia. Export Growth: Determinants and Prospects," Middle East and North Africa Region, Washington, D.C. : World Bank.

———1995a. *Global Economic Prospects and the Developing Countries*. Washington D.C. : World Bank.

———1995b. "Lebanon – Achieving Competitiveness in A Global Economy," Middle East and North Africa Region, Washington, D.C. : World Bank.

Zarrouk, Jamal, 1996. "Policy Implications of the Uruguay Round for the Arab Countries," in Said El-Naggar (ed.), *The Uruguay Round and the Arab Countries*. Washington, D.C.: International Monetary Fund.

Part II

Economic Growth, the State, and the Private Sector

5 From Boom to Bust – and Back? The Crisis of Growth in the Middle East and North Africa

John Page

From the 1960s through the first half of the 1980s the Middle East and North Africa enjoyed rising prosperity. Indeed, between 1965 and 1985 the Middle East and North Africa led all other developing regions except East Asia in per capita income growth. By the second half of the 1980s, however, growth had collapsed. In the Maghreb and Mashreq regions economic growth barely kept pace with population growth. In the GCC countries and Iran per capita incomes declined. Since the beginning of the 1980s economic growth has been unable to create sufficient job opportunities for the region's rapidly expanding labor forces – today more than 10 million people are unemployed.

This chapter examines the sources of growth and decline in the Middle East and North Africa in an international context. Three main messages emerge. First, the region is not exceptional in terms of its long-run growth performance, but it has experienced an unprecedented economic crisis since 1985. Second, the high rates of physical investment that characterized the region during 1960–79 planted the seeds of the region's subsequent abrupt collapse. The dominance of the public sector, both as the engine of accumulation and the primary mechanism for resource allocation, created a legacy of poorly performing investments, low productivity, and rigid industrial structures that were unable to adapt to the external shocks of the past decade. Third, restoring growth will require raising private investment – the public transfers of the past will continue to decline – and improving the efficiency of investment through greater integration with the global economy.

Despite the current growth crisis in the Middle East and North Africa, the historical picture contains both positive and negative elements. In the past the region as a whole outperformed all other regions except East Asia in both per capita income growth and equality of income distribution. But the cycle of economic expansion followed by contraction – boom and bust – was more pronounced in the Middle East and North Africa than in other regions.

GROWTH AND EQUITY IN THE LONG RUN – IS THE MIDDLE EAST EXCEPTIONAL?

The relationship between relative income level in 1960 and per capita income growth for a sample of 119 countries during 1960–85 is shown in Figure 5.1. The figure also plots an estimated nonlinear relationship between initial income and growth. The figure shows that worldwide per capita income growth is essentially independent of the level

Figure 5.1 GDP growth, 1960-85, and GDP per capita, 1960

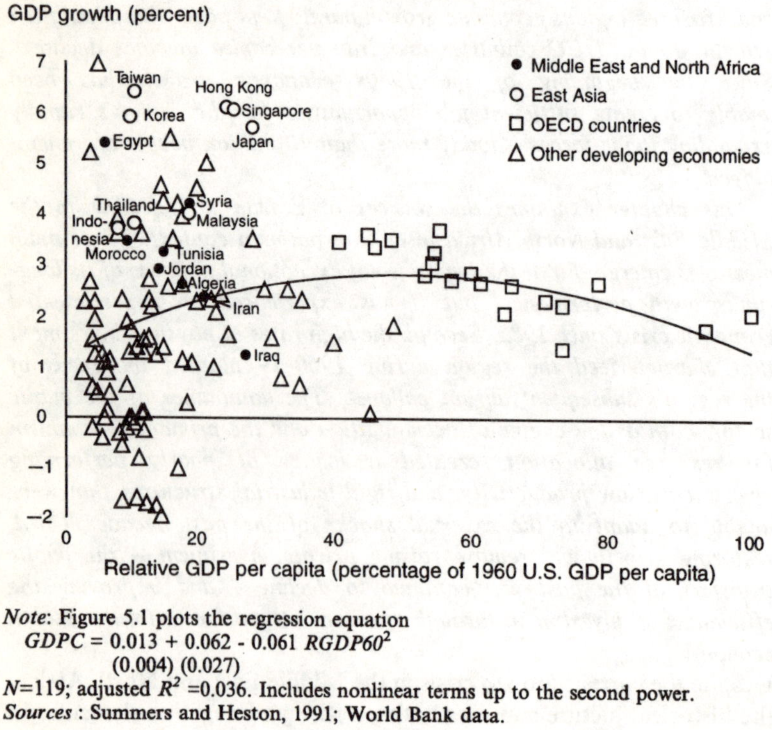

Note: Figure 5.1 plots the regression equation
$GDPC = 0.013 + 0.062 - 0.061\ RGDP60^2$
$\qquad\qquad (0.004)\ (0.027)$
$N=119$; adjusted $R^2 =0.036$. Includes nonlinear terms up to the second power.
Sources : Summers and Heston, 1991; World Bank data.

of relative income in 1960.[1] The figure also shows that while the per capita incomes of OECD countries tend to converge, developing countries are not catching up to the OECD countries. Per capita income growth in the poorest countries is lower than in the middle-income countries.

How do Middle Eastern and North African countries fit into this picture? Except for Iran and Iraq the region's major economies were above the predicted values of their growth rates for their level of relative income, and they were among the few developing countries to have per capita growth rates equal to or greater than the industrial economies over the twenty-five year interval. Egypt was among the world leaders in income growth, ranking with Hong Kong, Japan, the Republic of Korea, Singapore, and Taiwan (China). Morocco, Syria,

Figure 5.2 GDP growth, 1965–89, and income inequality

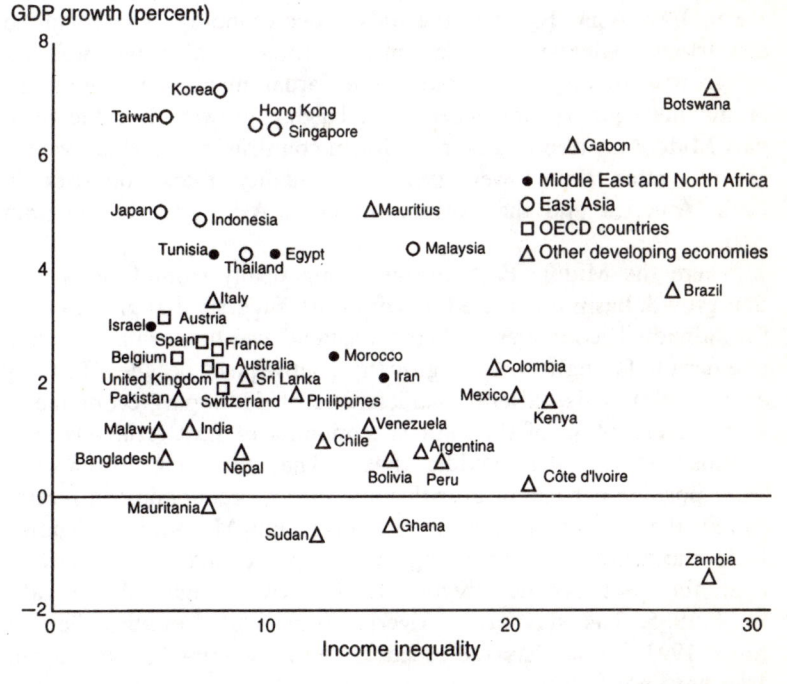

Note: Income inequality is measured by the ratio of the income shares of the richest fifth and the poorest fifth of the population.
Source: Page, 1995.

and Tunisia had growth rates that were similar to those of Indonesia, Malaysia, and Thailand.

The region also does well when income distribution is added to the long-term growth picture. Figure 5.2 ranks forty-five economies per capita income growth and the ratio of the income share of the richest fifth of the population to the income share of the poorest fifth during 1965–89.[2] Income inequalities ranged from about 5:1 (most high-income countries) to nearly 30:1. Of developing regions East and South Asia were in the range of 5–10:1, while Latin America and the Caribbean and Sub-Saharan Africa were in the range of 10–20:1. Except for Iran and Morocco all the economies in the Middle East and North Africa for which data are available had levels of income inequality that were similar to East Asian and OECD countries, with ratios of the income share of the richest fifth to the poorest fifth at less than 10:1.

Six countries had particularly high growth (more than 4 percent per capita) and low relative inequality (index of less than 10). Five are in East Asia. Egypt is the only other economy. The Maghreb countries – Algeria, Tunisia, and Morocco – also did well on the growth-equality distribution, while Jordan maintained high levels of income equality but experienced lagging growth. For the most part Middle Eastern and North African countries had higher average growth rates and lower average inequality than countries in Latin America and the Caribbean, South Asia, and Sub-Saharan Africa.

Where the Middle East diverges dramatically from East Asia is that growth has not persisted. Recent work suggests that growth rates for individual economies are highly unstable over time, with growth in one decade failing to predict growth in subsequent decades (Easterly *et al.*, 1993). This pattern, characteristic of developing economies – with the exception of the miracle economies of East Asia – is most pronounced in the Middle East. The economic turnaround from positive per capita growth until 1985 to economic contraction since is the most pronounced in the world. Only Morocco and Tunisia have succeeded in maintaining modest per capita income growth over the past decade. Egypt, which grew at East Asian rates until 1985, has stagnated. Algeria, Iran, and Jordan collapsed. Since 1993 Jordan has succeeded in restoring growth; Algeria and Iran have not.

SOURCES OF GROWTH, 1960–85

Accumulation of physical and human capital and the productivity with which these factors are combined are the keys to sustained growth. This section examines long-run patterns of investment in physical and human capital, contrasting the Middle East and North Africa's performance with a large sample of other countries. It then uses a cross-country growth regression to account for differences in per capita income between eight countries in the Middle East and seven in East Asia.

The region's record of accumulation

The relationship between income level in 1960 and average investment rate in 1960–85 is shown in Figure 5.3. The estimated nonlinear regression relating initial income level to investment is also shown. There is substantially more regularity in the relationship between investment

Figure 5.3 Investment as a share of GDP, 1960–85, and GDP per capita, 1960

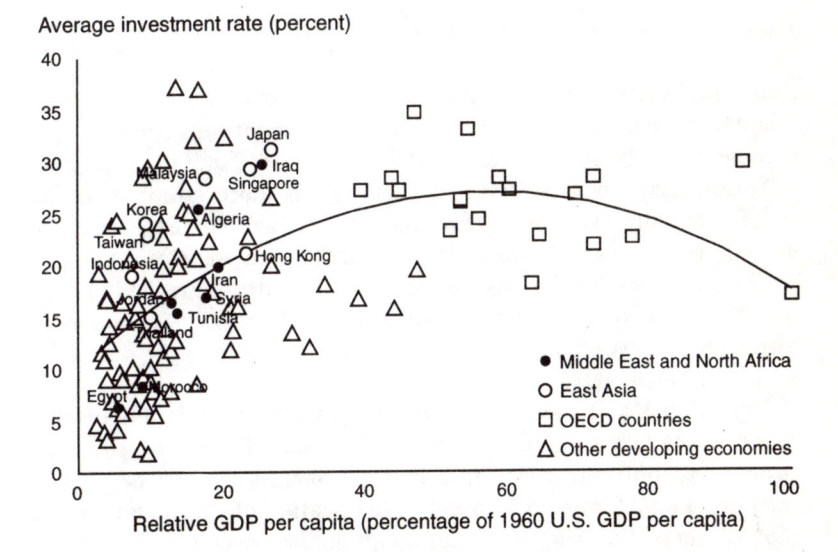

Note: Figure 5.3 plots the regression equation
$$INV6085 = 10.125 + 59.120\ RGDP60 - 51.881 RGDP60^2$$
$$\qquad\qquad (1.383)\quad (10.344)\qquad\quad (12.593)$$
$N = 119$; adjusted $R^2 = 0.295$
Sources: Summers and Heston, 1991; World Bank data.

Figure 5.4 GDP per capita and primary enrollment, 1960

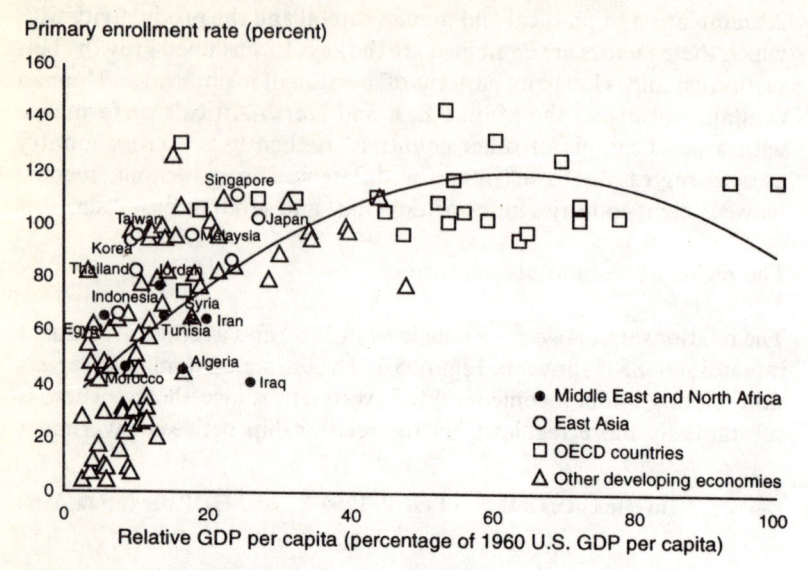

[Figure 5.4: Scatter plot of Primary enrollment rate (percent) on y-axis (0 to 160) versus Relative GDP per capita (percentage of 1960 U.S. GDP per capita) on x-axis (0 to 100). Markers: ● Middle East and North Africa, ○ East Asia, □ OECD countries, △ Other developing economies. Labeled points include Singapore, Taiwan, Korea, Japan, Malaysia, Thailand, Jordan, Indonesia, Syria, Iran, Egypt, Tunisia, Algeria, Iraq, Morocco.]

Sources: Summers and Heston, 1991; World Bank data.

share and relative income than in the relationship between growth and relative income. The investment rate for all countries increases with income up to about 70 percent of U.S. GDP in 1960 and then declines.

Middle Eastern economies conform much more strongly to the cross – country pattern of investment rates than to the pattern of growth rates. Iran, Jordan, Syria, and Tunisia lie close to their predicted values on the basis of the cross-country regression. Egypt and Morocco are the negative outliers among the region's economies – although not extreme ones – while Algeria and Iraq show unusually high investment rates.

Figures 5.4 and 5.5 summarize the pattern of variation of two measures of human capital with initial income. Figure 5.4 plots the primary school enrollment rate in 1960 against relative per capita income, while Figure 5.5 presents the scatter of Barro and Lee's (1993) average measure of education attainment over 1960-85 against initial income. The two figures tell somewhat different stories about human capital formation in the region. When primary school enrollment rates are correlated with relative income the region's economies generally conform to the cross-country pattern, although Algeria and

Figure 5.5 Average education stock, 1960–85, and GDP per capita, 1960

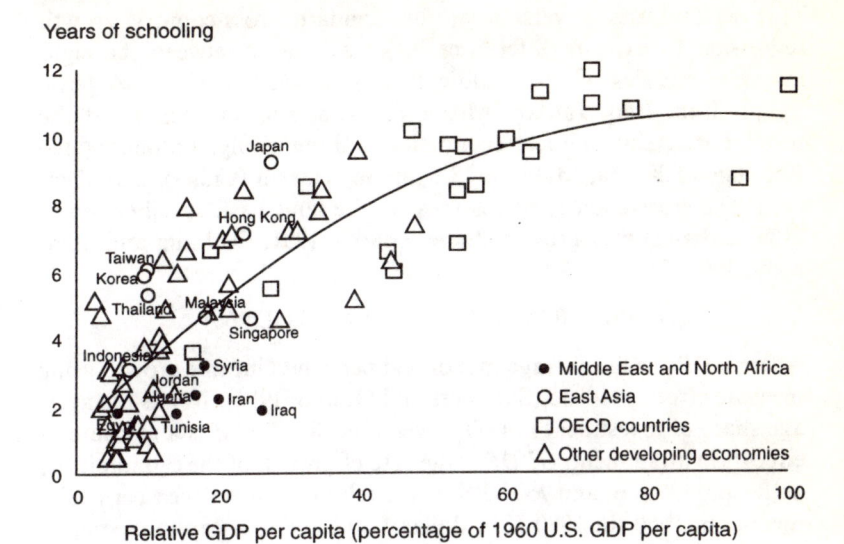

Sources: Summers and Heston (1991); Barro and Lee (1993).

Iraq are notable negative outliers. Egypt and Jordan, on the other hand, had higher enrollment rates than would have been predicted on the basis of their relative income levels in 1960.

The region performs quite poorly, however, in terms of education attainment. None of the economies reached its predicted value for the average education stock (years of schooling per person). The contrast with East Asia is particularly notable. Singapore is the only East Asian country below its predicted value. Indonesia – the East Asian economy with the lowest average education stock and lowest relative income – has a higher education attainment level than all the Middle Eastern and North African countries, despite their higher relative incomes.

At least two factors account for the differences between the region's relatively good track record on access to education and its much poorer record in terms of education output. First, the rapid expansion of primary enrollments only occurred during the late 1950s and early 1960s, so the average education stock changed slowly between 1960 and 1985 – the region was catching up from a late start. Second, high dropout rates in some countries – especially among women – also explain why increased access was not translated into increases in average years in school.

Explaining differences in growth in a cross-country framework

This section uses a version of the standard cross-country growth regression to explain differences in growth rates between the eight major economies of the Middle East and North Africa – Algeria, Egypt, Iran, Iraq, Jordan, Morocco, Syria, and Tunisia – and the seven East Asian miracle economies – Hong Kong, Indonesia, the Republic of Korea, Malaysia, Singapore, Taiwan (China), and Thailand. The cross-country regressions use the same basic specification as other cross-country growth studies (Barro, 1991; De Long and Summers, 1991; Dollar, 1991):

$$GDPG = f(INV, PRIM, GPOP, RGDP60) \qquad (1)$$

where *GDPG* is the average rate of real per capita income growth using measures from 1960–85 (Summers and Heston, 1991), *INV* is the average share of investment in GDP over 1960–85, *PRIM* is a measure of education attainment, *GPOP* is the rate of growth of the economically active population, and *RGDP60* is the relative gap between per capita income in 1960 (in 1980 U.S. dollars) and U.S. per capita income in 1960.[3] Mankiw, Roemer and Weil (1992) have demonstrated that this specification corresponds to the transitional dynamics of an enhanced neoclassical growth model with human capital.

Table 5.1 Output, growth, and investment, 1960–85
(dependent variable, rate of growth of real GDP per capita)

Variable	1960-85	1960-70	1970-85
Intercept	−0.0046	0.0081	−0.0128
	(0.0079)	(0.0091)	(0.0109)
RGDP60 (relative GDP per capita, 1960)	−0.0308	−0.0355	−0.0277
	(0.0099)	(0.0114)	(0.0137)
PRIM60 (primary enrollment rate, 1960)	0.0296	0.0193	0.0362
	(0.0064)	(0.0073)	(0.0088)
GPOP6085 (growth rate of economically active population, 1960–85)	−0.0526	−0.2766	0.0923
	(0.2103)	(0.2416)	(0.2888)
INV6085 (investment rate, 1960–85)	0.0639	0.1198	0.0273
	(0.0224)	(0.0257)	(0.0308)
Number of observations	113	113	113
Adjusted R^2	0.3328	0.3399	0.1803
RMSE	0.0154	0.0176	0.0211

Note: Coefficient (standard error).
Source: Author's calculations.

The basic results on the relationship between accumulation and growth are shown in Table 5.1. The estimated equations compare favorably with other studies using similar specifications. The overall fit of the regressions is good, and the coefficients of the variables are of the expected sign and are significant at conventional (0.05) levels.[4] The *RGDP60* variable indicates that, after controlling for the effects of investment and education, economies that were relatively poor in 1960 grew significantly faster than those that were richer. An economy at 50 percent of the level of U.S. per capita income in 1960 grew about 1.6 percentage points faster than the United States, controlling for education and investment.

Figure 5.6 uses the cross-country growth regressions to explain differences in per capita income between the Middle East and North Africa and East Asia over 1960–91. If the eight major economies of the Middle East and North Africa had the same rates of investment and education attainment as the East Asian miracle economies, how much more would they have grown? While the addition growth would have been impressive, it remains disappointingly small compared with the actual achievement of the East Asian economies.

Per capita incomes in the Middle East and North Africa increased from $1,521 in 1960 to $3,342 in 1991. Raising the average rate of investment to East Asian levels – increasing it by an average of 7.6

Figure 5.6 Accounting for differences in growth due to differences in accumulation, 1960–91

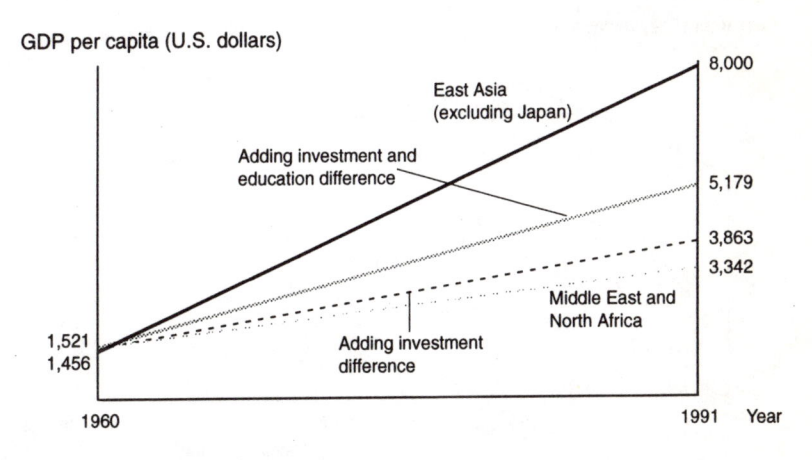

GDP per capita (U.S. dollars)

- East Asia (excluding Japan): 8,000
- Adding investment and education difference: 5,179
- 3,863
- Middle East and North Africa: 3,342
- Adding investment difference
- 1,521
- 1,456

1960 — 1991 Year

Source: Author's calculations.

percentage points over the period – increases per capita income in 1991 from $3,342 to $3,863. Adding the levels of human capital in East Asia to the higher investment levels – by projecting an increase in the primary school enrollment rate in 1960 of 33 percent-results in a further increase, to $5,179. Per capita incomes in East Asia grew from $1,456 to $8,000 over the same period. Thus more than half the difference in growth rates (55 percent) cannot be explained by East Asia's superior performance in accumulating human and physical capital. Rather, it is due to differences in the productivity with which that capital was used.

WHY THE CRASH? INVESTMENT YIELDED TOO LITTLE

If the Middle East and North Africa is not exceptional in terms of its long-run growth, it certainly is in terms of the depth of its economic contraction. This contraction is not, however, entirely attributable to the decline in investment that took place as a consequence of the fall in oil prices.

In a cross-country perspective the decline in investment in the Middle East and North Africa during the 1980s was not exceptional. Investment as a share of GDP was higher in the Maghreb and Mashreq than in Latin America or South Asia, and the reduction in

Figure 5.7 Investment and GDP growth, Middle East and North Africa, 1970–89

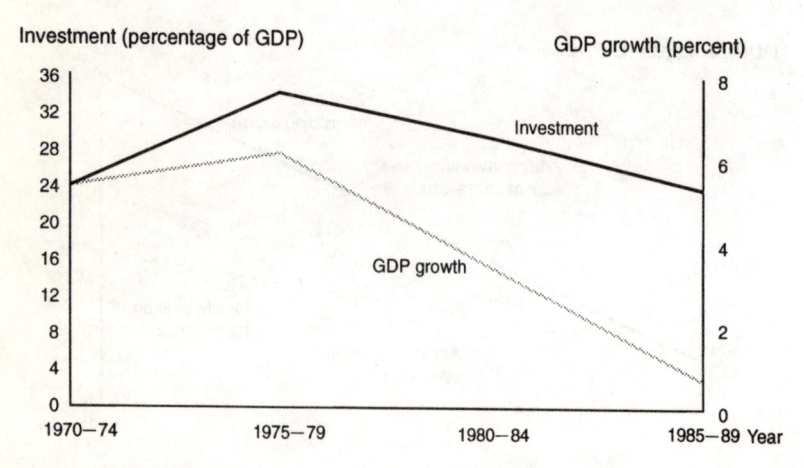

Source : World Bank data.

investment rates was less dramatic than in those regions. Thus the collapse in performance in the Middle East and North Africa was much greater than could easily be explained by declining levels of investment (Figure 5.7). It was instead the product of a dramatic decline in productivity.

Declining productivity over the past thirty years can be attributed primarily to the role of the state in the region's economic development, supported by the nature of the capital inflow into the region's economies. The state dominated Middle Eastern and North African economies in a way that was rivaled only by the economies of Eastern Europe and the former Soviet Union. Except in Lebanon the state acted as the primary agent for accumulating resources and allocating them to investment. The role of the state was abetted by the importance of public (official) external flows in financing public investments. In addition, private external flows, mainly in the form of worker remittances, were channeled into investments in nontradable sectors. With large portions of new investment going either to nontradables such as housing or quasi nontradables such as public industries protected by quantitative import restrictions, the economies of the region were ill-prepared to adapt to the terms of trade shocks of the 1980s.

Total factor productivity change

The residual measure of productivity derived from the cross-country regressions above is analogous to the more traditional concept of total factor productivity (TFP; see Pack and Page, 1994). This section uses a recent set of estimates of TFP to examine TFP change in the region in an international context (Nehru and Dareshwar, 1993). Figure 5.8 plots TFP growth rates for eighty-seven countries against relative income levels in 1960. The data show three things:

- The range of TFP growth rates for high-income countries is quite compact, especially compared with low- and middle-income countries.
- Nearly a third of the low- and middle-income countries in the sample had negative TFP growth rates during 1960–90.
- The low- and middle-income countries exhibit very little productivity-based "catch-up."

These are not promising results for the developing world. Despite considerable evidence on the potential for developing countries to achieve rapid growth through the adoption of known, best practice technolo-

Figure 5.8 Total factor productivity growth, 1960–90, and GDP per capita, 1960

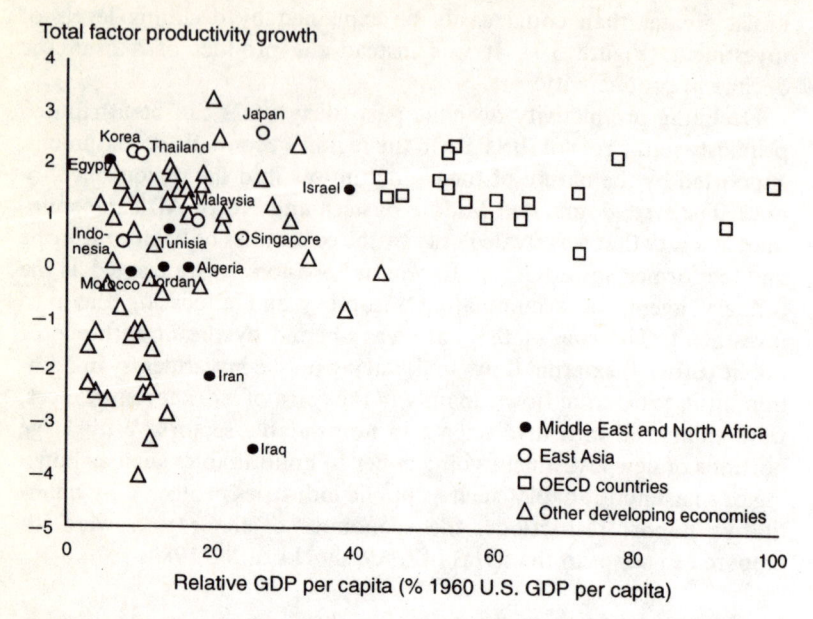

Source: Nehru and Dharesr, 1993.

gies, few countries have realized these potential gains.[5] Catch-up, where it occurs, is due primarily to higher rates of factor accumulation.

The Middle East and North Africa's TFP performance is typical of the pattern for low- and middle-income countries. Egypt has one of the highest TFP growth rates in the world – equal to that of Korea – but the other countries in the region have low or negative rates of TFP change. None is keeping pace with rates of productivity change in industrial economies, and hence any catch-up to high-income countries between 1960 and 1985 was wholly due to higher rates of accumulation.

Why does Egypt, where economic competitiveness has been a recurrent concern over the past ten years, do so well in these estimates? The answer is necessarily speculative; errors in data may be the cause. But there is also a plausible explanation based on more detailed TFP estimates for Egyptian industry (see Handoussa, Nishimizu, and Page, 1986). The "open door" policy of 1973 allowed rapid expansion of capacity by Egypt's public industrial sector and exposed it to external competition for the first time. This move resulted in rapid TFP change between 1973 and 1983 as output expanded without much expansion of investment or employment.

Jordan experienced rising TFP until 1980, but even at its peak the TFP growth rate was lower than that of the average OECD country. Productivity in Jordan has since fallen, and is now estimated to be less than 1 percent a year (World Bank, 1994). Tunisia's TFP growth rates exhibited a similar pattern. Estimates of TFP growth rates for Moroccan industry for 1985–90 validate the aggregate results. TFP growth at the sectoral level was close to zero, contrasted with OECD productivity growth rates in the same sectors in the range of 1–2 percent.

The state as entrepreneur

Of the nearly $55 billion that flowed into the Middle East and North Africa on a net basis during the 1970s, more than 90 percent accrued to the public sector. This inflow helped finance a rapid expansion of the region's public sectors. Public investment and total aid flows as a share of GDP for the Mashreq – Egypt, Jordan, and Syria – between 1970 and 1990 were closely correlated. Public investment rose when aid flows increased and fell when they diminished. Public money from external donors went into public projects.

Public investment as a share of GDP in the Middle East and North Africa has consistently been higher than the levels in other developing regions (Figure 5.9a). Between 1974 and 1982 there was a public investment boom in the Middle East, followed by a bust in the second half of the 1980s. Nevertheless, even today public investment remains substantially higher in the Middle East and North Africa than in any other part of the developing world.

By contrast, private investment in the Middle East and North Africa has been consistently lower than in the rest of the developing world (Figure 5.9b). East Asia and the Middle East and North Africa are mirror images when it comes to investment behavior. In the East Asian miracle economies private investment is the engine of growth, and has been for the past twenty years. While public investment as a share of GDP is about the same as the average for low- and middle-income countries, private investment is a stunning 7–10 percent higher. In the Middle East and North Africa private investment levels only reached the average of low- and middle-income countries in 1982 and remained similar thereafter.

Figure 5.9 Investment, various regions, 1970–88
(a) Public (b) Private

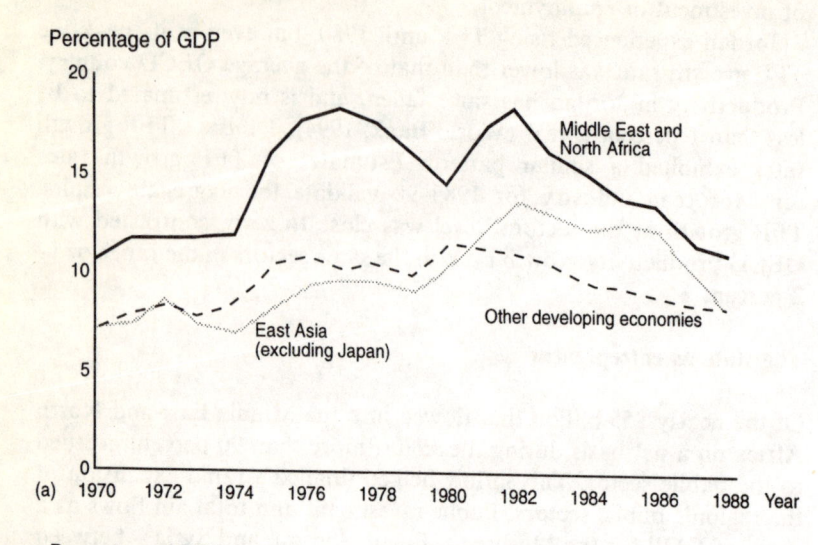

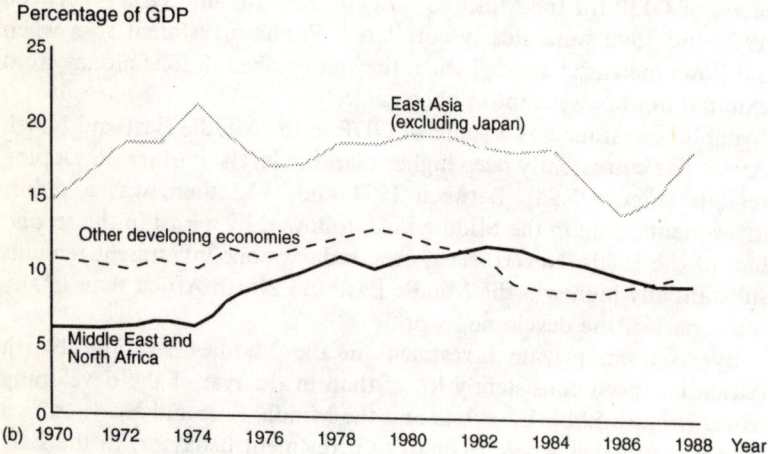

(a) Percentage of GDP — Middle East and North Africa; East Asia (excluding Japan); Other developing economies; 1970–1988.

(b) Percentage of GDP — East Asia (excluding Japan); Other developing economies; Middle East and North Africa; 1970–1988.

Sources: Diwan and Squire, 1992; World Bank data.

When the flow of official external capital began to shrink, inappropriate domestic policies were put in place to ration increasingly scarce resources, leading to an inefficient incentive regime, inflation, and capital flight. The magnitude of capital flight – the exodus of mainly private capital – attests to the private sector's unfavorable assessment of domestic policies. The average annual outflow in the 1980s is estimated at $1.6 billion in the Maghreb and $4.5 billion in the Mashreq.

Building houses and blocking imports – investment in nontradables

In the past remittances from workers abroad have been the most important source of external funding for the private sector throughout the Middle East and North Africa. Migration has played an important role in alleviating pressures in domestic labor markets and redistributing wealth from the oil-rich countries of the Gulf to the labor-surplus countries of the Mashreq. Remittances have been substantial, especially for Egypt, Jordan, and Lebanon. In the Mashreq, the major labor-exporting group of countries in the region, remittances have stayed above 10 percent of GDP since the late 1970s.

Two factors – the investment preferences of migrants and the incentive structures of the region's economies – combined to channel a disproportionate share of the region's investment into nontradable goods. Comparing five Middle Eastern and North African countries (Algeria, Egypt, Indonesia, Jordan, and Tunisia) and two East Asian ones (Indonesia and Korea), only Tunisia's share of gross investment in tradables and nontradables was comparable to East Asia's. All the other countries in the region put more than two-thirds of their total investment into nontradables.

Much of this investment went toward housing. Middle Eastern and North African economies are, by and large, better housed than other countries at similar income levels. This higher level of housing reflects the preference of migrants for housing investments; target savings for home construction are an important motivation for many migrants from the Mashreq to the Gulf and from the Maghreb to Europe.

But the high rates of investment in nontradables also reflect an incentive regime that favors other nontraded goods. The high levels of exogenous inflows of foreign exchange from natural resources, official flows, and migrant remittances have pushed real exchange rates lower, moving incentives in favor of nontraded goods production. Governments have responded to this Dutch disease by increasing the effective exchange rate for importables through high tariffs and quantitative import restrictions.

Measures of real exchange rate overvaluation are notoriously difficult to construct and interpret. Dollar (1990) uses the international comparisons of price levels for 121 countries compiled by Heston and

Summers (1988) to construct an index of "outward orientation." But Rodrik (1993) argues that the Dollar index actually measures exchange rate misalignment. If this is true, the region's economies are the worst-performing in the world (except for Sub-Saharan Africa) with respect to exchange rate management. When excess demand for foreign exchange emerges governments in the Middle East and North Africa have usually responded by maintaining a fixed nominal exchange rate and introducing or increasing trade and foreign exchange controls. Exportables are therefore doubly unprotected, denied both a competitive exchange rate and neutral relative incentives.

During the 1960s and 1970s governments in the region also made extensive use of quantitative restrictions to limit competition between imports and public industrial enterprises. The legacy of such policies persisted into the 1980s, with manufacturing being shielded by higher levels of protection (through nontariff barriers) than in other regions (Figure 5.10). Quantitative restrictions on imports break the link between international and domestic prices and effectively convert tradable goods into nontradables. Over time they also tend to diminish incentives for cost discipline and technological upgrading, resulting in lagging productivity growth (Nishimizu and Page, 1991).

The consequence of the region's tilt toward nontradables during the boom was that when the major terms of trade shock (embodied in a drop in oil prices) hit, the region's production structures were not sufficiently agile to shift production toward other tradable goods.

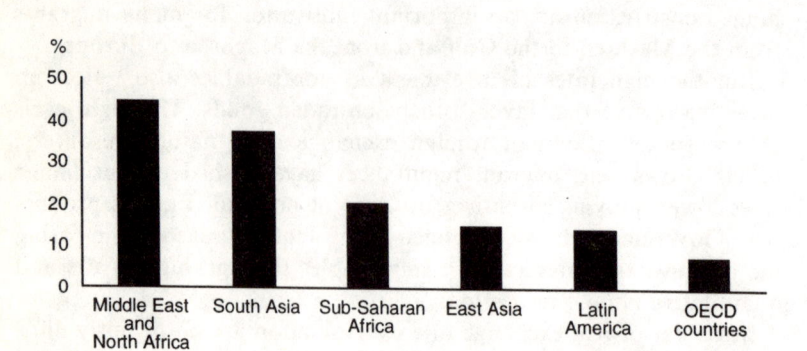

Figure 5.10 Quota coverage, various regions, 1985–88

Source: World Bank data.

Thus expenditure switching policies were of limited usefulness, and the major burden of adjustment fell on expenditure reduction. External demand could not substitute quickly for domestic demand, exports did not respond to exchange rate changes, and domestic economic activity contracted dramatically. Moreover, lagging productivity growth in the region's industrial base meant that regional industries were losing cost competitiveness more or less continuously during the boom. Real wages had to fall substantially – as they did in Egypt, Jordan, Morocco, and Tunisia – to restore competitiveness.

COMING BACK – RESTORING LONG-TERM GROWTH

Restoring long-run growth to the region will require increasing investment and improving productivity. The key reforms necessary to increase the quantity of private investment are well known. Macroeconomic stability, an incentive structure conducive to private sectordevelopment, a transparent regulatory framework, and an open trading environment are the elements that have proved successful elsewhere – notably in East Asia – in securing private sector-led growth.

Where will more investment come from?

Financing for higher rates of investment could come from domestic or external sources. While there is room for redirecting public expendi-

Figure 5.11 Total aid, worker remittances, and foreign direct investment in the Maghreb, 1970–90

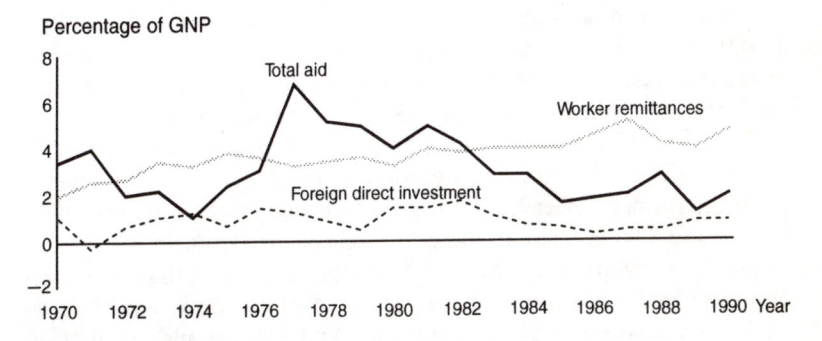

Source: World Bank data.

Figure 5.12 Total aid, worker remittances, and foreign direct investment in the Mashreq, 1970–90

Source: World Bank data.

tures, the scope for increased public savings is limited by the need to maintain consumption levels. Thus external financing will continue to be necessary. Figures 5.11 and 5.12 attempt to put the external financing picture into historical perspective. Each figure – one for the Maghreb and the other for the Mashreq – shows foreign aid, workers remittances, and foreign direct investment. While the historical experiences of the two groups differ in detail – for example, foreign direct investment is substantially more important in the Maghreb – they tell a similar story. Aid has fallen as a source of investment, remittances have remained constant, and foreign investment has increased, but only slowly.

Circumstances are unlikely to allow countries to regain the levels of public sector financing achieved in the late 1970s. Assistance from Arab, OECD, and multilateral sources is likely to be constrained. The Soviet Union and the former Eastern European bloc have ceased to be a source of capital and are, indeed, now competing for the limited quantities of international assistance. Relatively low oil prices, the fall in reserves resulting from the Gulf war, and rising domestic expenditures make it unlikely that Arab aid will increase dramatically in the near future. OECD countries are facing the dual problem of difficult domestic fiscal situations and extraordinary demands for assistance from the former Soviet Union and Eastern Europe. Multilateral institutions are also unlikely to increase levels of net flows. In some cases multilateral institutions have reached exposure levels that limit new lending.[6] In the Mashreq – the region to which aid flows have historically been most significant – flows from Arab sources and members of the Council for Mutual Economic Assistance declined substantially during the 1980s, and a modest rise in assistance from the OECD countries has failed to offset this decline.

Thus revenue-raising efforts should focus on private flows. Private capital flows from the Gulf could be significant. The considerable private assets held in OECD countries could be attracted to the labor-surplus countries of the region if conditions are sufficiently appealing. The Gulf war, with its attendant movement in populations, dramatically reduced the level of remittances as Iraq, Kuwait, and Saudi Arabia released millions of Arab workers. For example, about 300,000 people returned to Jordan during 1990–91. Despite an increase in intra-Arab migration since 1993, the evidence points to one fairly robust conclusion-remittances will decline as a share of GNP.

In the Gulf a mixture of political considerations and underlying economic fundamentals suggests that, while the nonnational labor force will continue to expand, the share of Arab migrants will continue to fall (World Bank, 1995). For example, if the nonnational labor force grows at the 1985–90 rate of 3 percent a year and the Gulf crisis results in an Arab share of only 20 percent, the 1995 number of Arab migrants in the Gulf would be well below the 1990 number. On the other hand better economic performance in the labor-surplus countries and hence better investment opportunities may encourage more remittances per worker. Continued growth in the Gulf should also translate into higher remittances per worker. The most favorable scenario is for remittances to stabilize at their current level, implying a steady decline relative to GNP.

Non-Arab portfolio and foreign direct investment could provide another channel for financing the restoration of growth. The region's track record in attracting foreign investment flows is poor, however, and capital flows have failed to keep pace with the globalization of financial markets. Portfolio investments to developing countries grew rapidly in the 1990s but have mainly gone to East Asia and Latin America. The Middle East and North Africa's ability to attract foreign direct investment FDI – critical for providing technology and skills – has been similarly disappointing, falling in the 1990s to levels comparable with Sub-Saharan Africa. Morocco has had some success in attracting foreign investment recently, but this has been more than offset by declining flows to Algeria and Egypt. The recent signing of association agreements with the European Union by Morocco and Tunisia and their eventual adoption by Egypt and Jordan may stimulate foreign investment, but without major changes in national financial markets and foreign investment regimes their impact is likely to be small (Page and Underwood, 1995).

Where can the region turn for increased investment in the short term? The recent exodus of private capital provides a potential solution. Residents of the region hold an estimated $100–500 billion in savings abroad (Diwan and Squire, 1992). For some countries – Egypt, Jordan, Syria – the amount exceeds GDP. International experience points to two factors that are critical in attracting flight capital back to the originating country. One is appropriate domestic economic policies. The other is an acceptable degree of international creditworthiness. These two elements are also the key elements in attracting foreign direct investment.

How can investment be made more efficient?

Greater volumes of investment alone will not allow a resurgence of growth to the levels needed in the region. The growth crisis is, after all, also a crisis of productivity. Increasing productivity requires improving the allocation of resources among sectors – moving resources to

Figure 5.13 Total factor productivity growth, 1969–89, and share of manufactured exports in total exports, 1960–85

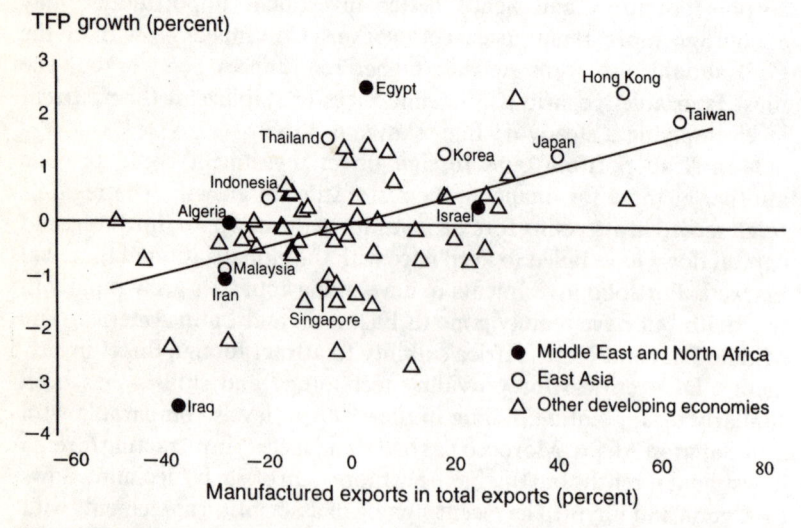

Note: TFP growth and manufactured exports in total exports are orthangonal on income per capita relative to the United States in 1960 (*RGDP60*), primary school enrollment in 1960 (*PRIM60*), and average rate of investment during 1960–85 (*NV6085*).
Source: Page, 1994.

areas of greater competitiveness – and increasing the productivity of individual firms and industries. International comparative studies suggest that the key to improving both dimensions of productivity is greater integration with the world economy.

Trade could be a major source of productivity growth, since import competition and exports enforce cost discipline and foster innovation. Manufactured exports are a powerful source of learning, especially where there are significant buyer – seller links between industrial and developing economies (World Bank, 1996; Pack and Page, 1994). There is a strong empirical association between economic growth and both the level of integration with the international economy and its rate of change. Figure 5.13 shows one effort to explain variations in TFP growth in terms of the share of manufactured exports in total exports (see Page, 1994). The figure is a partial scatter of the rate of TFP growth on the share of manufactured exports in total exports, controlling for three factors that are thought to influence TFP change – income relative to the United States in 1960, primary school enrollment in 1960, and average rate of investment during 1960–85. The estimated linear rela-

Figure 5.14 Changes in real trade, various regions, 1960–94

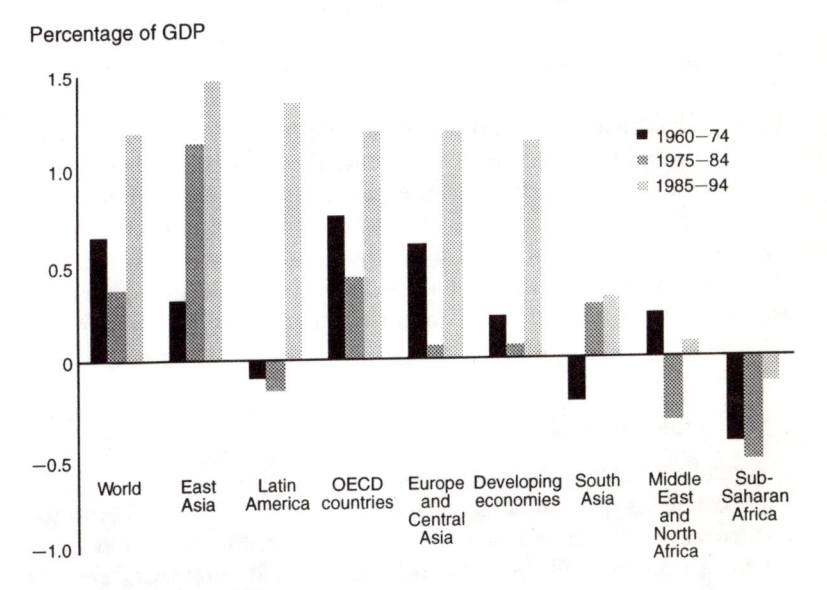

Source: World Bank, 1996.

tionship fits the data rather well and shows two important things. First, as the share of manufactured exports in total exports increases, the rate of productivity change increases. Second, Middle Eastern and North African countries are near the extreme low end of the distribution in terms of their (orthogonal) shares of manufactured exports.

The Middle East and North Africa has failed to keep pace with the changing global economy. While trade has risen rapidly in other parts of the world – especially over the past ten years – the region's trade has stagnated (Figure 5.14). Intraregional trade has stayed at less than 10 percent of total trade since the mid-1980s. Manufactured exports per capita have stagnated. World trade in 2000–10 is projected to grow at nearly 6 percent; in the Middle East and North Africa it is expected to grow by just 3.5 percent (World Bank, 1994).

The region's economies are still quite closed. Average tariffs are high, and nontariff barriers remain important in some countries (World Bank, 1994). Institutions that facilitate trade – customs, financial services, export promotion – are far less developed than in the rapidly integrating economies of East Asia and Latin America. Although Morocco and Tunisia have recently signed integration agreements with the European Union and Egypt and Jordan are negotiating agreements, the slow pace of trade liberalization allowed under the European treaties will continue to allow the region to lag behind.

Policies to restore growth

Raising investment rates and enhancing productivity will require sustained efforts by governments in at least three areas. Increasing private investment flows will require removing the state from many activities and refocusing its efforts into others. The business environment must be improved for both foreign and domestic private investors. Improving productivity may be most quickly achieved through an export-push strategy that increases integration with the world economy.

Reducing the role of the state

The public sectors in the Middle East and North Africa remain large. Algeria and Egypt have levels of public ownership comparable to the transition economies of Eastern Europe. Jordan, Morocco, and Tunisia have smaller public sectors, but state-owned enterprises are still large compared with Latin America or East Asia. The state-including the public administration – plays a large role in the formal labor market. The state dominates the financial sector (through public commercial banks) in all countries except Jordan and Lebanon. Accelerated privatization, both as a signal of government commitment to private sector development and to reduce costs to the private sector of publicly provided goods and services, is therefore critical.

Fiscal constraints will limit further investment in industrial capacity by governments in the region, but they will also limit the expansion of infrastructure. Strategies that attract private investment in infrastructure are therefore critical, but are underdeveloped in all the countries of the region. Egypt and Morocco have announced some limited concessions in power generation. Jordan is moving slowly to privatize telecommunications. But the impact of these initiatives is limited by their slow implementation and partial nature.

Empowering the private sector

Attracting a reflow of flight capital and channeling private investment into efficient activities are critical if growth is to resume. Key elements of this process for all countries in the region include:

- Reforming regulatory, legal, and civil service frameworks to reduce the administrative burden on the private sector, secure contracts and property rights, and promote competition.
- Improving supervision and prudential regulation of the banking system, increasing entry of foreign banks, and privatizing state banks to promote competition and increase efficiency.
- Fostering the concept of public–private partnerships among the region's civil services and political elites to promote rapid growth while preserving social equity.

Pushing exports

Successful exporters in East Asia have used four tools that are absent from most of the region's economies:

- Gradual but sustained reductions in domestic protection, increasing the relative incentives for investment in exports.
- Automatic and timely duty free access to intermediate and capital goods for exporters through well-functioning duty drawback and temporary admission schemes.

- Automatic access to export financing at competitive interest rates.
- Sustained attention by governments to improving the institutions – from export promotion agencies to customs services – that affect the daily business lives of the export community.

None of these policy actions is beyond the capacity of Middle Eastern and North African governments. But none has pursued them aggressively. If the crisis of diminished expectations in the region is to be addressed, more must be done. The region's economic boom carried with it the seeds of its economic collapse. Restoring growth cannot be achieved with business as usual – it will require fundamental economic reform.

Notes

1. Dollar (1991) finds a similar pattern using a sample of 114 countries and the absolute level of per capita income in 1960, though he finds a clearer pattern in which the poorest countries have the lowest per capita income growth rates, middle-income countries have the highest, and high-income countries are in between. However, he also reports low significance of his regression results.
2. Because the timing and frequency of observations on income distribution vary among the countries in the sample, the ratio of the top to bottom quintile is taken at the date closest to the midpoint.
3. The studies cited have introduced other variables to address different questions-equipment investment (De Long and Summers, 1991), trade orientation (Dollar, 1991), and endogenous investment (Barro, 1990). These variables are not included here.
4. The magnitude of the coefficient on investment (INV) is similar to that reported by Dollar (1991) for a sample of 114 economies (0.113). The magnitude of the coefficient for education ($PRIM$) is about half that given in Dollar's results, and the coefficient for the relative gap between 1960 per capita income and U.S. per capita income ($RGDP60$) is similar to the results obtained by Dollar and by De Long and Summers (*1991*).
5. For a concise review of the arguments for technologically-based catchup see Pack (1993c).
6. In others, such as the Arab multilaterals, new lending is limited by capital constraints.

References

Barro, Robert J., 1990. "Government Spending in a Simple Model of Endogenous Growth," *Journal of Political Economy*, 98 (5, pt.2):S103–25.
——— 1991. "Economic Growth in a Cross Section of Countries," *Quarterly Journal of Economics*, 105(2):407–43.

Barro, Robert J. and Jong-Wha Lee, 1993. "International Comparisons of Educational Attainment," paper presented at a conference on how national policies affect long-run growth sponsored by the World Bank (February), Washington D.C.

De Long, J. Bradford, and Lawrence H. Summers. 1991. "Equipment Investment and Economic Growth," *Quarterly Journal of Economics* 106(2):445–502.

Diwan, Ishac and Lyn Squire, 1992. "Economic and Social Development in the Middle East and North Africa," *Middle East and North Africa Discussion Paper*, 3., Washington, D.C.: World Bank.

Dollar, David, 1990. "Outward Orientation and Growth: An Empirical Study Using a Price-Based Measure of Openness," World Bank, East Asia and Pacific Region, Country Department I, Washington, D.C.

────── 1991. "Exploiting the Advantages of Backwardness: The Importance of Education and Outward Orientation," Washington, D.C.: World Bank.

Easterly, William, Michael Kremer, Lant Pritchett, and Lawrence H. Summers, 1993. "Good Policy or Good Luck? Country Growth Performance and Temporary Shocks," paper presented at a conference on how national policies affect long-run growth sponsored by the World Bank (February), Washington, D.C.

Handoussa, Heba, Mieko Nishimizu, and John M. Page Jr, 1986. "Productivity Change in Egyptian Public Sector Industries After the Opening, 1973–1979," *Journal of Development Economics* 20:53–73.

Heston, Alan and Robert Summers, 1988. "A New Set of International Comparisons of Real Product and Prices: Estimates for 130 Countries," *Review of Income and Wealth*, 34(1):1–25.

Mankiw, N. Gregory, David Romer, and David Weil, 1992. "A Contribution to the Empirics of Economic Growth," *Quarterly Journal of Economics*, 107(2):407–38.

Nehru, Vikram and Ashok Dhareshwar, 1993. "A New Database on Physical Capital Stock: Sources, Methodology, and Results," Washington, D.C.: World Bank.

Nishimizu, Mieko and John M. Page Jr., 1991. "Trade Policy, Market Orientation and Productivity Change in Industry," in Jaime de Melo and Andres Sapir, (eds.), *Trade Theory and Economic Reform: North, South and East: Essays in Honor of Bela Balassa*, Oxford: Basil Blackwell.

Pack, Howard, 1993a. "Exports and Externalities: The Source of Taiwan's Growth in Taiwan," Philadelphia: University of Pennsylvania.

────── 1993b. "Industrial and Trade Policies in the High Performing Asian Economies," background paper prepared for *The East Asian Miracle*, World Bank, Policy Research Department, Washington, D.C.

────── 1993c. "Technology Gaps between Industrial and Developing Countries: Are There Dividends for Latecomers?," In Lawrence H. Summers and Shekhar Shah (eds.), *Proceedings of the World Bank Annual Conference on Development Economics 1992*, Washington, D.C.: World Bank

Pack, Howard and John M. Page Jr., 1994. "Accumulation, Exports and Growth in the High-Performing Asian Economies," *Carnegie–Rochester Conference Series on Public Policy* 40:199–236.

Page, John M., Jr., 1994. "The East Asian Miracle: Four Lessons for Development Policy," in Stanley Fischer and Julio J. Rotemberg (eds.), *NBER Macroeconomics Annual, 1994*, Cambridge, Mass: MIT Press.

Page, John M., Jr., and John Underwood, 1995. "Growth, the Maghreb and the European Union: Assessing The Impact of the Free Trade Agreements on Tunisia and Morocco," paper prepared for the International Economic Association's Eleventh World Congress, Tunis.

Rodrik, Dani., 1993. "King Kong Meets Godzilla: The World Bank and *The East Asian Miracle*," paper prepared for the Overseas Development Council, New York.

Summers, Robert and Alan Heston, 1991. "The Penn World Tables (Mark 5): An Expanded Set of International Comparisons, 1950-88," *Quarterly Journal of Economics*, 105(2).

World Bank, 1994. "Jordan: Consolidating Economic Adjustment and Establishing the Base for Sustainable Growth," Middle East and North Africa Region, Washington, D.C.: World Bank.

——— 1995. *Claiming the Future: Choosing Prosperity in the Middle East and North Africa*, Middle East and North Africa Region, Washington D.C.: World Bank.

——— 1996. *Global Economic Prospects and the Developing Countries*, International Economics Department, Washington, D.C.: World Bank.

6 The State and Economic Transition in the Middle East and North Africa

John Waterbury

The pace and structure of transition and reform in the Middle East and North Africa are a source of frustration for members of the international donor and financial communities. Some countries in the region have made strides toward market-oriented policies and institutions, only to backpedal when faced with difficult economic choices. Other countries have avoided institutional and structural transformation, or been absorbed in the exigencies of a war economy. Whatever the approach, crises eventually force fiscal and political adjustment.

This chapter assesses the region's unique prospects and challenges, and the likelihood of a more rapid pace for reform. Leaders will have to adjust their approaches to respond to regional conflicts, the rise of political Islam, and the search for new sources of revenue. In addition, more vocal citizenries and human capital investment needs will require more responsive and accountable governments. Still, the region's cultural and political traditions are deeply entrenched, making rapid transformation unlikely.

In recent years the World Bank and other institutions in the international donor and financial communities have expressed general dissatisfaction with the economic performance of the countries in the Middle East and North Africa. Implicitly or explicitly, these complaints suggest that the donor community's efforts to promote reform in the region have been inadequate.

Are these observers bothered by the rate of change, or by the quality of change? If it is the rate of change, this implies that the region is an underachiever relative to its factor endowments. This understanding suggests that the policy pieces are in place, but that a sense of urgency and political will are not. But if the problem is one of quality, the challenge is far more structural, involving issues of institutions, governance, and culture. The solution to a quality problem demands far more than political will and a heightened sense of urgency.

Of course, it is somewhat artificial to separate the issues that determine the quality of reform from those that determine the pace of reform, for the two may be intimately linked. It is also artificial to separate political and economic reforms. Yet in the Middle East and North Africa these distinctions are warranted and useful.

I have argued elsewhere that the Middle East and North Africa may be characterized by a type of exceptional politics that will make the transition to greater accountability and democracy relatively difficult (Waterbury, 1994). I do not believe, however, that this exceptionalism extends to the economic sphere. Thus I view the problems facing the region mainly as one of the rate of change.

CHANGE HAS BENEFITS – AND COSTS

What are the costs of underachieving or lagging behind? As important, what are the benefits? Lagging means falling behind in the global competition for enhanced efficiency, technology, and dynamic comparative advantage. But moving ahead too quickly also has costs. Since the 1950s India has maintained its "Hindu rate of growth." India could have done much better, but it has chosen to grow slowly in order to maintain political stability and sustainable growth. What unacceptable costs could be attributed to this underachieving that would convince Indian politicians to move more urgently?

Mexico, on the other hand, has forced the pace of change – and appears to be paying a heavy price for it. It could be argued that Mexico is paying the price of success, and that it got most of its fundamentals right. But Egypt could defend its slow and cautious approach by pointing out that it has protected its economy from "hot money," sudden explosions in inflation, and the dumping of thousands of workers into the ranks of the unemployed.

To recapitulate: if the problem is one of culture, institutions, and governance, the challenge is long term and not well suited to the kinds of advice the World Bank provides. If it is one of the rate of change, then we have to ask how bad 'slow' is: what are the real costs of what Richards (1991) called dilatory reform?

Each country follows its own path

The Middle East and North Africa is more economically diverse now than at any time in the past fifty years. During the 1950s, 1960s, and 1970s the dominant development paradigm was based on import-substituting industrialization and corporatist, authoritarian politics. Some regimes called themselves socialist, others did not, but the differences among Egypt, Iran, Jordan, Morocco, Sudan, and Tunisia were less pronounced than their shared political and economic characteristics. In many ways pre-Likud Israel (that is, pre-1977) could be placed in this group as well.

The economic crises of the late 1970s and early 1980s shattered this paradigm. Economic strategies were overhauled, but no new dominant model emerged. Israel and Turkey became the region's earliest and most determined reformers, reining in their public sectors, stimulating their private sectors, and aggressively promoting exports. Egypt sought to develop a protected private sector without diminishing the size of its public sector. Algeria initially sought reform by fragmenting the public sector. Iraq went to war, Syria toyed with "crony capitalism" within a state-dominated economy, Lebanon dissolved into civil war, and the Sudanese economy collapsed.

Politically, homogeneity reigned. Until the late 1980s authoritarian police states remained the order of the day. Except for Turkey (and Israel, which has avoided authoritarianism), none of the countries has made a credible move away from that model. The alternative to authoritarianism has not been democracy, but rather civil war or the partial collapse of the authoritarian state: witness Algeria, Iraq, Sudan, and the two Yemens. Still, generalizations are risky. Each countries' experience with economic reform has been different.

Toward what targets should the region's economies be headed? Ratios (debt–GDP, primary deficit–GDP, exports–GDP, tradables and nontradables–GDP), inflation, unemployment, literacy rates, and infant mortality rates all measure economic and social progress, but in different ways. I have not seen any work from the World Bank that examines the tradeoffs involved in moving toward progress on all fronts. The general view is that all ships rise with the tide, and that the tide is driven by the four ratios listed above.

The move to market depends on initial conditions

In comparing Middle Eastern and North African countries, both among themselves and with other developing countries, it is important to define the initial conditions for reform, the dynamics of transition, and the success or failure in transforming institutions. Initial conditions must be carefully specified so that the pace and nature of transition can be estimated. Inasmuch as the initial conditions are highly diverse, so too are the pace and nature of the transitions.

Among the Middle East and North African countries, Morocco has the oldest and most experienced entrepreneurial bourgeoisie. It was well entrenched long before the establishment of the French Protectorate in 1912 and managed to survive the colonial experience with most of its assets intact. As a result of its early progress, Morocco is structurally and ideologically better positioned to promote market-oriented reforms than any other country in the region. It is not surprising that Morocco has been successful in its efforts to stabilize and open its economy; rather it is surprising that it has not gone further.

If the region's viable private sectors are placed along a continuum, Turkey, Morocco, and Israel appear to the left – manifesting the highest viability – with Iran somewhat to their right. All the other major countries in the region, despite efforts to stimulate their private sectors, fall to the far right of the scale.

Egypt set the development pattern for several Middle East and North African countries (Algeria, Iraq, Libya, Sudan, Syria, North Yemen, and even Tunisia). This pattern involved partial expropriation of foreign and indigenous private interests and the construction of a large public sector to control industry, banking, and external trade. Socialist – populist ideologies were used to justify the anti-private sector ideologies and redistributive policies of these regimes.

Dealing with crisis

Because those who benefit from the status quo have no incentive to change it, change – in this case the move toward transition – is unusual, perhaps even unnatural. A transition may develop from enlightened self-interest on the part of key actors, but that is unlikely. Rather, it is generally crisis that leads beneficiaries to espouse or promote change. Thus the agents of change must be clear on the nature of the crises, how they are perceived by leadership, and how they are first addressed.

Crisis is a perceptual phenomenon. Objective measures do not determine what is and is not politically sustainable. Sudan has been in economic crisis since the late 1970s; but only in 1985 did it force a change of government – and even then it may have been more

Nimeiri's increasing flight from reality than the economic situation that accounted for his deposition.

Crises may be perceived as conjunctural, and hence remediable through temporary emergency measures. When crises are perceived as structural, the question becomes whether to deal with them gradually or all at once. The approach chosen – and several in between – does not obviate further crises but rather determines their characteristics.

Matters have to get very bad for far-reaching and accelerated change to take place. Turkey's triple-digit inflation and debt crisis in 1979 provided the impetus for the reforms undertaken over the next five years. The collapse of oil prices and the bloody riots of 1988 drove Algerians to accelerate a process that had begun more cautiously around 1982. The beginning of the *intifada* in 1987, the termination of Saudi assistance in 1988, and the halving of worker remittances between 1986 and 1991 pushed Jordan to adopt a serious stabilization plan.

It is easier for challengers to the status quo to benefit from a crisis than it is for political incumbents. The Turkish generals in 1980 (and Turgut Özal after 1983) could blame economic and political crises on their predecessors and claim that the social pain brought by reforms should be attributed to them as well. Crises are thus almost always political as well as economic. Sudden changes in inflation and unemployment generally set the economic context, while near-civil war (as in Turkey in 1978–79), riots (Jordan and Algeria in 1988), or a revolt of the professional classes (Sudan in 1985) set the political context.

Incumbents are doubly handicapped if they must admit to and deal with crises. First, they must assume some of the blame for the situation (unless it is clearly the result of something beyond their control, such as falling oil prices or rising interest rates among their principal trading partners). Second, dealing with the crisis may require striking at the foundations of the coalitional interests that helped keep them in power in the first place. This is the dilemma of Hafez al-Assad (Syria) or Hosni Mubarek (Egypt), but if the crisis is sufficiently profound – as in Algeria in 1988 – then even an incumbent like Chedli Ben Jdid can take bold measures to deal with it. The lesson that the World Bank and other reformers might draw from this is that it is best to either advise challengers once they have taken power, or to wait for the crisis to deepen until the incumbents have no choice but to deal with it.

Such crises, curiously, engender creative activity. Through broadly based economic stress, they numb the population as a whole and disarm the defenders of the status quo, which is no longer viable. It is in such a situation that incumbents can risk far-reaching change. Those who do so successfully form small, technocratic "change teams" that transform general reform directives into policy. They control key financial and economic agencies (the central bank, the ministry of finance, the planning agency, the ministry of commerce, and so on). If backed by the head of state, such teams can push through a reform package that neither mass constituencies nor entrenched beneficiaries will have the power or the legitimacy to fight (see Waterbury, 1993).

For many years the change team brought together in Mexico by Pedro Aspe and Carlos Salinas was the quintessence of this model. Perhaps the first model was the "Berkeley mafia" recruited after 1965 by President Suharto of Indonesia. More recently and less emphatically, Prime Minister Rao of India has used Manmohan Singh and Montek Ahluwalia to play a similar role. In the Middle East only Turkey, in the mid-1980s, assembled a change team. Özal placed Ruştu Saracoğlu, Ali Tigrel, Yavuz Canevi, Bülent Gültekin, and others in key policy positions that allowed institutional transformation to begin. Elsewhere in the region, no other head of state has adopted a reform program as his own. Without that kind of support, technocrats will not risk their careers and reputations in the name of structural reforms.

In democratic or democratizing systems, the first generation of reformers may sacrifice itself politically or, sensing its dwindling popular support, seek salvation by watering down or abandoning the reform program. In 1989 Turgut Özal, who relinquished the prime ministership to become president, to some extent washed his hands of his change team, of his Motherland Party, and of his reform program. Political leaders who do not have the hubris to believe that they will survive will never initiate the reform process. Even under authoritarian systems, their chances of survival are not good. But politicians, we should perhaps be thankful, do not always think comparatively.

The World Bank does not have a lot of choices in these matters. It is unthinkable that the World Bank would stand aside so that a crisis could deepen sufficiently to allow it to leverage bold reform measures. Only if a country fails to meet its obligations to the international financial institutions – as has Sudan – can they stand aside. Failing that, the institutions are forced to help incumbents mitigate crises without really dealing with their structural causes. The crisis may thus merely be postponed. This form of interaction characterizes the World

Bank's and the U.S. Agency for International Development's dealings with Egypt.

PATHS TO TRANSFORMATION

A schematized representation of possible transitions can be built around two variables: the quality of government and the coherence of macroeconomic policy (Figure 6.1). The assumption is that good governments can do a lot with bad policies, as the Republic of Korea did with its drive into shipbuilding and heavy chemicals in the late 1970s, and that bad governments can wreck good macroeconomic policies. The transition paths in Figure 6.1 lead, more or less rapidly or in a more or less crisis-driven way, to institutional transformation.

Depending on the size and weight of the public sector, the necessary and sufficient components of successful transition consist of:

- Proper macroeconomic policies centered on hard budget constraints.

Figure 6.1 Pathways to institutional change

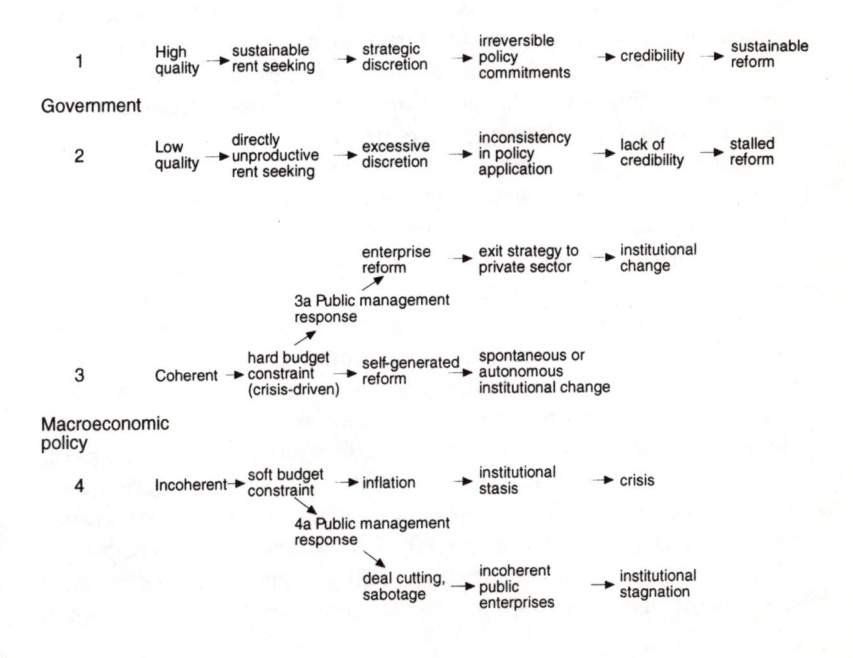

Government
1. High quality → sustainable rent seeking → strategic discretion → irreversible policy commitments → credibility → sustainable reform
2. Low quality → directly unproductive rent seeking → excessive discretion → inconsistency in policy application → lack of credibility → stalled reform

Macroeconomic policy
3. Coherent → hard budget constraint (crisis-driven) → self-generated reform
   3a Public management response → enterprise reform → exit strategy to private sector → institutional change
   → spontaneous or autonomous institutional change
4. Incoherent → soft budget constraint → inflation → institutional stasis → crisis
   4a Public management response → deal cutting, sabotage → incoherent public enterprises → institutional stagnation

- Incentives and regulatory changes that encourage private sector growth.
- Benign neglect of public enterprises so that in relative terms they are constantly losing ground to the private sector. Where the public sector is very large, as in Egypt, and generating constant demands for significant budgetary transfers, benign neglect may not be possible without risking a surge in the public deficit, monetization of the domestic debt, and the crowding out of the private sector. But even in Egypt it may be more important to get macroeconomic policies right than to tinker with the reform or restructuring of public enterprises in order to privatize them.

Figure 6.1 assumes that some forms of rent-seeking are inevitable, but that they can be contained so as not to cripple reform. It also assumes that some government discretion (or lack of transparency) is both inevitable and desirable – politics without discretion is an oxymoron. The newly industrializing economies of East Asia are instructive in this respect: rife with rents, policy discretion, and opaque procedures. We can describe their success but not fully explain it.

Path 1 assumes an effective government apparatus that is able to monitor and discipline its own agents so that rent-seeking does not cripple economic reforms. It is a government that retains means of intervention (some public credit, tariff policy, regulation, monetary policy, and even industrial policy) so that it can use discretion in a growth-promoting way. This government makes policy commitments that are credible and, hence, the reform process is sustainable. The Mexican government followed this path between 1985 and the spring of 1994, and it may get back on it fairly quickly.

Path 2 assumes an ineffective government in which rent-seeking is crippling (or directly unproductive; see Bhagwati, 1982), a fact that may be explained by or is the result of excessive policy discretion (instead of picking winners, the government picks favorites). Policies and policy implementation are, or are perceived to be, inconsistent, resulting in a lack of credibility in the government's commitment to particular policies and to the reform process as a whole. Reforms stall and the economy returns to crisis. Turkey has followed this path, having launched a reform process in response to the 1979 crisis and, between 1987 and 1994, drifting back to crisis as political expedience drained the government's reform effort of coherence and credibility.

Next is macroeconomic strategy. Paths 3 and 4 are determined by coherent and incoherent strategies, and each contains a subpath delineating how public officials and managers behave in the two scenarios. Path 3 assumes coherent economic strategy and an effective government apparatus. Together the two apply hard budget constraints to both public and private enterprises. The move to hard budget constraints may be crisis-driven – such constraints are seldom adopted merely because they make good economic sense. Faced with hard budget constraints, managers seek ways to reform their enterprises to ensure financial survival. Alternatively, they prepare their firms for privatization and try to ensure their own survival in the new property regime. Paths 3 and 3a thus produce an internally generated, or spontaneous, set of changes that ultimately leads to institutional transformation, bringing with it fundamental changes in public and private balances, in the functioning of financial intermediation, in contract practices, and in the behavior of firms.

In the Middle East, only Turkey moved a good distance along path 3 before reversing the steps it had taken. Israel might appear to have kept to this path since 1977, but its extraordinary level of strategic rents per capita and as a share of gross domestic product (GDP) makes it less clear how far it has actually gone.

Path 4 assumes incoherent macroeconomic strategy and a government lacking a credible commitment to reform. No effective hard budget constraints are introduced. The banking system, whether public or private, is laden with nonperforming loans and is essentially insolvent, as are its principal clients in the public and private sectors. Public managers and private interests respond to their principals' lack of credibility by cutting deals with them and by sabotaging whatever reform measures are taken (for example, public enterprises deliberately take on more debt in order to stave off privatization). Public firms undertake no meaningful reforms, so firms of varying technological obsolescence clutter the landscape. The initial result is institutional stagnation, followed by crisis. Egypt has traveled paths 4 and 4a, although the anticipated crisis has been repeatedly postponed.

As mentioned earlier, the international financial institutions must decide whether to wait until the crisis deepens, and then bring their full weight to bear to accelerate the reform process, or to help the dilatory reform muddle along. But there really is no choice; help for muddlers cannot be avoided. The real question is, can it do some good?

The paths in Figure 6.1 are descriptive in that they do not explain why a government develops the policy coherence and efficacy to proceed down path 1 or, conversely, to proceed down path 4. It is easier to explain – and achieve – institutional stagnation than sustainable reform, but regardless of the path that is initially pursued, the endpoint is either institutional transformation, or deep crisis followed by institutional transformation. A kind of inevitability is at work. It can be obfuscated by oil or strategic rents, but the real questions are how quickly the crisis will manifest itself, what measures the government will adopt to avoid it, and how politically difficult it will be to manage once it has been declared.

LEGACIES OF THE WAR ECONOMY

Until now I have treated the Middle East and North Africa as if it were a regional cluster of states without discernible cultural and institutional peculiarities. In fact, the region exhibits both. The most important factor affecting the region is the incidence of war, both conventional and civil, that has been experienced since 1948.[1] Few families in the Middle East have not been touched by bloody conflict. Only China, North and South Korea, and Vietnam can claim such a violent recent past. This fact both shapes the style of political leadership and participation and establishes patterns of resource use that appear to inhibit growth.[2] In short, since 1948 the Middle East and North Africa has had praetorian leadership (a term coined by Samuel Huntington in the late 1960s) espousing sacred causes, supporting the buildup of huge military establishments, and suffering the physical effects of prolonged periods of combat. Only Tunisia and the United Arab Emirates are exceptions to these generalizations. Every other country has experienced significant periods of civil or conventional war, or both.

Public policy in the region is hostage to security fears and war preparation. Political debate is nearly impossible when dissent is branded as treason, and when opponents are seen as agents of one's enemies. Discussions of macroeconomic issues may be depicted as revealing strategic information to the enemy. It was not until 1973 that the Industry Committee of Egypt's Majlis as-Sha'ab was allowed, in closed session, to see the accounts of about a dozen of Egypt's 200 or so state-owned enterprises.

This praetorianism has eroded significantly over the past decade or so. Other than Israel, no military establishment can claim resounding success. Indeed, most realize that they are held in increasing contempt by their civilian constituents. They also have not been spared by economic crisis. While uneven, the share of military spending in GDP has been declining in the Middle East and North Africa (except in Sudan, Tunisia, and possibly Turkey). Even Iraq's outlays are estimated to have dropped from about 70 percent of GDP in 1981 to about 20 percent in 1989 (*Middle East Report*, March – April 1995, p. 9). As defenders of the status quo, the military has been delegitimized by economic crises. It increasingly holds sway by brute force and intimidation.

The militaries' loosening grip on regional wealth is a positive trend for those seeking far-reaching economic reform and greater political liberalization. Still, the trend is limited. And we must not forget that repressing one's own people does not cost nearly as much as preparing for war with one's neighbors. In Algeria the share of military outlays in GDP has fallen to about 2 percent, well below that of Morocco or Tunisia. But in pursuing its internal war with the Islamic Salvation Front, Algeria's regime today is probably the most praetorian in the Middle East.

It is also worth remembering that most, if not all, of the security concerns that gave rise to arms races and oversized militaries still exist. Despite the declaration of principles and the Israel – Jordan peace treaty, no state proximate to the Arab-Israeli theater is going to disarm significantly. And other regional rivalries are as intense as ever (Box 6.1). In addition, large-scale conventional forces are currently deployed in the southern Sudan and eastern Anatolia. Thus, although crisis has eroded the resource base of the Middle East's military forces, they will continue to claim a sizable share of national wealth. The regional peace dividend will be limited because there is not likely to be much real peace. Enhanced regional stability, however, may increase investor confidence and produce a significant flow of foreign direct investment.

It would not be unreasonable for the international donor community and the international financial institutions to refuse credits to

---

Box 6.1 Regional conflicts in the Middle East and North Africa

Iran–Iraq
Iraq–Saudi Arabia
Syria–Iraq
Egypt–Sudan
Syria–Turkey
Yemen–Eritrea

Saudi Arabia–Yemen
Turkey–Greece
Iran–Israel
Egypt–Israel
Algeria–Morocco

countries that spend more than 5 percent of GDP on their militaries. The problem, of course, is that weapons exporters – the United States foremost among them – see countries that spend large portions of their GDP on defense as their most promising markets.

Two other issues are as important as the magnitude of resources devoted to military spending. The first is the invasion of the civilian economy by the military, which can use its cheap labor and powers to intimidate to crowd out private or civilian construction firms, farmers, vehicle and consumer durables manufacturers, and so on. The second issue involves a range of rent-seeking privileges afforded the military through ownership or control of foreign trade companies, real estate, housing construction, banking operations, and contraband trade.

The macroeconomic impact of high military spending is not clear, in the Middle East or elsewhere (Lamb and Kallab, 1992). Within the Middle East and North Africa countries with traditionally low military expenditures (Tunisia) have not outperformed those with high outlays. One reason may be that in nearly every case the claims of the public sector, military and civilian, have been uniformly high and, since the 1970s, have together dampened growth.

Accountability and governance structure

Whether military or, far more rarely, civilian (Israel, Lebanon, Tunisia, sometimes Turkey and Sudan), governments in the Middle East and North Africa have seldom been accountable to their citizens. That may be changing, because the economic crises of the 1980s and the decline in strategic rents following the end of the cold war have forced several governments to raise taxes on their citizens, whether through direct or indirect levies. Increased taxation may elicit greater demands for accountable government, or it may encourage flight or exit as much as confrontation with public authorities. For many of those involved in or sympathetic to political Islamic movements, the issue is one of holding incumbent governments to account.

Many of the sympathizers, militants, and, above all, leaders of these movements are middle-class citizens, often with professional training. As states attempt to deal with economic crises by increasing their domestic revenues as well as by reducing expenditures on employment, education, and production and consumer subsidies, the middle-class constituents who would have benefited from these subsidies will make their displeasure known. The past three or four decades of import-substituting industrialization have produced large middle classes just about everywhere in the region, and their political voice cannot be muted indefinitely.

I do not want to overstate the relationship between taxes and political accountability. The historical record just about everywhere is ambiguous on this point. Moreover, the trend everywhere is to rely less on direct taxes, whose political impact is likely to be the greatest, and more on indirect taxes, especially the value-added tax. Indirect taxes are popular revenue sources because the individuals who pay them are not as aware of them. The political message of indirect taxes is that it is better to tax citizens using a kind of subterfuge than to engage them directly through taxes on incomes and wealth, which may move them to scrutinize political performance.

Despite these guarded observations, a more promising political and economic context is manifesting itself in the Middle East and North Africa. States are less reliant on external rents because of falling petroleum prices, reduced worker remittances, and fewer strategic rents following the end of the cold war. Now that governments must turn to their own citizens for revenue, they may ultimately be forced to treat them as citizens. Neither authoritarianism nor militarism has passed from the scene, but their costs are widely recognized, and a modicum of financial discipline has been applied in several countries. These trends should continue. There are no prospects for a revival of external rents; hence governments and middle classes must pursue a more balanced accommodation than has prevailed in the past.

Are accountable governments important for growth? That too is not clear. The first three decades of the Korean and Taiwanese (China) "miracles" developed under strong, authoritarian regimes. For private entrepreneurs and investors the issue is one of credibility and predictability. Authoritarians can act arbitrarily, deny property rights, and negate contracts. This style of leadership has been the norm in the Middle East and North Africa. The potential for profit may be so great that investors will take a chance (that is what has driven capital flows into China) or there may be an economic and legal enclave that the regime can credibly commit not to touch (such as the petroleum sector or a free trade zone). Otherwise, authoritarians foster forbidding environments in which to risk wealth.

More democratic governments are less prone to arbitrary actions, more wedded to legal procedure and the honoring of contracts, and hence more predictable and credible than authoritarians. But the electoral cycle may drive them to monetary and fiscal incoherence, thus introducing another kind of unpredictability. In fact, most times-series and cross-national data fail to turn up strong correlations between regime type and economic performance. But investors' perceptions are more important than data.[3]

Human capital investments

The Middle East and North Africa region has lagged significantly in education, training, and research relative to its levels of aggregate and per capita wealth. The lag has been especially detrimental for women. This regional feature is as significant as the military factor, but its effects are no easier to measure. Women in the Middle East and North Africa are as well regarded as those in other, more successful late industrializers, including Japan. But the East Asian economies, for whatever reason, gave women access to primary education and literacy generations ago (although that did little to alter gender relations). The Middle East is moving toward universal literacy, and women are creeping up the educational ladder. The economic impacts of this slow progress – slower than what these economies could sustain – is not yet clear.

The increasing educational mobility of women may have a curious side effect. It is often the public sector and civil service, including the corps of teachers, that is most open to women. If economic reforms reduce the size of the civil service and of public recurrent budgets, women may stand to lose the most. Whether reform programs will be resisted along gender lines remains to be seen.

THE POTENTIAL OF ISLAMIC POLITICS

It is impossible to capture the socioeconomic dynamics of contemporary Islam in a few paragraphs. Still, some observations are relevant to any discussion of the region's future. Most Middle Easterners are comfortable with large, activist states and highly personalized leadership. No historical or philosophical traditions warn against such states; to the contrary, the ends-oriented or mission-driven state has been valued throughout the history of the region. At the same time, the region's historical and cultural tradition lacks a well-articulated theory of checks and balances. If one accepts that this form of government can be good, and that their leaders have important missions to accomplish, then why should their power be fettered?

Since the Second World War most Middle Eastern states have failed in their self-proclaimed missions for military strength, industrialization, prosperity, and so on. These failures have not led to a questioning of the use of concentrated public power, but rather – with the exception of a few isolated liberals – to a search for the right leaders and for appropriate corrective measures.

Contemporary political Islam shares this spirit. Despite the denials of the Islamic leaders in the region, I believe that their goal is to substitute themselves for the failed incumbents, and to reinvent the mission their adversaries first defined. Political Islamic movements espouse anti-imperialism (anti-Westernism), liberation of the *umma*, or community of believers (as opposed to a more narrow nationalism), revolution and redistribution, the defeat of Zionism, an end to corruption, and a process of rapid economic development that embraces advanced science and technology. "Islam is the solution" has meaning in the sense that this mission will now be fulfilled because Muslims, submitting to God's will and laws, will be able to do what the secularists, who make their own laws, could never do.

As Iran has shown, Islamic government and a large, interventionist state are fully compatible. When Necmettin Erbakan, the head of Turkey's Salvation Party in the 1970s, was minister of industry in coalition governments in the mid-1970s, he spent much of his time forming hastily conceived state-owned enterprises in key constituencies. Once in power, political Islamic movements will likely be as fascinated with the tools of intervention, the ability to orient the flow of investment, and the control of national wealth as were their secular predecessors.

Ideology

Political Islamic leaders, if they are elected, will have fewer ideological constraints to deal with than their predecessors. These movements have seldom embraced socialism, and Islam gives divine sanction to differences in wealth among believers. Thus the urge to redistribute and the reluctance to divest may be somewhat less among Islamists than among those whom they challenge. For example, the government of Sudan has repeatedly declared its willingness to implement the stabilization and structural programs – including privatization – espoused by the International Monetary Fund and the World Bank, despite the potential distributional and economic hardships they may bring.

Still, I would be deeply surprised if any of these movements produced the functional equivalent in religious and economic philosophy of Chile's Pinochet. Moreover, their obsession with spreading the Islamic revolution and with preparing for a final showdown with Israel could resurrect the praetorian pattern of national resource use, now in decline. It is somewhat reassuring, however, that Iran now devotes a far smaller share of its GDP to the military than it did under the Shah.

Islamic movements share with their secular adversaries a populist mindset that is suspicious of all things foreign (see Addi, 1995). Any such movement is likely to severely restrict the entry of foreign investment into their economies. They may be more protectionist than the incumbent regimes, and they will likely view indigenous public and private sectors as strategic assets. By the same token, such movements could pursue politically inspired foreign investment policies, promoting their Islamic business sectors abroad and using their own version of the Overseas Private Investment Corporation (OPIC) to foster Islamic enterprise in other states.

These distinctive characteristics of potential Islamic government in the Middle East and North Africa will be swamped by the exigencies of economic crisis. There is no "Islamic way" of dealing with crises and undertaking structural adjustment. Pious Muslims are no more tolerant of high inflation and unemployment than the less pious. And it is no more feasible for Islamic governments to revert to inward-looking, state-led import-substituting industrialization than it is for the secular governments of the region. The imperatives of containing public spending and deficits, keeping inflation within a narrow band, and sending credible signals to the international banking community are as powerful for Islamic governments as for any other.

Institutional patterns

Having entertained the possibility that a number of states in the Middle East and North Africa might one day be run by Islamic governments, I hasten to note that I do not have any idea how likely that outcome is. In Algeria, where many believed that a government run by the Islamic Salvation Front (FIS) was merely a question of time, the presidential election of fall 1995 has challenged that assumption. Algerians voted in large, uncoerced numbers for Amin Zeroual, the incumbent president and determined opponent of the FIS. Through lack of imagination and leadership, the Egyptian regime is unnecessarily exposed to an Islamic challenge. Still, I do not foresee a wave of Islamic states washing across the region. There is some likelihood, however, of considerable preemptive Islamization, no matter how superficial. Sadat began the process in Egypt in the early 1970s, Nimeiri bungled it in Sudan, Qaddafi has always manifested his own quirky variant in Libya, Saddam Hussein (Iraq) wrapped himself in Sunni Islam when he went to war with Iran, and Turgut Özal distanced his government from Atatürk's secular legacy. The kings of the region have always claimed religious legitimacy.

Thus, in a pattern that is reminiscent of the strategy followed by the Christian and Social Democrats in Europe to contain the communist threat (by borrowing parts of the Marxist agenda), the regimes of the Middle East and North Africa have borrowed pieces of the Islamic agenda – from increasing separation of the sexes to selective application of the *shari'a*, including in the banking sector. Europe's communists never succeeded in winning control of any government. They remained perpetually in the opposition, which meant that they could always claim they had the solution. Nevertheless, their support dwindled continuously, and when their policies on public enterprise and regulation of the private sector were discredited, they lost ground even though they had never implemented the policies for which they were obliged to share the blame. Political Islam in the Middle East and North Africa could suffer a similar fate, but only if real elections become institutionalized.

Islamic movements have opportunistically stepped into the "service gap" opened by incompetent and fiscally strapped states. Islamic associations collect *zakat*, mobilize volunteers, receive funds from abroad, and organize medical clinics, daycare centers, primary schools, disaster relief, and so on. Incumbents see such service provision as a political threat and challenge, and they are not wrong to do so. But they are wrong in how they have tried to meet the challenge. Typically, they have exploited the full panoply of restrictive laws drawn up during the socialist-populist authoritarian era to harass and sometimes coopt Islamic associations.

Such laws should be scrapped and replaced with new, liberal laws of association. In Egypt, Law 32 of 1964 gives extraordinary powers to the Ministry of Social Affairs to register, monitor, audit, and dissolve all private charitable, voluntary, and development associations. The grip of the ministry over an important part of Egypt's civil society has not relaxed much since the law was enacted (see Sullivan, 1994; Salim, 1991). While this may have inhibited the formation of some Islamic associations, it has also thwarted the establishment of non-Islamic associations that might relieve the government of some social welfare tasks and compete with Islamic groups for space in the vacuum created by the government. Europe's complex civil society prevented a stark confrontation between governments seeking to rebuild devastated economies and communist vanguards seeking to seize power immediately after the Second World War. In their futile efforts to control everything, governments in the Middle East and North Africa have stunted the very elements of civil society that might save them. Even if Islamic associations are advancing, wittingly or not, a political agenda, they are providing valuable and needed services. For that they should not be condemned or combated.

CONCLUSION

For at least a generation to come, the Middle East and North Africa's experience with war, its sense of prolonged confrontation with the West, and the nonresolution of several regional military rivalries will mean that the rationale for large, quasi-militarized states will continue to hold sway. It follows that the economies of the region will be thoroughly politicized, not only in terms of distributional issues but also in terms of the belief that the state must manage its citizens' resources in order to deal with external enemies and enhance security. The reform of large state structures, difficult enough when the debate is confined to economic tradeoffs, is nearly impossible when it becomes embroiled in national security issues. Even opposition parties may not want to see their states retreat from dominant positions in the economy or relinquish control over "national" assets.

That kind of outlook may diminish with time. The end of the cold war, the diminution of power maneuvering in the Middle East, and the possible settlement to the Israeli-Palestinian dispute will slowly transform the region's potential. Most states in the Middle East and North Africa have made progress in human resource development and in structural reforms. Whether this pace is too slow remains to be seen. While in some ways the countries in the region are similar to scores of other developing countries, there are important differences. These differences make the likelihood for accelerated reforms problematic, if not unlikely.

Notes

1. This is not to suggest that all the wars have been regionally generated or that the culture of the region is predisposed to conflict. To the contrary, nearly all the conflicts have involved extraregional intervention, if not provocation, of one kind or another.
2. The relationship between military spending and growth is not entirely unambiguous. (See Lamb and Kallab, 1992.)
3. Przeworski (1995) has carried out some of these analyses and found a moderate correlation between democracy and enhanced economic performance. He feels that this correlation may be spurious, in that democracies cannot survive truly poor economic performance while authoritarians can. Thus democracies that drive their economies into crisis tend to stop being democracies and disappear from the tail of the distribution.

References

Addi, Lahouari, 1995. *L'Algérie et la Démocratie*, Paris: Editions de la Découverte.
Bhagwati, Jagdish, 1982. "Directly Unproductive, Profit-Seeking Activities," *Journal of Political Economy*, 90 (5): 988-1002.
Lamb, Geoffrey and Valerina Kallab (eds.), 1992. *Military Expenditure and Economic Development*, World Bank Discussion Paper, 185, Washington, D.C. : World Bank.
Przeworski, Adam, 1995. "Symposium," *World Politics*, 48(1): 16-21.
Richards, Alan, 1991. "The Political Economy of Dilatory Reform: Egypt in the 1980s," *World Development*, 19 (12): 1721-30.
Salim, Amir, 1991. *In Defense of the Right to Form Associations*, Cairo: Modern Commercial Publishing Co. (in Arabic).
Sullivan, Denis, 1994. *Private Voluntary Organizations in Egypt: Islamic Development, Private Initiative, and State Control*, Gainesville, Fla.: University Press of Florida.
Waterbury, John, 1993. *Exposed to Innumerable Delusions: Public Enterprise and State Power in Egypt, India, Mexico, and Turkey*, New York: Cambridge University Press.
———1994. "Democracy without Democrats?: The Potential for Political Liberalization in the Middle East," in Ghassan Salamé (ed.), *Democracy without Democrats?*, London: I.B. Tauris.

7 Supporting Private Sector Development in the Middle East and North Africa

Robert E. Anderson and Albert Martinez

The public sector dominates most Middle Eastern and North African economies. Extensive government involvement in investment, enterprises, finance, and infrastructure provision constrains economic development, lowers productivity, and discourages investment – domestic and foreign. To recover growth, governments in the region must quickly adopt policies that modernize the financial sector, privatize the provision of infrastructure services, and restructure the regulations, laws, and fiscal incentives that govern economic activity.

Until the late 1970s gross domestic product (GDP) growth in the Middle East and North Africa exceeded population growth, resulting in rising *per capita* incomes throughout the region. By 1980, however, population growth exceeded increases in GDP in all the countries in the region except Morocco and Tunisia. For countries outside the Gulf Cooperation Council (GCC), recent growth rates have been insufficient to absorb the growing labor force, resulting in unemployment.[1]

In order for countries in the region to attain growth rates that enable per capita incomes to rise, both the level of investment and the level of efficiency will need to increase. Governments need to redefine the role of the public sector, limiting public investment to specific areas, moving quickly toward privatization, and creating business environments that encourage investment, minimize transaction costs, and maximize the utilization of market mechanisms.

PRIVATE INVESTMENT, PUBLIC INVESTMENT, AND GROWTH

During the 1970s and most of the 1980s the public sector's role in the economies of the Middle East and North Africa grew. Heavy public

Figure 7.1 Per capita income growth, various regions, 1965–93

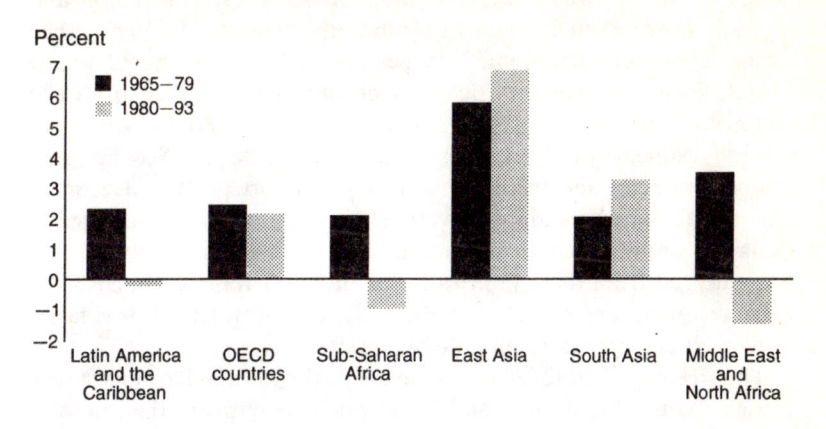

[Bar chart showing percent per capita income growth by region for 1965–79 and 1980–93: Latin America and the Caribbean, OECD countries, Sub-Saharan Africa, East Asia, South Asia, Middle East and North Africa.]

Source: World Bank data.

sector investment achieved average annual growth in GDP per capita of 3.5 percent during 1965–79. This strategy did not, however, result in sustained growth.

Although the ratio of investment to GDP in the Middle East and North Africa fell during 1980–93, it remained higher than that in OECD countries that experienced positive growth over the same period. Still, average per capita GDP in the region declined between 1980 and 1993 (Figure 7.1). Productivity figures partly explain the poor performance: GDP growth per unit of capital stock and GDP per worker fell during this time, and both measures lag behind comparable figures for many other regions.

Government domination of the economy

Public policy in the Middle East and North Africa is driven by the belief that the state is the most effective agent for stimulating economic development. Even the region's most market-friendly economies believe that private entrepreneurial activity should be closely regulated and controlled. Accordingly, nationalization and public ownership of the means of production figure prominently in public policy, and the state has sought to become the primary supplier of investment–even in sectors where there has been no evidence of market failure.

Governments in the Middle East and North Africa influence economic activity in two ways. First, public sector investment is large and typically crowds out investment by the private sector. In 1990 public sector investment represented 46 percent of total investment in the Middle East and North Africa-a much higher share than in OECD countries (where public sector investment represented 17 percent of total investment) or developing countries (38 percent). Second, government policies and institutions do not support private investment and are designed to allow governments to influence private sector decisions about resource allocation. The business environment that has emerged from these policies is one in which transaction costs are high, resources are allocated inefficiently, the informal sector is large, and small enterprises proliferate.

The strategy of state-led development in the Middle East and North Africa has produced more and larger public enterprises than in most other countries. The dominance of public enterprises can be measured in various ways. In the four countries for which data are available public enterprises account for a much larger share of GDP than is the average for other middle-income countries (Figure 7.2). If only nonagricultural economic activity is considered, the dominance of public enterprises becomes even larger. Public enterprises also account for a disproportionately large share of investment, suggesting that public enterprises control future development by deciding which sectors and industries will grow and expand.

Figure 7.2 Share of public enterprises in economic activity, various countries, 1986–91

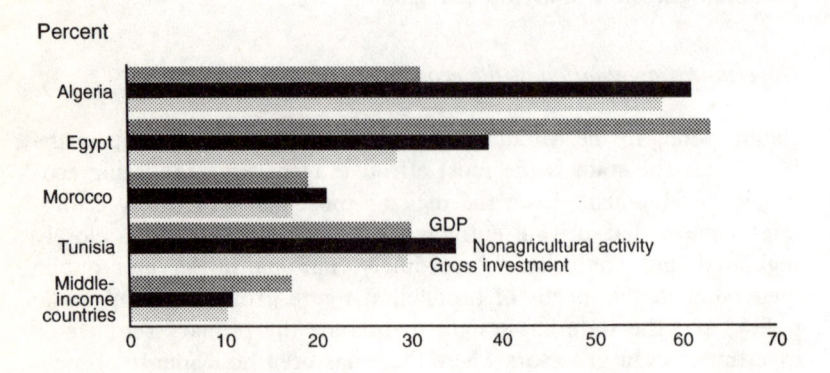

Source: World Bank, 1995a.

The public policy challenge: defining public–private boundaries

Infrastructure and other types of public sector investment generally have a positive and significant relationship with GDP growth. When the public share of total investment approaches 40 percent, however, public investment becomes a burden to the economy and the economic rate of return on investment projects falls (Easterly and Rebelo, 1993; World Bank, 1991a). The challenge for governments is to identify areas in which investment is critical but private investment is inadequate. A second role of government is to improve the environment in which private businesses operate by creating an incentive structure and institutional framework that facilitates private sector investment.

Public enterprises retard economic development

One explanation for the decline in growth in countries with a legacy of state-led economic development is that the productivity of public investment declines over time. During the early stages of development investment is required for heavy industry (such as steel and large factories) and capital-intensive industries (such as mining, electricity generation, and oil refining). Investment projects are large and relatively few in number. At the later stages of development investment projects are smaller and greater in number, and are more likely to involve small enterprises producing consumer goods, high-technology products, and services. Governments may be better able to cope with the more rudimentary investment projects that characterize the early stages of economic development and less able to cope with the more sophisticated and rapidly changing investment projects in the later stages of development.

A related reason that heavy reliance on public enterprises retards economic development is that enterprises in which the government owns a significant share tend to perform less well than other enterprises. A comparative study of industrial companies in Jordan for 1981–90 found that enterprises in which government ownership was less than 15 percent had higher productivity, greater sales growth, and higher profitability than enterprises in which the government owned more than 15 percent. In Morocco the fourteen largest public enterprises incurred losses that amounted to 2.1 percent of GDP. In Yemen government transfers to public enterprises account for as much as 2 percent of GDP.

Because of poor accounting and data collection, governments in the region may not even know the true extent of the losses incurred by public enterprises, and even enterprises that show a profit may do so only because they are protected from competition. Often the losses of public enterprises are financed through bank loans by state-owned banks. The extent of the losses financed in this way is hidden from view and difficult to estimate. In Tunisia, for example, only three or four enterprises receive subsidies from the budget, but other public enterprises receive loans from banks to cover their losses. The size of these loans is not known but is probably substantial. Since loss-making enterprises can probably never repay such loans, the losses of public enterprises contaminate the loan portfolios of the banks. This makes privatization of the banks impossible until the government recapitalizes them.

The reasons for low efficiency and high losses by public enterprises include price controls, overstaffing, patronage, lack of competition, lack of capital, and inflexible and bureaucratic civil service rules and procedures. Of course, not all public enterprises are inefficient loss-makers. On average, however, their performance is generally worse than that of privately owned enterprises.

PRIVATIZING THE ECONOMY

Two strategies have been advocated for improving the performance of public enterprises: reforming public enterprises (but retaining state ownership) or transferring them to private owners. In the first strategy the government must change the way it manages public enterprises. The problem with this strategy is that governments too often fail to keep reforms in place and allow public enterprises to slip back into their old ways of operation. (Examples of countries in which reforms resulted in initial improvements in performance but were followed by a deterioration include Bangladesh, China, the Republic of Korea, and Pakistan.)

Because of the large number of publicly owned enterprises in the Middle East and North Africa, full-scale privatization would be complex and difficult. Progress toward privatization has been even slower than might have been expected, however. Only Morocco and Tunisia have made significant progress, and even there fewer than 10 percent of public enterprises have been transferred to private owners. By contrast, developing countries in other parts of the world have been able to privatize a much larger number of enterprises and have gen-

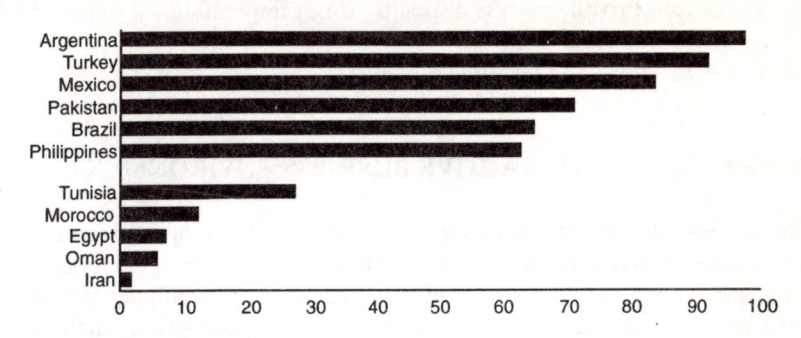

Figure 7.3 Privatization transactions, various countries, 1988–93

Country	Transactions
Argentina	~98
Turkey	~92
Mexico	~84
Pakistan	~70
Brazil	~65
Philippines	~62
Tunisia	~26
Morocco	~11
Egypt	~6
Oman	~5
Iran	~1

Note: Privatization transactions are defined as any sale of shares in state-owned enterprises.
Source: World Bank data.

erated more revenue from privatization than the countries of the Middle East and North Africa (Figure 7.3).

The large number of public enterprises in the region suggests that more radical approaches to privatization are needed. To speed up the privatization process, governments in the Middle East and North Africa should take the following steps:

- *Centralize*: Privatization activities should be centralized in a single privatization agency reporting directly to the highest levels of government. The head of the agency should be a champion of privatization who has implemented successful privatization programs in other countries. Allowing branch ministries to manage privatization is likely to slow the process, since they lack incentives and skills.
- *Simplify the process*: The use of a simple, transparent auction process will speed up privatization. New private owners should be chosen based on their willingness to pay the highest price. Restrictions on potential buyers, complicated postprivatization conditions, and numerous criteria and procedures for selecting the best buyer should be avoided.
- *Sell privatization to the public*: Successful privatization programs have used professional public relations campaigns to convince the public that privatization is in its long-run best interest. This approach helps counter special interest groups that may feel threatened by privatization and try to block the program.

- *Reward managers*: Boards of directors and managers of public enterprises should be rewarded for successfully implementing privatization. Privatization is difficult – if not impossible – if opposed by senior management.
- *Use consultants and investment bankers.*

CREATING AN ATTRACTIVE BUSINESS ENVIRONMENT

In an increasingly integrated global economy with open domestic economies, enterprises will have to compete against foreign suppliers in both export and domestic markets. Competitiveness will depend on the availability, quality, and cost of factors of production, such as skilled labor and efficient infrastructure services; the existence of competitive conditions that provide the impetus for constant innovation and opportunity seeking; the effectiveness of institutional arrangements that minimize transaction costs; and the presence of internationally competitive supporting and related industries (Porter, 1990).

Foreign investors perceive that the business environment in the Middle East and North Africa has been deteriorating since 1980. The *Institutional Investor* rating of five of the six countries in the Middle East and North Africa studied declined between 1980 and 1994, and the gap between countries in the Middle East and North Africa and countries outside the region widened (Table 7.1).

Table 7.1 Investor ratings, various countries, 1980–94

Country	1980	1985	1990	1994
Algeria	56	53	39	23
Egypt	34	34	24	32
Jordan	42	36	31	26
Lebanon	23	12	7	24
Morocco	40	23	26	39
Tunisia	48	43	36	43
Indonesia	55	49	48	52
Malaysia	72	65	60	67
Thailand	53	52	62	61

Note: Ratings are on a scale of 0–100.
Source: *Institutional Investor*, various issues.

Figure 7.4 Foreign direct investment inflows, various regions, 1982–93

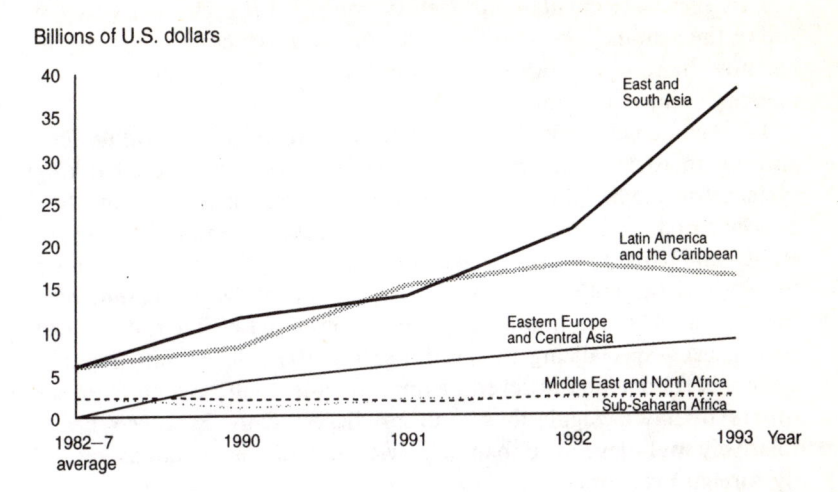

Billions of U.S. dollars

[Line graph showing FDI inflows from 1982–7 average through 1993 for: East and South Asia (rising to ~40), Latin America and the Caribbean (~17), Eastern Europe and Central Asia (~10), Middle East and North Africa (flat, low), Sub-Saharan Africa (flat, low).]

Source: World Bank data.

Investor assessment of risk is reflected in flows of foreign direct investment. Since 1982 foreign direct investment flows to the Middle East and North Africa have been flat, and the region's share of foreign direct investment flows in 1993 was very small compared with Asia and Latin America (Figure 7.4). To attract foreign investment, the countries of the Middle East and North Africa will have to convince foreign investors that the business environment in the region has improved.

Country (political) risk is a significant component of investor perceptions. Interviews with foreign investors (including expatriates) emphasize the need for regional peace, rule of law, and policy predictability. Domestic investors view constraints differently, emphasizing finance (cost and access), taxes (level and administration), skills availability, and legal and regulatory costs. Some of these issues are discussed below.

Modernizing the financial sector

An efficient financial system is critical to the development of a modern market economy. Until recently government policies in the Middle East and North Africa undermined financial sector development. Over the past few years many countries in the region have instituted significant reforms, including liberalization of interest rates, reduction of state control of credit allocation, and movement toward indirect and market instruments of monetary control. Financial markets are still in their infancy, however, and the financial structure in the region has not changed significantly, mainly because of the continued dominance of state-run banks.

The main characteristic of the financial systems in the Middle East and North Africa is the reliance by the private sector on the banking system for credit. Banking systems in the region are fragmented, concentrated, and government-owned. In Egypt five public banks (of eighty-one banks) control 70 percent of the system's assets. In Tunisia the state is the majority owner of five of the six largest commercial banks. The Algerian financial system is composed of five state-owned banks, each specializing in specific sectors. The Jordanian financial system is fragmented in several compartments, each isolated from the others by laws, regulations, and privileges. Only Morocco has a relatively well-developed banking system, with many banks owned by foreign investors.

Securities markets do not play a significant role in private finance in the Middle East and North Africa. Commercial banks provide credit (mainly short-term) to the private sector, and development banks provide most medium- and long-term credit. Commercial bank funding comes mainly from deposits and to a certain extent from rediscount facilities. Money market activity is limited, restricting the ability of banks to increase liquidity as needed and thereby forcing them to hold short-term assets. There is almost no market for long-term instruments.

Equity markets are also underdeveloped. Jordan has shown considerable success in the development of its equity market, however, with the Amman Financial Market (a stock exchange) experiencing impressive growth since its establishment in 1978.

The private sector share of domestic credit declined over 1970–93, and represented a much smaller portion of domestic credit than in other regions, particularly East Asia. Short-term credit accounts for a large share of total commercial banking credit (85 percent in Algeria, 60 percent in Tunisia, and 80 percent in Morocco in 1991–92), and the private sector has long complained about the lack of long-term credit. To address this vacuum in the financial market, many governments have introduced specialized institutions, typically government-owned lending institutions with special access to long-term financing at below-market rates. This strategy tends to impede the development of market solutions to the problem. Instead, governments should try to address the fundamental constraints to long-term lending: the lack of long-term project assessment capabilities, the high cost of collateral recovery, the lack of sources of long-term funds, and the lack of interest-hedging instruments.

In recent years there has been significant progress in liberalizing interest rates, facilitating better mobilization of deposits and allowing banks to charge higher rates for riskier projects. Still, intermediation margins for non-GCC countries are typically much higher than for OECD countries. In Algeria the relatively high spreads (8.5–13.0 percent for short-term loans) reflect the lack of competition in the banking system. The relatively low spreads in Morocco (about 4 percent) reflect government control over interest spreads.

Reforming the banking system

Reform of the banking system, the most important component of the financial system in the region, would improve resource mobilization, fund allocation, and monitoring of enterprises. The fundamental structural problem is the dominance of the public sector in commercial banking activities, which impairs efficiency, credit allocation, and, to a lesser extent, deposit mobilization. A comparative study of state and private banks in Tunisia found that performance of private banks was notably better than that of banks with significant government ownership. Governments should actively pursue bank privatization while striving to improve the regulatory and supervision framework.

To increase competition in the banking sector, the countries of the Middle East and North Africa must open up the market to foreign banks, which would increase competition and result in significant technology transfer and training; eliminate market fragmentation by eliminating the privileges accorded to specialized banks; and increase competition from financial markets. Providing enterprises with alternative sources of funds (such as commercial paper) and developing nonbank financial institutions (such as leasing companies) would create even greater competition in the banking system.

Much has been done to create the proper regulatory framework for the banking system. However, supervision capacity in many countries remains poor, and the information infrastructure remains inadequate. The development of accounting and auditing systems – in both banks and enterprises – must be accelerated. Some countries still require banks to hold a certain percentage of their assets in government securities. Legal reform would ease some of the problems with respect to collateral and guarantees.

Central banks should accelerate the move toward market-based instruments of monetary policy. Many countries still use some of these instruments to influence credit allocation, in the process undermining the development of a sound financial market.

Developing financial markets

Medium- and long-term government securities are the basis of modern bond markets. Because government borrowing in the Middle East and North Africa accounts for a large share of domestic credit (Table 7.2), market-priced government securities could become the building blocks for financial market development, establishing a yield curve and a benchmark for investors in assessing other securities.

Table 7.2 Government borrowing, Middle East and North Africa, 1980–93 (percent)

Country	Central government share of domestic credit			
	1980	1985	1990	1993
Algeria	33	30	40	69
Egypt	57	46	47	41
Jordan	11	18	33	25
Lebanon	10	36	40	33
Morocco	61	59	58	45
Tunisia	15	14	12	9

Source: World Bank data.

Commercial legislation (especially company and contract laws) and securities regulations require restructuring in many countries in the region. In some countries differential tax treatment of financial instruments has induced distortions. Disclosure regulations and accelerated development of accounting and auditing systems would also help create a more business-friendly environment. Regulatory barriers to foreign investor participation should also be reviewed.

Several key institutions are needed for the smooth functioning of financial markets. An efficient and secure payments and settlement system is essential. Trading systems and a set of market-trading conventions are needed to match bids and offers. Institutions that participate in financial markets need to develop competent treasury operations. Finally, credit rating institutions need to provide information so that small investors can participate in financial markets.

Improving the availability and efficiency of infrastructure services

Providing infrastructure services to business is crucial to establishing an environment that is conducive to investment. Various studies have documented business complaints about losses resulting from infrastructure deficiencies (from such problems as electricity shortages, malfunctioning telephone lines, and undeveloped roads). Some businesses may choose to purchase their own equipment (using expensive satellite or radio telephones, for example, to limit their dependence on the telephone system), thus adding to the cost of doing business in a country with an unreliable infrastructure.

The quality of infrastructure services greatly affects the international competitive position of businesses in a country or region. Studies show that investment in infrastructure has significantly reduced the cost of manufacturing in a number of high-income countries (Aschauer, 1993) and that the return on investment can be as high as 60 percent (World Bank, 1994).

The quality and quantity of infrastructure services in the Middle East and North Africa is about the same as in other countries at the same level of economic development. This provides little reason for complacency, however. With the increased globalization of the economy, international businesses can choose to operate almost anywhere around the world. Poor-quality infrastructure services will likely discourage many international firms from establishing operations in the Middle East and North Africa. If the countries in the region want to achieve a high level of economic development, they must develop their infrastructure to the same level found in high-income countries.

Most infrastructure services in the Middle East and North Africa are provided by government ministries, special agencies and authorities, or public enterprises. Can these institutions be reformed to improve the quality and efficiency of infrastructure services? How can the large amounts of investment capital be raised to finance needed expansion and improvements in infrastructure services? Three options for reform are worth considering.

A consensus is growing in many countries that privatization by selling to private investors is the best option for most infrastructure services, particularly if competition is possible. Even if competition is not possible, privatization may be appropriate if a regulatory structure can be put in place to set price levels and quality of service standards. If complete privatization is not possible, private participation can still be encouraged by leasing state assets to private operations or contracting out functions to private companies.

Reforming regulations, laws, and fiscal incentives

Regulation of the private sector in the Middle East and North Africa has developed to support state intervention in and control of the economy and to direct investments to favored sectors. The results have typically been lack of competition, high transaction costs, inefficient industries, and rent-seeking activities. In Egypt, for example, changes in production techniques or introduction of new products requires submission of an establishment and operation license. Securing such a license is a time-consuming process in which the regulatory agency examines various aspects of the firm's operations (internal plant layout, workforce deployment, composition of internal safety committees, and so on). A World Bank study found that up to 30 percent of the average manager's time in Egypt is spent resolving problems with regulatory compliance. In Morocco it typically takes six months and as many as thirty-five separate documents to complete the formal steps for commercial establishment. Information about procedures is difficult to obtain, and the regulatory maze is particularly difficult for small entrepreneurs.

Regulatory reform

World Bank experience with reform suggests that macroeconomic policy reforms such as those being developed in many countries in the Middle East and North Africa are a precondition for increased private sector investment and economic growth. By themselves, however, such reforms are insufficient (Alavi, 1990). A business environment should be put in place that enhances competition, reduces transaction costs, and allows market forces to determine resource allocation.

Although eliminating unnecessary and burdensome regulations can bring major benefits, a well-designed regulatory system still plays an important role in market economies. A strategy of dismantling many of the current regulations while building a system that addresses the needs of a more global economy is required. Some of the issues that need to be addressed by a new regulatory system include the establishment of intellectual property rights, to encourage investment in information and knowledge capital; environmental protection, to offset externalities; and provision of infrastructure services, to allow privatization and competition in sectors that have monopoly characteristics. The first two issues will have to be dealt with as countries in the region join the World Trade Organization (WTO).

Legal reform

An effective legal framework lowers transaction costs by establishing the basis for property rights and providing a mechanism for contract enforcement and dispute resolution. Surveys and anecdotal evidence indicate that the economic costs of an ineffective legal system are substantial.

Two areas of the legal system require reform. First, laws need to be changed. Much of the existing legislation was developed during the period of control, inwardness, and direct government participation in the economy, and is ill-suited to a dynamic, private sector-dominated, open market economy. Changes in the financial system, new trade agreements, and the growing importance of intellectual property rights also suggest the need to revise current laws.

Second, enforcement and administration of laws tend to be slow and cumbersome in the Middle East and North Africa. In Egypt, Jordan, and Lebanon it takes 2–2.5 years to settle the average commercial case, compared with 1.2 years in Canada. Businesses that avoid using courts for contract enforcement must search for alternative mechanisms, or incorporate the uncertainty associated with a deficient legal system into their costs. Reasons for judicial inefficiency include the lack of qualified judges, the poor state of the legal profession, and outmoded procedures and systems.

Investment promotion

Fiscal incentives promote investment in certain sectors in almost all Middle Eastern and North African countries. Recent analysis has questioned the efficacy of many investment incentive programs. A

1993 World Bank report concludes that the administrative burden associated with complicated incentive structures (such as those in the Republic of Korea or Singapore) exacts high social costs (World Bank, 1993). The study highlights the success of Hong Kong, which used low but uniform taxes on corporate incomes to encourage investment rather than fine tune incentive structures through the tax system. A recent survey of empirical studies found that investment promotion objectives are not well served by reducing corporate taxes in developing countries (Boadway and Shah, 1992). The same survey concluded that investment tax credits, investment allowances, and accelerated capital consumption allowances also require careful attention to the design and close monitoring of their impacts on investment and government revenues. Given the clear impact of tax incentives on investment, greater emphasis should be placed on the more fundamental constraints – lack of stability, weak institutions, and crowding out by the private sector.

CONCLUSION

The strategy of state-led development in the Middle East and North Africa has not achieved sustained growth. The productivity of physical assets and human capital has fallen in recent years. A move toward private investment and policies that encourage private domestic and foreign capital are essential if the region's growth rates are to recover.

Increasing the level and efficiency of investment in the region will require action on two fronts. First, privatization should be implemented rapidly to reduce inefficiency and crowding out of the private sector. This effort will require governments to redefine the role of the public sector and limit public investment. Second, a supportive business environment should be established to encourage investment, minimize transaction costs, and maximize utilization of market mechanisms. Legal and regulatory systems, financial systems, and infrastructure services all require major reforms.

Note

1. This chapter focuses on non-GCC countries and is based largely on World Bank studies of Algeria, Egypt, Jordan, Lebanon, Morocco, and Tunisia. Unless otherwise stated the Middle East and North Africa refers to non-GCC countries.

References

Alavi, Hamid, 1990. "Industrial Competitiveness: Determinants and Indicators," *World Bank Industry Series Paper*, 29, Washington, D.C.: World Bank.

Aschauer, David A., 1993. "Public Infrastructure Investment: A Bridge to Productivity Growth?," *Public Policy Brief*, 4, Bard College, Jerome Levy Economic Institute, Annandale-on-Hudson, New York.

Boadway, Robin and Anwar Shah, 1992. "How Tax Incentives Affect Decisions to Invest in Developing Countries," *Policy Research Working Paper*, 1011, Washington, D.C.: World Bank.

Easterly, William and Sergio Rebelo, 1993. "Fiscal Policy and Economic Growth: An Empirical Investigation," *Journal of Monetary Economics*, 32(2): 417–58.

Porter, Michael, 1990. *The Competitive Advantage of Nations*, New York: Free Press.

World Bank., 1991a. *Developing the Private Sector: The World Bank's Experience and Approach*, Washington, D.C.: World Bank.

────── 1991b. *World Development Report 1991: The Challenge of Development*, New York: Oxford University Press.

────── 1993. *The East Asian Miracle: Economic Growth and Public Policy*, A World Bank Policy Research Report, Washington D.C.: World Bank.

────── 1994. *World Development Report: Infrastructure for Development*, New York: Oxford University Press.

────── 1995a. *Bureaucrats in Business: The Economics and Politics of Government Ownership*, A World Bank Policy Research Report, New York: Oxford University Press.

────── 1995b. *World Debt Tables 1994–95: External Finance for Developing Countries*, vol.1, Washington, D.C.: World Bank.

Part III

Sectoral Issues: Human Resources, Poverty, and the Environment

8 A Human Capital Strategy for Competing in World Markets

Fredrick L. Golladay, Sue E. Berryman, Jon Avins, and Laurence Wolff

In order to restore growth and improve the living standards of their rapidly growing populations, the economies of the Middle East and North Africa must increasingly compete in world markets. Doing so will not be easy–today's global markets are forcing dramatic changes in the organization of work and the skills required of workers. To create the skills that workers need, education and training systems will have to change what they teach, how they teach, whom they teach, and when they teach. The share of each country's student-age population that completes a quality education will have to grow–by substantial percentages in some countries. Because the costs of meeting these targets will overburden the public budgets of most countries, governments should develop a system of mixed public and private financing, at least for higher education. The financing mechanism should promote externally efficient education, internally efficient operations of schools and universities, and equitable access to education.

After a quarter-century of strong output growth the economies of the Middle East and North Africa entered a period of economic stagnation around 1985. During the 1960s output across the region had grown by about 6.2 percent a year. Growth was led by public sector investments in manufacturing, particularly in the Mashreq region (Egypt, Jordan, Lebanon, and Syria). Development was concentrated in modern, capital-intensive production. Public enterprises were focused on the production of undifferentiated goods, including raw materials and intermediate goods. These enterprises remained economically viable under the protection of high trade barriers; firms that were unable to cover costs with operating revenue received generous subsidies. This development strategy generated a respectable rate of growth, but it also consumed inordinate amounts of capital while producing relatively few jobs.

Between 1973 and 1985 growth continued at about 4.2 percent a year, led by the boom in oil exports from the Gulf. Gross domestic product (GDP) in the six countries of the Gulf Cooperation Council (Bahrain, Kuwait, Oman, Qatar, Saudi Arabia, and the United Arab Emirates) increased by about 8 percent a year during this period. This spectacular performance was due largely to a sharp rise in oil prices–between 1973 and 1983 the price of a barrel of crude oil increased tenfold (in current dollars). The explosion in oil revenue spilled over into other Arab countries, with the number of Arabs working in the Gulf increasing from about 0.5 million in 1973 to nearly 3.0 million in 1985. The economies of the labor-exporting countries were stimulated by the inflow of worker remittances, fueling growth in the construction sector. Housing starts in Jordan, for example, increased by 230 percent between 1973 and 1985. Construction activity also increased substantially in other countries, including Egypt, Lebanon, and Syria. The boom flowed over into other sectors as workers in the Gulf and those who profited from the construction boom purchased goods and services from other sectors.

Even the less developed countries of the region benefited from the expansion. While Egypt, Iraq, Jordan, Lebanon, and Syria sent teachers, engineers, administrators, and doctors to the Gulf, Yemen sent mechanics, masons, carpenters, and laborers. By the 1980s about a third of Morocco's foreign exchange earnings were coming from worker remittances. The other Maghreb countries (Algeria and Tunisia) relied less heavily on employment abroad, but still earned a significant amount from remittances. During the 1980s worker remittances to the Maghreb totaled about $5 billion a year.

The collapse of oil prices in 1985 and a simultaneous slowdown in the demand for petroleum products brought the boom in the Mashreq to an end. In the United Arab Emirates, for example, per capita income fell from $33,600 in 1984 to $18,800 in 1992. The drop in oil export earnings reverberated throughout the Middle East, and worker remittances dropped sharply. This decline intensified after the Gulf war in 1991; the number of Arabs working in the Gulf shrank by more than two-thirds. The economies of the Maghreb were less affected by the oil boom and bust and thus were less traumatized than those in the Mashreq by the subsequent economic adjustments.

In order to adjust to these new economic realities and achieve greater prosperity in the twenty-first century, the Middle East and

North Africa will have to adopt a more outward-oriented development strategy. The scarcity of natural resources (including freshwater and agricultural land) in the face of rapid population growth will force the region to import an increasingly larger amount of food and basic materials. To pay for these imports, the region's economies will have to increase their export earnings substantially. This push to increase exports will come at a time when many developing countries are entering world markets with goods produced by low-skilled laborers. Thus the countries of the Middle East and North Africa will have to broaden the range of goods they produce and increase productivity in order to raise per capita incomes.

The quality of the region's stock of human capital has played a minor role in its pursuit of prosperity in the past, but it will be pivotal in the future. The emphasis on capital-intensive production and import substitution during the 1960s dampened labor absorption and guided production into low-skill areas. The fundamental weaknesses of these development initiatives were obscured by the oil boom during 1970-83. The key to success in the emerging economic environment will lie largely in the capacity to identify profitable economic opportunities and respond quickly to these opportunities with high-quality goods and services. This will require a labor force that is well trained and highly flexible.

COMPETING SUCCESSFULLY IN THE INTERNATIONAL ECONOMY

More than half a billion workers in the developing world will enter the labor force in the next fifteen years. Nearly all of these workers will have attended primary school and will be literate and numerate. More than 150 million will have completed secondary school. As these workers, qualified to perform basic manufacturing tasks, enter the labor force, global markets for mass-produced goods will become intensely competitive. Workers from countries such as China and Indonesia will be willing to work for much lower wages than those that prevail in the Middle East and North Africa.

Middle Eastern and North African countries will be able to compete directly with the emerging economies only if they allow average real wages to decline. For a brief period of time average incomes can rise even as average wages fall if labor force participation rates increase. In recent years economies as different as Morocco and the

United States have increased output and per capita incomes by bringing secondary workers – primarily women, but also teenagers – into the labor force. Given the low rate of labor force participation among women in the Middle East and North Africa, this option could generate immediate gains. But the viability of this strategy will diminish over the next two decades as labor force participation reaches its saturation point. At that point income gains will have to come from increased productivity.

Customer demand has changed

Suppliers in the Middle East and North Africa face a dynamic profile of customer demand as they move into higher-wage international markets. In agriculture, manufacturing, and services international customers now expect a large, varied, and high-quality basket of goods, fast delivery of orders, and low prices. In response, suppliers must place a premium on diversifying goods and services, making products and processes more innovative, lowering production times and costs, and meeting quality standards consistently. Thus employers often must change the organization of work, and workers must acquire different and in some cases higher levels of skills.

Computerization has been the main reason for this changing profile of customer demand. The shift from mechanical to electronic production technologies has changed the opportunities and ultimately the basis for economic growth. Mechanically based technologies are inflexible, making the retooling necessary to offer different products expensive and time-consuming. Long production runs were needed to keep unit costs down. Computerized technologies are flexible; retooling is achieved through the much cheaper process of reprogramming. Modern car manufacturers, for example, now produce utility vehicles, passenger cars, and light trucks on the same assembly line on the same shop floor on the same day. Computer-based technologies allow a shift from product orientation to customer orientation, and the replacement of mass markets with niche markets. These changes are often described in relation to the manufacturing sector, but the implications are equally profound for service industries and agriculture. In both cases the consumer has the opportunity to choose from a rapidly expanding range of goods that are customized to individual circumstances and preferences. In short, corporate growth strategies predicated on increased sales of standardized goods and services are being replaced by strategies predicated on an imperative to customize goods and services. Producers that seek to sell mass-produced goods will face stiff competition from low-wage economies.

The fierce competition of world markets imposes three imperatives on producers that hope to succeed internationally. The first is speed: successful companies will be able to push new items into markets more rapidly than their competitors. As mass markets have evolved into niche markets and as customer demand has become less predictable, retailers have learned to seek and reward suppliers who can fill smaller orders more rapidly. In turn, suppliers have been forced to reduce product development, production, and distribution times. Toyota, for example, cut its domestic manufacturing, distribution, and sale cycle from six weeks in 1982 to eight days by 1987.

The second imperative is low-cost production. Facing intense price competition from low-wage economies, producers must maximize production efficiency by improving the mix and use of labor and capital. The corporate downsizing and restructuring that is occurring in OECD countries reflects adjustments in the mix and use of labor and capital in response to changes in products, processes, and markets. Some of the competitive disadvantages created by low-wage competition can be overcome with superior management of production processes. Firms can reduce middle management jobs by shifting supervisory and managerial functions to workers on the floor as their qualifications improve.

The third imperative is continuous innovation. Successful firms must monitor the preferences of customers, stay abreast of new processes for improving goods and services, and relentlessly pursue opportunities for reducing costs. International trade rapidly spreads information on new quality standards, products, services, technologies, management systems, and market opportunities. Producers must continuously monitor and respond to these changes. Trade also drives up quality and consistency standards, because customers can easily find alternative suppliers with better products or lower maintenance requirements.

Customer demand affects work and skill requirements

Changes in production technology and marketing have profound implications for how work is organized and what skills are required to perform well on the job. Mechanical technologies work, break, and are repaired in ways that can be observed visually, and literacy skills are rarely necessary to operate and maintain them. By contrast, computer-based technologies are less observable and more complex. Their functions and structures are represented and communicated by symbolic materials such as manuals, diagrams, and other abstract materials. Workers require greater literacy to use these materials than they do for mechanical devices and electromechanical controls. The installation of computers in factories and offices has also significantly reduced the manual processing of routine data, thus driving down the need for low-skill clerical workers.

To improve speed and quality, reduce costs, and respond quickly to process, product, and market possibilities, suppliers integrate, pare, and innovate. The result is a more tightly integrated workplace, less downtime, and continuous adjustment. Producers integrate traditionally separate functions (for example, design, production, and marketing) to reduce the time lost when departments operate independently. They broaden job descriptions to give each worker authority over more of the tasks involved in responding to customer demand. They flatten organizational hierarchies and decentralize responsibility to reduce the time that is lost going up and back down hierarchical levels, simultaneously cutting middle management and supervisory jobs. The jobs of low-skill workers begin to incorporate some of the supervisory, planning, repair, maintenance, and quality control functions that were once reserved for managers or specialists.

These changes in the nature and organization of work have begun to change the type and level of skills required of workers. Workers need a broader knowledge of their jobs, better problem-solving skills, and greater initiative, flexibility, and adaptability in response to change. At all job levels they must understand their company's priorities in order to make sensible decisions. Since organizing for speed and cost reduces the "buffers" and "slack" (for example, extra time and inventory) that prevent short-run problems in one unit from spreading to others, they must perform their work tasks well and minimize errors.

Wherever these changes have occurred, they have ultimately reduced the number of low-skill jobs. But they have also increased opportunities for workers who are able to perform a broad range of tasks and to acquire additional skills quickly. The restructuring of production has also changed what workers must know and how they must use what they know. Although these changes have occurred gradually over decades in OECD countries, the pace of change is increasing and the long-term trends are becoming clear. Employment has grown more rapidly in the high- than in the low-skill occupations in OECD countries. Between 1975 and 1990, for example, high-skill occupations in the United States grew by 65 percent; low-skill occupations, by 24 percent. Occupational growth projected from 1990 to 2005 shows the same pattern (Berryman and Bailey, 1992). Consistent with these changes in occupational structure, workers with a college education reap greater economic returns to their education, while those with a secondary school education or less face declining real earnings (Figure 8.1). Analyses suggest that skill-intensive technological change is the single most important determinant of the growing wage gap between more and less educated workers (Bound and Johnson, 1995; Krugman, 1994; Berman, Bound and Griliches, 1994; and Katz and Murphy, 1992). In the United States a substantial share of college-driven wage premiums is correlated with the higher wages paid to workers who use computers (Krueger, 1993).

EDUCATION, TRAINING, AND ECONOMIC COMPETITIVENESS

Middle Eastern and North African countries face a future in which education and training will assume greater economic significance than in the past. As the region's economies shift toward the production and

Figure 8.1 Earnings gap between U.S. college graduates and high school graduates, 1965, 1975, and 1985

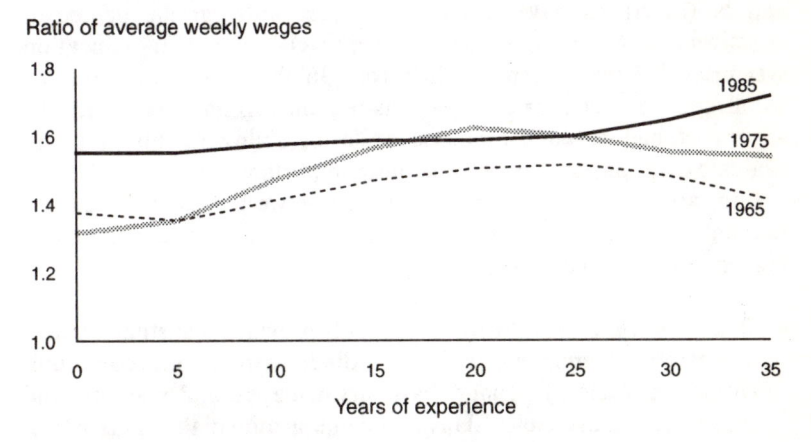

Source: Murphy and Welch, 1988.

export of higher-skill, higher-wage goods and services, skill requirements will change. This shift will necessitate rethinking education and training systems, including the role of informal learning. Studies have shown that the manner in which work and learning are organized within companies has a greater effect on the productivity of workers than do the skills that workers bring to their jobs (Adler, 1993a, and 1993b). Still, the knowledge and skills of workers strongly affect the options available to employers and the returns on any learning opportunities that they provide.

Firms competing in higher-wage international markets must employ more productive workers – workers who not only possess foundation skills, but are able to use them in particular ways. Competing in world markets implies change and uncertainty, demanding flexibility, problem-solving, and judgment by workers. These capabilities, known as higher-order cognitive skills, are applied in resolving problems that are not routine – where the path of action is not fully specified in advance. Such problems require the application of multiple, sometimes conflicting criteria. They also require the ability to deal with uncertainty using a self-regulated thinking process. A basic knowledge of mathematics is important, but even more so is the ability to apply mathematical tools to a wide range of novel problems.

Education is the primary instrument for transmitting knowledge, developing skills, and instilling attitudes and values. Schools also try to impart the social and cultural values required to ensure a coherent and cohesive political and social system. Schools in the Middle East and North Africa have served these roles with varying degree of effectiveness. As the next century approaches, however, education systems will have to expand their role. In the information age the recollection of facts, for example, has become less important with the advent of high-speed computers, while an ability to interpret and evaluate information has become more important.

Four areas can be used to assess the fit between a country's education and training system and the human capital required to compete in higher-wage international markets:

- *What does the system teach?* Do schools provide most students with a mastery of enabling skills – reading, writing, oral communications, a foreign language, basic mathematics, and scientific and technological principles? Have students acquired the skills necessary to interpret text on unfamiliar topics, to identify analogies and

patterns in information, and to assess the logical and empirical validity of statements in a broad range of subjects?
- *How does the system teach?* Do students have some control over learning? Is learning placed in a meaningful context? Does learning encourage the exploration of new or unfamiliar topics? Or is learning passive, fragmented, decontextualized, and organized around the aim of finding the "right" answer?
- *Whom does the system teach?* Does a growing share of the population have access to quality education at different levels? Or is access restricted largely to the children of the elite, particularly at higher levels of education? At any given level, does the quality of education differ sharply according to the social class of the students?
- *When does the system teach them?* Does the education system lay the foundations for continuous learning? Are opportunities for formal mid-career education and training available for people who want to upgrade their skills or change career direction? Are options for informal education readily available?

The absence of comparable data on the education systems of the Middle East and North Africa makes it difficult to evaluate their systems along these criteria. But anecdotal data suggest that the region's education and training systems differ greatly when assessed against these criteria. Some are more exclusive, selecting for and preparing the middle and upper classes. These systems set high – possibly unrealistically high – standards in examinations that determine a student's promotion into the next grade or level. Other countries have more inclusive systems, ensuring greater access. But the quality of such systems is frequently poor, which pushes up nonattendance rates and thus limits their coverage. To improve competitiveness countries in the Middle East and North Africa will have to seek broader participation in education and more sound educational quality within a sustainable public finance framework.

What the system teaches

Pre-university education should impart fundamental skills – literacy, oral communication, basic mathematics, higher-order cognitive skills, the basic principles of the physical and biological sciences, and the history and tradition of the national culture. Industrial countries are increasingly including computer skills in this basic package. Postsecondary and occupationally oriented programs should build on these fundamentals by imparting professional, technical, and occupational skills. School-based or firm-based occupational training is no substitute for solid fundamental skills, however (Mincer, 1989). Students should not enter occupationally oriented programs without the fundamentals unless the programs build these skills in the context of applied subjects.

Several benchmarks can be used to assess the performance of education systems in achieving these objectives. One is school curriculums – what subjects are taught. Another is "time on task," defined as instructional (or homework) time spent on each subject. A third dimension consists of the performance standards set for students, as indicated by the standards and questions on national exit or transition examinations. The final benchmark pertains to students' performance on these examinations, as well as on international comparative examinations.[1]

How the system teaches

The "how" of education refers to the design of the learning situation – to pedagogical strategies. The development of higher-order cognitive skills and initiative is particularly sensitive to how learning is organized. Current thinking on pedagogy rests on a powerful research base – the cognitive sciences – and there is little reason to believe that culture is more important in determining how human beings learn most effectively. In fact, some of the central principles in the cognitive sciences were established on the basis of cross-cultural studies. At the same time little information is available on how pedagogical strategies differ across countries and whether different cultures are able to achieve effective learning outcomes with pedagogies that work poorly in other cultures.

Many countries, including those in the Middle East and North Africa, use a traditional organization of learning: the teacher plays the active and expert role, students play the role of passive receivers of knowledge, and the objective is to learn the correct answers to fairly fixed questions in problem situations with little or no meaningful context (Table 8.1). One of the characteristics of this traditional learning organization is decontextualized learning, which contrasts with learning anchored in experience or a meaningful context (Box 8.1). The new pedagogy in mathematics and reading captures this contextualized learning organization by developing active inquiry, encouraging real-world problem-solving, emphasizing critical thinking, and fostering self-regulated learning.

Table 8.1 Traditional instruction and its effects on learning

Characteristic	Effects on learning
Passive learning. The teacher, as expert, acts as the source of knowledge and controller of learning. Learners are the passive receptacles of wisdom.	• Learners do not interact with problems and content and thus do not get experiential feedback. Students do not have a chance to make choices and judgments, to exert control, to formulate problems, or to make and learn from mistakes. • Being dependent on teachers for guidance and feedback undermines students' confidence in their logic and problem- solving abilities, discourages displays of initiative, and inhibits the development of cognitive self-management skills (knowing how to learn), which are essential to solving problems.
Fact-based learning. The focus is on getting the right answer rather than on developing understanding.	• Students resort to superficial accomplishment, figuring out the answers that teachers and tests want–but often at the expense of real learning. • Answers can be right for the wrong reasons, and a focus on the right answer means that the processes by which students reached the answer are not examined. • In their search for the right answers, teachers view student errors as failures rather than as opportunities to strengthen understanding. • An emphasis on the "right" answers means that learning does not focus on how to think about problems or on different ways of solving them.
Decontextualized learning. Material is taught without context or meaning in the belief that fundamentals that are learned in the absence of specific context can be applied to a wide range of specific situations.	• The lack of real-world context for abstract ideas eliminates the intuitive meaning that allows students to hook into and take possession of abstract ideas. • Decontextualized instruction maximizes forgetting, inattention, and passivity because it inhibits sense-making and meaning-making.

> **Box 8.1 Using context to learn concepts**
>
> Asian teachers rely much more heavily on context than U.S. teachers, both in terms of using concrete objects and real-world problems. Sendai teachers were twice as likely and Taipei teachers five times as likely as Chicago teachers to use concrete objects when teaching fifth-grade mathematics. U.S. teachers tended to introduce mathematical concepts and rules abstractly, only later (if ever) turning to real-world problems that involved those ideas.
>
> For example, the U.S. teachers would start a lesson on fractions by defining "fraction" formally and naming the elements of fractional notation ("denominator" and "numerator"). Asian teachers were more likely to introduce new mathematical ideas by first relating a real-world problem to the quantification needed for a mathematical solution. For example, a teacher might start the lesson by asking students to estimate how many liters of water a beaker contains, the amount always being some part of a whole liter. The teacher then helps the students translate their visual appreciation of "parts of" into fractional notations. The terms fraction, denominator, and numerator are mentioned only at the end of the lesson, once they have been connected to real-world experiences. Thus the Asian teachers understand that concrete experiences are not sufficient for learning – they must be linked to formal notation and abstract concepts. But real-world experiences provide the intuitive meaning that allows students to understand and take possession of abstract ideas.
>
> *Source*: Stigler and Stevenson, 1991.

The traditional pedagogy is suited to the skill requirements of organizations structured hierarchically around the performance of narrow and repetitive tasks. But this pedagogy begins to fail as enterprises change in response to the demands of international customers, especially in creating higher-order cognitive skills. Alternative paradigms for teaching and learning fit the skill requirements of new workplaces much more effectively (Table 8.2). They emphasize instruction that makes the student more responsible for his or her learning, that focuses on the processes by which answers are reached (not just on finding the right answers), and that uses context to give intuitive meaning to abstract ideas.

Table 8.2 Traditional and new approaches to working and learning

Traditional approach		New approach	
Workplace	School	Workplace	School
Passive order-taking in a hierarchical work organization; workers are closely supervised	Teachers as experts convey knowledge to passive learners	Workers are expected to take responsibility for identifying and solving problems and for adapting to change by learning	With teacher guidance and support, students assume responsibility for learning, in the process developing skills on how to learn
An emphasis on limited responses to limited problems and on getting a task done	An emphasis on facts and getting the right answers	Workers deal with nonroutine problems that must be analyzed and solved	A focus on alternative ways of framing issues and problems
A focus on specific tasks independent of the organizational context or business strategy	The material that is to be learned is stripped of meaningful context	Workers are expected to make decisions that require an understanding of the broader context of their work and their company's priorities	Ideas, principles, and facts are introduced, used, and understood in a meaningful context

Source: Berryman and Bailey, 1992.

Whom the system teaches

To support competition in higher-wage markets and to restrain growing income inequality, countries in the Middle East and North Africa must increase the share of their student-age populations who complete a quality education at each level. Except for Morocco, Saudi Arabia,

Table 8.3 Gross enrollments, Middle East and North Africa, 1992 (percent)

Country	Primary enrollment Total	Primary enrollment Males	Primary enrollment Females	Secondary enrollment Total	Secondary enrollment Males	Secondary enrollment Females	Tertiary enrollment total	Number of females per 100 males Primary	Number of females per 100 males Secondary	Number of females per 100 males Tertiary
Regional average	97		89	56		51	15	79	72	63
Algeria	99	*103*	92	60		53	12	83	81	44
Egypt	101	*109*	93	80		73	19	81	81	52
Iran	109	*118*	104	57		49	12	89	78	45
Iraq	96		87	48		37				64
Jordan	105	96	105	91		62	19	96	117	118
Lebanon	*112*	*115*	*110*	63		64				44
Morocco	69	78	57	28		29	10	68	70	58
Syria	109	*115*	103	50		43	19	87	71	71
Tunisia	117	*123*	112	43		42	11	87	82	68
Yemen	76	*110*	43	31	19	7		31	18	40

Note: Italicized figures are for most recent year for which data were available.
Source: World Bank, 1994, 1995; UNDP, 1994.

and Yemen, nearly all children between six and twelve years of age are enrolled in primary school in the Middle East and North Africa (Table 8.3). But of those who enter first grade, only about 80 percent complete the primary level. Although the region's enrollment rates for girls have improved dramatically in the past two decades, they still lag behind those of boys in all countries in the region, especially in rural areas and in Morocco and Yemen.

If enrollment targets that slightly exceed those of middle-income countries today are used as benchmarks, countries in the Middle East and North Africa will have to set a goal of 100 percent enrollment in primary school (ages 6–11) and 90 percent enrollment in lower secondary school (ages 12–14) by 2010 if their labor force is to be economically competitive in the next generation. Enrollment rates for the region conceal unknown levels of nonattendance and reflect a large number of repeaters. Thus the targets for the primary and lower secondary levels should pertain to completion of each level, and might be set at 95 percent for primary and 80 percent for lower secondary school. Only about 80 percent of primary school students currently complete primary school, and transition rates between the sixth and seventh grades are less than 70 percent of primary school completers (58 percent of the age-relevant cohort), with the worst performance found in the Maghreb. Since available data do not distinguish between lower and upper secondary enrollments, the gap between the 80 percent target for the completion of lower secondary education and current performance cannot be estimated.

Current performance in upper secondary cannot be estimated for the same reason. The region's average enrollment rate for lower and higher secondary levels (ages 12–17) was 56 percent in 1992, about the same percentage as in middle-income countries. But enrollment in the lower secondary grades is undoubtedly higher than in the higher secondary grades. Based on current enrollments in middle-income countries, the region's enrollment goals for upper secondary education over the next fifteen years should be 50 percent, a target that several countries in the region may have already met. The enrollment target for the tertiary level should be about 20 percent – slightly higher than the enrollment rates for upper-middle-income countries in 1992, and 5 percentage points higher than the 1992 percentage for the region – which is also almost being met by some countries in the region.

These quantitative goals cannot be divorced from quality issues. Educational quality should not be sacrificed to increase enrollment; quantity should be expanded only if quality can be ensured. The quality of higher education systems in several Middle Eastern and North African countries is poor or declining, due in part to the funding problems that have accompanied growth in enrollments. Nearly all Middle Eastern and North African countries offer free public higher education to all eligible students, and only in Iran, Jordan, and Lebanon are a significant number enrolled in private higher education. As enrollments in higher education have increased, public resource investments have not kept pace. The result has been declining unit costs and quality.

In vocational education the challenge for the region is to move from training that is dominated by social and supply objectives and financed and provided by governments to policies and programs that respond to market forces. Vocational schools should provide training that is useful to employers in the private sector, but should be supported and guided by the state. As unemployment rates for young workers have increased, many countries in the Middle East and North Africa have responded by offering secondary vocational education training. Unless youth unemployment is structural – a function of a mismatch between the supply of and demand for skills – training will not improve the job opportunities of graduates. In many countries the low rate of job creation is the fundamental problem. If vocational education is used simply as a form of social control, in that it keeps youths "off the streets" and reduces enrollment pressures on the universities, the price in external efficiency and opportunity costs is high. Students often do not receive quality training that they can use in the labor market and, by taking students out of academic secondary education, these programs reduce their chances of improving their fundamental skills.

In Egypt, for example, 61 percent of secondary-level students attend vocational or technical schools. Although these schools cost significantly more than general secondary schools, only 10 percent are adequately equipped; they also have too few teachers, and students are poorly motivated. The main purpose of these schools appears to be to keep students from attending higher education institutions. These programs are producing a supply of technical secondary school graduates that exceeds the demands of the economy. In fact, the demand for this type of worker could be met for several years from the current pool of unemployed workers with technical school credentials. International estimates indicate that technicians comprise only 5–6 percent of the production workforce, even in technically demanding industries. Egypt's system produces five to seven times this number. Furthermore, the technical education system is designed to meet formal sector needs in a country that still has a huge informal economic sector. A logical response in Egypt would be to downsize technical programs, increase general secondary education, and encourage enterprise-based training and apprenticeships.

When the system teaches

International competition will generate rapid change in the workplace and will increasingly require workers to acquire new skills throughout their lives. Education and training systems in the region must expand their "customer" base to include experienced workers. This means curricular flexibility – recasting programs of study as individual courses or modules that can be combined in different ways to meet different needs – and flexibility in training times and places – offering courses at different times and finding ways to retrain as close to the workplace as possible. Morocco, Tunisia, and Yemen, for example, are seeking to redirect public resources from pre-labor market programs to those directed at workers, and shifting to joint public-private financing in the process.

MEETING THE COSTS OF EDUCATION TARGETS

While a compelling economic case can be made for producing more qualified workers, implementing these changes in the education system will impose a financial burden that many governments will be unable to shoulder. Thus policymakers should pursue opportunities for reducing costs and explore alternative sources of funds for education.

How much will the targets cost?

The total annual cost of achieving the education expansion and improvement goals set forth earlier will be about $18 billion in 2010 in Egypt, Iran, Jordan, Morocco, and Tunisia (all costs are calculated in constant 1986 U.S. dollars).[2] This amount represents a 190 percent increase over the amount spent in the early 1990s by these five governments (Table 8.4). The most significant efforts will have to be made in Morocco, which will have to spend more than four times its 1992 level, and in Iran and Tunisia, which will have to spend nearly

Table 8.4 Public spending on education, Middle East and North Africa, 1990 (percent)

Country	Education as a share of GNP	Education as a share of total public spending	Primary and secondary school spending as a share of all education spending	Higher education spending as a share of all education spending
Regional average	5.2	21.0	74	18
Algeria	9.1	27.0		
Egypt	6.7		70	30
Iran	4.1	22.4	72	14
Iraq			77	21
Jordan	5.9	18.0	50	39
Lebanon		11.7		
Morocco	5.5	26.1	84	16
Syria	4.1	17.3	74	23
Tunisia	6.1	14.3	76	19

Note: Not available.
Source: UNDP, 1994.

three times 1992 levels. Spending in Jordan and Egypt will be less dramatic – about twice their 1992 levels. All projections reflect World Bank projections of population growth. If fertility declines more rapidly than is now expected, the cost of primary education would decline. But the impact of fertility on total education spending would be modest since the unit costs of primary and lower secondary schooling are small compared with the costs of upper secondary and tertiary instruction. The driving force behind the large increases in education spending over the next two decades will be the expansion in secondary and tertiary enrollment.

Population growth

The rate of population growth in the Middle East and North Africa is more than twice that of East Asia. Only Sub-Saharan Africa reports higher rates of fertility and natural population growth. While the growth rate will determine the size of the age cohorts entering primary school after the turn of the century, all of the children who will be educated in the next six years have already been born. Even the oldest of these new cohorts of children will not reach upper secondary school until 2009. Thus the impact of population growth on enrollment and costs for postprimary education until 2010 can be determined based on the size of the current school-age population.

Enrollment at virtually every level of education will thus expand rapidly in nearly all the countries in the region even if enrollment ratios do not increase. For the region as a whole the primary school-age cohort will increase by 21 percent, or about 13 million children. Several countries will have significantly higher rates. In Jordan, for example, the size of the primary school-age cohort will be more than 40 percent larger in 2010 than in 1995; in Iran it will be about 50 percent larger. The exceptions to this pattern are in countries whose birth rates have fallen substantially over the past decade. In Tunisia, for example, the number of primary school students will be only slightly greater in 2010 than it is now; in Egypt it will decline slightly if the enrollment ratio does not rise.

But even in countries whose population growth is slowing, the demand for secondary and tertiary slots will continue to increase to accommodate the current cohort as it moves through the system. Egypt and Tunisia will have the smallest increases in secondary school-age populations – about 10 percent in both countries. Other countries will see much greater expansion. The secondary school-age cohort will grow by about three-quarters in Iran, by more than half in Jordan, and by a third in Morocco.

Enrollment in higher education will expand significantly everywhere if current enrollment ratios are maintained. Except for Lebanon, the university-age populations in all the countries in the region will be at least a third larger than they are now. In Jordan and Tunisia these populations will increase by nearly half; in Iran and Yemen they will grow by about 80 percent.

If the amount spent per student stays the same, the financial requirements associated with enrollment growth driven solely by population growth will be about $2.5 billion a year by 2010 for the five countries. Total spending will be $8.6 billion a year. In Jordan and Morocco population growth alone will increase spending by about 45 percent and 25 percent, respectively, over 1992 costs. In Egypt and Tunisia, where population growth will have a small impact on the total cost of primary education, the proportional increases are smaller, at about 12 and 14 percent. The largest rate of increase will be in Iran, whose expenditures will increase by 65 percent, or $1.8 billion a year.

However, it is unreasonable to assume that the costs of education will stay the same over the next two decades, since growth in per capita income will likely fuel increases in teacher salaries. To capture the effects of changing salary levels, we have adjusted the costs of education by incorporating the projected rate of increase in real per capita income. This change in the assumptions underlying the analysis, combined with the effects of population growth, causes education expenditures to increase by about $6.1 billion a year by 2010, implying that costs will more than double. Countries that have the brightest economic prospects will see the largest changes. In Iran, for example, total expenditures for education will be 2.3 times their 1992 level, assuming that the real cost per student stays the same. In Jordan and Morocco total expenditures will nearly double over their 1992 level, given constant real costs per student.

The effects of increasing the quality of schooling can also be assessed. Increasing per student spending by 5 percent would give schools nearly twice the instructional materials. The cost would be about $840 million a year in 2010.

Enrollment ratios

As discussed earlier, competing successfully in world markets will require a workforce that is able to adjust rapidly to emerging market opportunities. Most workers in the high-performance economies of the future – not just the managers and senior engineering staff – will need to be able to function effectively without detailed guidance. Improving the human capital of the region's labor force will require enrollment targets that slightly exceed the enrollment ratios of middle- income countries today. By 2010 enrollment in primary school must be universal, enrollment in lower secondary education must be 90 percent, in upper secondary 50 percent, and in tertiary education 20 percent.

Most of the countries in the region have already achieved universal access to primary education. And the curricular and instructional improvements that are needed at this level will have only modest implications for the operating costs of the region's education systems. But given the rapid population growth over the past two decades, the enrollment ratio targets for secondary and higher education will have major financial consequences, even for countries that have already reached the target ratios. Meeting these targets will require nearly doubling enrollment in Iran, tripling enrollment in Morocco, and increasing it by about half in both Jordan and Tunisia. In tertiary education enrollment will have to more than double in Iran and triple in Morocco and Tunisia. In Egypt enrollment in higher education will have to increase by about 150 percent. Jordan will require the smallest increase, about 75 percent of its current base. For the region as a whole secondary school enrollment will have to increase by 8 million people between 1992 and 2010-an increase of 62 percent over the entire period, or 2.7 percent a year. Regionwide, enrollment in higher education will have to expand by 3 million students, or about 6.2 percent a year.

Implications for education expenditures

When combined with expanding school-age cohorts, as well as unit cost increases to maintain salary levels and to provide additional learning materials, the financial implications of these targets are considerable. Three countries – Iran, Jordan, and Morocco – will have to more than double their spending on primary education. The cost of supplying secondary education will rise by about 125 percent in Jordan, 140 percent in Tunisia, 175 percent in Iran, and nearly 400 percent in Morocco. Tertiary education costs will increase by between 1.0 and 6.3 times.

How will the targets be financed?

The five countries for which financing requirements have been analyzed spend about $6.1 billion a year on education (1986 dollars). As the school-age population cohorts expand, the enrollment targets will require a spending increase of about 7 percent a year, to $17.1 billion by 2010. While the returns from these investments are likely to be significantly higher than those from investments in plants and equipment, most governments in the region will be unable to finance these outlays from public funds. Some resources would be freed by increasing the efficiency of the education system, but allocations to the sector still must increase. Strong economic growth is likely to be the most important source of additional funds. In addition, the structural adjustment and privatization programs under way throughout the region will allow governments to shed some financial burdens, freeing funds for public use. Still, countries will also have to mobilize private funds from user fees for public institutions and expand the role of private institutions.

Efficiency

The region's higher education systems are inefficient and absorb a large share of the education budget in both the Mashreq and Maghreb regions. The long-standing policy of subsidizing university students' food, housing, and other living expenses is an obvious candidate for reform. These subsidies benefit relatively well-off members of society and are not necessary to achieve reasonable goals for university enrollment. The rationale for providing these subsidies is thus weak.

Inefficiencies can also be found in other parts of the education system. Student–teacher ratios at the primary level throughout the region are relatively generous compared with other countries. Except for Iran, student–teacher ratios at the secondary level are particularly generous and unit costs relatively high compared with other middle-income countries. Morocco has especially high unit costs in secondary education, with the share of secondary education in the public education budget among the largest in the world. But ensuring full funding for basic education should not necessitate lowering student–teacher ratios, which appears to be the strategy throughout the region. Indeed, experience in various countries suggests that lowering student–teacher ratios has little positive effect on learning. Rather, an appropriate mix of inputs – especially books and teaching – should be identified.

The persistently high rates of repetition and dropout represent sources of loss that should be attacked. To this end, instruction should be improved, more realistic standards for performance adopted, and aggressive policies to reduce absenteeism pursued. These activities will cost money, but will increase dramatically the effectiveness and efficiency of education systems.

Forces to encourage an efficient use of public funds for education throughout the region have been weak, with numerous political obstacles, for example, to restricting the hiring of new teachers. But continuing these inefficiencies will impose increasingly severe fiscal difficulties. At the same time there will be increasing social pressure to raise public school enrollments and to retain public financial support for secondary and higher education. Efficient public funding requires foremost that basic education be fully financed and that it receive the right mix of inputs; public funding for higher levels of education should be the residual in the government budget. Some countries, such as Jordan and Tunisia, appear to be providing an adequate amount to basic education.

Private resources in private institutions

Although significant, efficiency gains in the public sector will not provide sufficient resources for national education systems. Moreover, private sector development should be pursued even in the absence of financial pressures on public funds, to encourage diversity and market-based responses. Public education systems already receive substantial private resources in countries that do not have many private education institutions – as evidenced, for example, by the preponderance of private tutoring in Egypt and in some countries of the Maghreb. When financial pressure on public funds is a factor, the alternative to increasing the use of private funds is to reduce quality drastically or to starve lower levels of education.

In Iran, Jordan, and Lebanon the private sector plays a significant role in higher education. In Lebanon private education has dominated the entire sector for years in the absence of an operationally viable

---

Box 8.2 Iran's Islamic Azad University

Iran's Islamic Azad University, a privately financed, nonprofit institution founded in 1983, is possibly the largest private education enterprise in the world. By all measures, the institution's growth has been spectacular during the past ten years. Student enrollments are up from 2,500 to more than 300,000, degree programs from 10 to 126, and the number of campuses from 9 to 116, in 105 cities.

The university's students represent half the higher education enrollments in the country, while the remainder attend the public, tuition-free system. Remarkably, this has been achieved without state support for recurrent expenditures, most of which are covered by tuition fees. The state has helped the university's capital development by providing land and building grants during campus start-up. Private donations from local businesses and civic groups also have been instrumental.

The rapid expansion, coupled with the near-exclusive reliance on student tuition for recurrent spending, has nevertheless led to some qualitative deficiencies. Only 14 percent of faculty are fulltime. Laboratories and libraries lack basic provisions. And central management tools are weak. The university's current long-term development plan, with its emphasis on educational quality enhancement, aims at redressing these deficiencies.

Source: World Bank, 1992.

central government. Private higher education in Iran has also grown rapidly over the past ten years, from a base of nearly zero to about 50 percent (Box 8.2). In Jordan 20 percent of higher education students are enrolled in private sector institutions. In the past five years private universities have been established or authorized in Egypt, Morocco, and Tunisia. A large number of private business and commercial training schools exist throughout the region. In most countries preschooling is provided privately. Governments should encourage private education services in order to mobilize additional funds for this priority area.

Private resources in public institutions

A strong case can be made for introducing fees in public higher education. A minority of the age-relevant group will attend universities in these countries. In most cases this privilege will greatly enhance their earnings prospects. The economic rationale for granting public subsidies to these students is thus weak.

User fees could, however, exclude capable students from poor families, thus limiting their economic and social mobility. The abrupt imposition of fees could also have serious political ramifications. Countries throughout the world have addressed these two concerns by introducing student loan programs or deferred payment schemes. These mechanisms allow students and their families to finance the cost of higher education over a longer period of time; some of the schemes impose a surtax on the incomes of those who have been trained. Although not all the countries in the region can fulfill the requirements for implementing student loans or deferred payment contracts, they may be able to introduce at least some features of these schemes.

Distributing funds to the university system

The manner in which public finances are made available to the education system affects both its financial well-being and its performance. Three allocation mechanisms are common: public funds may be allocated directly to institutions under a line-item budget, a program budget may be adopted to provide funding based on the historical or standard costs of specific teaching activities, and funds may be distributed as grants to students or provided to institutions on the basis of enrollment. A financing system of line-item budgeting is likely to produce an education system that is neither sensitive to costs nor responsive to the demands of students or labor markets. If institutions receive funds on the basis of standardized program budgeting, they tend to offer a similar range of programs and quality of instruction. The absence of differentiation among institutions will impede flexibility in the system as a whole, making it unlikely to respond to new challenges in the labor market. Student-based financing ensures that the funding allocations among institutions reflect the students' assessment of each institution. Student-based financing also encourages diversity and increases access among poor students.

CONCLUSION

The education reforms that have been proposed in this paper will be difficult to implement. Experience with education reform elsewhere demonstrates that even modest changes in the content of education, methods of instruction, or access to schooling often provoke vigorous opposition. The political sensitivity of education policy reflects the nature of education's three main functions: socializing children to the community and the nation, developing the skills needed for economically productive activity, and equalizing opportunity. Discussions of schooling thus center around people's dreams for their children and their concepts of civic duty and harmonious society. Education inevitably becomes a magnet for wider social issues, such as the inculcation of moral values and the enhancement of national pride. In addition, education systems are major purchasers of construction services, furnishings, equipment, and other materials, as well as the largest employer of government workers. Consequently, virtually everyone has an interest in education policy, and these interests often conflict. Education reforms thus often disrupt existing power relationships, social contracts between governments and the governed, and truces that have emerged among interest groups.

In all countries, for example, curricular changes are always politically charged. The curriculum represents an agreement among the nation's different interest groups about what the country's children need to know in order to participate in the adult community. Changing that agreement disturbs what is often a fragile consensus – for example, the balance between secular and religious interests.

In some ways the pedagogical changes discussed earlier are more far-reaching than are the changes in curriculum. Resistance to these changes can be expected from some teachers. Under the new pedagogy they will be required to exchange a familiar role, in which they control the class, for an unfamiliar one, in which the student is the center of learning. School administrators and parents also tend to resist the new pedagogy. Both often judge the quality of education by the orderliness of the classroom. The new pedagogy, which gives greater responsibility and power to students for their own learning, creates less regimented and seemingly more chaotic classrooms.

Most education reforms fail because the process is poorly managed. But those failures have yielded important lessons.[3] The design and management of education reform can be improved significantly by drawing on those lessons. First, successful reform requires sustained leadership from high-level officials. These leaders must acquire the respect of interest groups and be willing to exercise their authority in resolving conflicts among these groups. Second, initiatives in several areas – including changes in curriculum, teacher training, testing formats, and the preparation of teaching materials – must be aligned and coordinated to support coherent reform. If examination systems do not reflect the objectives of the reformed curriculum, or teachers do not possess the skills required to teach new content, the reform is likely to fail.

Third, to inform their decisions, leaders must be provided with multiple and unbiased ways of measuring the technical and political progress of reform. Numerous decisions are required to direct reform; they will be made poorly in the absence of accurate feedback on the status of reform. Fourth, education reform must be monitored and refined continuously during the course of reform. Managing the conflicts that surface during implementation often requires modifying the original plan in order to broaden support for change. In addition, the implementation of a reform often reveals defects in its technical design. Inflexibility will solidify opposition and create serious technical weaknesses in the new program. Leaders' willingness to rethink the content of reform during implementation is thus critical to success.

For several years Tunisia and Jordan have pursued reforms that incorporate what are thought to be several requirements for successful change. Tunisia's leadership started reform in secondary education with a two-year, broadly participatory process of goal discussion and formation among members of Parliament, government, employers, teacher unions, and other interest groups. Once the various actors had reached agreement, it was embodied in a law. Leaders addressed the need for the stability of goals, partly by legislating that only the prime minister and president together could change any part of the law in the subsequent five years. But the most stabilizing action was the participatory process for framing the goals of the reform itself. The process created a consensus among groups with the power to try to change or circumvent the goals. The Tunisians then aligned the curriculum, examinations, and teacher in-service training with the goals.

Reform in Jordan has had three signal characteristics. One has been the visible and consistent leadership of the King and Crown Prince, who chaired all seventeen meetings of a year-long National Conference on Educational Development. Another has been the time frame for reform: the national conference produced a ten-year reform strategy. The third has been the development of a serious monitoring and assessment capacity to provide feedback on reform.

Notes

1. Jordan is the only country in the Middle East and North Africa to have participated in the 1991 International Assessment of Educational Progress. Jordan ranked last of the fifteen countries participating on both mathematics and science exams. The results for different cognitive processes are especially interesting. Jordan's students performed better on "conceptual understanding" of mathematics and "knowledge" of science (referring to a grasp of facts and concepts) than on "problem-solving" in mathematics and "integration" in science. The last two skills rely heavily on the higher-order cognitive skills that are essential to internationally competitive economies.

    The comments of a Moroccan official on secondary science teaching in Morocco are consistent with Jordan's results (Institut International de Planification de l'Education 1994, p. 157):

    > The objectives of science teaching do not seem to be well perceived by teachers, especially with regard to the relative importance of each objective. The majority of physical science teachers give a priority to knowledge development and consider the capacity to reason and to resolve problems only in fourth or fifth place among the objectives. This has direct consequences on teaching methodology.
    >
    > Our analysis also concludes that the science program, especially in natural science, is excessively detailed. The high proportion of secondary teachers who are required to give supplemental classes to cover the program is one indication of this excess. The excess detail, linked with the pressure of examinations, according to teachers, is what prevents them from putting in practice the active and experimental method recommended in the official instructions.

2. These countries account for 60 percent of the region's population (65 percent excluding the Gulf states).

3. See, for example, Sarason, 1991; Montenegro, 1995; Consortium on the Productivity of Schools, 1995; and Fullan, 1987.

References

Adler, P., 1993a. "Learning Bureaucracy: New United Motor Manufacturing, Inc," in *Research in Organizational Behavior*, Greenwich, Conn.: JAI Press.
———1993b. "Time and Motion Regained," *Harvard Business Review*, 98, Cambridge, Mass.
Berman, E., J. Bound and Z. Griliches, 1994. "Changes in Demand for Skilled Labor within U.S. Manufacturing Industries: Evidence from the Annual Survey of Manufacturing," *Quarterly Journal of Economics*, 109: 367–97.
Berryman, Sue E. and Thomas R. Bailey, 1992. "The Double Helix of Education and the Economy," Columbia University Teachers College, Institute on Education and the Economy, New York.
Bound, J. and G. Johnson, 1995. "What are the Causes of Rising Wage Inequality in the United States?" *Federal Reserve Bank of New York Economic Policy Review*, 1(1): 9-17.
Consortium on the Productivity of Schools, 1995. "Using What We Have to Get the Schools We Need," Columbia University Teachers College, Institute on Education and the Economy, New York.
Fullan, M. G. 1987. "Implementing Educational Change: What We Know," paper presented at a World Bank seminar for the implementation of education change, Washington, D.C.
Institut International de Planification de l'Education, 1994. *La Formation Scientifique au Maroc: Conditions et Options de Politique*, Paris: Ministère de l'Education du Royaume du Maroc.
Katz, L. and K. Murphy, 1992. "Changes in the Relative Wages, 1963–1987: Supply and Demand Factors," *Quarterly Journal of Economics*, 109: 35-78.
Krueger, Alan B., 1993. "How Computers Have Changed the Wage Structure: Evidence from Microdata, 1984–89," *Quarterly Journal of Economics*, 108: 33-60.
Krugman, Paul, 1994. "Technology's Revenge," *Wilson Quarterly:*, 56-64.
Mincer, J., 1989. "Labor Market Effects of Human Capital and its Adjustment to Technological Change," Columbia University Teachers College, Institute on Education and the Economy, New York.
Montenegro, Armando, 1995. "An Incomplete Educational Reform: The Case of Colombia," Washington, D.C., World Bank.
Murphy, K. and F. Welch, 1988. "Current Population Survey, 1964–86," Washington, D.C. : U.S. Bureau of Labor Statistics.
Sarason, S. B., 1991. *The Predictable Failure of Educational Reform*, San Francisco, Calif.: Jossey-Bass.
Stigler, J. W. and H. W. Stevenson, 1991. "How Asian Teachers Polish Each Lesson to Perfection," *American Educator* (Spring): 12-20.
UNDP (United Nations Development Programme), 1994. *Human Development Report*, New York: Oxford University Press.
World Bank, 1992. "Higher Education Policy Paper," Washington, D.C.: World Bank.

──── 1994. *Social Indicators of Development*, Baltimore, Md.: Johns Hopkins University Press.
──── 1995. *World Development Report 1995: Workers in an Integrating World*, New York: Oxford University Press.

9 Poverty in the Middle East and North Africa

Willem van Eeghen

Compared with the rest of the developing world, poverty in the Middle East and North Africa – whether expressed in levels of spending or consumption – is limited. Only about 5 percent of the region's population is classified as poor, and the region compares favorably with the rest of the world in terms of income equality. Still, the countries in the region have the potential – and, with the right strategies, can develop the resources-to do even better.

This chapter analyzes the significant changes in the number of poor that have occurred in the region in recent years and assesses the policies and programs that have been used to alleviate poverty. Rapid economic growth remains the most powerful instrument for reducing poverty, especially in the Middle East, where growth has an above-average impact on lowering the number of poor. Other tools – including better poverty monitoring systems, more secure social safety nets, labor-intensive growth and flexible employment patterns, investments in education and health, and better-targeted assistance program – are secondary but also can play a role. In addition, in order to effectively guide antipoverty policies, further research is needed on the design of poverty monitoring systems and social safety nets, the role of private transfers in alleviating poverty, and the determinants of inequality and their relationship to poverty reduction.

In the five years since the completion of the World Bank's *World Development Report 1990: Poverty*, poverty assessments have been completed for four Middle East and North African countries – Egypt, Jordan, Morocco, and Tunisia. These assessments provide data that yield insight into the extent of and government response to poverty throughout the region. The analysis here supplements that information by drawing on household expenditure surveys from six countries (Egypt, Jordan, Morocco, Tunisia, and, supplementarily, Algeria and Iran) to derive lessons about poverty in the region. The analysis indicates that economic growth has been the most important determinant of poverty performance in the Middle East and North Africa. But every country must make greater progress on several fronts – supporting labor-intensive economic development, building human capital, and targeting benefits – to keep poverty reduction policies on track.

POVERTY'S REACH

According to several basic indicators, poverty in the countries of the Middle East and North Africa is limited, and is less extensive than in other countries at similar stages of economic development. These indicators – incidence (or head count), poverty gap, severity of poverty, and income inequality – suggest that the region is not experiencing the growing poverty that is afflicting many other countries in the developing world (Appendix 9.1 p. 249). But these indicators mask three important trends that have adverse implications for the region's long-term progress in human resource development. First, not all of the six countries studied here saw poverty decline during the period of analysis; Iran and especially Jordan experienced an increase in poverty over the past ten years. Second, populations throughout the Middle East and North Africa – particularly women – still have

Table 9.1 Poverty in the Middle East and North Africa, 1985, 1990, and 1994

Country	1985 Number (thousands)	1985 Share of population (percent)	1990 Number (thousands)	1990 Share of population (percent)	1994[a] Number (thousands)	1994[a] Share of population (percent)
Algeria	400	1.83	290	1.16	439	1.60
Egypt	3,465	7.45	2,936	5.60	3,438	6.05
Iran	3,005	6.48	4,987	8.94	4,394	6.94
Jordan	110	4.16	413	12.60	589	13.83
Morocco	1,569	7.11	625	2.49	432	1.58
Tunisia	336	4.63	233	2.89	148	1.60
Total	8,885	6.06	9,484	5.59	9,440	5.01
Regional total	10,291	6.06	10,995	5.59	11,028	5.01

Note: Poor is defined as average spending of less than $1 a day at 1985 purchasing power parity.
a. Preliminary estimate.
Source: World Bank data.

limited access to basic health care and education. Third, economic growth in the region is not filtering down to several traditionally vulnerable groups: rural residents who do not own land, uneducated members of female-headed households, the elderly, and the handicapped.

Using a common definition of poverty (per capita spending of $1 a day at 1985 purchasing power parity prices, or PPP), about 5.6 percent of the total population of the Middle East and North Africa was poor in 1990 (Table 9.1).[1] This translates into about 11 million people. Although the number of poor people increased by about

Table 9.2 Poverty in various regions, 1985 and 1990 (percent)

Region/country	Year	\$21	\$30.42	\$40	\$50	\$60	Mean income
Middle East and	1985	2.82	6.06	10.94	17.42	24.77	128.80
North Africa	1990	2.32	5.59	11.07	18.37	26.27	124.09
Algeria	1985	0.59	1.83	4.94	10.63	18.01	136.06
	1990	0.43	1.16	3.01	6.78	12.32	155.67
Egypt	1985	2.70	7.45	13.48	21.19	30.21	93.33
	1990	0.55	5.60	13.76	24.45	35.36	97.75
Iran[b]	1985	4.67	6.48	8.86	11.95	15.63	176.33
	1990	5.93	8.94	12.99	18.16	24.08	133.17
Jordan	1985	0.68	4.16	11.48	20.60	29.74	116.83
	1990	3.09	12.60	24.54	36.52	47.17	86.12
Morocco	1985	2.25	7.11	15.88	27.04	38.25	95.42
	1990	0.24	2.49	8.78	17.14	25.70	124.07
Tunisia	1985	1.02	4.63	10.86	18.34	25.89	136.39
	1990	0.79	2.89	7.02	12.66	18.84	149.98
East Asia	1985	4.89	15.72	29.94	43.69	54.63	70.93
	1990	4.86	14.71	26.81	39.05	49.27	80.26
Latin America	1985	13.23	23.07	31.97	40.05	47.03	117.49
	1990	17.21	27.77	37.01	45.22	52.13	109.66
South Asia	1985	36.76	60.84	75.12	84.00	89.46	33.30
	1990	33.31	58.60	74.25	83.82	89.36	34.65
Sub-Saharan	1980	31.65	51.40	64.98	74.09	80.15	48.63
Africa	1985	33.44	52.89	65.55	74.11	80.00	48.92

a. Per person per month, expressed in 1985 purchasing power parity.
b. Distribution is based on the results of a HHBS for urban areas.
Sources: Chen, Datt and Ravallion (1993); World Bank staff calculations.

700,000 between 1985 and 1990 (and by another 35,000 between 1990 and 1994), the percentage of poor people in the region is actually declining. The number of poor people depends on the poverty line chosen for analysis: the higher the poverty line, the more people defined as poor. If a poverty line of $50 a person a month is used, the number of poor is much larger: about 40 million, or 20 percent of the region's population.

Whatever the poverty line used, the incidence of poverty in the Middle East and North Africa is lower than in other parts of the developing world (Table 9.2). And the percentage of *very* poor in the region has declined, with an increase in the proportion of those at the higher poverty lines of $40–$60 of monthly expenditures. Similarly, mean incomes in the region are higher than in other parts of the developing world. Given that poverty normally falls with rising mean incomes, this also indicates that poverty in the region is relatively low.

Compared with other countries that have roughly the same percentage of poor people (head count index) as the Middle East and North African countries studied here, the depth and the severity of poverty are also relatively limited in the Middle East and North Africa (Table 9.3). These small poverty gap and poverty severity indexes imply that the

Table 9.3 Incidence, depth, and severity of poverty, various countries (percent)

Country, year	Head count index	Poverty gap index	Poverty severity index
Colombia, 1980[a]	15.83	6.41	3.58
Venezuela, 1989	13.96	4.37	2.03
Jordan, 1992	**14.90**	**3.71**	**1.29**
Indonesia, 1984[a]	15.86	3.50	1.22
Malaysia, 1984	12.03	2.98	1.00
Morocco, 1990/91	**13.10**	**2.70**	**0.81**
Argentina, 1989[a]	7.20	1.93	0.77
Peru, 1985	7.16	1.77	0.69
Tunisia, 1990	**7.40**	**1.74**	**0.63**

Note: Based on domestic poverty lines. Comparator countries were chosen based on similar head count indexes.
a. Urban data.
Source: World Bank, 1995c.

> **Box 9.1 With perfect transfers, poverty could be eliminated**
>
> How much money would be needed to lift all the poor people in the Middle East and North Africa above the poverty line, given perfectly targeted transfers? In Morocco it would take only $25.7 million a year (0.08 percent of GDP) to lift each poor person above the domestic poverty line. In Tunisia it would take $2.4 million (0.01 percent of GDP), and in Jordan $7.7 million (0.16 percent of GDP). These amounts are considerably lower than the amounts spent on food subsidies, which are well above 1 percent of GDP.
>
> Transfers required to eliminate poverty under perfect targeting
>
> | Country, year | Poverty gap index (percent) | Number of poor (thousands) | Transfer required (millions of U.S. dollars) | Transfer as a share of GDP (percent) |
> |---|---|---|---|---|
> | Jordan, 1992 | 3.71 | 551 | 7.71 | 0.16 |
> | Morocco, 1990/91 | 2.70 | 3,738 | 25.68 | 0.08 |
> | Tunisia, 1990 | 1.74 | 600 | 2.37 | 0.01 |
>
> *Source*: Author's calculations.

actual transfers needed to move all poor people above the poverty line would not require a significant amount of resources (Box 9.1).

Income inequality

Income inequality in the Middle East and North Africa is relatively limited compared with other countries (Table 9.4). Gini coefficients compare favorably with countries in East Asia and Latin America; only Sri Lanka and Pakistan have less inequality. A similar picture emerges of income inequality according to the consumption ratio.

Poverty in the Middle East and North African countries for which we have data is more pronounced among largely traditional geographic, occupational, and demographic groups. Except for Jordan, poverty is most pronounced in rural areas, especially among those who own little or no land. But poverty is also rising in urban areas, especially among the self-employed engaged in small-scale trading activities. In all countries there is are groups of vulnerable people – the elderly, the handicapped, and members of multi-person female-headed housholds – who are hardly affected by overall economic growth.

Table 9.4 Income inequality, various countries (percent)

Country, year	Gini coefficient	Income inequality
Algeria, 1988	38.70	7.10
Jordan, 1992	43.30	8.30
Morocco, 1991	39.57	7.01
Tunisia, 1990	40.23	7.85
Chile, 1989	57.90	17.00
Malaysia, 1989	48.60	11.67
Pakistan, 1991	31.15	4.73[a]
Peru, 1990	43.87	10.50[b]
Sri Lanka, 1991	30.21	4.42
Thailand, 1990	47.14	8.31[c]

Notes: Income inequality is defined as the ratio of the top quintile of household income to the bottom quintile of household income.
a. 1990.
b. 1986.
c. 1988.
Source: World Bank, 1995c; World Bank data.

Basic social services

Despite its favorable poverty status among several developing countries, a different picture emerges about the region's poverty of opportunity-access to such basic services as health care and education (Shafik, 1994). In all countries poverty is strongly correlated with a lack of education. In Tunisia, for example, 90 percent of the heads of poor households did not complete primary school. Although the six countries studied here have made great progress in their social indicators over the past decade, they still lag behind other groups of low- and middle-income countries along some indicators (Table 9.5). And not all of the countries studied here are as socially advanced as their mean incomes might suggest. Whereas Tunisia and Jordan perform comparatively well, Algeria and Morocco do not. On the whole, the relatively favorable picture of poverty throughout the region is not mirrored by social indicators.

Table 9.5 Social indicators, various countries, 1993 (percent unless otherwise indicated)

Indicator	Algeria	Egypt	Iran	Jordan	Morocco	Tunisia	Lower-middle-income countries	Middle-income countries	Latin America	East Asia
Per capita income (U.S. dollars)	1,780	660	2,120	1,190	1,040	1,720	1,590	2,480	2,950	820
Population growth[a]	2.7	2.0	3.2	4.9	2.2	2.3	1.7	1.7	2.0	1.5
Infant mortality (per 1,000 live births)	53	64	35	27	66	42	75	74	82	77
Adult female illiteracy	55	66	57	30	62	44				
Primary school enrollment	99	101	109	105	69	120	103	104	106	117
Secondary school enrollment	60	80	57	91	28	43	52		45	52

Note: a. Average annual growth rate for 1980–93.
Source: World Bank data.

DETERMINANTS OF POVERTY

The favorable overall picture of poverty in the region masks important differences and sometimes rapid changes in poverty among the countries in our analysis. Of the four countries for which poverty assessments have been undertaken, three (Egypt, Morocco, and Tunisia) experienced a marked decline in poverty. Each had positive economic indicators and directed significant public spending to the social sector. Jordan, on the other hand, saw poverty increase sharply, reflecting sluggish GDP performance. These important changes took place over a fairly short period of time.

The analysis here assesses the determinants of these trends along dimensions that are linked to the extent of poverty: country policies, economic growth, income distribution, social sector spending and assistance programs, and food subsidies. To identify the determinants and to distinguish between growth and distributional effects, the discussion analyzes the time periods between two successive poverty surveys for each country, using domestic poverty lines.

Policies

This section draws on information from the World Bank's poverty assessments to show how economic indicators have affected social indicators in each country. The discussion is a prelude to a more specific analysis of the relationship between poverty and economic and social policy.

Egypt

The joint impact of economic growth and active social policies led to a substantial decline in poverty in Egypt. Rural poverty fell from 44 of the population in fiscal 1975 to 35 percent in fiscal 1982; in urban areas poverty fell from 35 percent to 27 percent over the same period. Poverty has since fallen even further (World Bank, 1995b). These reductions can be attributed to an average GDP growth rate of 7.5 percent a year during 1975–82, and to large social investments in education, health, water supply, and housing (comprising 22 percent of the total public investment program). Social sector spending reduced crude death rates by half, increased life expectancy from forty-six to sixty-two years, and reduced infant mortality from 179 to 60 per 1,000 live births.

Another positive social indicator was an increase in the daily per capita supply of calories, from 2,400 to 3,300. Part of this increase was due to an extensive – and expensive – set of consumer subsidies, most of which went toward wheat and flour. Evidence suggests that these subsidies protected food security and benefited the poor. In urban areas the subsidies accounted for 13 percent of the total expenditures of the lowest-income households; in rural areas this income effect was even higher, reaching 18 percent of total household expenditures.

It soon became clear, however, that public spending levels were unsustainable and had to be reduced. In the early 1980s the total subsidy budget accounted for 13 percent of GDP; by 1993 it had been reduced to about 2 percent. Although it is difficult to estimate the impact of this reduction on the poor, it must have been substantial, given that 40 percent of household expenditures in poor families goes toward subsidized foods (World Bank, 1995b).

Morocco

The percentage of people below the domestic poverty line in Morocco fell from 21 percent in fiscal 1985 to 13 percent in fiscal 1991. The decline was particularly pronounced in rural areas, from 32 percent to 18 percent. Some of this decline can be attributed to shifting employment patterns. Following the real effective depreciation of the exchange rate, real wages in export-oriented sectors dropped by 2.6 percent while employment expanded by 25.0 percent, largely due to a sharp increase in low-skilled jobs (World Bank, 1994b). In the domestic sectors, however, real wages increased and employment expanded by just 2 percent. Both the domestic and the export-oriented sectors saw a sharp increase in the use of temporary workers as firms responded to changing economic conditions. An expansion of manufacturing activity also led to a large migration from rural to urban areas.

Despite some progress in Morocco's social indicators, they remain well behind those of comparator countries. Achievements in education are particularly disappointing, with an overall primary school enrollment of 69 percent and a female primary school enrollment rate of just 57 percent. In addition, many social indicators reveal considerable disparities across regions and between urban and rural areas.

Tunisia

As in Morocco, real wages in Tunisia have declined. But disposable household income has increased because of income generated from an increase in self-employment, greater labor force participation, and large social transfers (World Bank, 1995e). Between 1985 and 1990 poverty within the general population fell from 11.2 percent to 7.4

percent. Roughly two-thirds of this drop can be attributed to the growth in consumption, and the rest to an improved income distribution. As in Morocco, increased consumption led to an expansion in such sectors as textiles, clothing, leather products, and tourism. These sectors created low-wage jobs for unskilled and temporary workers, which helped keep poverty under control.

Sustained fiscal adjustment was an important element of Tunisia's economic policies during 1985-90. The government was able to protect social expenditures, however, keeping them at about 18 percent of GDP while allowing expenditures in other categories to fall. Social spending helped smooth adjustment, reduce poverty, and improve the income distribution.

Jordan

Of the four countries under analysis, Jordan is the only one in which poverty increased – from 3 percent in 1987 to 15 percent in 1992. Economic contraction was the main cause. Between 1986 and 1992 mean household expenditures fell by 27 percent. Spending by poor households declined even more rapidly, by 36 percent. Income inequality also sharpened, with the Gini coefficient rising from 0.36 in 1986 to 0.43 in 1992. Part of this increase in inequality may be due to returnees from the Gulf in 1991; the returnees generally were wealthier than the average Jordanian. Still, most of the increase in poverty was the result of declining incomes; a much smaller portion can be attributed to growing income inequality (World Bank, 1994a).

Social spending in Jordan does not mirror its economic performance. Although spending on education, for example, fell by an average of 6 percent a year between 1987 and 1990, the annual drop in GDP was much larger – 8.3 percent. Overall, unit costs in both education are health are comparatively low. And judging by its indicators, Jordan was able to protect the quality of its educational and health services during the difficult years. In fact, its social indicators are still among the highest in the region. There is evidence that public expenditures on health and education have been targeted effectively at the poor. The real issue, however, is whether these expenditures are sustainable given Jordan's population growth rate (see Table 9.5).

Economic growth

The experiences of these four countries highlight the link between economic growth and poverty reduction. The contrast across the

Figure 9.1 Change in poverty and real GDP per capita, various countries

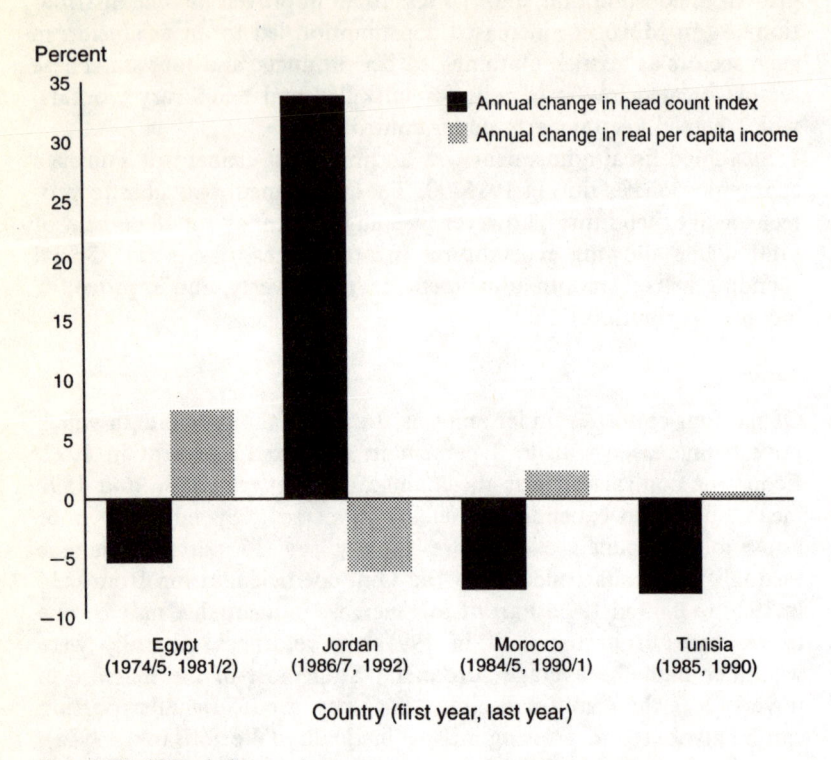

[Bar chart showing annual change in head count index and annual change in real per capita income for Egypt (1974/5, 1981/2), Jordan (1986/7, 1992), Morocco (1984/5, 1990/1), and Tunisia (1985, 1990).]

Source: World Bank data.

countries is striking: Egypt, Morocco, and Tunisia had sustained GDP growth per capita and saw poverty decline; Jordan had a sharp drop in GDP growth per capita and saw poverty increase. Although the growing number of returnees from the Gulf undoubtedly made it more difficult for Jordan to contain poverty, its average GDP growth overall has also been the lowest of the four countries, with consequent effects on the extent of poverty (Figure 9.1).[2] How does this strong relationship between poverty and economic growth manifest itself in these countries, and what does it portend for poverty reduction efforts in the region?

Growth was labor intensive

Growth in Morocco and Tunisia was labor-intensive, benefiting the poor. Macroeconomic and structural reforms changed the incentive structure, causing exports to become more competitive and the relative price of labor to capital to decline. Because real wages were kept in check, employment expanded rapidly. This new employment included both temporary and low-skill, low-wage jobs in such export-oriented manufacturing sectors as textiles, leather, and agro-industries. Employment also expanded in the informal sector.

The influx of low-skill workers into the labor force caused labor productivity to fall, however. Seen against wide unemployment, stagnation or even decline in labor productivity is not necessarily worrisome so long as total employment expands. In Morocco and Tunisia declining labor productivity reflected a rational use of surplus labor and sharp increases in employment and labor participation; the poor clearly benefited.

Poverty responds rapidly to growth

Across the region, poverty seemed to react more rapidly to changes in growth than in other parts of the developing world, as suggested by growth elasticities (Table 9.6). The higher a country's growth elasticity,

Table 9.6 Growth to poverty elasticities, selected countries

Country	Elasticity
Middle East and North Africa	
Algeria	−3.38
Jordan	−2.51
Morocco	−6.16
Tunisia	−3.52
Latin America	
Paraguay	−4.95
Honduras	−0.73
East and South Asia	
Singapore	−4.62
India	−0.81
Africa	
Côte d'Ivoire	−2.29
Zambia	−0.21

Note: Elasticities estimated using the $1 a day poverty line (at 1985 purchasing power parity). The comparator countries used here have the highest and lowest elasticites for their respective regions.
Source: World Bank, 1995c.

the lower the actual growth rate it needs to reduce the number of poor. These elasticities suggest that poverty reduction efforts that rely on rapid growth could achieve rapid results in the Middle East and North Africa.

Growth has a greater impact than income redistribution

The relationship between poverty and growth and poverty and income redistribution can be approximated by breaking down the changes in poverty into a growth component (the change in poverty that would have been observed if income distribution had remained the same), a redistribution component (the change that would have occurred had average income not changed), and the residual (the interaction between the growth and the redistribution effect). Consistent with international experience, the effects of economic growth outweigh those of income redistribution (Table 9.7). Among the three countries

Table 9.7 Growth and income redistribution as components of changes in poverty, Jordan, Morocco, and Tunisia (percent)

Country	Growth	Redistribution	Residual
Jordan	51.8	41.0	7.2
Morocco	80.3	−20.1	39.8
Tunisia	81.2	35.2	−16.4

Source: World Bank, 1995c.

for which we have data, the income redistribution effect was the most important for Jordan. Changes in income distribution between 1987 and 1992 helped increase poverty, indicating that the slowdown in economic growth was not compensated for by a more favorable income distribution. The relative importance of the income redistribution effect was smaller for Morocco and Tunisia, but the effect worked in different directions. In Tunisia income redistribution helped reduce poverty. In Morocco the reverse was true.

Income inequality

Although growth almost always reduces poverty, the link between growth and a more equitable income distribution is much more ambiguous. Jordan is the only country among those studied in which poverty increased and income inequality grew (Table 9.8). But a

Table 9.8 Poverty and income inequality, Jordan, Morocco, and Tunisia (percent)

Country	Year	Gini coefficient	Income inequality
Jordan	1986	36.19	6.02
	1982	43.30	8.30
Morocco	1985	39.10	4.02
	1991	39.57	7.01
Tunisia	1985	43.52	7.00[a]
	1990	40.23	7.85

Note: Income inequality is defined as the ratio of the top quintile of household income to the bottom quintile of household income.
a. 1975.
Source: World Bank, 1995c.

reduction in poverty is not always correlated with a more equitable income distribution. For example, income inequality seems to have increased in Tunisia as poverty fell. This trend suggests that income distribution has become more equal for middle-income households, while widening at the lower and higher ends. That is, growth has lifted people out of poverty, but those with higher incomes have benefited proportionally more from it. In absolute terms, however, the Middle East and North Africa's income inequality indicators remain low compared with those of other countries.

Social sector spending

It is almost impossible to reduce poverty over the long run unless investments are made that increase the human capital of the poor. Good education and health care help the poor lead more productive lives, increasing the return on public investment.

In the countries studied, however, large public expenditures on the social sectors have not yielded positive outcomes. Public spending on education, for example, was 7.3 percent of GDP in Tunisia, 7.1 percent in Jordan, 4.9 percent in Morocco, and 3.9 percent in Egypt – much higher amounts than in comparable countries. Yet these investments have generated poor returns according to such social indicators as school completion rates and employment among graduates. Similarly, public spending on health averages 2.4 percent of GDP (World Bank, 1993c), about the same as in Latin America or the formerly socialist economies of Eastern Europe. But returns have been disappointing, as evidenced by the region's low health indicators. Based on outcomes in other countries, Middle East and North Africa clearly has room to improve the effectiveness and quality of its social sector spending.

Besides increasing the returns to public investment in the social sectors, there is also a need to protect current spending levels, particularly for primary education. Average spending per primary student in Jordan, for example, amounts to about $166 a student in constant 1990 dollars (World Bank, 1994a). About 90 percent of this amount goes to teacher salaries; less than $8 a year (per student) is spent on textbooks and other supplies. This is much less than in countries that are competing with the Middle East and North Africa, and barely adequate to upgrade the quality of primary education. The limited data show that, despite fewer cuts in spending in the social sectors than on overall public spending, real spending per capita in the social sectors has declined in recent years (World Bank, 1995c). The only exception is Tunisia.

Governments need the resources to provide for education and health care. In this sense, GDP growth not only reduces poverty directly, it also provides the tax base necessary to carry out government-funded social programs. Jordan illustrates this case. Suppose that real spending per student remains constant between now and 2004. At zero percent GDP growth, maintaining spending would require a budgetary reallocation of about 15 percent of total government spending now to almost 30 percent by 2004. Effecting this reallocation would be virtually impossible. Maintaining social sector spending is critical to improving poverty indicators – but without GDP growth, funding is problematic.

Social assistance programs

The governments in the Middle East and North Africa have introduced a range of public assistance programs in an effort to directly address poverty (Appendix 9.2, p. 251). These include programs of direct assistance to the poor as well as extensive subsidies for such items as basic food and health. It is difficult to quantify the extent to which these efforts have helped alleviate poverty. The data to support a full poverty incidence or cost-effectiveness analysis often are unavailable; more analytical work will be required to determine how public spending affects the poor throughout the region. Unlike the clear relationship between poverty and economic growth, the link between poverty and social spending is less obvious or direct. In

Jordan, for example, an extensive set of social programs did not prevent poverty from rising dramatically between 1989 and 1992. By contrast, Morocco's social programs are less developed than Jordan's, yet poverty in Morocco declined sharply between fiscal 1985 and fiscal 1991.

Poor targeting makes for leaky programs

It is hard to design comprehensive social assistance programs that guarantee a minimum standard of living for everyone. Program coverage generally is vulnerable to leakage. Some programs, such as cash transfers to the poor and formal social security schemes, reach only some of the truly needy. General subsidies, which are meant to benefit everyone, leak disproportionately to the nonpoor. And the budgetary costs of these universal programs are often high and unsustainable. Food subsidy programs are a good example. Egypt spent more than 7 percent of its GDP on food subsidies in 1989. In Jordan and Morocco these subsidies were nearly 5 percent of GDP. These large amounts are well above the total transfers required to bring each poor person above the poverty line of those transfers were targeting perfectly (see Box 9.1). In Jordan, which had the highest incidence of poverty among the countries analyzed, it would take about 8.8 million Jordanian dinars to lift each poor person above the poverty line; the wheat subsidy alone in 1990 amounted to 50.0 million dinars.

In practice, the problem is more complicated than a simple transfer of budgetary resources away from the general public and toward the poor. First, it is extremely difficult to identify the poor. Second, changes in poverty occur rapidly; the transfer of funds to the poor requires extremely good monitoring. Third, the costs of exclusion – the chance that the genuinely poor are not being reached – are enormous in terms of lost human lives. Fourth, social assistance programs that reach large parts of the population (such as food subsidies) are politically difficult to abolish, as illustrated by the recent food riots in Egypt and Morocco.

Direct assistance – too broad or too narrow

Most direct assistance programs for the poor are also faring poorly, covering only a small portion of the poor or providing amounts that are too small to lift people above the poverty line. Jordan's National Assistance Fund covers only 22,000 households. By contrast, Egypt's social assistance program reaches an estimated 2.7 million beneficiaries, but it offers a small average payment to beneficiaries, covering about 5 percent of the absolute poverty line. Moreover, administrative costs can be high – in Egypt they reached 12 percent of total costs.

Private transfers often ensure survival

There is also evidence that government transfers tend to crowd out private transfers and reduce labor supply. In fact, private transfers – help provided by friends and family – are often a more significant source of income for the poor than government transfers. In Jordan, for example, they were about three times as high in 1992 (World Bank, 1994a). In Morocco an estimated 180,000 people (5 percent of the total) would be poor if not for private transfers from relatives working abroad (World Bank, 1994b). Experience in countries outside the region also suggests that financial help from relatives can be an extremely important safety net.

Food subsidies

There is evidence that food subsidies reach most of the poor and improve their nutritional status. Yet virtually every country in the Middle East and North Africa was forced to cut food subsidies when they became fiscally unsustainable. Egypt reduced them by more than 5 percent of GDP between 1989 and 1993 (World Bank, 1995b). Jordan cut them from 98 million Jordanian dinars in 1990 to 15 million dinars in 1992. In Morocco they fell from 4.5 percent of GDP in 1981 to 0.5 percent in 1993. Because food comprises a large share of the consumption of poor households, reductions in food subsidies undoubtedly affect many poor consumers. In Morocco and Tunisia, however, the reductions helped ease fiscal pressures, which in turn contributed to growth and reduced poverty.

Jordan and Egypt responded to cuts in food subsidies by designing new methods of delivery. Jordan introduced food coupons, which were offered to all households to allow them to purchase limited quantities of rice, sugar, and powdered milk at special stores. In practice, only one-third of the population used the coupon system. Egypt offered ration cards to deliver food subsidies, which in principle were available to everyone. Many poor people, however – especially the illiterate – found the administrative steps required to obtain a ration card an overwhelming obstacle. Tunisia introduced an innovative self-targeting scheme (Box 9.2).

> **Box 9.2 Tunisia uses quality differentiation to distribute food subsidies**
>
> Self-targeting mechanisms are based on the principle that only those who need the subsidy will choose to benefit from it. Tunisia used this approach when it restructured its food subsidy program to include a quality differentiation element. Goods consumed heavily by the poor continued to be subsidized, but they were made unattractive to other consumers. Subsidized milk, for example, is packaged in cheap cartons that are less attractive to wealthy consumers. At the same time, the sale of higher-quality versions of the products was liberalized. Subsidies for semolina, some types of bread, and brown sugar were maintained, but subsidies for couscous, pasta, baguettes, and cube sugar were eliminated. This program not only reduced costs by about 2 percent of GDP, it also targeted the poor 1.2 times more effectively.
>
> Despite this success at reducing costs, nutritional intake in Tunisia declined – caloric intake by 23 percent, and protein intake by 17 percent. Simulations show that the loss in caloric intake was 1.2 times greater among the poorest quintile than among the wealthiest. Given budgetary constraints, Tunisia eased the negative effect on the poor by targeting the subsidies more effectively. But the poor could not be protected from the overall price increases brought about by the reforms and the subsequent reduction in caloric intake.
>
> *Source*: World Bank, 1995d.

ESSENTIAL POLICIES AND PROGRAMS

The effectiveness of social policies, including reductions in poverty, depends heavily on adequate public resources. In turn, growth-oriented policies are the most effective vehicle for expanding the revenue base and for directly reducing poverty. Although budgetary reallocation toward spending categories that benefit the poor is desirable, massive budgetary shifts from the least to the most pro-poor programs are unlikely – too many vested interests are at stake. Still, social outcomes in the Middle East and North Africa must be improved. The region's governments must recognize that economic growth is essential if social programs are to be sustainable. Without growth, poverty is bound to increase, and the funding of social programs will run into problems. The preconditions for high growth are well known: a stable macroeconomic framework, fiscal discipline, the elimination of market distortions, incentives to promote private sector activity, outward-looking trade policies, and investments in education and infrastructure.

Growth is the most effective antipoverty tool

Egypt, Jordan, Morocco, and Tunisia's experiences suggest that economic growth is still the primary vehicle for reducing poverty. When average GDP growth is weak, a difference of 1 percentage point in annual GDP growth between now and 2004 has huge poverty implications – a reduction of about 8 million poor people for each additional percentage point of GDP growth. The additional impact on reducing poverty is smaller when GDP growth is strong. At that point interventions that are targeted precisely at the poor become important antipoverty tools.

World Bank projections of annual GDP growth for the region average about 3.2 percent. At this rate about 11 million people will be living below the poverty line ($1 a day at 1985 purchasing power parity prices) in 2004, and about 40 million people will be living below their domestic poverty line. This number is only slightly less than it is today. To make any significant impact on the number of poor, governments must push for 5 percent growth in GDP.

Growth must be labor-intensive

Growth itself is not enough. It must also be labor-intensive and lead to an expansion in employment. As such, it is important that wages be kept flexible. A move toward labor-intensive growth might reduce real wages and labor productivity. But, as illustrated by Morocco and Tunisia, this drop in real wages and labor productivity is essentially a reflection of an increase in the participation of low-skilled labor and temporary workers in the production process. Total output expands; the poor participate in this expansion and benefit from it.

Several accompanying policies can contribute to labor-intensive growth and the flexibility of labor. Minimum wages should not be set too high, and should reflect wages that are being paid in the informal sector. In addition, many Middle East and North African countries have banned private employment offices, relying instead on a public sector monopoly of employment services. These should be abolished. In some cases it might also be desirable to establish a limited compulsory unemployment insurance scheme, which makes it easier for firms to shed redundant labor in the event of changing economic circumstances.

Social spending and safety nets

Without major improvements in health and education, there will be no long-term growth, and without growth there will be no reduction in poverty. As pointed out earlier, returns on spending in the social sectors have been low, suggesting much room for improvements in service quality. But a major increase in spending will also be required to bring education levels up to international standards. To create the human capital needed to support economic growth, compete internationally, accommodate a growing population, and allow for quality improvements, Middle East and North African countries would have to spend about $26 billion a year on education by 2010 (World Bank, 1995a). This amount represents a 200 percent increase over the amounts spent in 1990. An increase of this magnitude can materialize only with strong GDP growth. Equally important, strong economic growth gives the private sector an incentive to invest in education, because private returns to education are high when economic growth is high. In turn, private education frees up scarce government resources and contributes to long-term growth. The cycle? No growth without expanded education, no expanded education without private sector involvement, no private sector involvement without growth, and no poverty reduction in the long run in the absence of either growth or education.

Social safety nets are also essential. Growth combined with an increased emphasis on education and health will not be enough to alleviate poverty for the widow, the landless laborer, or the female-headed household. Effective social safety nets have proved extremely difficult to design, and much more work is required to come up with practical recommendations. Without economic growth, however, social safety nets are likely to fail. Social safety nets would be forced to cover a growing number of people as resources were becoming increasingly scarce – an unmanageable task. Either the amount of assistance per person becomes too small (as in Egypt) or coverage is too limited (Jordan).

Improved cash transfers

The advantage of cash transfers is that they do not create price distortions and their costs are relatively transparent. Such transfers could be increased if target groups could be better identified. This system should be limited to the truly needy, however. Compared with other assistance programs in the Middle East and North Africa (notably food subsidies), cash transfers are still relatively limited, at less than 0.2 percent of GDP. These often have been restricted to the "visibly" poor, such as widows and orphans. They could be expanded by increasing, say, the coverage of Jordan's National Assistance Fund or the benefits offered by Egypt's cash transfer program (World Bank, 1995b).

Despite their benefits, cash transfers have two important drawbacks: they generate disincentives to work, and they substitute for private transfers. They also require a reliable poverty monitoring system for identifying the poor and responding to changes in the distribution of poverty. Processing cash transfer applications also takes time (sometimes several months), and for many people in the region the notion of receiving money from the government carries a stigma. Many Middle East and North African countries lack the administrative capability to deal with these issues.

Self-targeted interventions

Self-targeting can be an effective way of reducing the costs of existing programs and improving their targeting of the poor. Governments that hope to capture the benefits of shifting from universal to targeted programs must recognize the tradeoffs between reducing budgetary costs and protecting the poor, however. In Tunisia, for example, the shift to targeted subsidies was associated with a decline in overall nutritional intake, especially among the poor (see Box 9.2). Still, the self-targeted subsidy scheme proved effective, essentially dampening the negative effect of price adjustments and ensuring that a larger share of the subsidies reached the poor.

Public works programs also can be an effective self-targeting mechanism. Care must be taken when setting wages, however. If wages are too high, the programs might attract the better-off, absorb limited resources for reducing poverty, or undermine job creation in the private sector. Public work programs are particularly effective during recessions, when other job opportunities are scarce. In Tunisia, for example, an extensive public works program employs an average of 75,000 workers at an average cost of about $170 a year. The program has been an important source of seasonal employment, especially among rural workers during drought years.

A DATA COLLECTION AND RESEARCH AGENDA FOR THE FUTURE

This review underscores the need for more information and analysis to guide antipoverty policies in the Middle East and North Africa. What areas should be the subject of more in-depth research?

Poverty monitoring mechanisms

Poverty must be monitored more effectively, based on core household budget surveys administered on a regular basis. Poverty indicators can change sharply over a short period of time, and poverty's emergence or disappearance is not confined to easily identifiable groups. Thus, although household surveys are time-consuming and policy is often slow to respond to them, countries should streamline their data collection efforts and analytical capacity in order to carry out annual surveys covering key household consumption data. These surveys can be supplemented by more detailed surveys once every five years or so.

Analyses of public spending

Although the common wisdom is that public spending on primary education and basic health care is pro-poor, too little information is available on the impact of other public spending on poverty, particularly the various subsidies on food, energy, water, public transportation, and housing. At a time when most countries are being forced to reduce subsidies and public spending, the impact of the specific types of public spending on the poor must be assessed and prioritized. Several studies of Morocco, for example, could provide a useful foundation for future work on incidence analysis (Van de Walle and Nead, 1995).

Social assistance programs

More research is required on the design of effective social safety nets. Whereas evidence of the impact of economic growth and social sector spending on poverty is convincing, too little is known about the overall impact of social safety nets. The effectiveness of public works programs also needs to be assessed.

Private transfers

Private transfers play an important role in protecting people against economic shocks. But too little is known about the importance of these transfers in the Middle East and North Africa, and whether they are crowded out by government spending. Work carried out on the Philippines could serve as an example (Cox and Jimenez, 1995).

Poverty and income equality

The link between changes in income inequality and changes in poverty also warrants further research. Despite a decline in absolute poverty, increases in income inequality often lead to social tensions and the perception that poverty is increasing. From a political – economic perspective, increased income inequality makes it more difficult to implement economic reforms, ultimately undermining attempts to reduce poverty. The challenge is to identify policies that increase income equality without undermining growth. In the end the only sustainable growth pattern is the one that is widely shared – and perceived as such.

Appendix 9.1 Some Common Measures of Poverty

Head count index — The proportion of the population that falls below a specified poverty line. Commonly measured according to the level of household expenditures or income.

Poverty gap index — The additional money the average poor person would have to spend to reach the poverty line, expressed as a percentage of the poverty line. The poverty gap measures the *depth* poverty.

Poverty severity index — Reflects income inequality among the poor, something that the poverty gap does not. For example, the poverty gap is the same when two people have expenditures of 50 percent of the poverty line as when one person has expenditures of 75 percent of the poverty line and another spends only 25 percent of the poverty line. In both cases the poverty gap is 0.5. The poverty severity index overcomes this problem by calculating the mean of the squared proportionate poverty gaps: 0.25 in the first case of our example, and 0.32 in the second case, where the first case is $[(1-0.5)^2 + (1-0.5)^2] = 0.25$ and the second case is $[(1-0.75)^2 + (1-0.25)^2] = 0.31625$. The higher the poverty severity index, the more severe the poverty and the greater the inequality among the poor.

Income inequality

Gini coefficient — The most common indicator of comparative income inequality, the Gini coefficient bases inequality on the cumulative distribution of expenditures across the population. Specifically, it measures the area between the 45

	degree line and the Lorenz curve, which shows the cumulative percentage of individuals (x axis) against the cumulative percentage of income (y axis). With perfect equality the Lorenz curve would be equal to the 45 degree line. A Gini coefficient of 0 is perfect equality, a Gini coefficient of 1 is perfect inequality.
Consumption ratio	Income inequality can also be computed as the ratio of the consumption of the richest 20 percent to the consumption of the poorest 20 percent. In a perfectly equal world each decile would have the same share of consumption, and the ratio would be one. The lower the ratio, the less severe the income inequality.

Appendix 9.2 Social Assistance Programs in the Middle East and North Africa

Country/program	Number of people affected	Impact	Budgetary cost	Leakage
Algeria				
Family allowance[a#]	6 million	Limited because of its small size.	1.25 percent of GDP.	Large because there is no link between family income and eligibility.
School allowance	All families with children aged 6-21.	Small because it only goes to families that contribute to social security.	0.2 percent of GDP.	Large because there is no link between family income and eligibility.
Health care	Almost the entire population. Free public health care is available to social insurance contributors (and their dependents) and noncontributors alike.	Large. The entire population benefits from subsidized health care.	2.6 percent of GDP.	Large because there is no link between income and eligibility.
Consumer subsidies	The entire population. Implicit and explicit subsidies cover basic foodstuffs, energy products, and public services. Subsidies are neither rationed	Large because subsidies are not targeted. Although food subsidies have protected national	Explicit subsidies on food dropped from 4.7 percent of GDP in 1991 to 3.4 percent in 1992, to 2.0 percent in 1994.	Large. More goods are consumed, in absolute terms, by the rich than by the poor. The richest tenth of house holds

Country/program	Number of people affected	Impact	Budgetary cost	Leakage
	nor targeted. Since 1992 administered prices for food items have increased 50–130 percent, and explicit subsidies have been eliminated on all foodstuffs except bread, semolina, and milk.	nutrition levels, they have encouraged overconsumption, waste, and the re-export of imported basic foodstuffs.		receives more than twice the subsidy of the poorest tenth, and the top half of households receives 60 percent of food subsidies.
Public works and cash transfers	About 7 percent of the population. The two schemes, introduced in October 1994, provide income support to disadvantaged segments of the population. The public works scheme provides compensation to those able to work; cash transfers provide support to those unable to work (the elderly and the handicapped).	The public works scheme, in 3,183 sites, has 260,000 beneficiaries. The cash transfers cover 277,000 elderly and handicapped.	Less than 0.5 percent of GDP in 1994.	Large. Public works programs are not well-targeted. The eligibility lists for the cash transfers are rarely updated, and eligibility criteria are very general. Some people receive multiple benefits.
Unemployment insurance compensation scheme	Introduced in July 1994 to facilitate industrial restructuring. By April 1995, 34,000 cases had been referred to the fund.	Targeted to retrenched workers.	Not available.	Not available.

253

Appendix 9.1 Continued

Country/program	Number of people affected	Impact	Budgetary cost	Leakage
Egypt				
Food subsidies	87 percent of the population.	Large, although some of the poorest residents are not reached because they cannot afford to provide the necessary documentation.	4.8 percent of GDP.	Large because almost the entire population benefits.
Social assistance	2.7 million.	Small because the payment is only 5 percent of the absolute poverty line.	0.15 percent of GDP.	None.
Casual workers scheme	771,000.	Covers only 30 percent of the poor.	0.16 percent of GDP.	None.
Electricity subsidy	The entire population.	Regressive (ranges from 19.2 percent to 86.4 percent of cost for the highest and lowest consumption groups, respectively).	1.71 percent of GDP.	Large because the entire population benefits.
Water subsidy	All users, but price discrimination favors low-volume users.	Large.	4.9 percent of GDP.	Large because higher-income people benefit by more than their share in the population.

Country/program	Number of people affected	Impact	Budgetary cost	Leakage
Education subsidy	The entire population, to varying degrees.	Poorest do not benefit proportionately.	4.9 percent of GDP.	Large because higher-income people benefit by more than their share in the population.
Jordan Education	The entire population.	Poor do not benefit proportionately.	5.4 percent of GDP.	Large, but benefits are regressive.
Health care	5.5 million visits.	Military personnel are the main users.	3.7 percent of GDP.	Moderate. The poor pay lower fees.
Cash transfers to the unemployed poor	22,400 households.	Relies on individual assessment and self-selection of the chronically poor.	0.25 percent of GDP.	Limited because extensive documentation is required and monitoring ensures that all beneficiaries deserve the transfer.
Food coupons	All households.	Self-selection.	0.48 percent of GDP.	Large because only a third of expenditures go to the poorest fifth of the population.

Appendix 9.2 Continueed

Country/program	Number of people affected	Impact	Budgetary cost	Leakage
Morocco				
Health care	The entire population.	Moderate. There are vast regional imbalances in health expenditures.	3.5 percent of total public expenditures.	Large. The richest fifth of the population appropriates 40 percent of public spending in health, while the poorest two-fifths receive less than 20 percent.
Certificates for health care	Aimed at providing free access to basic services to the poor.	Fail to meet their objectives because the authorities have little knowledge of recipients' socioeconomic background.		Large.
National mutual aid activities		Targets the poor through nutrition assistance, preschool education, vocational training, and aid.	0.7 percent of total central government budget expenditures.	
Food support and nutrition programs	2.5 million. 875,000 children receive food at school.	Poor children are less likely to benefit since they are more likely to reside in rural areas and to not attend school.	0.5 percent of GDP.	Large.

Country/program	Number of people affected	Impact	Budgetary cost	Leakage
Public works program	Initiated in 1961; employs an average of 50,000 people a year.	Public works are in agricultural development, basic infra-structure, and social equipment. Workers are remunerated at the minimum wage and in some cases partly in food.	Not available.	None. Although there are no established targeting mechanisms, the public works program appears to reach the poor.
Women's programs	56,000 poor and illiterate women.	The programs consist of vocational training and technical and financial assistance to women's workshops and cooperatives.		
Tunisia General Compensation Fund	Until 1990 subsidies for food, animal feed, and fertilizers were available in unlimited quantities to the entire population. In fiscal 1991 the government introduced self-targeting mechanism, raised retail prices, and lowered the production costs of subsidized commodities.	Food subsidies are regressive as a percent-age of income. In 1993 they contributed more than seven times more to the purchasing power of the poor than to the rich, compared with about five times in 1990.	Self-targeting mechanism lowered expenditures on subsidy program from 3 percent of GDP in 1990 to 2 percent in 1993.	Large because anyone can buy subsidized products. Self-targeting mechanism reduced leakage, but further steps should be taken to sharpen the effectiveness of the reform.

Appendix 9.1 Continued

Country/program	Number of people affected	Impact	Budgetary cost	Leakage
Direct transfers	Targeted through indicators. Include food aid in school cafeterias and food rations for preschoolers, financial aid to the handicapped and the elderly poor, and cash transfers to poor families.	Services 300,000 preschoolers, 5,000 handicapped people, 4,700 elderly poor, and 101,000 needy families.	0.43 percent of GDP in 1994.	Large because eligibility lists are rarely updated and eligibility criteria are very general. Some people receive multiple benefits.
Health care	Basic health care is available to almost the entire population, regardless of income. The state provides free or subsidized health care to the poor through *Assistance Medicale Gratuité*.	Provides more or less uniform subsidies to the entire population. Subsidized health care provides strong incentives to evade paying into the social security system.	5.2 percent of GDP.	Large. More than half of the population enjoys free or heavily subsidized health care.
Public works program	Provides employment for the poor. Employs an average of 75,000 workers a year, one-third in urban areas and two-thirds in rural areas.	The programs, the largest and most effective employment programs for unskilled workers, have helped alleviate poverty in urban and rural areas. In urban areas public works mostly involve	About 0.12 percent of GDP in 1994.	None. Public works programs have been effective in targeting the poor through self-targeting mechanisms: setting wages below the minimum wage and locating in predominantly poor areas.

Country/program	Number of people affected	Impact	Budgetary cost	Leakage
		road maintenance, sewer cleaning and installation, removal of wastewater, and cleaning of public roads. In rural areas they mostly involve road work, soil conservation, and forestry activities.		

a. A reform of Algeria's social assistance programs in 1993 has resulted in some improvement from the results reported here.

Notes

1. Purchasing power parity is the adjustment of data on the money incomes of workers to reflect the actual power of a unit of local currency to buy goods and services in its country of issue, which may be more or less than what a unit of that currency would buy of equivalent goods and services in foreign countries at current market exchange rates.
2. Strong empirical evidence that economic growth is highly correlated with poverty also comes from an evaluation of the social impact of adjustment operations in thirty-three countries. In each of the nine countries with negative growth, poverty increased; in twenty-one of twenty-four countries with positive growth, poverty was reduced noticeably (World Bank, 1995c).

References

Chen, Shaohua, Gaurav Datt and Martin Ravallion, 1993. "Is Poverty Increasing in the Developing World?", *Policy Research Working Paper*, 1146. Washington, D.C.: World Bank.

Cox D. and E. Jimenez, 1995. "Private Transfers and the Effectiveness of Public Income Redistribution in the Philippines." in Dominique Van de Walle and Kimberly Nead, (eds.), *Spending and the Poor*, Baltimore, Md.: Johns Hopkins University Press.

IMF (International Monetary Fund), 1991. "Algeria: Comments on IMF Report on Social Safety Nets," Washington, D.C.: International Monetary Fund.

Nead, Kimberly and Dominique van de Walle, 1995. "Public Spending and the Poor Theory and Evidence," Washington, D.C.: World Bank.

Ravallion, Martin, 1992. "Poverty Comparisons: A Guide to Concepts and Methods," Washington, D.C.: World Bank.

Ravallion, Martin, Gaurav Datt, Dominique van de Walle, and Elaine Chan, 1991. "Quantifying the Magnitude and Severity of Absolute Poverty in the Developing World in the Mid-1980s," *Policy Research Working Paper*, 587, Washington, D.C.: World Bank.

Shafik, Nemat, 1994. "Big Spending, Small Returns: The Paradox of Human Resource Development in the Middle East." World Bank, Middle East and North Africa Region, Washington, D.C.: World Bank.

Van de Walle, Dominique and Kimberly Nead, 1995. *Spending and the Poor*, Baltimore, Md.: Johns Hopkins University Press.

World Bank, 1991. "Egypt: Alleviating Poverty During Structural Adjustment," Washington, D.C.: World Bank.

———1993a. *Poverty Reduction Handbook*. Washington, D.C.: World Bank.

———1993b. "Tunisia: The Social Protection System, " Washington, D.C.: World Bank.

———1993c. *World Development Report 1990: Investing in Health*, New York: Oxford University Press.

―――――1994a. "Jordan: Poverty Assessment," Washington, D.C.: World Bank.

―――――1994b. "Poverty, Adjustment, and Growth of Morocco," Washington, D.C.: World Bank.

―――――1995a. *Claiming the Future: Choosing Prosperity in the Middle East and North Africa*, Middle East and North Africa Region, Washington, D.C.: World Bank.

―――――1995b. "Egypt: Social Welfare Study (Strengthening The Social Safety Net)," Washington, D.C.: World Bank.

―――――1995c. *The Social Impact of Adjustment Operations*, Operations Evaluation Department, Washington, D.C.: World Bank.

―――――1995d. "Tunisia: From Universal Food Subsidies to a Self-Targeted Program," Washington, D.C.: World Bank.

―――――1995e. "Tunisia: Growth, Policies, and Poverty Alleviation," Washington, D.C.: World Bank.

10 Environmentally Sustainable Development in the Middle East and North Africa

Hamid Mohtadi

Oil has shaped economic development throughout the Middle East and North Africa. This reliance on oil, abetted by the aridity of the region's land, has produced a distinct pattern of environmental degradation. Oil has allowed the countries in the region to pursue inward-oriented policies that protect the industrial sector at the expense of natural resources and the environment; it also has supported massive energy subsidies, causing an overreliance on highly polluting fossil fuels. This chapter assesses the impact of these policies on the region's environment and its peoples' health and proposes policy and institutional reforms, including better-defined property rights, improved information flows, increased public education, and an eventual move outward- and market-oriented economic development.

The extensive environmental degradation of the past forty years has heightened concern about the global environment. Problem areas include the rapidly depleting ozone layer, the greenhouse effect, acid rain, deforestation and desertification, the loss of vegetated land, municipal and hazardous waste, air and water pollution, a declining fish population, and the loss of animal species. During 1945–90, a period in which the world's population doubled, nearly 11 percent of the Earth's vegetated soil (1.2 billion hectares) was degraded. Furthermore, deforestation increased by 50 percent during the 1980s, reaching an annual average of 17 million hectares (WRI, 1992). Among these lands, tropical rainforests-which are particularly crucial because they support a vast range of plants and animals and affect the Earth's climate-are being lost at even faster rates. During the 1980s, for example, an estimated 9 percent of the world's tropical forests were lost (FAO, 1991). Similarly, between 1965 and 1990 the atmospheric concentration of carbon dioxide and methane (two greenhouse gases) increased by 11 percent and 23 percent, respectively (WRI, 1992).

Figure 10.1 Environmental indicators at different country income levels

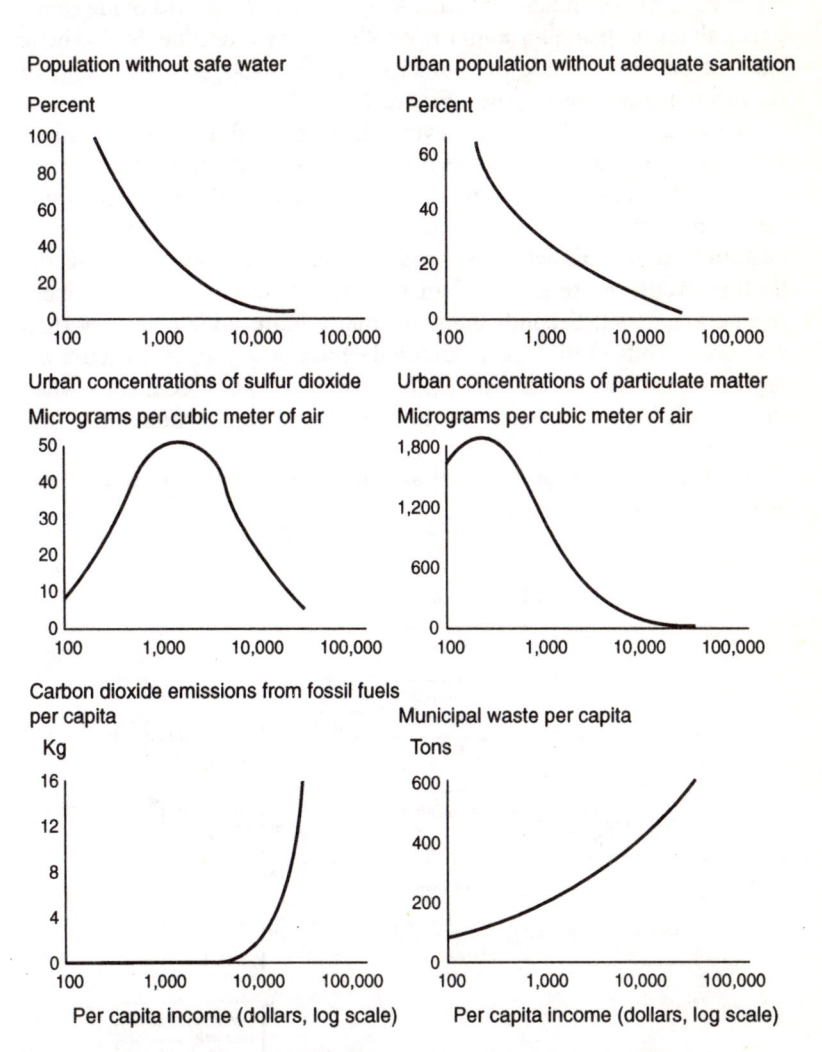

Population without safe water
Percent

Urban population without adequate sanitation
Percent

Urban concentrations of sulfur dioxide
Micrograms per cubic meter of air

Urban concentrations of particulate matter
Micrograms per cubic meter of air

Carbon dioxide emissions from fossil fuels per capita
Kg

Municipal waste per capita
Tons

Per capita income (dollars, log scale)

Note: Estimates based on cross-country regression of data from the 1980s.
Source: World Bank, 1992, based on Shafik and Bandyopadhyay, 1992.

What does the future hold for the state of the environment? One way of answering this question is to study environmental trends as countries grow. Studies that use this approach suggest a mixed picture (World Bank, 1992; Shafik and Bandyopadhyay, 1992). Certain indicators, such as those reflecting the provision of safe water or urban sanitation, indicate that economic growth has a positive environmental impact. Other indicators, such as measures of sulfur dioxide or air particulates, indicate an initial rise followed by a decline. Still others, such as carbon dioxide or municipal waste levels, show no sign of relenting as economies grow (Figure 10.1).

The conclusions from such evidence must be drawn with caution. For example, falling indicators do not necessarily imply environmental improvement, for two reasons. First, many environmental processes are cumulative over time, and thus even a declining flow of pollution may still lead to catastrophic cumulative results if the decline occurs more slowly than the rate at which the environment regenerates itself. Second, there are many more poor countries than rich ones. Thus even if the long-run declines in Figure 10.1 accurately represent the future environmental profile of poor countries when they reach higher incomes, worldwide production of pollutants that

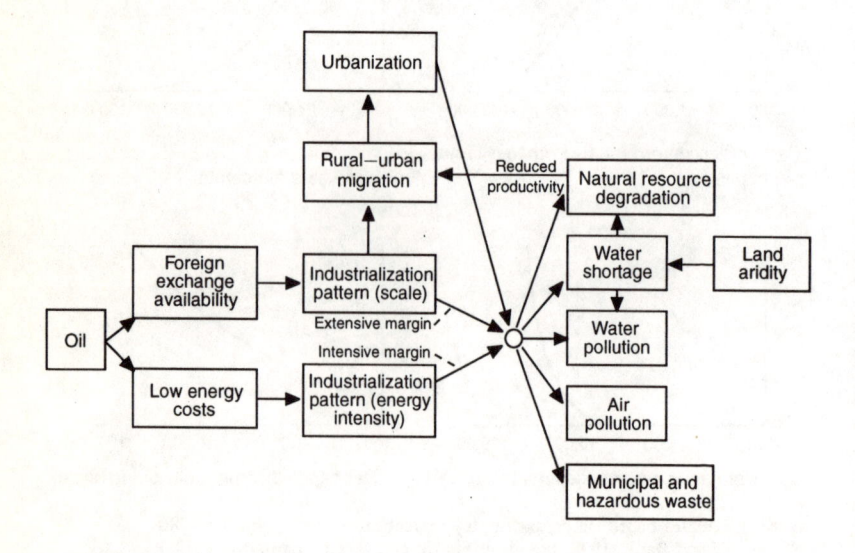

Figure 10.2 Economic development and the environment in the Middle East and North Africa

exhibit an inverted "U" pattern (such as sulfur dioxide) might still increase.

The countries of the Middle East and North Africa occupy a place of importance in this global environmental perspective and thus must fulfill certain responsibilities, both regionally and globally. Several factors warrant an analysis of these countries as a group. First, because it shapes economic behavior, economic policies, and socioeconomic transformations (including urbanization patterns), oil has important implications for the quality of the environment in many of these countries. Second, the aridity of land and the scarcity of water play significant roles in the region's environmental profile. The interaction between these two factors produces a pattern of environmental degradation that is unique to the region (Figure 10.2).[1]

ECONOMIC DEVELOPMENT AND THE ENVIRONMENT

Industrialization and urbanization are the two primary determinants of the ecological profile of the Middle East and North Africa. Each has an impact on the quality of air and water, and together they influence the type of natural resource degradation that occurs throughout the region.

Industrialization

During 1970–91 many countries in the region experienced extremely high rates of industrial growth, largely as a result of substantial foreign exchange revenues from oil and the availability of oil as a cheap energy source for domestic use (World Bank, 1995). All the countries in the region except Israel, Jordan, Lebanon, and Morocco are net exporters of commercial energy.

For the most part the pursuit of industrialization in the region has been predicated on inward-oriented policies that protect the industrial sector at the expense of natural resources, mainly in the form of energy subsidies for electric power plants and transportation. Annual fossil fuel subsidies in the region total nearly $14 billion, and electricity subsidies are nearly $12 billion (World Bank, 1995). The comparative inefficiency of energy use in the Middle East and North Africa reflects this policy bias. Countries in the region use nearly twice the energy as countries in Latin America and the Caribbean for the same dollar of gross domestic product (GDP) produced.

Table 10.1 Estimated pollution loads by sector, Middle East and North Africa (thousand tons)

Sector	Sulfur dioxide	Nitrogen oxides	Solid particulates	Carbon monoxide	Hydrocarbons
Power	1,600	1,000	200	150	50
	(39)	(34)	(17)	(<1)	(<1)
Industry	2,000	780	770	60	330
	(49)	(26)	(65)	(<1)	(10)
Refineries	1,100	80	50	10	300
	(27)	(<5)	(<5)	(<1)	(10)
Cement and steel	150	300	600		
	(<5)	(10)	(50)		
Other	750	400	120	50	30
	(18)	(13)	(10)	(<1)	(<1)
Road transport	200	1,100	120	16,000	3,000
	(5)	(37)	(10)	(>90)	(>80)
Residential	300	100	100	20	10
	(7)	(<5)	(8)	(<1)	(1)

Note: Numbers in parentheses are percentages.
Source: World Bank, 1995.

This pattern of industrialization implies a use of fossil fuels that is both intensive and extensive. Pollution loads from the main sectors – power, industry, refineries, cement and steel, transportation, and residential – confirm this pattern (Table 10.1). Industrial policies contribute to these profiles. For example, sulfur dioxide emissions from power plants account for nearly 40 percent of regional emissions. Many power plants use fossil fuels, about 45 percent of which consist of heavy fuels with a high sulfur content. Consumption of these fuels in the Middle East and North Africa grew by 1.7 percent a year during the 1980s (World Bank, 1995). Similar links exist between the use of heavy fossil fuels and nitrogen oxide gases.

Industrial discharges also affect water quality. In Egypt, for example, industrially generated wastewater from Greater Cairo dumps large quantities of mercury and organic waste into local lakes that are used for agriculture. In Jordan industrial waste from battery-charging processes enters municipal sewers, creating high concentrations of lead. In Oran, Algeria industries discharge mercury and cadmium into the local bay; in Morocco pollution from refineries and paper and chemical industries is discharged into Sebou river (World Bank, 1995). The severe and often toxic nature of these industrial discharges is compounded by rapid urbanization and the scarcity of water.

Urbanization

In addition to its direct impact on the environment, industrialization has indirectly contributed to urban pollution by accelerating the pace of urbanization. In the past twenty-five years the region's urban population rose by more than 400 percent, from 32 million to 132 million people. Rural–urban migration alone has been 4–6 percent a year. Excluding secondary cities – whose growth may reflect reclassification as rural communities expand and are reclassified as urban – the urban population in primary cities grew by 3.8 percent a year during this period (World Bank, 1995). Aside from births, rural – urban migration is largely responsible for this rapid urbanization. Rural–urban migration is caused largely by urban "pull" factors but is exacerbated by rural "push" factors (Mohtadi, 1986, 1990) and natural resource degradation.

To the extent that the pattern of natural resource degradation and rural push is caused by rural outmigration, a vicious circle emerges. Moreover, rural outmigrants come increasingly from the younger and more productive segments of the rural population, imposing an even greater productivity loss. This unstable pattern may explain the existence of megacities in the Middle East and North Africa. Although these disproportionately large cities are emerging in other developing countries, the rapid industrialization of the "oil" countries in the Middle East and North Africa is likely to have contributed to this effect.

Urbanization exacerbates the environmental degradation caused by industrialization. For example, the pollution of nearly all local water sources in the Middle East and North Africa is caused by both industrial discharges and untreated residential waste (World Bank, 1995). In addition, one of the by-products of urbanization – a massive vehicle population – contributes a large share of air pollution, compounding the already high levels of fossil fuel emissions from industry. Road transport systems as a whole are the largest single source of air pollution in major cities (Table 10.2).

Auto pollution in the Middle East and North Africa poses a more serious environmental threat than in other regions, largely because of the aging vehicle population. Imports of new cars have fallen considerably in recent years due to foreign exchange problems from terms of trade shocks, declining oil prices, and regional and local conflicts. Many of the vehicles that were bought during the 1960s and 1970s lack adequate emissions control systems, and many have engines that run on leaded gasoline. In Egypt, Iran, and Syria the average vehicle is

Table 10.2 Road transportation and air pollution, selected cities

City	Year	Total pollutants[a] (thousands of metric tons)	Carbon dioxide	Hydrocarbons	Nitrogen oxides	Sulfur dioxide	Particulates	Total
Ankara, Turkey	1980	690	77	73	44	3	2	57
Kuala Lumpur, Malaysia	1987	435	97	95	46	1	46	79
Los Angeles, California	1982	3,391	99	50	64	21	—	87
Manila, Philippines	1987	500	93	82	73	12	60	71
Mexico City, Mexico	1987	5,027	99	89	64	2	9	80
Osaka, Japan	1982	141	100	17	60	43	24	59
Sao Paulo, Brazil	1987	2,110	94	76	89	59	22	86
Seoul, Republic of Korea	1983	—	15	40	60	7	35	35

— Not available.
Source: Faiz, Sinha, and, Walsh, 1990.

fifteen years old; compared with new vehicles their emissions are twenty to twenty-five times higher for hydrocarbons and carbon monoxide, four times higher for nitrogen oxides, and five to ten times higher for particulates (World Bank, 1995). Perhaps the most sinister toxic pollutant comes from the lead contained in gasoline, which is intensified by the fuel inefficiency of older cars. For example, airborne concentrations of particulates and lead in the region's megacities often exceed World Health Organization (WHO) guidelines by 200–500 percent (World Bank, 1995).

The impact on natural resources

The interaction between urbanization and industrialization – the determinants of natural resource degradation – suggests a combined approach toward addressing the several categories of natural resources.

Water scarcity, use, and quality

Countries in the Middle East and North Africa are distinguished by the aridity of their land and the scarcity of water. Combined, these two factors increase the inefficiency of water allocations and make water pollution even more severe. The availability of renewable water resources in the region has declined from 3,500 to 1,500 cubic meters per capita since the 1960s, and at current population growth rates will drop to 700 cubic meters per capita by 2025 (World Bank, 1995). These figures include even the ostensibly water-rich countries of Algeria, Morocco, and Tunisia, where water exploitation is technically feasible.

Water use is critically affected by population growth, urbanization, and water-intensive agriculture. Agriculture accounts for 57 percent of the water used in the region, industry for 7 percent, and the domestic sector for 6 percent (World Bank, 1995). Yet despite industry's smaller share, the sector has the predominant negative impact on the quality of the available water, due to its intensive discharge of industrial pollutants. And in the coastal areas of the Red Sea and the Persian Gulf, offshore oil exploration, oil traffic, and tourism are harming the deep water and its fish populations.

Deforestation and desertification

About 4.3 percent (38 million hectares) of the region is forested. Iran contains nearly half this total and suffers from the highest rate of deforestation, about 200,000 hectares a year (World Bank, 1995). Its rapid deforestation is being caused by pressure to convert forest land into agricultural land in response to one of the highest population growth rates in the world – nearly 3.9 percent. Alarmingly, the trend toward deforestation does not appear to be slowing. The Iranian government recently announced that parts of the forested land in the Caspian coast will be denationalized and given to 30,000 farmers for cultivation; this policy is similar to the one adopted by Brazil in the 1970s and 1980s that led to irreversible rainforest damage. If such policies continue, they will eventually lead to the total loss of forested land in the area.

Like deforestation, desertification in the region is often caused by pressure for food in response to rapid population growth rates. Desertifcation's most immediate causes include overgrazing of land and the conversion of productive pastures into unsustainable crop cultivation (World Bank, 1995).

EMPIRICAL ANALYSIS

Oil, because of its direct (by encouraging excessive energy use) and indirect (by supporting inward-oriented policies that protect the industrial sector) effects, is a crucial determinant of environmental quality in the Middle East and North Africa. This section assesses these effects by using a formal regression analysis that examines the relationship between oil export revenues and economic openness, as well as the impact of oil and economic openness on the intensity of energy use per dollar of GNP produced. Since higher energy use is associated with higher levels of pollution, the environmental implications of this analysis are self-evident.

The statistical sample and model

The sample is based on ninety-seven countries taken from World Bank (1990) for which data were available on the following variables:

y_1 = Population (million)
y_2 = GNP per capita (U.S. dollar)
y_3 = Energy use per capita (kilogram of oil equivalent)
y_4 = Export shares devoted to fuels and other raw materials
y_5 = Total exports (U.S. dollar)

y_6 = Total imports (U.S. dollar)
From these, the following variables were constructed:
GNP = $y_1 \cdot y^2$
z_3 = Energy use per dollar of GNP = $y_1 \cdot y_3$/GNP
z_4 = Exports of fuels and other raw materials relative to GNP = $y_4 \cdot y_5$/GNP
z_5 = Imports plus exports relative to GNP = (y_5+y_6)/GNP
z_6 = A measure of nonfuel and raw material economic openness = z_5-z_4
DM = Dummy variable for countries in the Middle East and North Africa

To examine the overall impact of fuel and raw material exports on energy use, we use the following linear model:

$$z_{3i} = \alpha_1 + \beta_1 y_{1i} + \gamma_1 z_{4i} + \epsilon_i \tag{1}$$

where y_1 controls for the possible effect of population on energy use. Since z_4 includes raw material exports as well as oil, a second version of (1) interacts z_4 with the dummy variable DM to focus more exclusively on the primary raw material exports of the Middle East and North Africa – that is, oil. Thus:

$$z_{3i} = \alpha_2 + \beta_2 y_{1i} + \gamma z_{4i} + \gamma 2' z_{4i} \cdot DM_i + \epsilon_i \tag{1a}$$

The impact of economic openness is examined next, for both cases above:

$$z_{3i} = \alpha_3 + \beta_3 y_{1i} + \gamma_3 z_{4i} + \delta_3 z_i^6 + \epsilon_i \tag{2}$$

$$z_{3i} = \alpha_4 + \beta_4 y_{1i} + \gamma_4 z_{4i} + \gamma_{4'} z_{4i} \cdot DM_i + \delta_4 z_{6i} + \epsilon_i \tag{2a}$$

However, economic openness (or lack of it) may itself be a function of the presence of oil revenue. To test this part of the hypothesis, $z6$ was regressed on an instrument of $z4$, such as $y4$ (share of oil and raw material exports in total exports). Thus we have the following equation:

$$z_{6i} = \alpha_5 + \beta_5 y_{1i} + \gamma_5 y_{4i} + \epsilon_i \tag{3}$$

Using y_4 rather than z_4 in (3) allows us to reexamine (2) and (2a), where the "fitted" (endogenized) values of z_6, obtained from this procedure, are substituted for the actual values of z_6. Otherwise, perfect colinearity would exist in (2) and (2a) if z_4 rather than y_4 were used to yield values of z_6. The new equations, with fitted (endogenized) values of z_6, are:

$$z_{3i} = \alpha_6 y_{1i} + \beta_6 y_{1i} + \gamma_6 z_{4i} + \delta_6 \hat{z}_{6i} + \epsilon_i \tag{4}$$

$$z_{3i} = \alpha_7 + \beta_7 y_{1i} + \gamma_7 z_{4i} + \gamma'_7 z_{4i} \cdot DM_i + \delta_7 z_{6i} + \epsilon_i \qquad (4a)$$

Finally, it is useful to examine the effect of openness (itself related to oil, per equation 3) to energy use without the direct effect of oil. This tests a "sequential" chain of causation in which oil exports are associated with an excessive pattern of energy consumption only indirectly – that is, by promoting inward economic policies – rather than the "parallel" chain of causation implicit in (3) and (4) in which oil export dependence reduces economic openness but both oil and openness affect energy consumption. The new equation is:

$$z_{3i} = \alpha_8 + \beta_8 y_{1i} + \delta_8 \hat{z}_{6i} + \epsilon_i \qquad (5)$$

The results

The analysis reveals several interesting patterns (Table 10.3). First, estimates of equation 1 reveal that countries that rely on exports of oil and other raw materials consume a significantly larger share of energy per dollar of GNP produced (the coefficient of z_4). Second, (1a) shows that when confined to the Middle East and North African countries whose primary raw material is oil, the statistical association (coefficient of $z_4 \cdot DM$) increases in size, although its significance declines slightly. In all the regressions population is significantly associated with a greater consumption of energy per dollar of GNP.[2]

Next, estimates of (2) show that oil and other raw material exports (z_4) are associated with greater energy use per dollar of GNP even in the presence of economic openness (z_6). In fact, economic openness is not associated with a rise in the pattern of energy use when introduced jointly with z_4. Similar to (1a), the estimate of (2a) also shows that when the focus is exclusively on the Middle East and North Africa, the coefficient of $z_4 \cdot DM$ increases in size but declines slightly in significance.

Another interesting result comes from the estimate of (3), in which the higher share of oil and raw material exports in total exports (the coefficient of y_4) is strongly associated with inward-oriented policies. The next question of interest is how this endogenized form of economic openness (or lack of it) is associated with energy consumption. Estimates of (4), (4a), and (5) suggest a sequential chain of causation over a parallel chain. The sequential chain is indicated by the significant and negative coefficient of z_6 in the estimate from (5), which excludes the z_4 variable, but by a general loss of significance among all equations in the estimates from (4) and (4a), which include both the z_4 and z_6 variables.

Table 10.3 Oil, economic openness, and energy consumption (dependent variable, energy use per dollar of GNP)

Independent variable	(1)	(1a)	(2)	(2a)	(3)	(4)	(4a)	(5)
Constant	0.33	0.33	0.32	0.30	0.55	0.61	0.42	0.81
	(7.69)	(8.15)	(5.13)	(6.45)	(10.73)	(2.21)	(1.54)	(4.59)
y_1	0.08	0.08	0.08	0.08	−0.04	0.06	0.07	0.04
	(3.39)	(3.42)	(3.39)	(3.54)	(−2.79)	(1.67)	(2.18)	(1.39)
z_4	0.75	0.60	0.74	0.58		0.37	0.49	
	(2.36)	(1.49)	(2.34)	(1.44)		(0.64)	(0.92)	
$z_4 \cdot DM$		1.00		1.07			0.92	
		(1.80)		(1.87)			(1.59)	
z_6			0.03	0.05				
			(0.34)	(0.89)				
y_4					−0.34			
					(−4.94)			
$\hat{z}_6$						−0.53	−0.16	−0.90
						(−1.02)	(−0.32)	(−2.52)

Note: Results are corrected for heteroscedasticity. Numbers in parentheses are *t* statistics. Variables are defined in the text.
Source: Author's calculations.

The empirical results suggest a sequential and triangular chain of causation in which oil and raw material exports are significantly associated with excessive energy consumption, such exports are also significantly associated with economic inwardness, and economic inwardness is associated with greater energy use.

WELFARE EFFECTS

Three damaging effects of environmental degradation are generally cited – ill health, the loss of productivity, and the loss of "amenities" (World Bank, 1992). Of these, health entails the largest human and social cost and presents the greatest challenge to policymakers. Traditional measures of national accounts often neglect to tally these costs, with adverse implications for accurate measures of national well-being.

Health effects

World Bank (1992) presents persuasive evidence of the adverse impacts of poor water and sanitation, air pollution, and solid waste on health in developing countries. In the Middle East and North Africa, for example, the impact of environmental pollution on health (including impairments and treatments) is estimated at nearly $11 million, while the combined impact on natural resource degradation (related to productivity loss) and the loss of tourism (related to amenity loss) is estimated to be slightly more than $2 billion.

Measuring environmental damage according to its health impacts is useful because an impact-oriented approach avoids the problems associated with the heterogeneity of environmental indicators. Furthermore, using an alternative social cost valuation approach that is based on contingent valuation and that attempts to gauge a society's willingness to pay for environmental protection has faced many obstacles (Hueting, 1989). (See Mohtadi and Roe, 1994, for further discussion and a model of the environment-health linkage in a dynamic endogenous growth context.)

Sulfur dioxides and air particulates

Sulfur dioxide, caused by the combustion of fossil fuels with a high sulfur content in metal smelters, industrial processes, and diesel engines, largely affects the lungs and respiratory system (WRI, 1992). Similar health impacts arise from suspended air particulates (smoke, soot, and dust) from fuel combustion, industrial processes, agricultural practices, and some natural sources; roughly half of particulates are generated by the conversion of sulfur dioxide into sulfates in the upper atmosphere. Although industrial countries have adopted several technological innovations to lower their sulfur dioxide emissions – Japan, for example, reduced its sulfur dioxide emissions by 40 percent between 1974 and 198 – developing countries have not yet done so. As a result 70 percent of the world's urban population is exposed to dangerous levels of sulfur dioxide and 66 percent is exposed to dangerous levels of air particulates (GEMS – WHO – UNEP, 1987). As mentioned earlier, air particulate levels in the Middle East and North Africa exceed WHO guidelines by 200–500 percent (World Bank, 1995).

Nitrogen oxides

Although both nitrogen dioxide and nitrogen oxide – which are emitted by vehicles and industrial processes (power stations and industrial boilers) – have mild health effects (nitrogen dioxide affects the lungs somewhat), their major hazard is that they synthesize photochemically with other organic compounds, producing low-level ozone. Ozone is a very active gas and is thus highly reactive, attacking cells and breaking biological tissues, especially lungs. It is also known to be a potent plant toxin (Holman, 1989).

Carbon monoxide

Carbon monoxide, which is produced primarily by the incomplete combustion of carbon-based fuels, reduces oxygen in the blood, causing perception problems, slower reflexes, headaches, and drowsiness (WRI, 1992). In most industrial countries catalytic converters are used to complete the burning process by converting carbon monoxide intro carbon dioxide, and thus the incidence of carbon monoxide in most industrial countries is declining. The United States, for example, reduced its ambient carbon monoxide level by 28 percent during 1980–9 despite a 39 percent rise in vehicle-miles traveled (U.S. EPA, 1991). Carbon monoxide is still a major pollutant in developing countries, however, including those in the Middle East and North Africa – primarily because they lack catalytic converters.

Lead

Lead is a highly toxic pollutant. In its ambient form lead comes primarily from fuel additives (leaded gasoline), metal smelters, and battery manufacturing. Its emission affects brain functioning, causing mental retardation in severe instances. A decline in leaded gasoline use in industrial countries has considerably reduced the lead content of blood among these countries' populations. A 50 percent drop in leaded fuel use in the United States during 1976-80, for example, reduced the average blood-lead content by 37 percent.

Developing countries in general, and countries in the Middle East and North Africa in particular, are far behind in the use of unleaded gasoline, and lead thus remains one the most potent health threats in these countries. Lead pollution in air, water, and food in Cairo alone has caused an estimated loss of 4.25 IQ points in children, 820 additional infant deaths from the exposure of pregnant women to lead, 6,500-11,600 heart attacks, 800-1,400 strokes, and 6,300-11,000 premature deaths (World Bank, 1995). In Iran the potential savings in health care costs as a result of reductions in lead pollution are three to four times the additional costs to refineries of producing unleaded gasoline. For the Middle East and North Africa as a whole (assuming a 50 percent urban concentration in gasoline use) health cost savings would be $1.5-2.0 billion, compared with additional refinery costs of $500 million (World Bank, 1995). In fact, 30 percent of the region's total health care costs (including nonenvironmental costs) stem from water and air pollution. Costs of this magnitude indicate the critical importance of addressing environmental issues in the region.

Environmental national accounts

Because common measures of national accounts – such as GDP – often ignore the negative "shadow price" of environmental externalities, they may not accurately reflect social welfare costs. Environmental national accounts are then needed to assess these costs. One advantage of such measures is that they differentiate among the performance of countries with similar growth records but with vastly different environmental records. A study in Japan, for example, found that environmental degradation was the greatest obstacle to translating economic growth into economic well-being. Economic well-being was measured by an indicator called net national welfare that captures not only elements that can be translated into monetary value but also makes deductions for environmental pollution, urban crowding, and other indicators of natural resource degradation (Uno, 1989; Kanamori, Takase, and Uno, 1977).

The welfare loss in Japan due to environmental pollution peaked in 1970, both absolutely and according to net national welfare, at 14.3 percent. By 1980 the loss due to pollution fell to 4.3 percent of net national welfare, and by 1985 to 3.0 percent. The basic point here is that in the face of adverse environmental effects, the measure of GNP does not necessarily reflect economic well-being, nor does GNP growth measure improved well-being. Thus an economy on a lower growth path that has internalized this externality may yield higher levels of well-being than a more prosperous country with significantly negative environmental indicators.

INWARD- AND OUTWARD-ORIENTED APPROACHES

When environmental degradation is caused by negative economic externalities, governments should adopt regulatory policies – such as taxes on polluters, incentives for using nonpolluting technologies, and quantitative restrictions on the amount of pollution – that mitigate it, since environmental degradation in this case is a result of market failure (Mohtadi, forthcoming).

The same cannot be said of regulatory policies that are implemented under inward-oriented, heavily distorted economies, as many countries in the Middle East and North Africa are. The potentially devastating outcome of inward-oriented economies is illustrated by Brazil in the 1970s. As mentioned earlier, deforestation has been widespread in Brazil's Amazon region – almost 600,000 square kilometers of the Amazon, an area larger than France, have been cleared since the 1970s (Bojö, Mäler, and Unemo, 1990). One of the main causes of this devastation was the Brazilian government's policy of supplying subsidized rural credit (Mahar, 1989) to compensate for the implicit taxation of agriculture, as reflected in the overvalued exchange rates and import controls that developed from inward-oriented, import-substitution policies. For example, Brazilian companies that invested their profits in an Amazon region that was targeted for development received a tax credit of up to 50 percent. These kinds of tax and policy schemes, which included low taxes on agricultural incomes to encourage the clearing of forested land, rules of land allocation that benefited squatters, land taxes that rewarded farms as productive and forests as unproductive, and tax regulations that encouraged livestock production, hastened deforestation in the Amazon (Binswanger, 1989). Similar disincentives to forest conservation exist in the Middle East and North Africa. As mentioned earlier, nationally forested lands are being privatized in Iran; other examples include threats to Jordan's rangeland from overgrazing and the conversion of pastureland to unsustainable agriculture. The main causes of deforestation are the increased pressure on agriculture from urbanization and inward-oriented policies that promote food self-sufficiency.

Second-best solutions in inward-oriented economies

Only by redirecting the inward orientation of the economies of the Middle East and North Africa will these countries achieve environmentally sustainable economic development. But because this strategy requires a long-term perspective, policies should be formulated that reduce the extent of environmental deterioration now, with an emphasis on those that can be implemented easily and are best suited to the area. An example is the removal of energy subsidies in Egypt, which has helped conserve water by increasing transportation and pumping costs and making farmers use water more efficiently. The innovative aspect of this policy is that a direct increase in the price of water would have been politically and administratively difficult for the government; removing energy subsidies was less sensitive and has achieved the desired results. In Jordan the removal of producer subsidies for domestically consumed crops would encourage farmers to grow soil-conserving crops such as olives and grapes, which would discourage overgrazing in the country's rangeland (World Bank, 1995).

In urban settings the impact of removing subsidies would be direct and immediate, because much of the industrialization in the region is based on energy subsidies. Eliminating $11 billion of energy subsidies in Iran, for example, would reduce environmental pollution and yield $4.5–5.0 billion in annual economic benefits by 2010 (World Bank, 1995).

Moving toward outward-oriented strategies

As discussed, inward-oriented policy distortions tend to hasten natural resource degradation. Evidence suggests that such distortions also slow the long-run growth rate. The slow growth of Latin American economies during the 1970s has been attributed to their inward-oriented policies, while the rapid growth of the East Asian economies has been attributed to their outward- oriented policies. More formal support for this view is available from econometric studies that link export promotion policies to growth (Bahmani-Oskooee, Mohtadi, and Shabsigh, 1991). It is thus possible to achieve the dual goal of preserving the natural resource environment and achieving higher growth by promoting greater economic openness and encouraging non-oil exports (in addition to oil exports). Certain steps in this direction by such countries as Iran and Turkey are encouraging.

To be sure, environmental degradation will still arise in outwardly efficient economies. But as mentioned earlier, the problem here is one of market failure, not resource misallocation. As such, it can be addressed with various regulatory incentives.

Reforming property rights

The kind of policy reforms that seek to preserve natural resources (such as forests and grazelands) generally differ from those that seek to reduce environmental pollution (such as air pollution). Efforts to protect natural resources often focus on the need to assign property rights. Whereas unlimited access to forests, pastureland, or fishing grounds tends to induce overuse, an ownership stake in a resource provides an incentive to maintain that resource. For example, providing land titles to farmers in Thailand has reduced damage to forests, assigning ownership titles to slum dwellers in Indonesia has tripled household investment in sanitation, providing tenure security to Kenyan farmers has reduced soil erosion, and allocating transferable fishing rights in New Zealand has reduced overfishing (World Bank, 1992).

Individual and community rights

It is important to distinguish between traditional common property systems, in which the community as a whole internalizes the externality from overuse, and open access systems, in which the free-rider problem prevails. This distinction is important because governments often nationalize natural resources in the name of eliminating open access, but in fact end up eliminating traditional common property arrangements and replacing them with inefficient controls (World Bank, 1992). Policy errors may occur in the other direction as well.

For example, replacing a traditional property rights arrangement with private property rights at the local level reduces – rather than increases – the extent to which externalities are internalized, and so leads to a deteriorating environment. Similarly, replacing national rights with private property schemes (as in Iran's nationalized forest lands) also reduces the extent to which the environment is preserved by reducing the degree of externalities.

Finally, when nationalization is unenforceable *and* traditional community rights do not exist, an alternative approach to property rights is to create new community rights – to decentralize structures of governance by involving individuals and communities and internalizing externalities without having to nationalize (World Bank, 1995). An example comes from the northwest coastal zone of Egypt, where community involvement (including female participation) has been sought to address overgrazing by tribal settlements. Given the region's historical regard for community values, collective approaches may need to be emphasized to redress future environmental degradation.

Property rights and atmospheric pollution

Although atmospheric pollution and natural resource degradation are very different problems, it is possible to view atmospheric pollution as an open-access problem and to devise a property rights approach in this area as well. An example of this approach comes from the "pollution rights" issued recently in the United States. Utility companies are allotted "rights" to pollute up to a certain level, and to sell and buy these rights from one other. The overall number of rights is fixed, however, and determined by the maximum level of allowable pollution.

Certainty and enforcement of property rights

From the standpoint of individual behavior, not only is the clarity of property rights reforms important (such as the delineation among individual rights, community right, and national rights), but so too is certainty in the enforcement of rights. Countries in the Middle East and North Africa are at different stages of legal reforms and enforce existing laws differently. For example, Jordan is revising its legal framework for pollution control and natural resource conservation (World Bank, 1995). By contrast, although Egypt's standards for water quality exceed those of the United States and many other industrial countries, these laws are not enforced (Batstone and

Kosmo, 1989). Since some enforcement difficulties result from the expense of monitoring at the national level, this problem could be mitigated by involving both the private sector and communities (World Bank, 1992). Tighter monitoring and enforcement in Algeria, for example, has already produced results. The National Chemical Enterprise plans to convert from chloro-alkalies processing to a method that does not discharge mercury, in recognition of the costs of treating and disposing the waste (World Bank, 1995).

Other means by which future uncertainty can be reduced should also help increase physical capital and improve the preservation of environmental capital. One such general factor is peace in the region, which should promote economic stability and reduce future uncertainty.

Outward-oriented economic policies and market failure

Even if the institutional and legal framework to guard property rights is in place and market reforms have removed economic distortions, the behavior of economic agents still might not be consistent with preserving the environment and protecting natural resources. Rational economic agents who act in their own interests or those of their households are likely to ignore the impact of their behavior on the larger community. But the collective effect of all agents is significant, and leads to environmental degradation and pollution.

Government pricing and quantity regulations can correct (internalize) these externalities when price and property rights systems are functioning properly. Interventions that induce socially optimal behavior by affecting the cost of market transactions are known as market interventions, and take the form of taxes, subsidies, user fees, and so on. This market-oriented approach to environmental regulation has proved successful where economies are relatively free of distortion and property rights are clearly defined.

Market and nonmarket interventions

Three types of policy interventions are available to policymakers: those that affect the price of resource use or the cost of pollution, those that affect the quantity of resource use or pollution, and those that specify the technology to be used (World Bank, 1992). Policies that stipulate standards and control (that is, nonmarket quantity regulations) have dominated in the past. Recently, however, interest

Table 10.4 Policies for changing environmental behavior

Type of policy	Variable affected		
	Price	Quantity	Technology
Incentive			
Direct	Effluent charges (Netherlands, Canada) Stumpage fees (Canada, United States) Deposit-refund schemes (beverage containers: northern Europe)	Tradable fishing permits (New Zealand) Tradable emissions permits (United States)	Technology taxes based on presumed emissions (water pollution control: Germany, France)
Indirect	Fuel taxes (Sweden, Netherlands) Performance bonds (hazardous waste: Thailand)	Tradable input or production permits (lead trading program: United States)	Subsidies for research and development and fuel efficiency (catalytic converters: United States, Japan, western Europe)
Regulation			
Direct	—	Emissions standards (United States, China) Quotas and bans (logging: Thailand)	Mandated technical standards (catalytic converters: United States, Japan, western Europe)
Indirect	—	Land zoning (Brazil) Quotas and bans on products and inputs (high-sulfur fuel: Sao Paulo, Brazil)	Efficiency standards for inputs or processes (fuel effiency standards: United States)

Source: Eskeland and Jimenez, 1991.

in using an incentive-based approach (price) has been revived. Recent examples include emissions trading rights for air pollutants in the United States; charges on fuels, automobiles, pesticides, and fertilizers in Northern Europe; and others (Table 10.4). In most cases a combination of regulatory (quantity-command) and market (price-based) policies are most effective (World Bank, 1992).

Public goods and investments

Although the emphasis placed on large public projects by governments and international agencies may have created inefficiencies in the past (due to underutilization), and although many of these projects were poorly planned from an environmental perspective, this trend is changing. Furthermore, certain public expenditures are likely to enhance environmental quality and are badly needed in many developing countries. An example is sewerage and sanitation, yet spending on these items accounts for substantially less than one-fifth of World Bank-financed projects (World Bank, 1992). Even less has been spent on treatment. As a result only 2 percent of sewage in Latin America is treated. Investment in the disposal of solid waste is also lacking; only about 5 percent of solid waste in developing countries is disposed of properly, compared with 25 percent in industrial countries. The countries in the Middle East and North Africa have similarly underinvested in municipal waste relative to their investments in water supply projects, thus reducing the benefits of the water supply projects by contaminating water resources. Less than 20 percent of the sewage in most of the region's countries is treated. While this is a better record than in Latin America, it lags far behind the rate the OECD rate of 60–70 percent (World Bank, 1995).

Improving information flows

Because many environmental pollutants also adversely impact personal health, an informed citizenry, acting in its self-interest, is likely to behave in ways that are consistent with an improved environment. Thus information on environmental pollutants is likely to spur demand for improved environmental quality. Whether this demand is manifested through the market or politically depends on the existence of markets that can reflect consumer preferences. Consider, for example, such agricultural inputs as pesticides, herbicides, and fertilizers. These inputs affect health, both directly from the residue they leave on foods and indirectly from their run-off into water systems.

This direct health impact and the health concerns it raises can be transformed in the marketplace as people demand food not laden with residue, inducing farmers to adopt growing techniques that do not involve pesticides and herbicides. Thus markets allow the negative externalities associated with such pollutants to be internalized. This process also reduces the environmental effects of such use – for example, by reducing the extent of the run-off (Mohtadi and Roe, 1994).

Thus the dissemination of information can lead to behavior that is likely to improve environmental quality. Because information is better understood and more efficiently absorbed by an educated citizenry, education should have a positive impact on environmental quality. At the same time, the contribution of education and human capital to economic growth is well documented. This issue has assumed special importance with the rise to prominence of endogenous growth theories (Lucas, 1988; Romer, 1990). These theories suggested that economies with higher initial levels of human capital grow more rapidly; empirical studies have supported these theories (Barro, 1991).

Education may thus be a key element of an overall win-win strategy that improves environmental quality and contributes to economic growth. Furthermore, a highly educated citizenry may even demand a greater amount of environmental information. The ability to access public information and act on it also implies a greater sense of belonging to the community and thus a greater likelihood to act in the interest of the social good. Finally, because it enables the poor to participate in economic growth, education is among the most effective instruments for reducing poverty (World Bank, 1990).

Political structure

While education is likely to enhance decisionmaking about one's health and the local community, larger public policy issues (for example, reducing levels of sulfur dioxide across a country) require input from a range of citizens and thus democratic structures. Evidence from Eastern Europe and the former Soviet Union indicates that in the absence of citizen input, environmental degradation may still occur despite a highly educated populace. In many nondemocratic countries in the developing world public policy not only does little to reflect citizen input, but these countries also lack the education levels of countries in Eastern Europe. The recent democratization of the Eastern bloc has caused environmental policies to improve in these countries, but democratization in many developing countries may be insufficient for informed and responsible environmental policy decisions, since education levels in developing countries are generally lower than in Eastern Europe.

Still, there are promising exceptions among the developing countries. For example, pressure from a well-informed citizenry has improved environmental quality in Curitiba, Brazil. In this city of two million people, the combination of an energetic mayor and an informed and involved public led to a number of environmental innovations, including the expansion of green spaces, widespread recycling, and careful scrutiny of industrial location and product mix to minimize pollution (World Bank, 1992).

CONCLUSION

Addressing environmental concerns in the Middle East and North Africa will require addressing the sequencing of reforms. For example, tax-based environmental regulations will be useless if prices do not reflect allocative efficiencies. Energy subsidies and other price liberalization schemes should thus be removed before problems of market failure are addressed. But legal and institutional strengthening must occur at the same time as liberalization policies, since many of these policies are based on incentives schemes and the legal protection of private property. Finally, other long-term reforms are needed to produce policies that are more environmentally friendly and that better reflect society's preferences. These include efforts to disseminate information on environmental and health hazards, educating the citizenry to enable it to respond to this information, and democratizing society to allow for greater public input.

Notes

1. Two additional features that are not discussed here further warrant the grouping of Middle East and North African countries. The first is the existence of the Mediterranean Sea and several shared rivers, which comprise environmental common areas for several of the countries in the region (for analysis of strategic policy games under cross-border pollution effects see Mohtadi, 1992; for a treatment of the global North-South issues see Diwan and Shafik, 1992). The second is the similarity among economic, cultural, and religious institutions, which induces common economic behavior and responses to economic incentive and disincentive schemes.

2. One plausible explanation for this may be that larger populations are associated with higher levels of urbanization and urban concentration, in turn implying higher levels of energy use by vehicles and road transport systems.

References

Bahmani-Oskooee, M., H. Mohtadi and G. Shabsigh, 1991. "Exports, Growth, and Causality in LDCs: A Reexamination," *Journal of Development Economics* 36:405–15.

Barro, R., 1991. "Economic Growth in A Cross-Section of Countries," *Quarterly Journal of Economics* (May):407–43.

Batstone, R., and M. Kosmo, 1989. "Industrial Pollution in the Mediterranean," *Working Paper* 5, World Bank, Environment Program for the Mediterranean, Washington, D.C. World Bank.

Binswanger, Hans, 1989. "Brazilian Policies that Encourage Deforestation in the Amazon" *Environment Department Working Paper*, 16, Washington, D.C. World Bank.

Bojö, J., K. Mäler, and L. Unemo, 1990. *Environment and Development: An Economic Approach*, Dordrecht, Kluwer Academic Press.

Diwan, Ishac and Nemat Shafik 1992. "Investment, Technology, and the Global Environment: Towards International Agreement in a World of Disparities," In P. Low, (ed.), *International Trade and the Environment* Washington, D.C.: World Bank.

Eskeland, G., and E. Jimenez, 1991. "Choosing Policy Instruments for Pollution Control: A Review." *Policy Research Working Paper*, 624, Washington, D.C.: World Bank.

Faiz, Asif, Kumares Sinha and Michael Walsh, 1990. "Automotive Air Pollution: Issues and options for Developing Countries" Policy Research Working Paper 492, Washington D.C.: World Bank.

FAO (Food and Agricultural Organization), 1991. "Second Interim Report on the State of Tropical Forests," paper presented at the Tenth World Forestry Congress, (September), Paris.

GEMS–WHO–UNEP (Global Environmental Monitoring System–World Health Organization – United Nations Environment Program), 1987. *Global Pollution and Health*, London: Yale University Press.

Holman, C., 1989. *Air Pollution and Health*, London: Friends of the Earth.

Hueting, R. 1989. "Options for Dealing with Defensive Expenditures," in Y. Ahmad, S. El-Serafy, and E. Lutz (eds.), *Environmental Accounting and Sustainable Income*. Washington, D.C.: World Bank.

Kanamori, H., Y. Takase and K. Uno. 1977. "Economic Growth and Welfare: An Estimation of NNW in Japan," *Research Report* 41 Japan Tokyo: Economic Research Center.

Lucas, R., 1988. "On the Mechanics of Economic Development." *Journal of Monetary Economics* 22:3–42.

Mahar, D., 1989. "Government Policies and Deforestation in Brazil's Amazon Region." in G. Schramm and J. Warford, (eds.), *Environmental Management and Economic Development*, Baltimore, Md.: Johns Hopkins University Press.

Mohtadi, Hamid, 1986. "Rural Stratification, Rural to Urban Migration, and Urban Inequality: Evidence from Iran." *World Development*, 14:713–25.

—— 1990. "Rural Inequality and Rural-Push versus Urban-Pull Migration: Evidence from Iran, 1956–1976," *World Development*, 18:837–44.

—— 1992. "Environment, Trade, and Strategic Interdependence: A Simple Model with Implications for NAFTA," *North American Review of Economics and Finance*, 3:175–86.

—— Forthcoming. "Environment, Growth, and Optimal Policy Design," *Journal of Public Economics*.

Mohtadi, Hamid and T. Roe, 1994. "Environment, Health, and Growth."*Working paper*, Economic Development Center, St. Paul: University of Minnesota.

Romer, P., 1990. "Endogenous Technological Change," *Journal of Political Economy* 98(5):S71–S102.

Shafik, Nemat and Sushenjit Bandyopadhyay, 1992. "Economic Growth and Environmental Quality: Time Series and Cross-Country Evidence,"*Policy Research Working Paper*, 904, Washington, D.C.: World Bank.

Uno, K., 1989. "Economic Growth and Environmental Change in Japan: Net National Welfare and Beyond." In F. Archbugi and P. Nijkamp, (eds.), *Economy and Ecology: Towards Sustainable Development*, Dordrecht Kluwer Academic Press.

U.S. EPA (United States Environmental Protection Agency), 1991. *National Air Quality Emission Trends Report, 1989*, Washington, D.C.

World Bank, 1990. *World Development Report 1990: Poverty*, New York: Oxford University Press.

—— 1992. *World Development Report 1992: Development and the Environment*, New York: Oxford University Press.

—— 1995. "Middle East and North Africa Environmental Strategy: Toward Sustainable Development," Middle East and North Africa Region, Washington, D.C.: World Bank.

WRI, (World Resources Institute), 1992. *World Resources, 1992–93*. New York: Oxford University Press.

11 Environmental and Natural Resource Management in the Middle East and North Africa

Bjorn Larsen

The depletion of natural (mostly nonrenewable) resources and the environmental and health problems posed by freshwater scarcity, air pollution, and the lack of safe water and sanitation pose threats to countries throughout the Middle East and North Africa. Policies in the region are having a deleterious impact on natural resource conservation and environmental quality, and reforms are required if the region if to achieve sustainable growth and widely shared access to basic environmental services. Although reform will involve adjustments – including cutting off subsidies and introducing cost recovery as a basic objective of service provision – the costs of inaction may be unaffordable. To make changes politically and socially acceptable, environmental and natural resource awareness must be strengthened, local participation of stakeholders must be encouraged, public information campaigns must be stepped up, and pricing and incentive reforms must be accompanied by credible commitments to improve service quality.

The governments in the Middle East and North Africa have done little to plan for their natural resource and environmental futures. Given their large, nonrenewable oil and gas reserves and arid and semiarid climates, countries throughout the region require management plans that protect their natural and environmental resources while contributing to economic growth. More important, scarce freshwater resources, increasing air pollution, and large rural areas without adequate water and sanitation services, combined with the region's rapid population growth and urbanization, pose serious health risks to the region's populations. Policy and institutional frameworks must be reformed to ensure environmental protection and provide incentives for conservation, private participation, and sustainable development.[1]

DWINDLING NATURAL RESOURCES AND THE REGIONAL ECONOMY

Countries that ignore environmental and natural resource issues do so at their own economic peril. In the Middle East and North Africa the depletion of nonrenewable natural resources (oil and gas) is producing negative national savings rates, especially in countries whose reserves are expected to last less than twenty to thirty years. Countries throughout the region also have neglected to save windfall revenues from high oil prices to increase their total physical capital stock.

Poor national savings rates

Most countries in the Middle East and North Africa derive a substantial share of their gross national product (GNP) from natural resources – primarily oil and gas production, but also agriculture. Yet they are depleting these resource bases, and so are depreciating their physical capital stock. (Appendix 11.1, p.306 provides definitions and calculations for accounting for the depletion of natural resources.) Although estimates of the depreciation of land, pasture, water, and forest resources in the region are limited, oil and gas production is primarily responsible for natural resource depletion in most countries. The consequence is a decline in national net savings rate throughout the region.

Evidence of the poor national savings rates as a measure of economic vitality comes from a comparison of Middle East and North African countries and East Asian natural resource extractors (Figure 11.1). The non-Gulf countries in the region – Algeria, Egypt, Iran, Syria, and Tunisia – compare poorly with China, Indonesia, and Malaysia, yielding three broad conclusions:

- Natural resource-extracting countries in East Asia have dramatically improved their net savings rate since 1986, primarily by increasing their gross savings rates and achieving higher income growth.

Figure 11.1 Net national savings rates in the Middle East and North Africa and East Asia, 1972–92

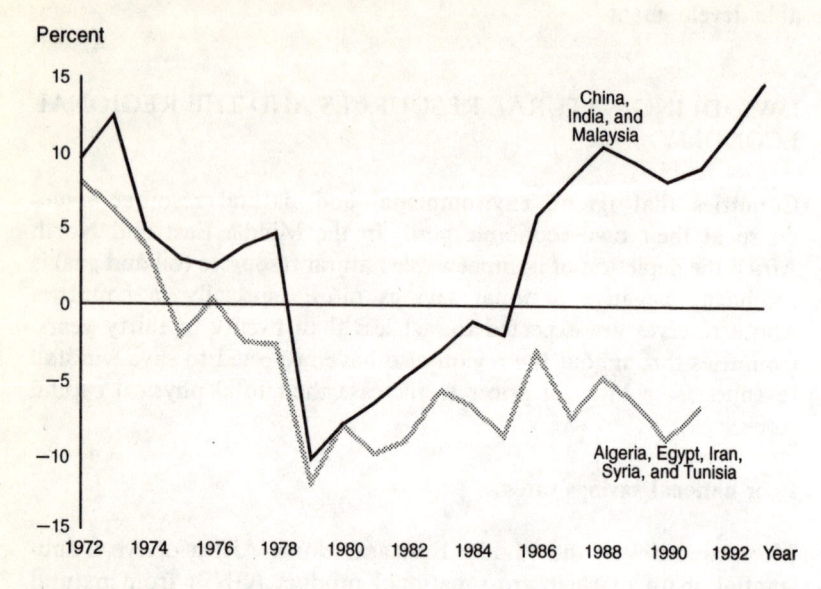

[Chart showing Percent on y-axis (-15 to 15) and Year on x-axis (1972-1992). Upper line labeled "China, India, and Malaysia"; lower line labeled "Algeria, Egypt, Iran, Syria, and Tunisia"]

Source: Author's estimates.

- The non-Gulf countries largely consumed the windfalls from high oil prices through the mid-1980s. Algeria and Iran, however, scaled back production after the 1979 price increase, which increased their net savings rates.
- Net savings rates in the nonrenewable natural resource-extracting countries in the Middle East and North Africa have been consistently negative since 1979 (except for Tunisia since 1987). The total capital stock, including produced assets and natural resources, has thus been declining, possibly eroding the basis for future economic growth in countries with small oil and gas reserves, such as Algeria, Egypt, and Syria.

Inefficient redistribution of resource rents

Governments throughout the Middle East and North Africa have redistributed resource rents from oil and gas extraction largely by subsidizing energy, water, and sanitation services and by investing in and protecting inefficient public industrial enterprises. Most countries in the region do not charge users for the provision of water, particularly in the agriculture sector, which consumes more than 85 percent of total water in most of the region. In addition, energy subsidies are still substantial in Iran, Saudi Arabia, and Syria.

The redistribution of resource rents through subsidies is expensive. It discourages conservation, and misused resources inhibit economic growth. Revenue from oil and gas production often seems to be viewed as a public good that can be redistributed at no cost through subsidized goods and services. Yet most countries in the region rely on distortionary taxes on trade and capital to finance additional government spending. Thus the marginal cost of the subsidies is the efficiency loss associated with the distortionary taxes, in addition to the efficiency loss associated with distorted consumption patterns for subsidized goods and services. High taxes on trade and capital also have adverse environmental impacts, since they tend to inhibit the adoption of cleaner technologies.

THE ENVIRONMENTAL CONSEQUENCES

Natural resource policies throughout the region are having grave environmental consequences. Many countries allocate scarce freshwater resources inefficiently to low-value users, increasing the pressures on nonrenewable water supplies and making expensive desalinization the only option for meeting urban demand. Subsidies for municipal water and sanitation services and wastewater treatment also mainly benefit urban residents, while most rural (often poor) populations lack even basic services. Average energy intensity throughout the region is 0.62 kilogram of energy per dollar of GDP which, combined with a heavy reliance on high-sulfur fuel oil in many countries, contributes to high levels of air pollution. Public enterprises, with few incentives to use resources efficiently and upgrade technology, are the source of most toxic air and water pollution. And lead pollution from energy-inefficient old vehicles (which are particularly pervasive in non-Gulf countries) has intensified pollution levels.

Freshwater resources

The Middle East and North Africa has less than 0.5 percent of the world's freshwater resources, but contains 5 percent of the world's population – a per capita endowment that is one-tenth the world average, and that is declining with rapid population growth. Eleven of nineteen countries use more than 100 percent of their renewable freshwater resources. The high-income Gulf countries are relying increasingly on desalinized seawater, while several other countries are drawing down groundwater reserves. And the quality of freshwater supply is being threatened by increasing salinity, industrial and municipal pollution, and agricultural chemical runoffs.

Water allocation

The drive for food self-sufficiency for rapidly increasing populations – abetted by low or zero irrigation water prices, agrochemical subsidies to farmers, producer price supports, and limited land- and water-use planning – has placed intense pressures on the quantity and quality of surface and groundwater resources. Conflict over freshwater resources may grow as municipal and industrial water demand increases, and as per capita water availability declines with population growth. Countries that are unable to afford seawater desalinization may be particularly squeezed. Improving water efficiency in the municipal and industrial sectors may help mitigate such conflicts, since unaccounted-for water in urban areas often exceeds 50 percent of supply. But such relief would only be temporary, and may depend on whether the costs of improved efficiency outweigh the opportunity costs of reallocating water from agriculture.

Water reallocation

Reallocating water from agriculture to the industrial and municipal sectors raises two concerns: the potentially adverse social impact on populations that derive income primarily from agricultural activities and the potentially adverse economic impact on agricultural productivity.

Because irrigated agriculture employs a fairly minor share of the regional labor force – except in Egypt, Oman, and Yemen – reallocating water to meet the growing demand of the industrial and municipal sectors is not likely to disrupt overall employment. And even if agricultural employment is a concern, reducing the degradation of rainfed cultivable land, which accommodates a substantially larger share of the labor force, may be far more critical to sustaining agricultural employment (Box 11.1). Egypt, Oman, and Yemen could ease adverse agricultural employment effects by fostering a dynamic private manufacturing and service sector to absorb a growing labor

> **Box 11.1 Tunisia: sustaining employment with effective natural resource management**
>
> The Tunisia Northwest Mountainous Areas Development Project, supported by a World Bank loan of $17.3 million, is helping populations in remote mountainous areas make better use of limited natural resources. The project will help restore sustainable range, forest, and farming activities; reduce soil degradation, erosion, and sedimentation in reservoirs; and increase the productivity and incomes of poor farmers. By using a participatory approach, the project will strengthen farmers' capacity to plan and implement natural resource protection measures and improve the responsiveness of rural service agencies to farmers' needs.
>
> The two largest components of the project focus on improving watershed and rangeland management and the rural infrastructure base. The watershed and rangeland management component promotes such measures as rotational grazing to support the regeneration of vegetation, fertilization grazing to improve hay and forage production, and reseeding with native forage species to reestablish rangeland productivity and promote agroforestry. These measures will help restore the natural vegetative cover, reduce runoff and soil loss, and improve soil fertility. The infrastructure component is providing isolated villages with access to markets and potable water and constructing and maintaining such basic services as rural roads, classrooms, and health centers.
>
> *Source*: World Bank, 1995.

force. Improving water efficiency in agriculture and switching production to higher-value crops also would smooth the transition.

The second concern is more valid. But the adverse economic impact of water reallocation on agricultural productivity could be mitigated – or even offset – if substantial water savings were realized with improved irrigation technology, greater distributional efficiency, and a move toward higher-value crops. And even if the impact on agriculture is negative, the overall economic impact of water reallocation would be positive if scarce water resources were diverted to higher-value sectors. For example, the average value added per cubic meter of water in industry is greater than in irrigated agriculture; agriculture generally cannot compete for scarce water resources on economic grounds. Although this conclusion should be viewed cautiously,[2] the striking differences in value added per cubic meter of water in agriculture and industry generally do not favor increasing water allocation to agriculture, particularly since the marginal cost of water is rising in most of these countries.

Urban air pollution

The urban population in the Middle East and North Africa has quadrupled in one generation, to more than 130 million. Growth has been most rapid in the region's more than 100 secondary cities (population between 100,000 and 1 million people), which grew more than 50 percent faster than the 19 largest cities (population of more than 1 million).[3] Excessive levels of air pollution are found not only in such megacities (population or more than 10 million) as Cairo and Tehran, but also in most cities with populations of more than 1 million, as well as in smaller cities that are heavily industrialized. Air concentrations of particulates, lead, and sulfur dioxide are often more than twice WHO guidelines in the region's large cities.

An estimated 60 million people in the urban areas of the Middle East and North Africa – almost 25 percent of the entire population – are exposed to air pollution levels that exceed World Health Organization (WHO) guidelines (Table 11.1). This figure is expected to reach 90 million by 2004 if the rate of urbanization continues and

Table 11.1 Trends in human exposure, Middle East and North Africa, 1980–2004 (million people)

Indicator	1980	1994	2004[a]
Excessive air pollution	35	60	90[b]
Unsafe water supply	60	45	30
Unsafe sanitation	90	85	85

a. Based on *per capita* investment levels in the 1980s and population growth of 3 percent a year.
b. Does not include cities that currently face no or minor air pollution problems, but that may be troubled in 2004.
Sources: WRI, 1995; World Bank, 1995.

immediate actions are not taken to curb air pollution. A rapid increase in adverse health impacts caused by air pollution can be expected from the combined effects of the growing number of people exposed to excessive air pollution and an increase in the level of air pollution emissions from various sources.

Premature mortality and illness from excessive air pollution are imposing substantial health care costs throughout the region. An estimated 1.5 million disability-adjusted life years (DALYs) are currently lost each year to excessive particulate and sulfur dioxide pollution.[4] Lead pollution from traffic is estimated to cost $1.5 – 2.0 billion in terms of impaired intelligence among children, premature mortality, and illness (World Bank, 1995).[5]

The major sources of air pollution are fossil fuels, lead additives in gasoline, and heavy industry. Air pollution is exacerbated by the use of fuel oil with a high sulfur content (often 3 percent in many countries), old vehicles without emissions control equipment, and industrial processes with poorly operated or nonexistent pollution control technologies.

Energy intensity

Average energy intensity in the Middle East and North Africa is 0.62 kilogram of energy per dollar of GDP, compared with 0.32 in Latin America and 0.26 in OECD countries. This disparity can be partly explained by the energy-intensive oil and gas production in the region, but it is also due to large energy subsidies to domestic consumers. These subsidies encourage energy-intensive economies and have provided little or no incentive to improve energy efficiency or conserve energy. Energy subsidies are still substantial in some countries, ranging from 5–10 percent of GDP in Iran, Saudi Arabia, and Syria. Egypt, which provided similar levels of energy subsidies until a few years ago, has for the most part raised energy prices in line with opportunity costs, although diesel fuel subsidies remain high.

The region does contain some success stories, however. Energy intensity in Morocco is only 0.27 kilogram of energy per dollar of GDP; in Tunisia it is 0.34. These two countries have achieved greater efficiency by pricing energy appropriately and by promoting policies that encourage energy conservation and improve consumption efficiency (Box 11.2). Countries in the region have the potential to generate substantial energy savings at little or no cost.[6] But savings will not be realized unless energy subsidies are scaled back and information dissemination campaigns are undertaken to promote energy efficiency.

> **Box 11.2 Morocco and Tunisia: energy efficiency and pricing policies**
>
> Energy intensity in Morocco is 0.27 kilogram of energy per dollar of GDP (koe/GDP); in Tunisia it is 0.34 koe/GDP. These Figures are about half the regional average (0.62 koe/GDP). Some of this difference can be attributed to energy-intensive oil and gas production in the other countries. Still, adjusting for this difference yields an estimated regional energy intensity of about 0.50 koe/GDP, which is 50 percent higher than in Tunisia and Morocco.
>
> The main reason for the high energy efficiency in these two countries is likely to be substantially higher end-user energy prices. Gasoline prices in Morocco were about $0.83 a liter in 1992, and $0.58 a liter in Tunisia, compared with $0.25 a liter in Lebanon, $0.14 a liter in Saudi Arabia, and less than $0.05 a liter in Iran (diesel prices follow similar patterns). Due largely to the high fuel prices in Morocco and Tunisia, fuel consumption per road transport vehicle is less than half the average in non-Gulf countries, and less than one-third the average in Iran. Prices for industrial fuel oils in Morocco and Tunisia are also substantially higher than in most countries in the region, providing incentives to conserve energy in the industrial sector.
>
> *Sources*: U.S. Department of Energy, 1992; OECD, 1994; author's estimates.

Energy consumption

During the 1980s energy consumption increased by an average of 6 percent a year. Oil and natural gas account for the majority of primary energy consumption in the region. Natural gas consumption, which is more environmentally friendly, increased to about 33 percent of primary energy consumption in 1991. But the consumption of heavy fuel oil – particularly fuel oil with a high sulfur content – remains high, particularly in the non-Gulf countries (Figure 11.2).

Figure 11.2 Share of heavy fuel oil in primary energy consumption, Middle East and North Africa, 1991

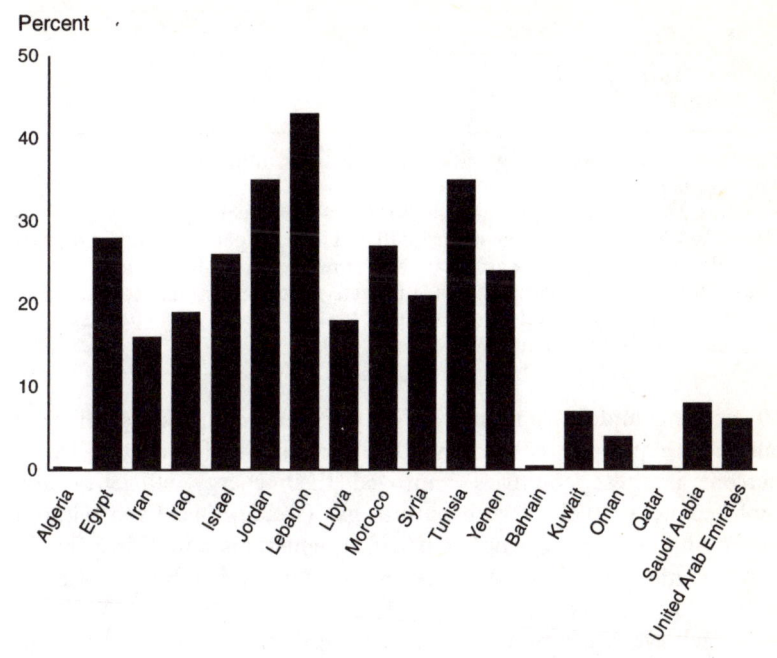

Source: OECD, 1992.

By contrast, Saudi Arabia reduced its consumption of heavy fuel oil consumption by 50 percent during 1982–91. The main reason for high-sulfur fuel's popularity is its cost – about $15 a ton less than for low-sulfur fuel oil. But these lower prices do not reflect the substantial health impacts of both sulfur dioxide and particulate emissions.

The region could achieve substantial emission reductions by improving energy efficiency and by substituting natural gas for high-sulfur fuel oil. These potential reductions were estimated for non-Gulf and Gulf countries under two scenarios: improved energy efficiency and the replacement of heavy fuel oil with natural gas (scenario 1), and the replacement of heavy fuel oil with natural gas alone (scenario 2; Table 11.2).

In non-Gulf countries the potential reduction in sulfur dioxide emissions is more than 70 percent under both scenarios – reflecting these countries' substantially larger consumption of high-sulfur fuel oil. Particulate reductions would be 60 percent under scenario 1 and

Table 11.2 Potential reductions in emissions from fossil fuel use (percent)

Emission	Non-Gulf countries		Gulf countries	
	Scenario 1	Scenario 2	Scenario 1	Scenario 2
Sulfur dioxide	75	72	75	50
Particulates	60	40	50	33

Scenario 1 – improved energy efficiency and substituting natural gas for high-sulfur fuel oil.
Scenario 2 – substituting natural gas for high-sulfur fuel oil.
Note: Uses Morocco's energy intensity (0.27 kilogram per dollar of GDP) as a base. Estimated reductions are relative to emissions from fossil fuel combustion only, and do not include process-related emissions from cement and steel plants and metal smelters.
Sources: Author's estimates; World Bank, 1995.

40 percent under scenario 2. For the Gulf countries particulate emissions could be reduced by 50 percent and sulfur dioxide by 75 percent if these countries improved their energy efficiency and replaced heavy fuel oil with natural gas (scenario 1). Even without improving energy efficiency, particulate emissions could drop by 33 percent and sulfur dioxide emissions by 50 percent by substituting natural gas (scenario 2).

To achieve Morocco's impressive energy intensity level, the countries in the region would have to reduce energy intensity (adjusted for the incremental energy intensity attributed to oil and gas production) by an average of 35 percent (see Box 11.2). Such a move would yield annual savings of $15 billion, assuming a uniform reduction of gasoline, diesel fuel, fuel oil, gas, and electricity consumption in each country. Although achieving a reduction of this magnitude would require increasing investment in more energy-efficient technologies, each country could likely reduce its energy intensity by at least 20 percent at nominal cost. The consequent net savings of a reduction of this size would also be substantial, perhaps as much as $10 billion a year.

Industrial pollution

The industrial sector – particularly cement and steel plants and metal smelters – is a major contributor to air pollution. It is also the largest source of toxic pollution, which is not captured by the health impacts estimated earlier. But toxic pollution is obviously a major concern.

Although industrial pollution coefficients are not available for Middle Eastern and North African countries, an industrial pollution projection model provides a preliminary assessment of the pollution load of toxic releases (Figure 11.3). As much as 80 percent of toxic releases from the industrial manufacturing sector come from three or fewer subsectors. These subsectors are predominantly industrial chemicals and metallurgy, but include petroleum refineries in Jordan, Kuwait, and Qatar.

Figure 11.3 Toxic pollution from industry, Middle East and North Africa, 1990

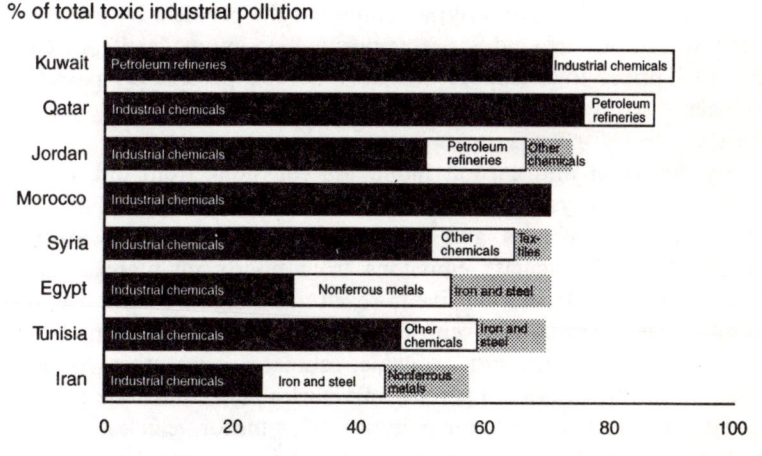

% of total toxic industrial pollution

Country	Composition
Kuwait	Petroleum refineries / Industrial chemicals
Qatar	Industrial chemicals / Petroleum refineries
Jordan	Industrial chemicals / Petroleum refineries / Other chemicals
Morocco	Industrial chemicals
Syria	Industrial chemicals / Other chemicals / Textiles
Egypt	Industrial chemicals / Nonferrous metals / Iron and steel
Tunisia	Industrial chemicals / Other chemicals / Iron and steel
Iran	Industrial chemicals / Iron and steel / Nonferrous metals

Source: World Bank, 1995.

The highly polluting industrial plants in the region are predominantly public enterprises that have long been protected by high trade barriers and soft budget constraints. The absence of competitive market forces has promoted inefficient resource use, slowed the adoption of less polluting and more productive technologies, and in many cases allowed economically unviable enterprises to remain in operation.

Given the right incentives, the region's countries have many immediate, relatively inexpensive options at their disposal to mitigate industrial pollution. Many of these measures would also reduce consumption of water, energy, and polluting substances in the production process, while improving product quality (Appendix 11.2, p. 303). In some cases more expensive, technologically complex measures will be required to combat pollution. To encourage enterprises to make these investments, governments will have to enforce strict environmental standards while providing tax and other incentives.

Traffic pollution

Although the share of particulate pollution for motor vehicles is not large relative to industry, human exposure is substantially higher because of the proximity of vehicles to people. Complicating matters is that fact that the vehicle fleets in several countries are, on average, more than fifteen years old. These vehicles lack emissions control systems, are poorly maintained, and are run by highly fuel-inefficient engines. Egypt, Iran, and Syria compound the problem by protecting domestic automobile industries, imposing high import tariffs, or keeping fuel prices low. Import tariffs of 50–100 percent on passenger vehicles discourage turnover, keeping old and highly polluting vehicles on the streets for years.

Hydrocarbon and carbon monoxide emissions from old vehicles without control systems are often twenty-five times higher than those from equipped vehicles, and their nitrogen oxide emissions are four times higher. Particulate emissions from poorly maintained diesel-fueled buses and trucks are five to seven times higher than those from similar, well-maintained vehicles. Although emission estimates by vehicle age group are not available, estimates from other countries suggest that the oldest 20 percent of vehicles may contribute as much as 80 percent of the total air pollution from motor vehicles.

Vehicles are also the major source of lead emissions. Leaded gasoline commonly contains from 0.3–0.4 grams of lead per liter, and lead emissions are often exacerbated by a 40–50 percent higher fuel consumption among older vehicles. Egypt recently announced that some retail fuel stations will begin to sell unleaded gasoline. But the supply is severely limited, and the price of unleaded gasoline will be higher than the price of leaded gasoline; most vehicle owners thus have no incentive to switch to unleaded. Unleaded gasoline has been available for some time in Tunisia, but the price incentive for substitution is also lacking there.

Safe water and sanitation

About 45 million people in the region are without safe water, and 85 million lack safe sanitation (see Table 11.1). These figures have dropped since 1980 in response to investment of $25 billion in water supply and sanitation during the 1980s. Still, the number of people without access to safe water and sanitation is unacceptably high. Unsafe water and sanitation is estimated to cause a loss of about 3 million DALYs each year, primarily as a result of child mortality and diarrheal diseases (World Bank, 1995).

About 90 percent of those living without safe water are in rural areas. In fact, the number of rural residents without safe sanitation increased by more than 5 million during the 1980s. Estimates suggest that about 80 percent of the investment in water and sanitation during the 1980s benefited urban populations, despite the fact that about half the region's population lives in rural areas. Water and sanitation services for urban residents are highly subsidized, at the expense of rural provision. Moreover, huge investments have been made in expensive municipal wastewater treatment plants that are often poorly operated and have a limited impact on health – while basic sanitation services are neglected in rural areas.

Public agencies control water and sanitation services. These agencies pay little attention to such demand parameters as willingness to pay for improved quality and convenience of services. The structure and level of investment in water supply, basic sanitation, and wastewater treatment would likely be quite different if these services were driven by market forces, even after the environmental externalities associated with wastewater pollution are accounted for.

Subsidies for water and sanitation services are often advocated on equity grounds. Yet subsidized services disproportionately benefit urban residents, whose income levels are substantially higher than those living in rural areas. Moreover, urban residents who do not have a piped water supply are often poor and must buy water from vendors, which is far more expensive than piped municipal water.

POLICY OPTIONS

Redressing the mounting problems associated with the depletion of natural resources and environmental degradation requires sweeping reforms in incentives and institutions. Making such reforms politically and socially palatable will require strengthening environmental and natural resource awareness, encouraging participation by stakeholders, enhancing the dissemination of information, and accompanying pricing and incentive reforms with credible commitments to improving the quality of services. Only a limited set of such reforms and measures are highlighted here; detailed recommendations for environmental management must be tailored to individual countries.

Achieving sustainable growth

Countries in the Middle East and North Africa cannot continue indefinitely to consume their capital stock. To reverse the decline in the sum of produced assets and nonrenewable resources, the following should be priorities on their policy agenda:

- Eliminating any remaining subsidies for natural resources (energy and water) and environmental services (municipal water and sanitation).
- Imposing hard budget constraints on public enterprises, whose consumption of scarce natural resources should be judged according to market-based criteria.
- Increasing reliance on the private sector to provide natural resource-based and environmentally related goods and services (such as water and sanitation) that are largely private in nature.
- Levying environmental taxes to discourage pollution and natural resource waste and to provide revenue that would allow taxation on investment to be reduced and thus foster private sector development.
- These measures would not only help reduce the depletion of natural resources and improve environmental quality, they would also increase allocative efficiency, enhance fiscal performance, and strengthen the basis for sustained economic growth. Combined with a more favorable economic and institutional policy environment for the private sector, these measures would help the region's economies increase their net savings rates, as have the natural resource-extracting countries of East Asia.

Addressing freshwater scarcity

As renewable freshwater resources in the region become more scarce and municipal and industrial water demand increases, per capita water availability will decline with population growth. In addition, the agriculture sector will face greater competition for freshwater resources, particularly given the substantially higher value added and willingness to pay per cubic meter of water in the municipal and industrial sectors. Several measures can ease the emerging conflict:

- Raising irrigation, municipal, and industrial water charges to cover the marginal cost of supply in the short run and to reflect social costs in the long run, thus moving intra- and intersectoral water-use efficiency toward more integrated water markets.
- Improving irrigation efficiency to the extent that is economically and environmentally desirable and encouraging higher-value crops with appropriate incentives, including social-cost pricing of water resources.
- Reducing unaccounted-for water in the municipal and industrial sectors.
- Evaluating options for mitigating any adverse effects of water reallocation on agricultural employment, such as increased conservation efforts on rainfed agricultural land.

Mitigating pollution

Substituting natural gas for heavy fuel oils can substantially reduce emissions of particulates and sulfur dioxide. Leaded gasoline can gradually be replaced by unleaded gasoline, preferably on a large scale, either by upgrading refineries or importing unleaded gasoline. Industrial and transport pollution mitigation requires a portfolio of both regulatory and enforcement measures and pricing and tax reform, as well as measures to improve the financial accountability of public enterprises. The following policies are among the most promising for achieving these goals:

- I mposing a pollution tax on high-sulfur fuel oil and regulations to restrict its use near population centers, thus encouraging the switch to cleaner fuels.
- Levying a tax on leaded gasoline to reflect the social cost of lead, thus encouraging vehicle owners to switch to unleaded fuel.
- Strictly enforcing environmental regulations for industrial enterprises and closing noncomplying plants, particularly in subsectors (chemicals and metallurgy) whose share of toxic industrial pollution is 70–80 percent of the total.
- Reducing taxes on capital, eliminating capital import tariffs and excise taxes, and allowing accelerated depreciation for tax purposes. Environmental taxes and incentives should be implemented

to encourage environmental investments and investments in cleaner production technologies.
- Replacing vehicle import tariffs in whole or in part with taxes on transport fuels, adapting annual registration fees to reflect the age of vehicles and their fuel use, and enforcing emission standards to limit the use of highly polluting vehicles.
- Targeting high-use vehicles, such as taxis, buses, and trucks, for rigorous inspection and maintenance programs.
- Internalizing the full cost of road transport (including the costs of road infrastructure and maintenance, air pollution, congestion, and traffic accidents) to mitigate the social cost of road transport and to improve the competitiveness of alternative transport modes, such as private buses.

Improving water and sanitation services

The Middle East and North Africa invested about $25 billion in water and sanitation during the 1980s. About 80 percent of these investments benefited urban residents; 60 percent of the rural population still lacks safe sanitation, and 30 percent lacks safe water. An additional $20 billion might be required to provide full rural and urban coverage. Several additional provisions are warranted:

- Service delivery should be subject to such demand parameters as quality, safety, and convenience.
- Services should be accompanied by health education and information, and behavioral parameters affecting health should be identified and made part of the overall design of service delivery.
- The private sector should be encouraged to participate in service delivery (through investment or operations and maintenance activities) to improve efficiency and customer satisfaction.
- Water and sanitation charges should cover the cost of high-quality service delivery and efficient resource allocation.
- Higher charges should be accompanied by higher quality and more reliable services to make the price increases socially acceptable.

CONCLUSION

The development challenges facing the Middle East and North Africa require a strategic vision and the mobilization of critical support from and participation by the constituent populations to make change sustainable. Consistent policies within each country can minimize the tradeoffs between economic growth and environmental quality, including health. Growth can build on complementarities that minimize resource waste and avoid costly corrective measures in the future. Environmental and natural resource issues should be considered as part of the economic and social development agenda, and their current status and projected trends should be a policy priority.

Appendix 11.1 Calculating Natural Resource Depletion Costs

Income growth is predicated on the accumulation of physical and human capital and on increased factor productivity. This chapter considers only the accumulation of physical capital; the comparative contribution to growth of factor accumulation and increased productivity is discussed in the growth literature.

The physical capital stock includes produced assets as well as renewable and nonrenewable natural resources (such as land, pasture, forests, water resources, oil, gas, and minerals). In order to accumulate physical capital, investment must be greater than capital stock depreciation. Investment, in turn, is given by:

$$I = S + NFB \qquad (1)$$

where S is gross national savings and NFB is net foreign borrowing. Gross national savings is the unconsumed residual of national income, including transfers – that is,

$$S = GNP - C - G \qquad (2)$$

where GNP is gross national product, C is private consumption, and G is government consumption. In order to accumulate physical capital and avoid foreign debt, a country's national savings must be higher than its depreciation of produced assets and depletion of the natural resource stock – that is, net savings must be positive:

$$S^n = S - D^p - D^{nr} > 0 \qquad (3)$$

where S^n is net national savings, D^p is the depreciation of produced assets, and D^{nr} is the depletion of the natural resource stock.

The net national savings rate (that is, S^n/GNP) accounts for the depreciation of produced assets (machinery, buildings, and so on) and the depletion of natural resources (oil and gas). A time-series analysis of the stock of produced assets is estimated based on the perpetual inventory method:

$$K_t = K_{t-1}(1 - d_t) + I_t \qquad (4)$$

where K_t is the stock, d_t is the depreciation rate, and I_t is the gross investment in period t. The initial period stock is estimated based on Nehru and Dhareshwar (1993). The depreciation rate is assumed constant at 4 percent a year, which is consistent with other estimates of stock depreciation.[7] Depreciation of produced assets in period t is thus:

$$D_t^p = K_{t-1}d \qquad (5)$$

The depreciation of the natural resource stock is given by the production of oil and gas. The value of oil production is based on international spot prices of crude oil. The valuation of natural gas production is less straightforward, because for the most part natural gas is not traded. Its value is approximated by the average of heavy fuel-oil spot prices and observed free-on-board prices of natural gas to the European market.

Appendix 11.2 Process-Technology Options for Controlling Pollution

EGYPT

The Rakta integrated pulp and paper mill in Alexandria makes writing and printing paper using rice straw. For every ton of rice straw pulp produced, two tons of black liquid waste are generated. A detailed environmental audit of the mill was conducted as part of the Mediterranean Action Plan. End-of-pipe treatment without in-plant measures would cost about $500 per ton of paper, a prohibitive Figure relative to the cost of producing a ton of paper (about $600). But a change in process technology – involving full scale-desilication and chemical recovery of black liquid – could be a viable alternative. Initial estimates indicate that the investment in process technology would have a positive financial rate of return. Although the return is less than 10 percent, it is preferable to end-of-pipe treatment, which simply adds to the cost.

SYRIA

Several process technology changes with short payback periods have been identified at the General Fertilizers Company in Homs:

- The primary reformer in the ammonia plant emits about 32 tons of nitric oxide a day. A purge-gas treatment plant would increase the production of ammonium nitrate by 5 percent and reduce nitric oxide emissions by about 90 percent. The investment cost is about $1 million, and could be recovered in two years.
- A scrubber to reduce nitric oxide emissions from the nitric acid plant would cost $750,000. The current concentration of nitric oxide in the process gas is on the order of 1,500 micrograms per cubic meter. About 6.0 tons of nitrogen dioxide are emitted each day, as are 2.5 tons of nitric oxide. The investment would pay for itself within three years.

- The urea plant emits about 8 tons of urea dust a day. An investment of $1 million in fabric filters would pay for itself within three years with the recovery of urea dust.

ALGERIA

Wastewater from the CELPAP pulp and paper factory accounts for about half the pollution load in Oued el-Harrach. If the factory recycled its water it would provide enough water for an additional 150,000 people, avoiding the cost of additional water supply.

The Enterprise National de la Petrochimie chloro-alkali production plant in Skikda uses an amalgam process that produces mercury pollution. Rebuilding the amalgam process to reduce pollution would cost about $30 million. Converting to membrane technology, which uses no mercury, would cost about $80 million, but with a payback period of three to five years.

TUNISIA

The Groupe Chimique company at Gabes could reduce sulfur dioxide emissions by scrubbing with ammonia and recovering ammonium sulfate. This approach would generate foreign exchange savings of about $1 million a year.

IRAN

The copper smelter at Sar Cheshme uses an outdated production technology based on reverbatory furnaces and Pierce-Smith converters. Because the smelter lacks sulfur emissions controls, an estimated 1,000 kilograms of sulfur are generated for each ton of copper produced-some 125,000 tons a year. The most common way of reducing sulfur dioxide emissions from this type of smelter is to produce sulfuric acid from the furnace gases; the resulting sulfur dioxide emissions would be about 100 kilograms per ton of copper produced.

Modern processes are more energy efficient and use half the energy per ton of copper produced compared with the reverbatory process. The processed gases from a modern technology such as the flash process also contain high concentrations of sulfur dioxide, which increases the recovery rate of sulfur. This process reduces emissions to about 30 kilograms per ton of copper produced. The most advanced processes have sulfur dioxide emission rates of less than 5 kilograms per ton of copper produced. Investing in modern processes would reduce sulfur dioxide emissions at a cost of $100 per ton. If the value of energy savings and sulfuric acid is included, such investment is likely to yield a positive rate of return.

Source: World Bank, 1995.

Notes

1. For a more detailed treatment of a broader range of environmental and natural resource issues, readers are directed to World Bank, 1995.
2. In some cases the value added of crops is substantially higher than the average, increased yields and improved water efficiency can raise value added per cubic meter of water, and the costs of redirecting water to other sectors can be exorbitant.
3. During 1985-90 secondary cities grew by nearly 6.0 percent a year. Annual growth in the largest cities was 3.8 percent.
4. DALYs are a combination of discounted and weighted years of life lost as a result of death at a given age, and disability as a result of morbidity, adjusted by severity (World Bank, 1993).
5. Other potentially significant sources of lead pollution include emissions from lead smelters, lead in water pipes, and lead in cans used in food production. Although these sources may contribute substantially to the total human intake of lead, they remain largely unquantified in most countries in the region.
6. In Iran's industrial sector, for example, the potential savings are 20–25 percent.
7. Alternatively, the depreciation rate could be estimated as a time-specific function of such variables as GDP growth, the structure of GDP, and changes in relative input and output prices, but doing so this would involve substantial practical difficulties.

References

Nehru, V. and A. Dhareshwar, 1993. "A New Database on Physical Capital Stock: Sources, Methodology, and Results," *Revisita de Economico*, 8(1):37–59.

OECD (Organization for Economic Cooperation and Development), 1992. *Energy Statistics and Balances of Non-OECD Countries, 1991 and 1992*, Paris: OECD.

────── 1994. *Energy Prices and Taxes, 1994*. Paris: OECD.

U.S. Department of Energy 1992. *International Energy Annual 1992*, Washington, D.C.

World Bank, 1993. *World Development Report 1993: Investing in Health*, New York: Oxford University Press.

———. 1995. "Middle East and North Africa Environmental Strategy: Toward Sustainable Development," Middle East and North Africa Region, Washington, D.C.: World Bank.

World Resources Institute, 1995. *World Resources 1994–95*, Washington, D.C.

Index

Abed, G.T. 9
accountability 170–2
Addi, L. 174
Adler, P. 204
Agency for International Development 165
Agreement on Agriculture 115
Ahlwalia, M. 164
air particulates 274–5
air pollution 294–300
Alavi, H. 190
Algeria 3, 97
  economic transition 161, 162, 163, 169
  environment and natural resource management 289, 290, 297
  environmentally sustainable development 266, 269
  exports 21
  growth crisis 136, 147, 151, 154
  human capital strategy 210, 214
  Islamic Salvation Front (FIS) 174–5
  markets and production 25, 28, 30, 32, 33, 34
  Mediterranean Initiative 36
  National Chemical Enterprise plans 281
  pollution control 309
  poverty 226, 227, 228, 231, 232, 237
  private sector development 180, 184, 186, 187, 188
  social assistance programs 252–3
  trade performance and reform 37, 108, 109, 110
  see also Maghreb
Anderson, R.E. 7, 178–92
Argentina 183, 229
Aschauer, D.A. 189
Asia 126
  goods and services trade 39
  markets and production 29
  private sector development 184
  trade patterns 50
  Uruguay Round and European Free Trade Area 49, 56, 58, 59
  see also Asian; Central; East; South
Asian developing countries 51–2, 54, 57
  change in exports by destination 86–7
  change in prices by sector 68–9, 76–7, 84–5
  change in sectoral exports by destination 70–1, 78–9
  factor reallocation 74–5, 82–3, 90–1
  structural change 72–3, 80–1, 88–9
Askari, H. 3
Aspe, P. 164
Assad, H. al- 163
assets 22
Association Council 123, 124
Atatürk, M.K. 175
atmospheric pollution 280
Avins, J. 7, 197–224

Bahmani-Oskooee, M. 279
Bahrain 44, 97
  environment and natural resource management 297
  exports 21
  markets and production 25, 28, 32, 33
  trade policy distortions 100
  see also Gulf Cooperation Council
Bailey, T.R. 203, 209
Bandyopadhyay, S. 263
Bangladesh 29, 182
banking system reform 187
Barro, R.J. 138, 139, 140, 284
Batstone, R. 280–1
Bazzari, M. 3
'Berkeley mafia' 164
Berman, E. 203
Berne Convention 118
Berryman, S.E. 7, 197–224
Bhagwati, J. 166
Binswanger, H. 278
Boadway, R. 191
Bojö, J. 277
Bound, J. 203
Brahmbhatt, M. 2, 15–45
Brazil 183, 268, 270, 277–8, 282, 285
business environment, attractive 184–92
  banking system reform 187
  financial markets development 188
  financial sector modernization 185–8
  infrastructure services 188–9
  investment promotion 191–2
  legal reform 191
  regulatory reform 190

Canada 191, 282
Canevi, Y. 164
capital 41–2
  see also human
carbon monoxide 275
Caribbean 18, 136
  environmentally sustainable
    development 265
  export earnings 20
  private sector development 179, 185
cash transfers, improved 246
Central Asia 18, 30, 153
Central Europe 97, 121, 124
  intraindustry trade opportunities
    111–13
  private sector development 185
  trade performance and reform
    105–13
Chang-Po Yang 2, 47–95
chemicals 29–30
Chen, S. 228
Chile 48, 100, 231
China 7, 42, 48, 49
  economic transition 168
  environment and natural resource
    management 289, 290
  environmentally sustainable
    development 282
  exchange rates 43
  human capital strategy 199
  markets and production 24, 29, 30
  private sector development 182
  trade policy distortions 99
Christian Democrats 175
clothing and textiles 29
Cobb–Douglas utility function 92
Colombia 229
commercial services 23
competition in international
  economy 199–203
competition policy 123
constant elasticity of substitution 92, 93
constant elasticity of transformation 92, 93
consumption ratio 250
Corm, G. 6, 9
Côte d'Ivoire 237
Council for Mutual Economic
  Assistance 106, 107, 150
Council for Trade in Services 115
Cox, D. 248
customer demand 200–3
Cyprus 36
Czech Republic 108

Dadush, U. 2, 15–45
Datt, G. 228
de Melo, J. 94
Dean, J. 99
deforestation 269–70
DeLong, J.B. 140
demand 92, 200–1
depletion costs 306–7
Desai, S. 99
desertification 269–70
development assistance, official 22
Dhareshwar, A. 143, 307
Diwan, I. 2, 47–95, 151
Dollar, D. 140, 147

East Asia 2, 5, 18, 58
  economic transition 166, 172
  environment and natural resource
    management 289, 302
  environmentally sustainable
    development 279
  exports 20, 144, 152
  goods and services trade 41
  gross domestic product 134
  growth crisis 134, 136, 141, 145, 148,
    149, 151, 154, 155
  human capital strategy 214
  income inequality 135
  investment 137, 146
  markets and production 24
  poverty 228, 230, 232
  primary enrollment 138
  private sector development 179, 185,
    186
  real trade 153
  total factor productivity 144, 152
  trade patterns 53
  Uruguay Round 47, 48, 58
  years of schooling 139
  see also China; Indonesia; Korea,
    Republic of; Malaysia
Easterly, W. 136, 181
Eastern Europe 42, 43, 65, 97, 121, 124
  change in exports by destination 86–7
  change in prices by sector 68–9, 76–7,
    84–5
  change in sectoral exports by
    destination 70–1, 78–9
  environmentally sustainable
    development 284–5
  exports 20, 40
  factor reallocation 74–5, 82–3, 90–1
  goods and services trade 41
  growth crisis 143, 150, 154

intraindustry trade opportunities
  111–13
poverty 239
private sector development 185
revenue prospects 22
structural change 72–3, 80–1, 88–9
trade patterns 51–5
trade performance and reform 105–13
Uruguay Round and European Free
  Trade Area 47, 48, 49, 56, 57, 58,
  59, 60, 61
economic agents 67
economic cooperation 124
economic development 264, 265–70
  deforestation and desertification
    269–70
  industrialization 265–6
  retardation 181–2
  urbanization 266–9
  water scarcity, use and quality 269
economic growth 235–8
  labor intensive 236–7
Economic Research Forum 1
economic transition and the state 159–77
  benefits and cost of change 160–5
  Islamic politics, potential of 172–6
  transformation, paths to 165–8
  war economy, legacies of 168–72;
    accountability and governance
    structure 170–2; human capital
    investments 172
education 7–8, 138, 139
education, training, and economic
  competitiveness 203–13
  cost of targets 213–21; enrollment
    ratios 216–17; implications for
    expenditures 217; population
    growth 214–16
  distribution of funds to university
    system 220–1
  finance of targets 217–20;
    efficiency 217–18; private resources
    in private institutions 218–20;
    private resources in public
    institutions 220
  how the system teaches 205, 206–9
  what the system teaches 204–6
  when the system teaches 205, 213
  whom the system teaches 205, 209–13
Eeghen, W. van 226–60
Egypt 2, 3, 5, 7, 9, 42, 49
  cash transfer program 246
  economic transition 160, 161, 162,
    163, 165, 166, 167, 175

environment and natural resource
  management 289, 290, 292, 294,
  295, 297, 299, 300
environmentally sustainable
  development 266, 267, 278, 280
Euro-Mediterranean economic
  area 121, 122, 123
exports 21
General Organization for Export and
  Import Control 102
goods and services trade 40
growth crisis: investment 143, 144,
  147, 148; long-run 135, 136; long-
  term restoration 151, 154;
  sources 140
human capital strategy 198, 210,
  212–13, 214, 215, 216, 219, 220
Law 32 of 1964 175
Majlis as-Sha'ab 168
markets and production 24, 25, 28,
  29, 32, 33
Mediterranean Initiative 36
Ministry of Social Affairs 175
pollution control 308
poverty 226, 227, 228, 232, 244;
  determinants 233–4, 236, 239,
  241–2
private sector development 180, 183,
  184, 186, 188, 190, 191
revenue prospects 23
social assistance programs 254–5
trade performance and reform 37,
  106, 108, 109, 110
trade policy distortions 98, 99, 100,
  101, 103–4
World Trade Organization 97, 114,
  116–17
see also Mashreq
Elbadawi, I.A. 6, 9
energy consumption 296–8
energy intensity 295–6
environment 7–8
environmental and natural resource
  management 288–310
  calculation of depletion costs 306–7
  freshwater resources 291–4
  national savings rates 289–90
  policy options 301–4; freshwater
    scarcity 302–3; pollution
    mitigation 303–4; sustainable
    growth achievement 302; water and
    sanitation services
    improvement 304
  pollution control 308–10

environmental (*Contd.*)
  resource rents 290–1
  safe water and sanitation 300–1
  urban air pollution 294–300
environmentally sustainable
    development 262–86
  empirical analysis 270–4;
    results 272–4; statistical sample and
      model 270–2
  indicators at different country income
    levels 263
  inward-oriented economies 278
  outward-oriented economic policies and
    market failure 278–9, 281–5;
    information flows, improvement
    of 283–4; market and nonmarket
    interventions 281–3; political
    structure 284–5; public goods and
    investments 283
  property rights reform 279–81; and
    atmospheric pollution 280;
    certainty and enforcement 280–1;
    individual and community
    rights 279–80
  welfare effects 274–7; environmental
    national accounts 276–7; health
    effects 274–6
  see also economic development
Erbakan, N. 173
Eskeland, G. 282
Euro-Mediterranean agreement 122–4
Euro-Mediterranean Economic Area 22,
  35, 121
Europe 18
  –Asia trade route 39
  environment and natural resource
    management 307
  environmentally sustainable
    development 282, 283
  real trade 153
  revenue prospects 21
  see also Central; Eastern; Euro;
    European
European Free Trade Area
  56–61
European Investment Bank 124
European Union 4, 10, 16, 44
  change in exports by destination 86–7
  change in prices by sector 68–9, 76–7,
    84–5
  change in sectoral exports by
    destination 70–1, 78–9
  European Commission 22, 121
  export growth 40

factor reallocation 74–5, 82–3, 90–1
free trade arrangements 5
goods and services trade 41
markets and production 24–5, 26, 29,
  30
revenue prospects 22
structural change 72–3, 80–1, 88–9
trade patterns 51–2, 54
trade policy distortions 102
see also Mediterranean Initiative;
  Uruguay Round
exports 152
  earnings 19–20
  obstacles 103–4
  per capita 16–18
  performance 106–10
  pushing 155
  see also nonoil
external environment 2–4

factor endowments 50, 67
Faiz, A. 268
financial cooperation 124
financial markets development 188
financial sector modernization 185–8
Finland 24
flight capital, repatriation of 41–2
food subsidies 242–3
foreign direct investment 3, 123, 149,
  150, 151, 185
foreign exchange earnings 16–18
former Soviet Union 6, 65, 121
  change in exports by destination 86–7
  change in prices by sector 68–9, 76–7,
    84–5
  change in sectoral exports by
    destination 70–1, 78–9
  environmentally sustainable
    development 284
  exports 20, 40
  factor reallocation 74–5, 82–3, 90–1
  goods and services trade 41
  growth crisis 143, 150
  markets and production 30
  revenue prospects 22
  structural change 72–3, 80–1, 88–9
  trade patterns 50–5
  trade policy distortions 101
  Uruguay Round and European Free
    Trade Area 49, 56, 57, 58, 59, 60, 61
France 282
freshwater resources 291–4
freshwater scarcity 302–3
future growth 5–7

General Agreement on Tariffs and
    Trade 40, 97, 106, 117, 120, 123,
    126, 127
  markets and production 30
  1994 disciplines 114–15
General Agreement on Trade in
    Services 97, 116, 117, 119, 120
Germany 282
Gini coefficient 249–50
Global Trade Analysis Project
    database 50
globalization *see under* world economy
    and implications for Middle East and
    North Africa
Goldin, I. 98
Golladay, F.L. 7, 197–224
goods and services trade 39–41
governance structure 170–2
government
  aid 123
  domination of economy 179–80
  procurement 123
  reduced role 154–5
  see also economic transition
gradualism 9–10
Griliches, Z. 203
gross domestic product 3, 65, 161, 276
  and agriculture 123
  cash transfers 246
  Eastern Europe 42
  Egypt 233–4
  and energy 265, 291, 295, 296
  and exports 16
  food subsidies 241, 242, 253
  growth 19, 31, 134, 135, 142, 178, 179,
    198, 244, 245
  and investment 137, 142, 145, 146,
    147, 151
  Israel 167
  Jordan 230, 235
  Kuwait 22
  Mashreq 145
  and military spending 39, 169, 170, 174
  Morocco 230
  per capita 16, 134, 137, 138, 139, 140,
    141, 144, 179
  public enterprises 180, 181
  public sector investment 180
  and social sector spending 239, 240
  Tunisia 230, 235, 243
gross national product 64, 115, 149, 150,
    151, 277, 306
  and energy 270, 271, 272
  natural resources 289

growth 178–82
growth as an antipoverty tool 244
growth crisis 133–56
  crash and investment decline 142–8;
    nontradables 146–8; state as
    entrepreneur 145; total factor
    productivity change 143–5
  long-run growth and equity 134–6
  restoration of long-term growth
    149–55; investment efficiency
    152–4; investment sources 149–51;
    policies 154–5
  sources (1960–85) 136–42;
    accumulation record 137–9;
    differences in cross-country
    framework 139–42
growth and labor intensiveness 244–5
Gulf Cooperation Council 2, 44
  Euro-Mediterranean economic
    area 122
  flight capital repatriation 41
  foreign exchange sources 17
  goods and services trade 40
  growth crisis 133
  human capital strategy 198
  markets and production 25, 26, 28,
    29, 30, 32
  population expansion 18, 19
  private sector development 178
  revenue prospects 22
  see also Bahrain; Kuwait; Oman;
    Qatar; Saudi Arabia; United Arab
    Emirates
Gulf war 150, 151
Gültekin, B. 164

Hamdouch, B. 3
Handoussa, H. 3, 144
Harrison, G. 113–14
head count index 249
health effects 274–6
Hertel, T.W. 50
Heston, A. 137, 138, 139, 140, 147
Hoekman, B. 3–4, 61, 96–128
Holman, C. 275
Hong Kong 135, 140, 191
housebuilding 146–8
Hueting, R. 274
human capital investments 172
human capital strategy 197–224
  competition in international
    economy 199–203
  see also education, training, and
    economic competitiveness

Hungary 108
Huntington, S. 168

imports 98–103, 146–8
income inequality 135, 230–1, 238–9, 248, 249–50
India 7, 42, 49
  economic transition 160
  environment and natural resource management 290
  exchange rates 43
  goods and services trade 41
  markets and production 24, 30
  poverty 237
Indonesia 42, 48, 135
  environment and natural resource management 289
  exchange rates 43
  growth crisis 140, 147
  human capital strategy 199
  poverty 229
  private sector development 184
  trade policy distortions 99, 100
industrial pollution 298–300
industrialization 265–6
information flows 283–4
infrastructure services 188–9
institutions, decay of 8–9
intellectual property rights *see* trade-related
International Monetary Fund 173
international shipping 92–3
investment 283
  decline 142–8
  efficiency 152–4
  in nontradables 146–8
  private and public 178–82
  promotion 191–2
  as share of gross domestic product 137
  sources 149–51
Iran 1, 2, 3
  economic transition 161
  education targets 213, 214, 215, 216, 217, 218, 219
  education, training and competition 210, 212
  environment and natural resource management 289, 290, 291, 294, 295, 296, 297, 299, 300
  environmentally sustainable development 267, 270, 278, 279
  exports 21
  growth crisis 133, 135, 136, 137, 140
  markets and production 25, 28, 30, 31, 32, 33, 34
  pollution control 309–10
  poverty 226, 227, 228, 232
  private sector development 183
Iraq
  economic transition 161, 162, 175
  environment and natural resource management 297
  export earnings 20
  growth crisis 135, 140, 150
  human capital strategy 198, 210, 214
  markets and production 25, 28, 32, 34
  trade policy distortions 101
  World Trade Organization 97
Islamic politics, potential of 172–6
  ideology 173–4
  institutional patterns 174–6
Islamic Salvation Front (FIS) 169, 174–5
Israel 4, 66, 97
  economic transition 161, 162, 167, 168, 170
  environment and natural resource management 297
  environmentally sustainable development 265
  exports 20, 21
  foreign exchange sources 17
  markets and production 24, 25, 26, 28, 31, 32, 33
  Mediterranean Initiative 36
  peace process 38, 39
  population expansion 19
  revenue prospects 23
  trade performance and reform 37, 108, 109, 110, 111
  trade policy distortions 100

Jalali, J. 2, 15–45
Japan 58, 59, 135, 172
  change in exports by destination 86–7
  change in prices by sector 68–9, 76–7, 84–5
  change in sectoral exports by destination 70–1, 78–9
  environmentally sustainable development 268, 275, 276, 277, 282
  factor reallocation 82–3, 90–1
  structural change 72–3, 80–1, 88–9
  trade patterns 50–4
Jdid, C. Ben 163
Jimenez, E. 248, 282

Johnson, G. 203
Jong-Wha Lee 138, 139
Jordan 2, 3, 4, 5, 42, 44, 97
  Amman Financial Market 186
  economic transition 161, 163
  environment and natural resource
    management 297, 299
  environmentally sustainable
    development 265, 266, 278, 280
  Euro-Mediterranean economic
    area 121, 122, 123
  exports 21, 40
  goods and services trade 40
  growth crisis: investment 144–5, 147,
    148; long-run 136; long-term
    restoration 150, 151, 154;
    sources 137, 140
  human capital strategy 222, 223;
    education targets 213–20;
    education, training and
    competiton 210, 212; international
    economy competition 198
  markets and production 25, 28, 29,
    31, 32, 33
  Mediterranean Initiative 36
  National Assistance Fund 241, 246
  peace process 38, 39
  poverty 226, 227, 228, 229, 230, 231,
    232; determinants 233, 235, 236,
    237, 238–9, 240, 241, 242; policies
    and programs 244
  private sector development 184, 186,
    188, 191
  revenue prospects 22, 23
  social assistance programs 255
  trade performance and reform 37,
    106, 108, 109, 110
  trade policy distortions 98, 99, 100,
    101, 102, 103, 104
  see also Mashreq

Kallab, V. 170
Kanaan, T.H. 3
Kanamori, H. 277
Karshenas, M. 3
Katz, L. 203
Kenya 279
Kheir-El-Din, H. 3
Kherallah, M. 98
Korea, Republic of 30, 99, 100, 268
  economic transition 165, 168, 171
  growth crisis 135, 140, 144, 147
  private sector development 182, 191
Kosmo, M. 280–1

Krueger, A.B. 203
Krugman, P. 203
Kuwait 44, 97
  environment and natural resource
    management 297, 299
  exports 21
  growth crisis 150
  markets and production 25, 28, 32
  revenue prospects 22
  trade performance and reform 108,
    109, 110
  see also Gulf Cooperation Council

labor intensiveness 244–5
Lahouel, M. 3, 101
Lamb, G. 170
Larsen, B. 8, 288–310
Latin America 99, 126
  environment and natural resource
    management 295
  environmentally sustainable
    development 265, 278–9, 83
  growth crisis 136, 142, 148, 151,
    154
  per capita growth 18
  poverty 228, 229, 230, 231, 232, 237,
    239
  private sector development 179, 184,
    185
  real trade 153
Lawrence, R. 4
lead 276
Lebanon 2, 6, 7, 8, 44, 97
  economic transition 161, 170
  environment and natural resource
    management 296, 297
  environmentally sustainable
    development 265
  Euro-Mediterranean economic
    area 121, 122
  export earnings 20
  growth crisis 147, 154
  human capital strategy 198, 210, 212,
    214, 215, 219
  markets and production 25, 28
  Mediterranean Initiative 36
  private sector development 184, 188,
    191
  trade performance and reform 37,
    108, 109, 110
  trade policy distortions 102–3, 104
  see also Mashreq
  legal reform 191

Libya 97
  economic transition 162, 175
  environment and natural resource management 297
  markets and production 25, 28
Lucas, R. 284

Maghreb 43, 44
  foreign direct investment 149
  foreign exchange sources 17
  growth crisis 133, 142, 147
  human capital strategy 198, 211, 217, 219
  markets and production 25, 26, 28, 32
  population expansion 19
  trade performance 37
  see also Algeria; Morocco; Tunisia
Mahar, D. 277
Malaysia 48, 99, 135
  environment and natural resource management 289, 290
  environmentally sustainable development 268
  growth crisis 140
  poverty 229, 231
  private sector development 184
  trade policy distortions 100
Mäler, K. 277
Malta 36
Mankiw, N.G. 140
markets *see under* world economy and implications for Middle East and North Africa
Martinez, A. 7, 178–92
Marxism 175
Mashreq 43, 44
  foreign direct investment 150
  foreign exchange sources 17
  gross domestic product 145
  growth crisis 133, 142, 149
  human capital strategy 197, 217
  markets and production 25, 26, 28, 32
  population expansion 19
  revenue prospects 21, 23
  trade performance 37
  see also Egypt; Jordan; Lebanon; Palestine; Syria
Mediterranean Action Plan 308
Mediterranean Initiative 4–5, 29, 34–9
Mexico 48, 100, 160, 164, 166, 183, 268
Mincer, J. 206
Mohtadi, H. 8, 262–86
Morocco 2, 3, 5, 6, 42, 97
  economic transition 161, 162
  education targets 214, 215, 216, 217, 218, 220
  education, training, and competition 209, 210, 211, 213
  environment and natural resource management 295–6, 297, 298, 299
  environmentally sustainable development 265, 266, 269
  Euro-Mediterranean economic area 122, 123
  exports 20, 21
  goods and services trade 40
  growth crisis 135, 136, 140, 145, 148, 151, 154
  human capital strategy, international economy competition 198, 200
  markets and production 25, 28, 29, 31, 32, 33
  Mediterranean Initiative 36
  poverty 226, 227, 228, 229, 230, 231, 232; data collection and research agenda 247; determinants 233, 234, 235, 236, 237, 238–9, 241, 242; policies and programs 244
  private sector development 178, 182–3; attractive business environment creation 184, 186, 187, 188, 190; private and public investment and growth 180, 181
  revenue prospects 23
  social assistance programs 256–7
  trade performance and reform 37, 108, 109, 110
  trade policy distortions 98, 99, 100, 101, 103, 104
  see also Maghreb
most favored nation status 114, 116, 118
Motherland Party 164
Mubarek, H. 163
Multifiber Agreement 2, 29, 42, 58, 65, 114
Murphy, K. 203

National Conference on Educational Development 223
national savings rates 289–90
Nead, K. 247
Nehru, V. 143, 307
Netherlands 282
New Zealand 279, 282
newly industrialized countries 49, 51–2, 54
  change in exports by destination 86–7

change in prices by sector 68–9, 76–7, 84–5
change in sectoral exports by destination 70–1, 78–9
factor reallocation 74–5, 82–3, 90–1
structural change 72–3, 80–1, 88–9
Nimeiri, G.M. al- 163, 175
Nishimizu, M. 144, 148
nitrogen oxides 275
nonoil export performance and potential 24–31
nonoil exports, required growth of 31–4
nontradables 146–8
North America 44, 57, 59
change in exports by destination 86–7
change in prices by sector 68–9, 76–7, 84–5
change in sectoral exports by destination 70–1, 78–9
factor reallocation 74–5, 82–3, 90–1
structural change 72–3, 80–1, 88–9
trade patterns 50–4
see also Canada; United States

oil 20–1
Oman 21, 100, 183
environment and natural resource management 292, 297
markets and production 25, 28, 32, 33
see also Gulf Cooperation Council
Organization for Economic Cooperation and Development
change in exports by destination 86–7
change in prices by sector 68–9, 76–7, 84–5
change in sectoral exports by destination 70–1, 78–9
education 138, 139
environment and natural resource management 295
environmentally sustainable development 283
European Free Trade Area 59
exports 20, 152
factor reallocation 74–5, 82–3, 90–1
gross domestic product 134, 137
growth crisis 136, 145, 148, 150
human capital strategy 201–3
income inequality 135
investment 137
markets and production 24, 26, 29, 30
private sector development 179, 180, 187
real trade 153
structural change 72–3, 80–1, 88–9
total factor productivity 144, 152
trade patterns 51–5
Uruguay Round 48, 59
World Trade Organization 114
Organization of Petroleum Exporting Countries 18, 21, 22
overseas assets, earnings on 22
Overseas Private Investment Corporation 174
Özal, T. 163, 164, 175

Pack, H. 143, 152
Page, J.M. Jr 5, 133–56
Pakistan 42, 43, 182, 183, 230, 231
Palestine 2, 4, 9
Liberation Organization 38
see also Mashreq
peace process 38–9
Peres, S. 4
Peru 229, 231
Philippines 183, 268
Pinochet Ugarte, A. 174
Poland 108
pollution
air 294–300
atmospheric 280
control 308–10
industrial 298–300
mitigation 303–4
traffic 300
population expansion 18–19, 214–16
Porter, M. 184
poverty 226–60
common measures 249–50
economic growth 235–8
elimination possibility with perfect transfers 230
essential policies and programs 243–7; cash transfers, improved 246; growth as an antipoverty tool 244; growth and labor intensiveness 244–5; interventions, self-targeted 246–7; social spending and safety nets 245–6
food subsidies 242–3
gap index 249
incidence, depth and severity 229
income inequality 230–1, 238–9, 248, 249–50
monitoring mechanisms 247
1985 227, 228
1990 227, 228
1994 227

poverty (*Contd.*)
  policies 233–5; Egypt 233–4; Jordan 235; Morocco 234; Tunisia 234–5
  private transfers 248
  public spending analyses 247
  severity index 249
  social sector spending 239–40
  social services, basic 231–2
  see also social assistance programs
price system 93
Primo Braga, C. 117
private sector empowerment 155
private sector support 178–92
  business environment, attractive 184–92
  private and public investment and growth 178–82; government domination of economy 179–80; public enterprises retarding economic development 181–2; public policy challenge 180–1
  privatization 182–3
  production *see under* world economy and implications for Middle East and North Africa
property rights 279–81
  see also trade-related intellectual
public enterprises retarding economic development 181–2
public goods 283
public policy challenge 180–1
public spending analyses 247

Qaddafi 175
Qatar 25, 28, 97, 297, 299
  see also Gulf Cooperation Council

Rao, Prime Minister 164
Ravallion, M. 228
Rebelo, S. 181
reform 190–2
regional options, evolution of 4–5
regulatory reform 190
resource rents 290–1
revenue prospects by source 20–3
Richards, A. 160
Riedel, J. 99
Riordan, M. 2, 3, 10, 15–45
Robinson, S. 94
Rodrik, D. 147
Roe, T. 274, 284
Roemer, D. 140
Romania 108

Romer, P. 284
Ruström, E.E. 5, 125
Rutherford, T. 5, 113–14, 125

Sadat, A. 175
Saddam Hussein 175
Salim, A. 176
Salinas, C. 164
sanitation 300–1, 304
Saracoğlu, R. 164
Saudi Arabia 97
  economic transition 163
  environment and natural resource management 291, 295, 296, 297
  exports 21
  growth crisis 150
  human capital strategy 209
  markets and production 25, 28, 32, 33
  trade performance and reform 100, 108, 109
  see also Gulf Cooperation Council
sensitivity analysis 61–5
services 123
Shabsigh, G. 279
Shafik, N. 1–10, 231, 263
Shah, A. 191
shipping, international 92–3
Singapore 48, 135, 140, 191, 237
Singh, M. 164
Sinha, K. 268
skill requirements 201–3
Slovak Republic 108
social assistance programs 240–2, 248, 251–9
  Algeria 252–3
  Egypt 254–5
  Jordan 255
  Morocco 256–7
  Tunisia 257–9
Social Democrats 175
social sector spending 239–40, 245–6
social services, basic 231–2
South Asia
  export earnings 20
  goods and services trade 41
  growth crisis 136, 142, 148
  markets and production 30
  per capita growth 18
  poverty 228
  private sector development 179, 185
  real trade 153
  trade policy distortions 99
  see also Bangladesh; India; Pakistan; Sri Lanka

Squire, L. 151
Sri Lanka 230, 231
state *see* economic transition; government
Stevenson, H.W. 208
Stigler, J.W. 208
Streifel, S. 2, 15–45
Sub-Saharan Africa
  export earnings 20
  goods and services trade 40
  growth 18, 136, 148
  human capital strategy 214
  poverty 228
  private sector development 179
  real trade 153
  trade policy distortions 99
Sudan 2, 6, 32
  economic transition 161, 162, 163, 164, 170, 173, 175
Suharto, President 164
Sukkar, N. 3, 6
sulfur dioxides 274–5
Sullivan, D. 176
Summers, L.H. 140
Summers, R. 137, 138, 139, 140, 147
Sunni Islam 175
sustainable growth achievement 302
Sweden 282
Syria 2, 3, 6, 7
  economic transition 161, 162, 163
  environment and natural resource management 289, 290, 291, 295, 297, 299, 300
  environmentally sustainable development 267
  exports 21
  growth crisis 135, 137, 140, 151
  human capital strategy 198, 210, 214
  markets and production 25, 28, 29, 33
  Mediterranean Initiative 36
  peace process 39
  pollution control 308–9
  trade performance and reform 37, 108, 109, 110
  trade policy distortions 100
  Uruguay Round 49
  World Trade Organization 97
  see also Mashreq

Taiwan 135, 140, 171
Takagaki, K. 2, 15–45
Takase, Y. 277
Tarr, D. 5, 113–14, 125

Thailand 30, 48, 135, 140, 184, 231, 282
Tigrel, A. 164
Togan, S. 6
total factor productivity 143–5, 152–3
tourism 23
trade 122–4
  patterns and initial conditions 50–6; factor endowments 50; structure 53–6
  -related intellectual property rights 97, 118–19
  see also world production; World Trade Organization
Trade Policy Review Mechanism 120
traffic pollution 300
Treaty of Rome 123
Triangle proposal 4
TRIPS *see* trade-related intellectual property rights
Tunisia 2, 3, 5, 6, 7, 42, 44
  economic transition 161, 162, 168, 169, 170
  environment and natural resource management 289, 290, 293, 295–6, 297, 299, 300
  environmentally sustainable development 269
  Euro-Mediterranean economic area 122, 123, 124
  export earnings 20
  goods and services trade 40
  growth crisis: investment 145, 147, 148; long-run 135, 136; long-term restoration 151, 154; sources 137, 140
  human capital strategy 222, 223; education targets 214, 215, 216, 217, 218, 220; education, training and competition 210, 213
  markets and production 25, 28, 29, 31, 32, 33
  Mediterranean Initiative 36
  pollution control 309
  poverty 226, 227, 228, 229, 230, 231, 232; determinants 233, 234–5, 236, 237, 238–9, 240, 242, 243; policies and programs 244, 246–7
  private sector development 178, 180, 182, 183, 184, 186, 187, 188
  revenue prospects 23
  social assistance programs 257–9
  trade performance and reform 37, 108, 109, 110, 111

Tunisia (*Contd.*)
  trade policy distortions 98, 99, 100, 101, 104
  World Trade Organization 97, 116–17
  see also Maghreb
Turkey 1, 2, 5, 6, 7
  economic transition 161, 162, 163, 164, 166–7, 170
  environmentally sustainable development 268, 279
  exports 21
  Mediterranean Initiative 36
  private sector development 183
  Salvation Party 173
  trade policy distortions 100
  Uruguay Round 47, 48, 49
Tyler, W. 3

Underwood, J. 151
Unemo, L. 277
United Arab Emirates 44, 97
  economic transition 168
  environment and natural resource management 297
  markets and production 25, 28, 32, 33
  trade performance and reform 108, 109, 110
  trade policy distortions 100
  see also Gulf Cooperation Council
United States 40, 170
  environmentally sustainable development 268, 275, 276, 280, 282, 283
  human capital strategy 200, 203, 208
Uno, K. 277
urban air pollution 294–300
urbanization 266–9
Uruguay Round 2, 3, 97, 117, 121
  and European Free Trade Area 56–61; first simulation 56–60, 62, 64, 68–75; second simulation 57, 60, 63, 64, 76–83; sensitivity analysis 61–5; third simulation 57, 60–1, 63, 64, 84–92
  export earnings 20
  goods and services trade 39
  growth crisis 141, 153
  markets and production 25, 29, 30
  revenue prospects 22
  see also World Trade Organization

Van de Walle, D. 247
van Eeghen, W. 6, 7

Venezuela 229
Vietnam 168

Walsh, M. 268
Walton, M. 49
war economy, legacies of 168–72
water
  allocation 292–4
  fresh 291–4, 302–3
  improvement 304
  safe 300–1
  scarcity, use and quality 269
Waterbury, J. 9, 159–77
WEFA Group 39
Weil, D. 140
Welch, F. 203
welfare effects 274–7
Wolff, L. 7, 197–224
work requirements 201–3
worker remittances 21–2
World Bank 1
  economic transition 159, 160, 161, 163, 164–5, 173
  environment and natural resource management 293
  environmentally sustainable development 270, 274, 283
  human capital strategy 214
  markets and production 31
  population expansion 19
  poverty 226, 233, 244
  private sector development 190, 191
  revenue prospects 21
world economy and implications for Middle East and North Africa 15–45
  export earnings 19–20
  opportunities 34–42; flight capital, repatriation of 41–2; goods and services trade 39–41; Mediterranean Initiative 35–8; peace process 38–9
  participation in globalization of markets and production 23–34; nonoil export performance and potential 24–31; nonoil exports, required growth of 31–4
  per capita export and foreign exchange earnings 16–18
  population expansion 18–19
  revenue prospects by source 20–3; commercial services 23; development assistance, official 22; oil 20–1; overseas assets, earnings

Index

on 22; tourism 23; worker remittances 21–2
World Health Organization 8, 269, 294
world production and trade 67–94
  change in prices by sector 68–9, 76–7, 84–5
  change in sectoral exports by destination 70–1, 78–9, 86–7
  demand 92
  economic agents and factor endowments 67
  equilibrium 93
  factor reallocation 74–5, 82–3, 90–1
  international shipping 92–3
  macroeconomic closure, choice of 94
  numeraire, choice of 93–4
  price system 93
  production 67, 92
  structural change 72–3, 80–1, 88–9
  trade-distorting policy 93
World Trade Organization 4, 190
World Trade Organization and European Union 96–128
  implications 124–5
  potential role of EU agreement 121–4
  trade performance and reform 105–13; export performance 106–10; intraindustry trade opportunities in Central and Eastern Europe 111–13
  trade policy distortions 97–105; export obstacles 103–4; import tariffs and protection 98–103; progress and possibilities 104–5
  Uruguay Round 113–21; commitments 116–18; General Agreement on Tariffs and Trade – 1994 disciplines 114–15; General Agreement on Trade in Services disciplines 116; maximizing potential benefits of membership 119–21; trade–related intellectual property rights 118–19

Yemen 97
  economic transition 161, 162
  environment and natural resource management 292, 297
  exports 21
  human capital strategy 198, 210, 211, 213
  markets and production 25, 28
  private sector development 181
  trade policy distortions 100, 101, 102

Zambia 237
Zarrouk, J. 122
Zeroual, A. 174
Zhi Wang 2, 47–95